Back Lives M

Ordinary People
in 19th Century Somers Town, London and beyond

Paul A Titley

Back Lives Matter

Ordinary People in 19th Century Somers Town, London and beyond

First Printing, 2023 Paultitley99@gmail.com

Other Books by Paul A Titley

Rolling It In Glitter (Arithmetic With Attitude) May 21st 2014

ISBN 978-1-4918-9785-0 (sc)
ISBN 978-1-4918-9784-3 (hc)
ISBN 978-1-4918-9786-7 (e)
Library of Congress Control Number 2014905281

Arithmetic With More Attitude Than You Can Shake A Stick At
July 27th 2016

ISBN 978-1-5246-3580-0 (sc)
ISBN 978-1-5246-3579-4 (e)
Library of Congress Control Number 2016909185

The Right To Remain Silent (Waived)
– a life exposed in doggerel and prose

https://www.amazon.co.uk/Right-Remain-Silent-waived-doggerel/dp/B08C453Y142020

ISBN 9798656680073

Awkward to Pigeonhole (Reflections on a Life) 2020

 ISBN 979 8582 996255

This is a small history of ordinary people whose lives were shaped by a broader history they almost certainly had no knowledge of and by events beyond their control or influence. It also considers the system which created the circumstances they found themselves in and which conditioned their normality. It is a commentary on unrepresented lives: impacted by revolutions (agrarian, industrial and political), by manufacturing and migration, and by the absence of social welfare and healthcare.

These ordinary people lived without the right to vote and without a voice. I hope this work speaks for them at least in some small way.

Please note: Footnotes which are highlighted in grey contain family history information which may only be relevant or of interest to family researchers.

Family history information: From the narrower perspective of my own family I would add that as we cannot know the thoughts and opinions of these who have gone before, I decided I would not compound the insufficiency: I determined, therefore, to present the gathered and collated information in a way which is factually accurate but also personally reflective, and thus indicative of my thoughts and opinions in the context of my own time. I doubt it will take you long to notice.

To the wider public I hope this is a novel read and one that I further hope you will enjoy.

To kith and kin: I hope that these unfamiliar names covered within the scope of this book will at length mean a little more to you – and, therefore, finally, perhaps, be strangers no more.

This was written for the pleasure of writing ... and - within the stretch of my imagination - to hopefully offer something worthy to those who embrace the joy of reading. It is dedicated to those I love: they know who they are.

INTRODUCTION: SOMERS TOWN LONDON. 19TH CENTURY

Kings Cross, Euston, St. Pancras: these three place-names are familiar to millions of travellers, tourists, commuters and, of course, to Londoners as both transport hubs and as areas within the capital, but Somers Town? Well, I would hazard a guess that name doesn't mean much even to most Londoners, but nevertheless Somers Town was the seed-bed of those three famous locations.

Formerly just farmland, it initially became a gentrified semi-rural development and was home to poets, writers, political activists, thinkers and philosophers. These refined and well-to-do folk are **not**, however, the focus of this work, but for general reference, should your curiosity be piqued, a brief roll-call of the area's noted residents would include William Godwin - the "father of political anarchism" - and the poet Wordsworth who lived in 15 and 25 Chalton St, respectively. Famous women would include Mary Wollstonecraft, author and advocate of female educational and social equality. The women's rights champion married Godwin, and gave birth there to their daughter Mary, the author of Frankenstein. It was here that young Mary Godwin was wooed by her future husband, the poet, Percy Bysshe Shelley. Somers Town was also the home of Catherine Despard, a political activist, who was the widow of the executed seditionist/Levellist/ egalitarian Colonel Despard, a friend and comrade of Horatio Nelson. Other notable residents included the Chartist John Arnott and the radical orator John Gale Jones (who both lived in Middlesex Street). And for good measure – despite him having lived in innumerable places – for about four years, it was subsequently, home and inspiration for a young Charles Dickens. They, perhaps, are the big guns but apparently it was also home and workplace to artists and engravers (cf Benjamin Smith, William Nutter, Edward Scriven, Samuel Witan & James Willmore).

This is not, though, as stated, a record of its famous residents: instead it partly charts the lives of one ordinary family, the Baxter's. Allow me to call them ordinary, but accept that what they and their kind endured required *extra*-ordinary fortitude and grit. The Baxters were numbered amongst the predominant set of much-less-well-off *other* inhabitants, who mainly lived hand-to-mouth and who – where they survived - lived there throughout Somers Town's metamorphosis from rural outpost to vital organ of the capital city. They were there when the Regent's Canal was still a novelty and during the period in which the area underwent the further colossal transformation that was the advent of the railways.

So, more generally this is a small record of the many ordinary people whose lives were shaped by a broader history they almost certainly had no knowledge of and by events far beyond their control or influence.

This book considers the lives of the Baxter family and of their contemporaries in relation to a wider socio-political reality. It further encompasses an overview of their lives and the facilities which were available to them. Their daily normality – what they could and could not do, what they had access to and what they were denied - were all bound up in the various laws and conventions which controlled them.

THE REINS OF CONTROL

Historic events, wars and battles etc. may be interesting from afar; and they were of course even a matter of life and death at the time for some.... especially those who were vying for the top position. For the main protagonists and for the chief contenders, these were high-stakes games, but generally the battles' outcomes made little if any real difference to those at the bottom of the social stack. Regardless of who was the winner, the consistent fact that can be relied upon over the centuries is that the money, the wealth, the rights and the power always remain within the privileged and ruthless top sector.

It is legislation, though, from bye-laws to Acts of Parliament, which more comprehensively affects the lives of ordinary people. Steady yourself for a moment here, because as a layman I have neither the capacity nor indeed any inclination to pick the bones and intricacies of Laws and Statutes, so do not fear on that account: you won't be bored rigid by technical legalese. A light overview, however, of some legislation will prove interesting, and enlightening.

Now, while legislation sometimes has an immediate and dramatic effect, quite often it is its lingering presence that impacts incrementally upon society, especially as it is added to or amended. Thus, over time laws create the circumstances, which condition the normality of successive generations. Of course, laws are made by the people in the higher levels of hierarchical systems to consolidate and maintain order: in effect, a good deal of most legislation was conceived to preserve that order, to protect (their) privilege and assets ... and to control people who had neither.

Within this very undemocratic system those at the bottom of the hierarchy were denied even the most basic rights and were, therefore, compelled to follow rules and Laws, which they were not allowed to shape. It is hard to imagine how few were the rights of the ordinary man at the beginning of the 19th century, but the ordinary woman – and indeed the not-so-ordinary women - had even less.

For example, the "law" determined that married women - being merely the property of their husbands - did not have rights to the man's other property... which included their own children. In this way a mother's access to her child was solely within the gift of her husband, who could legally restrict or deny her access as he saw fit. This restriction was probably more relevant to middle-class and wealthier people but it is indicative of the status of women across the social spectrum.

In all but the most exceptional circumstances any wealth, land or property owned by a single woman was generally lost or transferred to her husband upon marriage. Divorce – even for the rich – required an Act of Parliament, and few women could extricate themselves from an awful or abusive relationship. Any attempt to free themselves would invite sanction such as the loss of access to children in conjunction with other punitive measures.

Later, other legislation would to some degree improve - but did not equalise - parental and ownership rights, and in turn slowly a more generalised right to legal separation and divorce emerged. Naturally the changes were heavily weighted in favour of the man (and primarily, of course, the bias favoured the wealthiest men first, and then percolated through males of the better classes, eventually filtering down through the social stack).

There are a few examples of legislation which were beneficial to the lower orders, but mostly laws would determine, command or prohibit their actions and their rights: for example, specific laws limited their right to vote, while others criminalised collective bargaining, such that as workers it was illegal to organise and combine – even peacefully - for the betterment of conditions and wages.

Ordinary people – the ones without wealth, property or assets – also had long-standing restrictions to their right to free movement: these had been imposed from the time of the Black Death (in 1348), but were upheld and amended throughout the 19th century. The legal restraints, which were designed to contain the worker, defined not just the limits of what workers could do or of where they could travel, but they also delineated the responsibilities of those in control. Undoubtedly this system impacted harshly on the Baxters and their poor 19th century contemporaries, who were described by a local writer, one Karl

Marx, as *the proletariat*. However, despite immediately having great benefits for the few, it was a system that also inadvertently became an increasing burden to those sections of society which Marx had classified as *the bourgeoisie*: the class of business (and property) owners. Perversely, perhaps, and unintentionally certainly, those who were in the "driving seat" and held the reins began to find themselves entangled in those straps.

It would be from a diverse range of legislation also that children gained some protection from the more overt abuses and dangers they faced at work; and for not altogether altruistic reasons they gradually gained rights to basic education. 19th century society and conditions did improve, but it was in piecemeal fashion, and overall change could not be considered to have been significantly achieved until the late 20th century: it was a much different world.

Some of the details which have been revealed to me in the pursuit of this work have forced me to think about the *system* that ordinary people endured <u>and</u> that we have inherited. Consequently those facts have shaped my opinion in regard to certain matters. For example, it seems to me, that in securing greater control of the ordinary people through the imposition of restrictions on their movements and actions, the wealthier classes had made themselves responsible for the infrastructure of containment. Thus, I would suggest, they became responsible for funding the workhouses and infirmaries, which with a rapidly growing population soon became an increasingly onerous financial burden. Having painted themselves into a corner, a way had to be found out: that way was the creation of a Welfare State; it was not entirely the result of altruism. This is admittedly the conclusion I have reached, and the opinion I espouse: other conclusions/opinions may of course be valid.

I do not doubt the good intention of the few Victorian philanthropists, of Charles Booth, the Rowntree's, Sydney and

Beatrice Webb and the latter's "Minority Report" (one of whose researchers was Beveridge) but neither do I doubt that self-interest and a desperate desire for self-preservation of the privileged few surpassed altruism as an engine of change. (An example of such resignation as to what might be necessary to sustain the position and comfort of the wealthy – in the face of the majority's poverty and unemployment – may be seen in a letter from Joseph Chamberlain in March 1886. Chamberlain, the President of the Local Government Board, which made him responsible for the administration of the Poor Law Relief, indicated his position in a letter to Beatrice (who was then Beatrice Potter). Her diary record of it *(See Bibliography: Diary p155)* states that in this he repeated his opinion that a 'rather crude' scheme of public works might be part of the price 'the rich must pay to keep the poor alive.' Schemes, perhaps, which kept the poor alive in order they could continue to do the dirty duties and filthy work the rich would not do; schemes which kept the poor with just enough (to lose) that they would not rise up and challenge privilege.

The Welfare State - when it was introduced - was a device which allowed the wealthier (and the not-so-poor property-owning rate payers) to breathe a sigh of relief: it absolved them of their former financial responsibilities to the poor and infirm. Of course, they did not all see it that way, and many were resistant to it. However, it would leave the wealthier free to enjoy their privilege at the minimum cost to themselves.

A Welfare State, though, could not have been imagined even in the wildest dreams of the Baxters and their ilk. They would have to endure much discomfort, and relief would not come for them in their life-time. Meanwhile, about them the development of Somers Town (and of both a mighty and mightily lauded Empire) continued.

There are more questions than answers (so an old song rightly asserts), and I had a great many questions. Of course, not all could be answered with certainty, but what was indisputable was that these Baxter families – along with tens if not hundreds of thousands of others – lived in the midst of great and vast changes; and unless they were deaf, dumb and blind they were front-line witnesses to the new industrialisation as it unfolded and as it reshaped the city and the world.

All of these changes to the landscape and infrastructure undoubtedly impacted upon them directly – feeding into all aspects of their lives: not all of which were advantageous to them. For our Baxters, their kith and kin, and for their neighbours, what we may view now as history was the fabric of their lives: their "first-hand" experience.

I hope you will find my interpretation of their time to be a reasonable "read." I particularly wanted to avoid infusing the text with dry mind-numbing litanies of recorded rites of passage: the intolerably bland dates of births, baptisms, marriages and deaths of obscure personalities and colourless, shapeless ancestors. However, some of these dates are essential to anchor the people to "the moment" within the wider perspective of their social, economic and physical environments and of world events, which again they may or may not have been oblivious to and yet which also had consequential impacts upon them.

Certainly a good deal of the area (which includes Euston, Somers Town, Kings Cross and Camden Town) has changed enormously since those Baxters and their families lived there. Now it is packed with huge office and housing developments, and is home to colleges and the great British Library. It is also an area that has attracted multi-national companies, which showcase their enterprises with buildings of varied and sometimes striking architecture. There are, though, amid the sprawl, still a few places, a few features and streets – or at least street-names – which do remain, and which would be familiar if not recognizable to those earlier inhabitants.

Of course, while the huge gas-holder storage tanks - which dominated the area for the better part of two centuries have been removed (albeit only recently) thankfully some of their skeletal frames have been sympathetically preserved and incorporated boldly into the new design. The canal still winds its way through, although no longer carrying the goods and traffic it formerly bore. The railways have continued to expand, such that St Pancras is currently an international connection; stations have been refurbished and the early Underground system has also been upgraded with many other lines added. The old features – other than the glorious St Pancras Hotel – have largely shrunk into the fabric of the newer additions.

Now we all have a tendency to take a great many things for granted and often hardly give them a second thought. In my own case, whilst I may not be a *local* in the strictest sense, these remnants of the Victorian age are within the three-mile radius in which thus far I have lived throughout my entire span; and yet it is only this particular research which prompted me to ask blindingly obvious questions that frankly had never occurred to me before.

"Why are there three railway stations cheek by jowl? Why were those gasometers located where they were? How actually did gasometers work? Why - exactly - were the canals built? And why were they built where they were?" Obviously, these days the canals are more regarded as leisure zones, but originally they performed specific functions, which made them – for a time – not just important, but vital. "What happened to change that?"

Those initial questions led to enquiries into aspects of infrastructure development, which I was aware could be seriously boring territory. I hasten to add that they are only lightly referred to and are included as background information: crucially there is nothing technically challenging or yawn-inducing (hopefully) in the details provided. They were, though, relevant to all those who lived in the area, to born Londoners and to migrants from near and far who would in turn spawn other Londoners.

That line of enquiry set the background of how the area developed but did not address the many basic human issues, the spirit of the age or consider the nature of society. It was, therefore, necessary to ask other questions which might inform their lives: what rights did ordinary men and women have as individual human beings? What rights did women have, and how were these affected by marital status? What had history bequeathed to them all?

Legal restraints have always been imposed upon people as workers, but what rights, if any, did they have? What were the regulations that controlled them – and which of these afforded them protection? The Factory Acts of the 19th century were a new concept – as indeed was the very notion of a factory – and there were certainly no Health and Safety "demands" upon employers. At the beginning of that century - in those *good old days* - employers had total and free rein: they were not "hamstrung" (as sly right-wingers would now have it) by such "ridiculous red-tape" as later bound those engaged on the construction of the London Olympic stadia, a project which for some apparently inexplicable reason had been completed without a single fatality. In the 19th century deaths, accidents and injuries at work were commonplace inconveniences for employers, while the workers had no recourse to representation or opportunity for litigation and compensation.

A look at what work people mainly did would obviously contrast with the present day, but I wondered on what scale or to what degree? Even with the change that had shifted many workers away from the land at the beginning of the 19th century, agriculture still accounted for a great deal of employment, and was in addition a cohesive social force for vast communities. This way of life also both supported and required the work of many associated and ancillary trades, such as blacksmiths, farriers, harness-makers, saddlers, wheelwrights and millers etc. Working the land then as now further required seasonal workers.

At the heart of all country, village, town and city environments other diverse trades flourished: basket makers, rope-makers, tinsmiths, cordwainers, glove-makers, cutlers, candle-makers, milliners/hatters etc. Along with all the tradesmen and women and skilled workers there were throughout the country huge numbers of daily-employed labourers.

There were also mining industries (for coal, tin and copper etc), which thrived and possibly enriched their owners, if not their workers. Whilst these men worked underground and were engaged in hazardous and unhealthy toil, they – like the workers who grafted generations later (even until the 1980's) – were only paid from the time they were actually *at* the rock or coal-face no matter how far down under the ground or however distant it was from the site entrance. In some cases that distance was 3 miles! Coal mining, though, had nevertheless been regarded as vital, not that this was signified in the wages of the miners. It had certainly allowed the Industrial Revolution to take place, powering steam engines, fuelling production as well as blast furnaces which turned iron ore into iron. Coal production was massive in the 19th century, reaching a peak of 292 million metric tonnes per year in 1913, when it also was employing around one million people. (The deposits are still there but now we only mine 2 million tones.) Similarly the tin mines have gone, although there are now thought to also contain lithium, an element much in demand for electric cars and batteries. *(See M. Garside)* The Victorians, however, knew nothing of lithium. Incidentally back in the 18th century the Mynydd Parys Mountain Mine in Anglesey, Wales, was the largest producer of copper in the world (see Bib: copper kingdom) and provided the copper sheathing for the hulls of British Navy warships - its fleet being completely coppered between 1778-82. (See Bib: mindat)

Whilst all of these jobs and trades were land-based, there was also much demand for river workers, for bargees, for fishermen and for seafaring men: occupations largely of that by-gone era. It was not uncommon for the census to record in the occupations' section, "mariner," a term which encompassed merchant seamen, Masters and Mates. There were also those seamen who were engaged and serving in the Royal Navy. (How many people, I wonder, currently know anyone with a working connection to the sea?) Of course, where the sea met the land there were ports and docks which bustled with workers.

As industrial and manufacturing methods developed, the simple cottage industries of family enterprises could not compete and their labour – if it was required - was swallowed up by huge-scale operations along with their expertise. Many traditional trades and skills disappeared as the trends of further mechanisation continued apace, such that now with computerisation most are non-existent (or have been out-sourced). The technological progress which began in that period would change the very nature of work.

At this point more questions forced their way to the fore: "What age did a young person became a full-time worker? What was considered a normal working week? What hours did adults and children work and what were their conditions like?" Here, though, I realized the assumption of people "at" work had not considered how they got "to" work, and what transport was available to them?

So, there was work, travel and then home, but what shelter was available to them, what housing did they have? What was their access to water and to sanitation? What was the effect upon them of migration (and of a vast population-increase) in regards to work, housing and social conditions? How did their conditions affect their rest and their play?

What age did - or could - people marry? What was their experience of mortality, of infant deaths, of lives cut short by disease and poor conditions? What was the toll of repeated pregnancies and how common was the occurrence of mothers dying in child-birth? In an age before the invention of "the Pill" (and of morning-after medication) what contraception was available to people and what part did abortion play in their lives?

What then also of their food, sustenance and drink? In cosmopolitan 21st century London and other British cities our citizens can wander down a High Street and eat "around the world" such is the availability and variety of international and global cuisine. Modern metro-citizens are seemingly careless of having a huge carbon footprint in relation to food supply but where did the city's food come from in the 19th Century? How was their food and other goods measured, weighed and paid for? What coinage did they use for purchases, and what systems of currency and mensuration were used to count their money and to weigh and measure goods etc.?

In 2001 Tony Blair, the UK Prime Minister, asserted that the Labour Party's top priority "is and will always be education, education, education," and two decades on the people of Great Britain currently expect children to be educated from at least the academic year in which a child becomes 5 years of age up until the age of 18. They are educated now at least to the extent that they can pass the exams, tests and get grades which governments, subsequent to Blair and Gordon Brown, have both determined and disparaged simultaneously. Back in the simpler times of the 19th century, though, what schooling was available for ordinary children (those not from the well-to-do classes) and what schooling did they actually get? Could they read, and if so what did they read; what was the availability of books and newspapers?

We now have many media outlets and organs, be they newspapers, radio, television, smart-phone, satellite/ internet etc., some of which are free to the user (usually for the price of having their opinion shaped and their biases moulded while being exposed to brand advertising). These present information as if it were reliable, factual and accurate. Despite their many forms which seemingly offer supposed independent commentary and opinion – their message rarely strays into anything likely to affect the vested interest of the "establishment" and of their proprietor. That intent is unlikely to have changed. We generally accept, however, that we have to read between the lines, but how, with few lines to read between, did those of the 19th century get "news"? What did they know of current affairs, of foreign affairs, of war, and famine?

I also wondered what they did for leisure; how poor or how wealthy were they. Whilst love may conquer many things, it tends to stagnate when steeped in poverty, becomes diluted to homeopathic proportions by violence, humiliation and hopelessness so... could they divorce? What happened when they became sick... or too old or infirm for work? We naturally acknowledge that death was a regular uninvited guest to most households: it played a large and constant part in their lives, and the increase in the overall population exacerbated the problem, but what impact did this have on how and where the dead were disposed of in the capital?

All those questions together shaped the work so that it grew beyond the limits of being solely *Baxter-family* specific; it became a generalized overview. In due course, the Baxter's and their contemporaries would move on and away from the area which had changed irrevocably, while their lives were perhaps only marginally different. They would migrate from Somers Town – for largely the same reasons they went there in the first place;

and this narrative also tracks their movements into other local areas until time caught up with them, as it must.

The book's content aims to offer a commentary of unrepresented lives impacted by the absence of social welfare and healthcare; of lives kept in ignorance – manipulated and controlled by a system governed by self-interest. These ordinary men and women lived without the right to vote and without a voice. I hope this work speaks for them at least in some small way.

Table of Contents

BONES: DEAR READER, A FEW FOREWORDS

Make no bones about it: family history is a rapidly growing hobby for many people, and –very much in its favour – it can be done by day or by night: come rain or come shine. The easy accessibility of on-line resources makes it, therefore, a very user-friendly activity; and while it is a vastly expanding amateur pursuit even more qualified researchers and assiduous social historians are also to be found doing those graveyard shifts. For hobbyist and social researchers alike - with or without burning the midnight oil - it is a compelling enquiry.

Family history research, for those who succumb to its charms, can be a wondrous shell. Whilst it doesn't always readily give up its pearls it is a treasury of an enquirer's social DNA: with meticulous attention, with luck and perseverance, it can open up a world of the past which is profoundly personal. Your prize is an initial introduction to people of fairly recent antiquity, but then each new acquaintance may subsequently reveal other strangers. Thus, the process allows you to remember strangers who have gone before. Ah, surely you may baulk at that statement and say that it is patent nonsense: for it is not possible to remember those whom we have never known... or is it?

In Egyptian mythology Isis searched for and collected the scattered bones – the body parts and limbs (the members) – of her murdered husband, Osiris; and, so the legend tells us, she then painstakingly pieced these organic bits back together, literally "re-membering" him. Bringing Osiris fleetingly back to life – for just long enough – she was able to conceive their son and avenger, Horus.

Well, the tale of Isis may be a slight digression, but having re-membered some of my dead relatives, I found these creatures also took on a life of their own. They soon and quietly re-orientated my enquiries and transformed the underlying purpose of my original endeavour; and weirdly, as already alluded to, the closer I looked, the more they compelled me to broaden the scope of my enquiry.

In doing so, these previously unknown-to-me souls have led me through portals of time to the shadows of the stories of the ordinary people who made me *ME* and possibly of similar people who made you *YOU*. Along these pathways I have caught glimpses of the era these strangers actually lived in. Thankfully, these have allowed me to find my own new understanding of that part of the past and enabled me to appreciate its greater relevance to the present in which you and I (and our contemporaries) live.

In some instances their unearthed circumstances could have reasonably induced a desire for an Isis-like retribution against someone or against a class of individuals (who still retain power, wealth, benefit and or influence), but instead they have encouraged me to content myself with just a gentle re-calibration of what exactly I understand as a history of the 19th century and beyond.

N.b. Any work which embraces the 18th and 19th centuries should consider people who were deprived of rights and or those who had little or none to lose in the first place. There is not, however, any particular emphasis on direct slavery within this book, because while it is a hot topic I feel it is worthy of much greater research and enquiry than I can commit to at this time. A question that I would be tempted to pose if slavery was part of my focus, and one I would encourage you to pursue, is to ask **not why** slave-owners in 1835 were paid government bonds/gilts as compensation under the *Slavery Abolition Act (1835)*, but ***who*** continued to receive those payments up until February 1st 2015?

And why, and by whose order, have those recipients continued to remain nameless and to enjoy shameless and profitable anonymity?

(See: Fowler. Naomi, and also I would recommend: Draper. Dr Nick: What does London owe to slavery? 28 Oct 2010 UCL Lunch Hour Lecture).

While this book was concerned primarily with the affairs and progress of one ordinary 19th century family – unremarkable strangers, if you will– their lives are to an extent largely representative of those of many other ordinary people. Crucially their common and shared experiences were shaped first by history (and by laws which emanated from past events) and subsequently by contemporary laws that were used to further control them. All these strangers were, of course, also affected by the social and environmental change that came with the development of the Somers Town area and by events that occurred in parallel to their simple goings-on (their daily struggles) within the rapidly changing capital. Individually and collectively many factors and events – sometimes from far-flung places - would all be significant to these people to varying degrees: for, ordinary or not, we are all tethered to the peg of history by the ropes of old agreements and laws, by current affairs and by the fibres of indefatigable avarice, which continue to bind our present and our future.

The narrative begins in an era that predates the vision of 19th century Victorian London which is usually portrayed in black-and-white movies - with their pervading images of polluting smog swamping the city's bustling inhabitants. This pre-pea-souper London was also a smaller entity, and did not extend much beyond the city proper – "the square mile" – from whence the wealthier people of the day then went off to places like Hackney and Battersea for the clean and clear country air.

This work is both an informal record of families who lived in London in Somers Town at the time of great change, and of others who – having had to abandon a rural life on the "land" and in their small villages – had flocked to the urban environment of the capital in search of work. In that period the population of

London had risen from 1.09 million in 1800 to 2.6 million in 1851; and the ramifications of that increase were enormous for both indigenous inhabitants and for the new immigrant population. Whilst London may have grown physically to incorporate other areas and hinterland these are the figures recorded in ONS sources (See Bibliography: ONS Old Bailey). By 1860 the population had reached 3 million. The magnitude of changes and their impact obviously gave rise to many logistical problems.

One such problem, which I will deal with presently in the section *At Your Disposal,* concerns a by-product of the burgeoning population: the pressing issue of huge numbers of deaths within the metropolis and what to do with the bodies.

I hope that this piecing together of the fragments of these ordinary people's lives – within the wider context of what was going on around them – is tolerably presented.

The personal events and individual tragedies which affected these people are used as examples: as references to a broader picture. They allow the scope of enquiry to be magnified, so it is not exactly the mere story of these simple people's lives; it is more a documentary flavour of the times in which they lived and of the domestic politics and social arrangements that impacted upon these strangers.

These were not famous people: they were just ordinary souls, who may or may not have been typical for their time. I have not attempted to put words in their mouths, nor – since they have apparently left no personal records or writings – can I tell you any of their thoughts; but I hope that the information provided is sufficient to allow a greater understanding of the general conditions they endured and of the struggles which beset them and their neighbours in 19th century London.

CAVEATS

Importantly, the following is not something to be read *at length*: I hope you find it a novel experience, but it is not a "novel," and you will surely find that quite often the butterfly of my attention has succumbed to flitting off to different nectar sources. You may, therefore, find it more palatable to take your time with it... to put it down and maybe return a little later would not be bad advice, although I must admit I am rarely given to taking advice myself.

The names of these strangers contained within regularly are unimaginatively repetitive and this can be very confusing... especially when a reader is tired. So, please remember.... a little at a time... less is more.... or be like the butterfly and flit off for a while. I will occasionally flag up when a digression is imminent (or where I believe a break might be suitable) with the inclusion of a butterfly. Consider this then whenever you see this symbol

A smaller butterfly indicates a return to a familiar track.

I have tried throughout to be consistent in only asserting facts where I am sure there is sufficient evidence to substantiate a particular claim: you – and the fullness of time - may judge how successful or not I have been. In other ways, in regard to the times they lived in, I have researched the areas and the social climate, and what I have written is my interpretations of that reading.

Recently I read Chaucer's Canterbury tales which were originally written over 640 years ago in 1381. At the end of the book (according to the version I read) he had commented that he hoped the reader enjoyed his stories; but in case they happened not to like them he also hoped that they would know that the writer had essentially tried to do his best. He further added that he hoped they also knew "that if he could have done better, he would."

Well, the tales have survived on their own merit, and I would admit that I found his comment rather quite charming. Of course, it could be read cynically as a preemption of criticism, but I feel more that it endures positively as a noble aspiration and remains a gentle encouragement to the reader at large: it is a call for tolerance and for generosity of spirit to be abroad in the world, which surely can't be a bad thing. Bravo Chaucer!

Howsoever, you read it or sample the following text, I can only hope you find it is worthy of your time.

At your disposal: Burial or cremation of the dead.

Demographic changes and their wider impact on services, facilities and infra-structure are currently monitored and considered by bodies such as the Office of National Statistics; thus a modern society plans strategically for the short and long-term. In the 19th century, though, and with few public services, I am not sure there was that much official oversight going on. That notwithstanding and whether or not they were utilised at the time, those demographics which were noted - and their consequent impact - have revealed some interesting details.

One of the associated problems of any rapid surge in population is a precipitant increase in local natural wastage. A greater concentration of people in an area must lead inevitably to an increase in the number of people who die there… and vitally, all those corpses crammed into the mid-19th century metropolis needed to be disposed of…. and the God-fearing society of Britain then almost exclusively favoured burial/interment as the means of disposal.

Of course, in other cultures and in other times, the dead were often consigned to fire; even the Old Testament of the Bible records Abraham's God instructing him to prepare a funeral pyre for his son Isaac, whom God had commanded Abraham to sacrifice. Fortunately, Isaac was reprieved; others were no doubt subsequently offered up, with the use of funeral pyres unaffected: for millennia they have continued to be used in many cultures as an option of dealing with human remains. However, the advent of Christianity and its later adoption in Britain had impacted on this method of disposal.

Apparently, cremation did not sit quite so well with the Christian belief in resurrection: a body of recognised bones and bits-and-bobs might (in Isis-fashion) reasonably be brought back to life, but a pile of ash….? Well –and despite the Book of Common

Prayer and its "ashes to ashes" phrase in the burial service – *that* seemingly was stretching things a little too far. Thus, for over a thousand years Britain had embraced the practice of burial, such that in the 1800's it was not only the traditional solution but also the normal – and almost the sole - method for despatching the dead. The few exceptions might include mariners, who passed on the briny, and for convenience and hygiene would mostly be "buried" at sea; the wealthy, also had the capital to opt for interment within vaults and mausolea. There were, however, not many who like Jeremy Bentham chose to be embalmed for public display.

Now space may have been the final frontier for the fictional crew of the Star-ship Enterprise, but in earthly terms - especially in regards to space on an island - terra firma remains a finite property. Where for centuries the Christian-departed of the British Isles had been buried comfortably within the consecrated grounds of their local church, the increased urban demand for such burial plots was outstripping the available supply of hallowed ground. With the population explosion (and subsequent huge numbers of people dying within inner-city parishes) churchyards, like St Pancras Old Churchyard and St Luke's in Old Street, London, were becoming swamped. The situation at the latter rapidly became quite desperate: existing graves were being double and triple-packed, and bodies were piled upon bodies. Increasingly these were planted nearer to the surface, and as a result the ground had "risen", and the dead were soon over-spilling. Complaints were made .... dogs, apparently, were retrieving bones.... rats were said to be feasting on remains....

In addition to this there were fears that decaying corpses were contaminating the water supply and those concerns were exacerbated by the cholera epidemics of 1848/9 and the 1850's, which also led to spikes in mortality rates. Even Bunhill Fields graveyard (whose very name was a corruption of *Bone-hill*), – and which had been the final resting place of non-conformists such as John Bunyan, William Blake and Daniel Defoe – had to be closed to further burials. It would seem that it was only in response to this growing problem and in order to accommodate the increase in metropolitan mortality that the Government first set aside land for *public* cemeteries. Also news to me was that there was then (either within or without a city on dry land) no alternative to interment or to being put in a crypt/mausoleum.

It may be interesting to note that whilst for centuries it had been quite permissible to burn someone alive at the stake, it was not deemed legal to cremate a *dead* body. In fact this would not change until February 1884 when a judgement by Mr Justice Stephen declared cremation legal "provided no nuisance is caused in the process to others." (See *Bibliography* Justice Stephen). That ruling, though, was a long way off, and in the meantime local government was ordered to provide municipal burial grounds. (Cremation and its path to acceptance are covered later in CREMATION NOTES. See index).

Despite my misgivings about a lack of official oversight of demographics there must have been some who were wary of the effects of increased population. In 1832 Parliament had after all passed an Act encouraging the establishment of private cemeteries outside central London. Subsequently, during the next decade seven cemeteries were established: the General Cemetery of All Souls was the first to be set out at Kensal Green, followed by West Norwood, Highgate, Abney Park, Brompton, All Saints (at Nunhead) and Tower Hamlets (at Bow). These cemeteries were soon resplendent with marvellous monuments, sculptures and memorial stones, such that these Victorian cemeteries are now known as the Magnificent Seven. The later Burial Act of 1852 required further new burial grounds in a list of urban parishes of London (the Metropolis).

One cemetery – Brookwood, which opened in 1854, near Woking in Surrey – even had its own railway station on a dedicated train line called the necropolis railway! (The cemetery had two stations: one which served the Anglican community, while the other was for non-conformists and other faiths.) The railway company offered 1st, 2nd and 3rd class tickets, with similarly designated carriages and waiting rooms; thus, even in death, class divisions were both observed and strictly operated. Such segregation ensured there was no mixing of nobs, wannabes (different knobs) and hoi-polloi.

Incidentally, third-class passengers and mourners were charged 2 shillings for a return trip, and of course no-one (dead or alive) travelled free. The deceased relative of 3rd-class travellers would be conveyed to their final destination upon payment of a third class "coffin-ticket" which cost a half-crown (2 shillings and 6 pence) ... one way, of course. {See: Clarke, John M..}

EXECUTION QUIRKS: BURNING THE LIVING. QUEER ENDINGS.

In England, it had been the custom to burn heretics alive as had been the fate, for example, of Joan of Arc in disputed territory in 1431 during the Hundred Years War. Admittedly the Maid was burnt in Orleans in the Loire valley but the punishment was carried out ***by*** the "English" Lancastrian/Plantagenet's and their allies, the Frankish Burgundians. (France, by the way, was not then a unified country as we may know it now.) Whilst this practice of burning heretics does not appear to have been widely used in England, it was certainly not unknown, and was later revived with some relish by Mary I (bloody Mary) in her 5-year reign (1553-1558). During this period she managed to burn some 274 people, including Bishops Latimer, Ridley and Cranmer. This method of execution fell largely out of favour and the last **man** burnt for heresy in England was in 1612. (Actually the last execution for heresy was by hanging in 1697.)

Burning at the stake in public, though, remained a legal punishment for **women** found guilty of high treason and also for the act of petty treason i.e., killing their spouse, or for the murder of an employer by his or her servant, or for a clergyman's murder of his religious superior: any circumstance, in fact, where someone of a lower status had had the gall or temerity to kill a person of a higher social status. Burning was also the women's punishment for witchcraft and for coining (counterfeiting).

Now, you may feel this was brutally unfair and even misogynistic, but a man's fate was as unenviable as it was gruesome: he was first hanged by the neck but **not** until he was dead, (meaning he was only partially throttled by temporary suspension by a ligature); then he was drawn (dragged along over the rough ground – tearing, grazing and shredding his skin) onwards through the streets to a place of further torture and merriment for the crowd. Then the unfortunate chap was allowed to catch his breath: a short rest during which he would be castrated and emasculated – no doubt the worst break he ever had - before having his stomach sliced open and his entrails/intestines/bowels pulled out; and, finally, before he bled out totally, he would be chopped into parts and beheaded. Women escaped this mutilation-fest because similar intestinal removal would have necessitated exposing their naked bodies (heaven forbid!), which perversely would have offended the delicate sensibilities of the perpetrators and the crowd. It was said to be "a violation of that natural decency and delicacy inherent at all times to be cherished in the sex." (See Bibliography: Devereaux. Simon,)

On the 18th of March 1789 Catherine Murphy, a counterfeiter, was the last woman in England to be burned at the stake. (She was reputedly – and mercifully (?) strangled first, and thus not literally burned to death). The penalty of burning at the stake was abolished the next year, 1790, just seven years before the birth at Ratcliff of my ancestor, one Francis Baxter, a cutler, who would later relocate to Somers Town in the 1830's.

Perhaps the methods of execution (which also included boiling) are a reminder of the not-too-distant brutality, the barbarity and the manner by which the lower orders were then kept in fearful check. They were further constrained into subjection by other laws, including the aforementioned petty treason, plus over 100 more minor other criminal offences which importantly also attracted a capital sentence, i.e. one which demanded forfeiture of their life. Also included on the list was homosexuality, so woe betide any gay Baxters. It may be interesting to note that whilst homosexual acts would remain illegal until 1967 (whereafter it was permissable between consenting adults above the age of 21), some extremely dubious progress towards liberality had slowly taken place in the interim. Prior to 1967 convicted homosexuals like Alan Turing in 1954 were still urged/compelled to undergo correctional therapy to "cure them" of their homosexuality: I believe that part of his deal to avoid imprisonment was that Turing *volunteered* or agreed through coercion to be "treated" by what was euphemistically called chemical castration. Back in the 1830's, though, such men who were found to be *guilty* were simply hanged.

Incidentally, there would still be public executions almost throughout the entire life of Francis Baxter the cutler until, that is, 1868 when - whilst capital punishments continued - they were contrived more decorously out of public view behind prison walls. With television, radio and motion pictures yet to be invented the mob, being starved of this distracting entertainment, were not best pleased.

WHAT IS IN A NAME? ITS RELATIVE..

Generally, you will share YOUR surname with only ONE of your EIGHT great-grandparents. There might also be the coincidence of same but unrelated surnames, but statistically that is the way it works. Likewise, in the next generation back yours will only be one that sits alongside fifteen others; and yet crucially you are equally related to each. The chances are that most people do not know the surnames of most of those fifteen others.

This narrative initially concerns one of my great-great grandparents who was a stonemason named Francis Baxter, who was the son of the aforementioned Francis Baxter (that cutler of Ratcliff); and, of course, it is about him and his family, who in turn, dear reader if you happen to be kin, are all part of *our* story. The events of these times and the general state of affairs will nevertheless be likely to have affected some of *your* ancestors.

The following script attempts to illuminate the lives of my 19th century Baxter ancestors and others – who lived, loved, toiled and for some who died – in the Somers Town and Kings Cross areas of London. The Baxters certainly lived there from at least the time when Victoria was just a slip of a teenage Queen.

So, working backwards from what is known as certain, which is the absolute prerequisite modus operandi of the genealogist, I found an early reference to these Baxters within this area in the 1841 Census (the first Census where names were recorded). Subsequently the birth certificates of the younger children shown then confirmed a presence in Somers Town at least from the ascendancy of Victoria to the throne in 1837.

The Baxters were found to be amongst what the Census described as a thickly inhabited area. New arrivals to that locale included people from abroad; many came from Ireland - even before the famines - but there were great swathes of the domestic population who had also relocated. The reasons for this huge influx of English workers to the capital (which similarly affected other towns and cities) were the changes in agriculture, the enclosures of land, urban industrialisation, and the development of canals and railways. Migration was about opportunity... sometimes it was also about fleeing from persecution... but for most and above all it was about escaping hunger and poverty. Few would achieve the latter.

In that 1841 Census Francis Baxter, the central focus of my attention in this piece, is shown as being 14 years of age. In our time – and especially with our notions of childhood – we would regard him as just a boy or perhaps as a teenager/young-adult, but for that period in which he lived he would already have been a full-time worker for quite some years. I hope the demands and growth of industrialisation had not necessarily affected him as directly as it did others who were caught in the traps of gluttonous industries which fed so enthusiastically upon cheap child-labour. However, there wasn't too much that intervened between the children's nursery and the progression to becoming a worker: there were few schools and fewer still that would have had any use for a fourteen year old. No, Francis at 14 years of age had no option but to be a worker.

Of course, the children of the poor and working-classes had historically worked before industrialisation occurred: this had taken the form of "house-work" (tidying and cleaning within the home) and where their input assisted the family enterprise. In the rural aspect children helped out and gave a hand in accordance with their ability and also where they could: on farms, for example, youngsters' activities were relatively light even though the actual work if done excessively might have tested older backs. With age, they would progress to ploughing and other hard physical tasks, but I don't believe they were worked literally into the ground – pragmatically their contribution was both necessary and essential. Their work input would initially have taken the form of collecting firewood and helping to plant seeds and sow crops such as beans and potatoes. They were also needed to scare the birds from the crops, which no doubt scatter-brained boys may have been only too keen to do. Children might gather mushrooms, or pick fruit or hops as the seasons determined. Boys were more likely to have been also employed to tend animals, to prevent the livestock from straying and also to help herd animals to market. Country-girls may have done some similar work but they would definitely have done domestic work, fed chickens and milked cows.

In the towns children helped in the home or did light tasks, but these were fairly gradual progressions. This was regarded as normal: it was not seen as exploitative or abusive, but was rather viewed as necessary practice which ensured the survival of the family. It was also seen as training or more probably as acclimatisation: preparation to taking on more adult roles. (There were, naturally, still many occasions where children – even very young children - were nevertheless worked excessively and unscrupulously.) *See Bibliography: The Museum of Childhood.*

Increasingly, though, in the early 19th century, the poor - and emphatically the children of the poor - had no option but to work or starve. Indeed, the advocates of the prevailing Workhouse-system were so keen on preventing idleness and encouraging a work ethic that there are reports of children at the age of 5 residing in the workhouse who were "introduced" to the spinning room! Can you imagine a five-year old being set to work? If that doesn't cause something to pop within you, stop reading: there is something wrong with you. Go forth... and seek some shred of humanity.... before you multiply...

It is slightly more probable that Francis's then recorded age is close to his actual age, since ages given at this stage of life tend to be less inaccurate than those given later. (On future records we find that years, like whiskers on an old great-aunt's chin, tend to get shaved off somewhat erratically.) Other sources down the years, though, indicate that Francis, who was to become a stonemason, was born sometime between 1823 and 1827.

NEW ARRIVALS, OLD FAMILIAR NAMES

Francis Baxter was certainly born during George IV's short reign (1820-30), an era which pre-dated the obligation to register births (which occurred in 1837), so that an official Public record of his birth is not available. Almost universally, though, various rites of passage *were* recorded within the framework of organized religion, and of course, tantalizingly these christenings and baptisms – being then more popular than they are currently – offer the genealogical prospector opportunity to dig further into their research.

However, opportunity can also be a double-edged sword, and we must be careful how we handle it if we are to identify the correct individual. A number of factors come into play. In the event that an adult, say a George Gates, has stated his place of birth in a census (and assuming that was correct) then you are required to look for a baptism of a child in a particular area within a certain time period. If George married before civil registration then you may be unlikely to know his father's forename. This is one difficulty. Another is that the same surnames may proliferate within an area, and the inhabitants may be distantly related even if they are unaware of a connection. Also, unfortunately in those days not only did rakes of non-descript horny-handed sons-of-the-soil named John Smith duly turn up to christen their cherished child, but with astounding regularity they unimaginatively named their male offspring after themselves, their brother or their dad. The situation is often compounded when adult siblings followed the tradition of naming their first sons after their dad, so that a granddad may have had three or four grandsons with the same name and all born sometimes within just a few years of each other. Female names, of course, follow similar trends with girls being named after aunts, mothers, grandmothers, as well as Queens and princesses.

Anyone enquiring into their "roots" will soon unearth often previously unknown ancestors, and in many cases they are helped by those Church and Public records, by ancestry sites, and other family history facilities. These can all be fantastic resources *provided they are used properly,* i.e. critically and accurately. However, should you hear someone declare they have traced their family tree back to when "would you Adam-and-Eve-it" fig leaves were the fashion or back to 1500-and-dot then be prepared to reach for a large pinch of salt – and do raise at least one eyebrow.

In the main the further back you enquire the less certain you can be; and with that in mind, while in both the censuses of 1851 and 1881 Francis Baxter gave his place of birth as Clerkenwell, there is no actual evidence yet to substantiate this assertion – neither within census returns, nor within known Church *records.*

A few further words of warning: a great deal of the "facts" and connections as presented by amateur researchers on the internet do not stand up to scrutiny; even where their sources are cited it is not unusual to find that these actually contradict the pronouncements they are meant to support. I would recommend that all assertions are tested for conclusive and verifiable proof.

Legal documentation, land-deeds, criminal records and litigation may provide confirmation of the identity of an individual, especially when they suitably cross -reference; but the necessary deeds which attend wealth and ownership are not generally applicable in the lives of the majority –and not in regards to most of "my" people.

Naturally those repetitions of names may frustrate attempts to identify particular ancestors, but even where the individuals have been confidently (and competently) identified we are often left with a gaggle of people within a family with the same names. This can easily cause confusion to readers of any written account of the families.

In the 1841 census, ref HO 107 685 19 folio 13, for example, our Francis is recorded as living at home with his mum, Elizabeth, and his Dad, another Francis Baxter. As previously stated to distinguish the two I have opted to associate them with their subsequent occupations, thus one is "Francis the stonemason" and the other is "Francis the cutler."

SOMERS' TOWN HOMES. THE AREA. THE GROWING INFRASTRUCTURE.

Young stonemason-to-be Francis (at 14 years of age) is shown in 1841 as the eldest child – or, importantly, at least he was the eldest of those children who were then within the family home. (His parents had married in 1820 and as his age would indicate a birth around 1827, there is every likelihood that other children preceded Francis - although whether they had survived is another matter.)

Home for Francis and his younger siblings was here in the Parliamentary Borough of Marylebone, in the parish of St. Pancras. In fact, were you to visit the British Library in London you would be treading in their spectral footsteps for that was the geographic location of their home. (It occurs to me to wonder if the Baxters or their neighbours possessed such a thing as a book...) To be precise the buildings then to be found at that National Grid reference were within John's Court, near Ebenezer Buildings, which it would appear was close to Marson Street. It lay off to the immediate west of Skinner Street, which is now the start of Midland Road.

Skinner Street may have been named because it led to the Skinners' Company Estate, whose land (which remained farm land until 1807) formerly straddled the New Road and stretched south-east to the Foundling's Hospital. It may also have got its name because when the Baxters were in the area it then housed a large population of labourers and trades people, amongst whom were workers in the skin trade.

A few skinners were specialists in ermine, sable and marten which by their exclusivity were the sartorial reserve of royalty and aristocracy. I believe some ancient laws/diktats outlawed the wearing of these by any upstarts who may have had access to such highly prized creature pelts. So there was even a hierarchy of fur: with squirrel and fox adorning the middle classes, while rabbit and cat did for the poor. I am not sure then of the availability of mink or of its social position. I also don't know how common or not was the use of rat fur, although it is currently being used as a substitute for cashmere. Beavers, being semi-aquatic rodents, were another matter: they could at least boast of especially good water-proofing qualities.

All this section of Somers Town which is to the immediate east of modern day Ossulston Street was a part of - or at least in close proximity to – the district known as the Brill. In the argot of the last few decades "brill!" has been used as a contraction of brilliant, but I suspect it was not this quality for which the area was so-called. I further wondered if there was some association with the smooth oval-shaped flat-fish which is a member of the Turbot family, but it seems not.

According to the Camden History Review, (See Hayes. David 2020), the name is thought to derive from an old French word, meaning a park or wood stocked with beasts of the chase. Mr Hayes states that by 1690 there was a rural tavern here, which was a popular resort of Londoners. The area surrounding, owned by Lord Somers, was called Brill Farm, and was developed from the late 18th century as Somers Town. Its eastern part, with a bustling street market had at its centre a rebuilt Brill Tavern, and was often referred to simply as The Brill.

The Brill Market (1850's)

In 1849 Kings Cross station opened for business, increasing the flow of people and travellers through the area. I am not sure if this had any effect on the local "Brill" and its trade. Apparently, though, by 1850 the Brill had become noted for its Sunday markets, and it attracted visitors and shoppers from many of the surrounding areas, including Hampstead, Holloway, Highgate, and Camden Town. One report claims visitors came from up to 6 miles away - which sounds a little too incredible bearing in mind the condition of roads and the poor means of transportation available.

Henry Mayhew, whose collection of articles, including the ones he had written in 1850-52 for the *Morning Chronicle,* were published as *London Labour and the London Poor,* was unusual in that he wrote about ordinary people and the street markets (like the Brill) which they used; he also considered the lives of street-vendors: the criers, the meat-dealers and sweet pie-men and those who sold various fruits and vegetables. At Brill Market, Mayhew reported that as many as 300 pitches every Sunday were selling meat, vegetables, clothes and shoes.

Christian groups were upset by this Sunday trade and lay-preachers would also be seen preaching the gospel and temperance as well as observance of the Sabbath. Strong advocates of this included Sabbatarian organisations like The Lord's Day Observance Society which had been co-founded in 1831 by the vicar of St. Mary's Islington (1824-1832), Daniel Wilson. Objections included the argument that Sunday work and trading was made necessary as a result of the long hours of "normal" work (Monday to Saturday). The Illustrated News in 1858 further commented that as men were not paid their wages until late Saturday night that facilities must be afforded to the poorer classes in purchasing food at other times... It hoped for change, and that they (the employers) would know the actual state of things and recognise the necessity of abolishing Sunday trading altogether.

The length of hours worked coupled with a purposely lax attitude to the timing of payment of their wages did not allow people enough time to shop for their vitals etc., such that this prevented them from keeping the Sabbath as a day of rest. To compound the problem men were further delayed by being required to wait for payment in a particular pub – in which and by no coincidence his employer often had a financial interest. Compelled to wait they bought drink – or borrowed the money on account – until the wage arrived, sometimes late in the evening. Of course the longer they waited the more they drank, and the more the employer/publican earned. This dubious device survived in many forms throughout the 20th century. I expect it still goes on in some places.)

The arguments against Sunday work and against Sunday trading caused some political and religious unrest. This persisted throughout the 19th century and beyond, but as employers were rather more enthusiastic about getting their pound of flesh than their employees' "moral welfare" which would necessitate allowing them more free time, the objections then had little effect.

Lack of regulation and an abundance of workers meant desperate competition for jobs; and the most direct way they could compete was to undercut each others' hourly wages to such an extent that they could not live on their wages without working the excessive hours demanded by their employers. Often the reward for their cheap labour – even that wage derived from working up to 16 hours-a-day – was insufficient to cover their outlay: these were not work-shy idlers, and gradually it became unavoidably evident that there now existed huge numbers of *working poor* who were living in chronic want. A few philanthropists were aware of their plight and were sympathetic to them; others were fearful that such a condition might lead to social unrest or even revolution. Despite that growing awareness little changed for the working poor. Too few people of influence were interested in their plight or their welfare, although some did worry about the effect their circumstances may have had on their morality and their souls.

Help was scarce, and self-help was encouraged as long as it did not include the "combination" of workers into groups. Laws had been made to prohibit such actions, and even when the restraints were repealed other restrictions would then be brought to bear. There were great efforts made to prevent workers organising and to prevent them forming a Trade Union where they could bargain collectively and offer their service and their labour for a consistent rate of pay.

As work was a six-day/ 12-16-hours-a-day-enterprise the street markets were open into the late evening. [1] Mayhew wrote about a Saturday night market scene with "hundreds of stalls," donkey-carts and barrows where the costers plied their trade on the crowded pavements and roads. He described the housewife "in her thick shawl, with the market-basket in her arm" walking slowly on and stopping to "cheapen [i.e. to haggle or bid to lower the price for] a bunch of greens." I wonder if Mayhew – decent man though he was – ever haggled *of necessity.*

Mayhew's attention also fell upon many enterprises including the sellers of dolls, of ice-creams and of poison for rats and other vermin. These, of course, were the normal costers (costermongers), but in addition he observed those at the bottom of the social barrel, who included the buyers of waste and refuse, the bone-grubbers and rag-gatherers. Few escaped his attention, certainly not the beggars of various kinds or even the cigar-end finders – whose scavenging contrived to manufacture and compose newly "whole" products for the more desperate smoker. Sadly, in 2022 I witnessed a woman doing the same in Stoke Newington.

---

[1] N.B. The OECD gives global figures for manufacturing workers in the 19th century as working 60-90 hours weekly on average. See Bibliography Gilmore. Oisín,

In the 1851 first edition of his reports of the poor's hectic and clamorous lives Mayhew also stated that "until it is seen and heard, we have no sense of the scramble that is going on throughout London for a living." At the beginning of his work "London Labour and London Poor" he stated that his earnest hope was "that the book may serve to give the rich a more intimate knowledge of the sufferings, and the frequent heroism under those sufferings, of the poor." Mayhew did not condemn these as apparent *low-lifes* but rather instead he beseeched those "who are beyond temptation to look with charity on the frailties of their less fortunate brethren." He was one of the few good guys, and he also encouraged those who are in high places "(*to*) bestir themselves to improve the condition of the class of people whose misery, ignorance and vice, live amidst all the immense wealth and great knowledge of 'the first city in the world.' This - to say the very least - was a national disgrace to us." Mayhew wasn't wrong.

The Illustrated News, a little later in 1858, described the area as reputedly formerly "Caesar's camp." It also remarked that in the Brill area on Sunday mornings from 7 – 12 there were "stands laden with fish, fruit, potatoes and everything that might be needed for a Sunday dinner." Provided, of course, that the punters had the necessary cash. It was also said to be a "fair old hullabaloo of criers." The famous "Cheap Jacques" was there at 19 Skinner Street: the shop, having recently returned to the area, sold dishes and those wares whose commercial, if not spiritual, descendant seems to have found its way down through the centuries to us now in 2022 as the ubiquitous "Pound shop."

Other noted shops in 1858 were Mr Adams' wearing apparel shop and Mr Bates the baker. One can only but pity his son ("Master Bates") – but perhaps that might be too modern an innuendo for those times. The general business of the Brill was apparently so busy that one pork butcher allegedly did not open on the Sunday morning - not as a result of any religious revelation but because he had sold out his complete stock of 60 pigs on the Saturday!

Of course amongst the throng of criers were still the street preachers' who did their utmost to save the people. Preachers were not uncommon in markets, and would remain so for many years to come. I recall a lay-preacher, who worked as a lift engineer, taking his lunch break to preach the gospel in Leather lane in the early 1970's.

The need to earn a living, or to supplement a poor wage, was ever-present. The 1858 report comments that adjacent houses to the Brill "with a yearly rent of £50 can make a living selling from the front rooms, and are not likely to abolish this Sunday trade and desist, and start going to church."

This practice would also survive for a long time: in Kings Cross Road in the 1980's a woman used to sell shellfish from her front room window opposite the Mount Pleasant Postal Sorting Office.

Incidentally the Brill nevertheless eventually disappeared without a record of its passing, dwindling into extinction as so many other markets and Wastes have done.

Other reports have it that "women went to the Brill to buy fish, meat, vegetables and even crockery, while men came to buy clothes and working apparel." Perhaps, they headed for Mr Adams' shop. (The report infers an apparent clear division of labour along gender lines – I would imagine anything to the contrary would have been a rare exception.)

These male shoppers were manual grafters of the same calibre as those who had toiled on the canals (– the same men who also dug the cuttings and created the embankments of the railways). Their job titles designated them as navigators, and in time this term would be shortened to "navvies."

Importantly, these men (the navvies, not the shoppers) had come from far and wide, from within the city and without – from home and abroad... all to seek and find work. Of course, there were waves of political refugees which did impact upon the area, but it is those who came primarily for work who are my current focus. This migration had been a constant feature: its incidence increased from the end of the 18th century and continued to do so in the 19th.

Incidentally, a conurbation could only be called a city if it contained a diocesian Anglican cathedral: this principle was established by Henry VIII and continued in England until 1888, when Birmingham was upgraded to city status, despite not having a cathedral. (Similarly, Belfast which was also without a cathedral had become a city the previous year.) In addition to this, population size was irrelevant: St David's in Wales is the smallest city with a population of 1850 in 2021, followed by St Asaph, the City of London, and by Wells.

An interesting footnote to migration from the country was the effect on the class system and food. Naturally each village and area had a hierarchy with the wider landlord (often being an actual Lord and peer of the realm) or the squire being the local landowner, who might lease some of his land to tenant farmers – who in turn employed farm labourers. Whilst these farmers (the Masters) might have more wealth than their workers, they nevertheless (in general it is supposed) considered that an efficient worker was a sufficiently-fed worker, and it was not uncommon for Master and men to share meals and to have a quite similar diet. The land they worked provided the food which may well have been sold on for the farmers' profit, but it also fed and sustained many in the local community. Importantly, there were seasonal foods that provided for diets possibly more varied than there are today, where carbon foot-print notwithstanding people are able to choose to eat the same foods all year around. It may seem there is a wider selection available, which many people do avail of, but before they were forced to give up certain foods and take up alternative local fruits and vegetables. In this process the variety of home-grown items has also diminished.

Of course, the system worked - and relied upon - the relative subservience of the agricultural worker and labourer, but not all the farmers saw themselves vastly different from their workforce: they often ate together, and went to the same church, they prayed together and probably enjoyed the same holy days, feasts and celebrations. Even within this agricultural hierarchy, mere farm labourers often had their own small vegetable garden: they might have even kept a pig to feed the family and had some hens for eggs.

The great land-grab that was known as land-enclosures also robbed or deprived ordinary people of their access to common land, etc., and this also forced them off the lands and away from the area. The combined effect of enclosure and the agrarian revolution therefore all reduced the need for workers in the countryside; consequently, workers left the land for the towns where the industrial revolution potentially had need of pure labour.

The difference these rural refugees found in the towns and cities was that the worker was no longer a part of an integrated community: here he and she were paid from the neck down, and a vast majority of employers (though, thankfully, not all and every one) had no great need or desire to share anything, nor had or felt any particular responsibility for his worker. If the worker starved to death, it was no great concern – there were many others waiting to fill that vacancy. The Mill and factory owners no longer shared meals with their workers, did not feast or celebrate with them and were for the most part entirely divorced from their workers' communities. Elizabeth Gaskell's 1854 novel, North and South, later sympathetically reflected upon this issue, but nevertheless actual concern for workers' well-being would hardly occur or even begin as a concept for the best part of two hundred years. This was perhaps the birth of – if not a further extension of – the British class system, which now incorporated a middle class as well as a wealthy class that was not based upon being "landed:" the new barons were industrial barons.

Furthermore, the ordinary country exile in the towns, now probably had to "buy" his food for the first time – instead of living off what he had grown, perhaps as a small-holder, or from the farmers' produce, and from what was commonly bartered for, shared and divided.

Bakers and Baxters

According to Food In England by Dorothy Hartley (©1954, reprinted 2003) when country people moved into towns they missed their weekly bread oven, so the local Baker had a regular custom to "take in baking" at a penny or so a dish. This was still commonplace when my parents were teenagers in the 1930's and 40's. The baker took in pies, cakes, puddings, joints of meat (for those lucky enough and prosperous enough to afford them), which were left with him and then called for when the oven was opened. Hartley states that "range" fireplaces did not have ovens until late into the 19th century. In her book (p581) she says that in many country places the practice of taking food to the bakery continued and the baker still obliged his customers at the time of writing (in the 1950's). She also mentioned a small bakers shop in Osnaburgh Square NW1 which was still serving the community thus up until the end of the Second World War

The Baxter surname, incidentally, is actually derived from those in the baking trade where the bakers' womenfolk were bake-sters - in the manner of spinners and their female spin-sters: its shadow may also be seen in misspellings of the name, where Francis was shown as Backster, Baxster, etc.

Following the work

Many of that great influx of migrants *had* travelled on foot or in horse-drawn carts, coaches and carriages or on pack-horses from rural/agricultural bases on "the land." They all came seeking a better life in the larger towns and cities, and naturally it was London that had seen the greatest influx during those earlier decades of the 1800's. People travelled from far and near, so while Francis Baxter may well have been born in relatively nearby Clerkenwell, I imagine that by the 1830's he and his father had found that their labour was similarly more sought after in Somers Town. They themselves may not have had to tramp the country and traipse hundreds of miles, but they still needed to go where the work was available; and transporting themselves daily to another adjacent parish or borough also still meant walking some miles to and from a hard day's slog – or else, they would need to up-stumps and relocate nearer to it. They couldn't just get a bus or jump on the "Tube," since these transport systems had not then been invented.

His father's (Francis the cutler's) roots had been in Ratcliff; perhaps this was historical and this family had resided there for a considerable time .... or maybe the cutler's father, a bricklayer, had also similarly been drawn to the area by the planned construction of the London Docks in the 1770's. Ratcliff or Ratcliffe, by the way, was situated on the north bank of the River Thames but it has since been absorbed within the modern-day districts of Limehouse, Stepney and Shadwell.

Whilst conjecture has a habit of filling in gaps in knowledge, what is a matter of record is that for a good portion of the stonemason's life - up until he was around fifty years of age – he appears to have been mostly resident in Somers Town and around the St. Pancras / Kings Cross /Camden areas of London. These areas, though, were part of a changing landscape.

SOMERS TOWN: FROM BUCOLIC IDYLL TO....

I can't imagine it was anything except the need to earn a living that drove the Baxters (and a little later people like the Titley's from Shropshire) to re-locate in North London. Somers Town, along with its surrounding areas, was definitely then in a constant state of development with huge building and infrastructure projects which therefore increasingly required - and attracted - labour. Somers Town inevitably changed from its

18th Century idyll, where it had been predominantly rural, and had grown expansively through a period of "refined" gentrification. That gentry, I hasten to add, did not include my Baxters and other ancestors.

As if to confirm the change in the area the Illustrated News in 1858 reported that some 60-70 or more years previous it was a piece of wild common or barren brick-field. However, contrary to the expected report of a semi-rural idyll, it seems to have been both close enough and yet sufficiently remote so as to attract dubious individuals and characters seeking "low entertainments." The article remarked that in those 1780's it was a location "whither resorted on Sundays the bird fanciers and many of the roughs from London to witness dog-fights, bull-baiting and other rude sports," which it maintained were "now (in 1858) happily unknown in the locality."

The construction of the New Road in 1756 (from Harrow Road, through what is now Marylebone Road and Euston Road) was originally built to assist drovers' traffic of cattle to Smithfield. It continued through what would become Euston to Battlebridge, at the King's Crossroads and thence either up Pentonville to Islington or through Grays Inn to Holborn. It may be that the King's Crossroads was merely abbreviated to King's Cross, but there are alternative reasons (later posited) described within.

In about 1788 bricks and kilns were to be found dotted here and there in the fields about. Possibly the geological material was Langley silt, also known as brickearth, which was a blend of silt and clay; if so, these were the source of London's "yellow stocks." (See Bibliography: Chivers. 2022) In 1788 Jacob Leroux, an architect, gained rights over the local brick-making and undertook a new building development in the area that would come to be called Somers Town. Reports are a little confusing but it appears that by 1794 Leroux had also gained the right to *sell* bricks – opening up the possibility that prior to this he may have only been permitted to make them for himself and his own construction purposes.

In the period from the late 18th century to the early 19th century some quite grand properties had begun to be built in this new Somers Town; one such construction was Leroux's *the Polygon*. It was accurately called and he didn't over-egg it: the 32 three-story houses built in 1793 were in a 15-sided shape located in what is Clarendon Square.

In 1796 William Godwin – said to be a proto-anarchist if not to be the father of political anarchism - had been living in Chalton Street when he met Mary Wollstonecraft, an unconventional free-spirit who had already had a child out-of-wedlock. She had also written Thoughts on the Education of daughters (1787) and then produced the Vindication of the Rights of Women in 1792 in reply or as a critical rebuke to Edmund Burke's Reflections on the Revolution in France. Whilst Thomas Paine's subsequent work Rights of Man totally eclipsed Wollstonecraft's, the latter's work nevertheless cemented her reputation as a feminist groundbreaker. Upon getting pregnant Godwin and Mary married and set up home together in the Polygon: at that point the development was a new row of houses "pleasantly seated near fields and nursery gardens." Pleasant it may have been but nevertheless Mary Wollstonecraft would die there in the next September of puerperal fever following childbirth: a great loss to them personally and to the furtherance of women's rights. Incidentally, there is also a later piece within entitled "PUERPERAL FEVER." See index and contents.

Her baby survived; also named Mary, she became friends with poets, authors and politicians. A successful novelist herself she was also involved in politics and with matters of gender equality and opportunity; one can only wonder how pleased or not she and her mother might have been with the 2021 statue erected in Wollstonecraft's memory in Newington Green,

Islington. The controversial tribute depicts a naked female, and is by an otherwise marvellous artist/sculptor, Maggie Hambling.

In the post-1789 period French aristocrats and clergy had headed off away from the egalitarian Revolution in their homeland which, if perhaps they had tarried, may well have taken their heads off; and so it was here in London they had found safety and a new home: with the really wealthy settling in the richer more established Portman and Manchester Squares, while the only-slightly less well-off went to Somers Town. (The poorer weavers and such went to Spitalfields.)

It was around this time that Abbé Chantrel established a chapel nearby to Phoenix Road, hoping no doubt for French Catholicism to rise from the ashes of the Revolution and the recent coup in France (on 18 Fructidor, otherwise September 4th, 1797) where thousands of refractory priests were arrested. It would seem this was not an unfounded hope because their community soon required a new and bigger Roman Catholic Church. With St Aloysius being consecrated in Clarendon Square in 1808 the area became something of an enclave, and French cafés apparently even began to emerge in Chalton Street. One can only wonder how business was, and whether their clientele extended beyond their own community. (I imagine they knew "their onions," n'est pas? Peut ệtre.)

By that first decade of the 19th century the Somers Town Estate had largely been completed in a grid plan which, at least in regards to the main streets, is still recognisable. Gradually, around the wealthier parts of the area, cheaper housing began to be put up by wage labourers. A great many were drawn by other employment opportunities, but such proximity and juxtaposition is always a necessary encroachment upon the *rich* because they rely upon the services of poorer workers and tradesmen, who are thus required to be relatively on hand and at their disposal.

Other changes continued to affect the area, and in 1809 the Workhouse (which had first opened here in 1731 but later had relocated elsewhere) returned to premises in Kings Road, as St Pancras Way was known. You may infer, I would suggest correctly, that the reintroduction of this facility was indicative of decline rather than of greater prosperity. Where Percy Shelley had wooed 16-year-old Mary Wollstonecraft Godwin in the local St Pancras churchyard in 1814 and on the banks of the River Fleet, by 1816 the ever deteriorating River was culverted as it passed the Church.

Over at Clarendon Square the Rev. J. Nerinckx had become pastor of St. Aloysius in 1815. He would be there 40 years (until his death) during which time he established schools and charitable institutions. These included a repository which would later operate as a soup kitchen twice a week. Jesus may have turned water into wine, but normal Christian charity would require money and ingredients to turn it into soup. It needed funding and it seems the Abbé managed to twist a few wealthy arms for sundry donations.

Immigration also continued such that by the 1820's there is another influx of people: artisans, writers, publishers, printers, furniture makers as well as Spanish refugees. These were said to number as many as 1000 families fleeing not from a disgruntled population as the French had done but escaping a despotic King (Ferdinand VII).

Around this time also Charles Dickens - not a stranger to poverty – had moved into Johnson Street (now Cranleigh Street) north of Clarendon Square. The Dickens family would subsequently be evicted for non-payment of rent and go to the Polygon, which being a destination for those in dire economic straits might also reasonably be presumed to have declined in status and condition. (Apparently in Bleak House the Polygon was the model for the home of Mr Skimpole. He describes "The Polygon where there were at that time a number of poor Spanish refugees walking about in cloaks, smoking little paper cigars..... The house was in a state of some dilapidation... two or three area railings were gone, the water butt broken, the knocker loose..." [see Bibliography: Gerryco.) In time the Dickens family would return to Johnson Street, but his father's luck and more often his choices were not always good and he accumulated debts which frequently forced the family to move. Naturally debt does not trouble all people equally. While some people crumble under the weight of debt and some are even driven to suicide, others are not so affected. In this regard I recall a saying of Oscar Wilde's, whose insouciant remark should encourage us all, "Whenever I sign an IOU, I think, thank God, that's settled."

When Dickens was 12 in 1824 his father was sent to the debtors' prison, the Marshalsea, in Southwark, apparently for a debt to a baker. He may have known the Lord's Prayer ("give us our daily bread") but it seems the bread he obtained wasn't a free gift. Howsoever it was received he omitted to pay for it. It strikes me that it was unlikely to have been a Somers Town baker because surely otherwise Dickens senior would have been sent to the Fleet Prison (which was in use until 1844). Alternatively he could have been committed to the Giltspur Street *compter* (a designated name for a debtor's prison) which was also in use until 1853. This compter was close to Christ's Hospital Boys' School in Smithfield, which indeed was actually opposite to Newgate Prison itself.

Social decline in Somers Town continued, while on the contrary apparently the country – i.e. the elite – prospered and infrastructure projects flourished. As poverty and desperation tends to foment unrest, it was hoped that the introduction of the Metropolitan Police Force by Sir Robert Peel, would combat and contain the lawlessness and reckless misbehaviours associated with the desperate poor; henceforth, "Peelers" or "Bobbies" (both names coined from those of Peel) would patrol the capital, at the ready to deal with miscreants. However, it was only just a few months after the Force's inception in 1830 that Police Constable Joseph Grantham met an untimely death in Somers Town off Skinner Street in Thomley's Place by Smith's Place. It was a summer night, but where some of the major streets were lit, albeit often by feeble gas light, the secondary lanes and back-streets like Smith's Place were dark and were, therefore, deemed to be dangerous. Now whether there was an actual danger to the peace or not, a little rowdiness had spilled out of a pub and into the street; an argument had begun which had involved one Michael Galvin (aka Duggan/Duffey) - a local (presumably Catholic) Irish bricklayer, who had been celebrating the completion of his apprenticeship on that very day. Poor fellow. It should have been a joyous rite of passage and a happy occasion, but apparently he was collared by the constable, and in the ensuing struggle the unfortunate officer had hit his head and died.

A local inquest was held in The Boot public house in Cromer Street, where the matter was considered by a jury of locals, who - reports claim - were drawn from a largely Irish Catholic group of residents. It has been suggested that the jury was comprised of those for whom the Gordon riots were a raw and unforgotten memory. Whilst a few decades had passed since the riots attitudes and prejudices were entrenched both within the local population and the ruling authorities, with the residents remembering anti-Catholic mobs ransacking their premises and committing arson and thuggery. Perhaps it was also uppermost in their minds that these actions unusually had failed to inspire the authorities to read the Riot Act, and thereby Catholics and their property went unprotected. The perpetrators - Protestant mobs - were allowed to enjoy a momentum of destruction and the violence continued for a week before the army began to respond effectively.

It is not unreasonable to assume that the general Catholic population may have felt that if the boot had been on the other foot the Riot Act would have been read immediately, and many Catholics would have been cut to pieces by the authorities. In such circumstances it seems a so-minded jury were unlikely to have been overly sympathetic to the representative of the Law; and duly they delivered their verdict that the officer had over-exerted himself! With a paper-thin skull the Police Constable was simply a fatality waiting to happen, and the offender - instead of swinging – was found guilty of assault and imprisoned for just over 7 months. Such a result would never be repeated; that was made sure. (An interesting blog by ex-policeman David Videcette is worth reading although he views the incident differently. see bibliography Videcette. David,)

Somers Town began to be developed quite a few years earlier than some of its surrounding areas, such as the Skinners' Company estate and the part of Battlebridge which was south of the New Road. In the 1820's this latter area had hardly been developed, although that is not to say no one had plans for it. An Italian teacher of music Signor Gesualdo (Gemaldo) Lanza (1779–1859) certainly had a grand scheme, which would combine cultural, social and residential elements. On a site between Birkenhead Street and Argyle Street he planned to include a centre for music and drama, residential properties, a theatre (the Grand Panharmonium), music and picture galleries, reading rooms, refreshment rooms and a ballroom. Around these was to be an open space for walks, and pleasure gardens complete with an overhead railway from which cars were suspended. You could fault neither Lanza's ambition, nor that of his associate one Stephen Geary. It opened in 1830, but for some reason it either failed or fell afoul of even bigger plans. Perhaps it just was not commercially viable or it could not compete with the potentially greater and quicker profits that a housing project could achieve. Whatever the cause within two years the cultural constructions that had been built would be demolished and the ground carved up into plots: amongst these was Argyle Square.

A copy of Lanza's plan, according to the London County Council survey (LCC 1952), is in the Crace Collection at the British Museum.

The whole area continued to be worked and expansion was relentless particularly after 1837 when Euston Station opened. The great problem of any settlement is the creation of waste in all its natural forms. Other societies and especially industrial ones tend to generate diverse and magnified amounts of detritus.

Of course the settlements around Somers Town had these problems. Perversely successful development contributed to the unappealing decline associated with the agglomeration of the huge dust heaps of Kings Cross, which were commented on by Dickens. These were mountainous eye-sore piles which any normal person, let alone nimby residents, would probably prefer to have been placed elsewhere. Nimby, in case it should fall into disuse, is an acronym for "not in my back yard."

The increased use of coal both in the furnaces of industry and in the grates of family homes had led to vast residues which were collected and gradually dumped to form those notorious heaps. While they were described as dust heaps, that rather undersells their contents. In time they would also contain all manner of local industrial and household rubbish and waste: ash, cinders, dust, breeze/brieze, and clinker as well as the whiff of human and animal waste, soil, etc. Just to add a soupçon of extra flavour, it also had a smattering of dead animals. Despite efforts to deplete the heaps they were continuously added to.

An old saying, though, has it that "where there's muck, there's brass" and this was true to an extent of the dust heaps. They proved to have value within and were scavenged for all and any valuable content. The clinker, for example, which was a stony residue of burnt coal from furnaces, was used as a common component of aggregates, of Portland cement, brickwork, block-work, paving and so on. Breeze and cinder were components that were used to make breezeblocks. Domestic waste (or soil/night soil) was sold to farmers for manure. (This pre-dated the age of plastic bottles, polythene bags and film wrappings which later generations would lay down daily by the million in landfill sites – or throw into hedges, rivers and seas - as ecological time-bombs for those in the future. Most things in the 19th century were at least wrapped in biodegradable paper.)

The Kings Cross heaps were said to be disappearing from around 1836 in response to an apparent need to rebuild Moscow, whose government is said to have agreed their purchase in 1826. I had felt initially that had seemed to be a dubious assertion given that there appeared to be no shortage of building work going on locally. Perhaps, though, the owners of the heaps got a better price from the Russians? Nevertheless great physical change was occurring in the area.

By 1849 a degree of deterioration within Somers Town was remarked upon (Cunningham 1849) such that the Polygon of that writer's acquaintance was now "enclosed by the dirty neighbourhood of Clarendon Square." This decline may have been inescapable for our Baxters but I doubt it would have been un-noticed. Like their contemporaries the Baxter men and boys (and the women and girls) would have known their local area – as they used to say – like the back of their hand.

The change from bucolic landscape to dirty neighbourhood occurred gradually over a 50-year period, but it had been brought about by initiatives which would eventually transform the area into north London's vital transportation hub, linking the capital with the west, the north and the east of Britain.

It perhaps began with the emergence of the canal system, whose origins grew from the success of the Bridgewater canal which had connected Worsley and Manchester in 1761. This canal had proved to be such a reliable and profitable mode of moving heavy cargoes between towns and cities that a canal system came to be seen as integral to the advancement of the British industrial revolution.

THE CANAL SYSTEM

By the late 18th century the extensive but rather individual canal systems in the North and in the Midlands were beginning to form into a significant network. This newly built infrastructure allowed heavy goods to be transported safely and more easily from and between important industrial and manufacturing centres. Naturally a highly-prized and desirable market was in London, and quid pro quo the capital itself also wanted easy access to those centres around the country.

The canal passage south, though, essentially stopped at Oxford and thus any trade to and from the capital had to proceed from Oxford via the river Thames. Unfortunately whilst the Thames is 215 miles in length (and therefore the longest river which is wholly in England) it frequently suffered from lack of water in its Oxfordshire and upper reaches, and therefore its shallow meandering sections made it poor for reliable navigation.

The partial solution was the subsequent construction of the Grand Junction Canal which brought the Oxford water traffic to within striking distance of the capital at Brentford. Further canal sections were then established which extended the water-borne services along the Paddington arm to and from Paddington Basin's wharves and warehouses. From there finally in 1820 the completion of the Regent's Canal opened up navigation from Oxford *through* Paddington, cutting through North London and around to the new Canal Dock at Limehouse. Here the Thames was a vast, fast and mighty river, and a portal to national and international trade. (The Regent's canal, like Regent's Park, was named for the Regent of George III, a.k.a. his grandson Prince George, later George IV.)

I think the barges were often operated as a family affair with the barge-driver (the bargee), his wife and kids on board and all doing their bit – they certainly weren't just passengers. All were called upon to help out in some way.

That *cut* (from Paddington across north London to the Thames) took the canal through Camden and Somers Town to the Battlebridge Basin at Kings Cross. (Incidentally, Battlebridge was eponymously named after a supposed battle here, in which Boudicca engaged the Romans near a bridge over the River Fleet.) From Battlebridge the canal passed through the 886-metre-long Islington Tunnel, which had no tow-path for the normally horse-drawn barges. Here the horse was uncoupled, to be led, possibly by the kids, over-ground across to the other end of the tunnel in Vincent/Duncan Terrace. Meanwhile – deprived of horse-power – propulsion necessitated the canal men or bargees to lie on their backs and "walk" the walls of the tunnel, thus pushing the craft on. This was known as "legging-it" - a term which has become familiar to Londoners especially.

From the tunnel the canal went down through to the City Road and Wenlock basins, which were close to where Titley and Baxter family members would much later have grocery and chandlers' shops. From the Wenlock basin the canal continued on to the Kingsland and Laburnum basins (near De Beauvoir Town and Haggerston) until eventually it joined the Thames at the Regent's Canal Dock (a.k.a. the Limehouse Basin). The Basin accommodated sea-going vessels which were serviced by two groups of men who worked there: watermen and lightermen. Watermen carried and transferred passengers, while lightermen "alighted" goods and cargoes to and from the sea-going vessels for onward transportation. The lightermen used flat-bottomed barges called lighters.

(Importantly, in addition to supplying coal to the numerous gasworks, the canals would later supply coal to electricity generating stations which were also positioned along the canal and provided electricity for domestic and commercial usage.)

John Nash's design for the whole canal had required the construction of just over 8 miles of waterway, seven canal basins, 12 locks and 40 bridges: it took eight years to build. A Government loan secured by the Regent's Canal Company was authorised with the requirement that 20,000 pauper workers were engaged in its construction. (See: Bibliography. Cosh. Mary, pg 187)

The completion of the network route to and from the capital naturally facilitated internal trade, but the shortened and reliable flow of water-borne traffic between the North, the Midlands and London right down to the Thames now not only sped up delivery times but may have also boosted imports and exports.

The Regent Canal basins along the route and their environs also became centres of trade, and henceforth Somers Town and Kings Cross were to become firmly established as integral parts of transport, construction and employment equations. Each development fuelled further activity and created more enterprise, which all led to increased competition for land, housing and labour.

Workers flooded to the area from far and wide; and the Baxters were amongst that early burgeoning population. More people also meant a greater demand for furniture – even of the most rudimentary kind; and timber was now able to be brought along the canal direct to waterfront timber-yards, factories and workshops or to the City Road basin for redistribution. The basin adjoined Shoreditch, which for up until 150 years afterwards would be a great centre of London furniture and chair-making.

John Richardson (Richardson. John, 1995 Pg 165) states that sailing barges brought bricks up from the Medway towns. These were transferred onto canal barges to be taken up into Hackney, Stoke Newington and Camden Town where fields and open spaces were soon filled with streets of houses. The Medway bricks supplemented the supply of more local brickfields.

One of the many other types of cargo brought along the canal was coal (mainly from Staffordshire). Cargo brought by canal could be relied upon to arrive – the barges were unlikely to suffer from storm battering and the insecurity etc that other supply lines were prone to; nevertheless, this coal came in addition to the supplies from the north east coalfields (coals *from* not *to* Newcastle) which was shipped via the North Sea. It was no coincidence that easy and reliable access to this energy source would also tempt other business ventures to the area.

Coal, Coke and the Gasworks

The gasometers at Three Mills, Bow; again, I would latterly note, they were built next to waterways: the River Lea and the Navigational Cut.

With coal now being brought more easily and reliably by canal, in 1824 the Imperial Gas Light and Coke Company seized upon the opportunity that proximity to this waterway afforded, and opened its gasworks just to the south of the canal in Somers Town. The gasworks' tanks – aka gasometers/gasholders – would in time loom over many of the houses in which our Baxters lived during the next three decades.

Those new gasworks and certainly their gasometers would survive for the best part of two centuries (and would serve as architectural backdrops to the lives of many Baxter descendants).

It transpires that the gasworks were used to produce and store flammable coal gas. It had been found that burning the coal at high temperature (crucially without the presence of oxygen, which made it, therefore, incombustible) produced gas that could then be purified and put into the gas holders. From these cylindrical storage tanks – the great gasometers - they were now able to pipe the purer gas out to consumers for lighting streets and buildings.

Naturally, daylight had been vital for most work, and with the use of oil and tallow lamps I imagine it had been possible to extend work beyond dusk; but "gas" potentially heralded the age of proper shift-work. A normal working day was already a 12-hour shift, but this capacity for more extended shifts would set in motion the treadmill of round-the-clock toil, which would now be more easily imposed, if not so easily accommodated by the workforce. (Of course, the use of oil and tallow lamps eventually almost totally gave way to this modern gas-lighting, as indeed gas would later cede to electric-lighting.)

The processes of burning coal at high temperature– and its purification to make coal-gas also created useful and profitable by-products: these included coke (which could again be further used as fuel), as well as commercially valuable commodities such as tar, ammonia, and sulphur. A win-win situation, perhaps – as long as you didn't consider people's lungs... So, there were even more opportunities for enterprise and for jobs... and as mentioned it all impacted commensurately on the continuing competition for land and housing: all of which in turn impacted upon our Baxters. Hard on the heels of the canal system was the rapidly emerging railway system, which in time would practically engulf our Baxters' neighbourhoods.

The Railways

The railways – like the canals – had also begun in piecemeal fashion serving distinct, but relatively "local" interests. In the north-east (in County Durham) George Stephenson's steam locomotive design for the Stockton and Darlington Railway in 1825 had been very successful.

Now, I am far from being a railway "buff," or as the enthusiast is known "an anorak," but the answers to my questions have led me to lines of enquiry I did not envisage. Some information is superficially technical, but it is necessary to understand how and why competition was driven: they should not overly trouble you. I believe the Baxters' lives and many of those other local inhabitants' lives were inextricably linked to this competition and to how it affected their immediate vicinity; I will, therefore, reference a short railway history in parallel to aspects of family lives.

Stephenson's engine and rolling stock initially ran on rails set at a gauge of 4 feet 8 inches (around 1422.4 mm). This gauge (i.e. the distance between the inside faces of the rails) proved to be a little too critical and made the trains a bit tight on the bends and therefore prone to derailment. It was soon "eased" by adding an extra ½ inch making the gauge 4 ft 8.5 inches (1435.1 mm) which helped to reduce problems; and thence for a time this design criteria was the automatic choice of many Railway companies, and thus it became known as "standard gauge." It was used for the Liverpool and Manchester Railway – the first intercity line in 1830 - and also for the Grand Junction Railway.

Independent railway companies developed separately, as they do, but gradually, (and mirroring the progress of the canal system,) expansion, mergers and interconnection of services plus the need for standardisation would become not merely financially desirable but would later also become commercially imperative. That realisation, though, was some way down the line.

In the meantime land was being bought up everywhere by the railway companies, and plans for development were being made by competing engineers; rivals fighting for contracts, wealth and fame: men who would in time become household names, and whose faces would later even feature on banknotes.

For over 13 years from 1990 George Stephenson graced the reverse side of the Series E £5 note.

Here he is looking like he lost a shilling and found a sixpence

While George was the engineer engaged by the Liverpool and Manchester Railway, his son Robert Stephenson, aged just 20, started his own eponymous and separate company. He went to Columbia to work as a mining engineer, which must have been quite some adventure and was also very brave in regards to his reputation as an engineer. (The young man couldn't telephone home for advice from Dad, nor could he use a computer search engine for clues and solutions to overcome a problem...) Hopefully he was learning from someone there.

Recorded histories sometimes offer different information, but it seems that father and son collaborated on the design of their new locomotive "the Rocket," which was built by Robert's company. They sold the Rocket and three other locomotives to the L&MR. As George Stephenson & Son, though, they jointly proposed surveying a railway link in 1832 to connect London (at Euston) with Birmingham; of course these were days when merchandising was more direct and the railway was named the London and Birmingham Railway (L&BR). It simply did what it said on the tin!

The owners of farmland in the St Pancras area, the Rhodes family, were big dairy farmers, who I believe were persuaded to sell their local farm. Dairy farms and cow-keepers were all necessary, but as the metropolis continued to grow and expand there was bigger profit to be made from that land. Local dairy farms could survive - as long as the dairy-farmer owned the land and for as long as he could resist the greater profits which could be made otherwise from building and development. (Similarly in a more modern context in the late 20th century the profits derived from the business of individual London Pubs, which had been affected by immigration/culture, demography and change of habits, were not sufficient to withstand realisation of the value of the property. Selling often immediately made money to an equivalent of 10-20 years of work. Sadly, it was no contest.)

The land occupied by many dairy-farmers was either sold or its use was converted directly by the farmer or land-owner, such that brickfields were created. On their land and on surrounding land their bricks could be used to build houses for sale or rent. This was both a long-term and a short-term investment, because there were demands for both temporary and also for more permanent construction in relation to housing and industry. One example of the change of use concerned one Samuel Rhodes, who also owned the Stonefield estate in Barnsbury, which as its name implies was easily turned into brickfields. Rhodes then began supplying the bricks necessary to build houses and develop the local area. Such projects were replicated elsewhere, and Rhodes accordingly bought land in Stoke Newington; the family also transferred some of their interests to Hackney and Haggerston in north-east London. They apparently also gave a 0.5 acre plot of land in Liverpool Road Islington for a school to be built next to St Mary Magdalene Church.

(It would seem there is some connection between this family and one Cecil Rhodes, the founder of the African country Rhodesia, as Zimbabwe was known for about 80 years. cf Mary Cosh: A History of Islington.)

Housing development and buildings for industry are, though, a different kettle of fish when compared to a vast and visionary infrastructure project such as the creation of a railway system, where even bigger stakes and potentially greater profits were in play. The railway company viewing the Somers Town lands must have made Samuel Rhodes an offer he couldn't refuse... or more likely one he was unable to resist.

Thus, the vacated land in Somers Town, previously known as Rhodes Farm, became the site of *Euston* Station; it seems this was so-named as a nod to the Fitzroy family, who owned a great deal of land in the area, and who held titles such as the Duke of Grafton and the Earl of Euston. [2]

---

[2] Fitzroy, of course, literally means "son of the King" and was the name given to illegitimate sons of a King, who could not be heirs to his throne. Naturally, all of those legal stances concerned the influences and interests behind every queen, whose marriages had been a deal, both financial and political, between her family and the King. The King could gallivant around but the Royal household – servants, ladies-in-waiting etc – were strategically placed so as to restrict the access of the queen to other men. This theoretically ensured the legitimacy of any issue and protected the family investment.

Nowadays, with modern techniques and DNA testing biological parentage is now provable, but historically – and if it matters – connections were only certain through the female line. I have some sympathy with the view that genealogy is only valid through maternal lines.

The Rhodes farm site was the intended terminal destination but because of the concerns of the elite that the mighty engines would scare their horses or otherwise wreak havoc in the district, the Railway Company was initially compelled to stop the locomotion of trains at Chalk Farm/Camden Town. Here the engines were disconnected from the carriages and an endless rope (3 inches thick and driven by a fixed engine) pulled the carriages from there into Euston: an awkward arrangement, which would continue until 1845.

In 1833 the Stephenson's main rival, 27 year old Isambard Kingdom Brunel, announced the construction of another railway - the Great Western Railway - which by 1841 would run 116 miles from the important port of Bristol, terminating in London at Paddington.

{Brunel was a *big-thinker* with many grand schemes: he also envisaged the GWR going the other way as it were from London... over rivers, across viaducts and bridges of his construction, through English vales and hills to Bristol and then across Wales to Neyland, where an iron ship - of his design - would take on-going passengers and freight over to New York. You certainly could neither fault his vision, nor most of his design.}

It is amazing to consider the youth of these great rivals, Stevenson and Brunel, and to marvel at their dynamism and their achievements. Of course they were both sons of engineers and great men, but such circumstances more often cast big shadows on the offspring – and rarely do heirs manage to fill parental boots. These sons, though, were exceptional in their own right.

Brunel's railway design had different engineering criteria from that of the Stephenson Company. Brunel preferred a wider gauge to both increase stability and to make the journey a smoother experience: set at 7 feet (later eased to 7 feet $^{1}/_{4}$ inches or 2140 mm) it became known as *broad gauge*. Theoretically it would also be able to operate at higher speeds and carry bigger goods wagons and therefore increase its freight capacity. (I assume it also used more materials, more labour and required greater installation time.) In a bold strategic gamble he apparently also decided to arch north of the Marlborough Downs, which was a daring move because it was not necessarily the shortest or easiest route. Whilst it offered no immediate advantage it fitted with Brunel's other plans, presenting the potential to incorporate lines to Oxford and Gloucester. Thus, it was by design not the most direct route; and whilst some commentators of the Victorian age who had a sense of humour are said to have dubbed the GWR "the Great Way Round," the line proved successful. Brunel's design led to expansions and was taken up by other companies, which also widened the scope of the broad gauge system.

By 1837 the L&BR at Euston-proper had become the first intercity railway in London, and soon the railways, offering a faster service for transporting people and goods, began to take traffic from the canals. The increased railway business and commercial success further encouraged up-grading of services and led to the general expansion of the railway system. This would provide work for our Baxters and their neighbours, but at the same time it would also threaten their accommodation as areas of land and sections of housing were cleared to make way for the railway and its associated infrastructure.

The last traces of an unhurried bucolic Somers Town had been trampled by the march of progress, and – short of a nuclear war – the area will never return to that earlier condition. It was lost forever then in the hurly-burly at the heart of a rising empire.

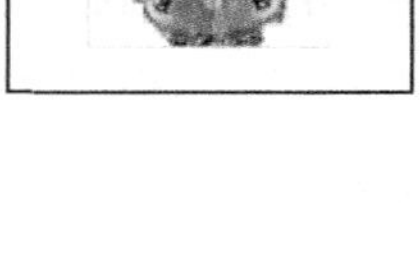

CLOTHING/ APPAREL, FASHION AND SIZE.

Ordinary working men like Francis Baxter would have trudged through Somers Town daily; trudged, that is, not for any reluctance to get to work (indeed everyone was only too glad to have *any* work to go to). They did so instead because the streets were not as city-streets are today with pavements (or sidewalks as Americans call them) and with tarmac covered road-surfaces: cobblestones in many cases were laid when dirt and mud became intolerable or impassable. Of course most of the other surfaces they walked across would be affected markedly by the weather.

I do not know what the dress-code requirements (if any) there were for those very few who worked in offices, but the vast majority of people then were manual workers – even if they weren't quite, as Napoleon is reported to have claimed, the nation of shop-keepers (or shop assistants). As such, most men would have worn hob-nailed leather boots, and I doubt all but the wealthy had any notion of leisure or casual footwear: all they possessed was strictly utilitarian. [There were no "trainers," as those sports' shoes now are known which are mainly worn for comfort and fashion more often than for any energetic endeavour. The noun *trainers* - in the sense of items of footwear - would not enter the UK market (or the British lexicon) until the 1980's.]
Incidentally, in the 1830's and 40's it had only been relatively recently that people again began to wear what I believe are called *chimal* footwear, that is shoes and boots which were made specifically to fit the right foot and the left foot: previously shoes were made to fit either foot, and were formed on "straight" lasts. (Cf American *Brogans*) There were instances where people worked bare-footed, although many people in diverse trades and especially factory workers wore wooden clogs. [In various parts of Europe this type of wooden shoe was known as a sabot. When the industrial revolution occurred there and machines were

introduced to replace workers, wearers of sabots threw them into the machinery to disrupt or break them. Hence, we have grown to use the term "sabotage".]

Fitted clogs and leather-covered wedges fitted under the arches of shoes kept feet directly off the cold ground, while over-shoes with iron rings on the bottom, which were called pattens, also stopped getting wet feet. St Margaret Pattens, a Wren church, in Eastcheap, has great examples of these. [3] Silk shoes had been fashionable in the mid 18th century but obviously these were for dainty trotters and richer hooves.

Men would also be attired in "hard-wearing apparel," accessorised by their sweat-catching neckerchiefs and sun-protecting/winter-warming hats. Construction workers would have to wait 150+ years before hard-hats, safety shoes and other PPE (Personal Protective Equipment) even began to become the norm: such items, that is, which now protect workers' eyes/sight/hands/lungs/bodies and their hearing. The best quasi-protective-shield available to Victorians was their neckerchiefs, which they may have pulled up over their noses and mouths.

Trousers, as we know them, were also a fairly recent invention in the early 19th century, and previously long "shift" shirts had been worn over hose or breeches, which mainly were knee-length. Pantaloons were also a fashion although I suspect these were made to clad wealthier legs. The materials used for

---

[3] Indeed two livery companies – patten makers and basket makers - have their home within the church, and both provide exhibits of their work within museum cabinets in the narthex. The church also still has impressive iron sword rests should you happen to arrive ready for action.

clothing were - as always - dependent upon class and wealth, and on their use or application: wool, cotton and linen were the main fabric for common people, whilst silk, cotton and linen were the preference for the wealthy. In the 21st century the cotton fibre-made *denim* is ubiquitous, but it was only in the mid-to-late 19th century that it came to be popular as a hard-wearing material rather than a fashion statement – and even then the fabric was widely taken up in the U.S., and not in the UK. [The fabric's unique weave, which combined variations of warp and weft, had originated in Nimes in Frances, and was marketed as *serge de Nimes*, meaning *sturdy fabric of Nimes*: this soon became corrupted in the English-speaking world as de Nims until it just squeezed itself – like so many wearers would subsequently - into "denims."]

So, there was little denim in England at that time.

Sturdy fabric was also supplemented with leather, or at least pieces of leather, worn as part of the shoulder piece across the back of a coat, such as a coal-heaver might wear. Other material was sackcloth – not necessarily that of Biblical fame – which was a very coarse, rough fabric woven variously from flax, hemp, or goats' hair. This was used mainly for sacks but apparently was often worn as a mourning and/or penitential garment.

Whilst not everyone worked outside, those who did were therefore more prone to the vagaries of the English weather. Given the range of occupations I imagine it is fair to assume that those who did work outside would represent a significant proportion, if not a majority. People would get wet, and it may be their situation would not afford any shelter nearby. I don't know what the attitudes of an employer might have been to any notion of "rain stopping play" let alone stopping work. If clothes got wet, they were at best damp for the rest of the day and were not conducive to good short-or-long-term health.

The difficulty of drying wet clothes has always been a strain upon time, effort and resources. Obviously the people of that time had no airing cupboards – or hot presses as the Irish call them – and they certainly had no tumble-driers or other such machines which we have access to in the 21st century. They dried their clothes either in the open air or in front of open fires, but their need or desire to remain dry is perhaps a primal instinct. Maybe that was paramount or conversely I wonder if they regarded damp clothes as inevitable.

To combat the problem of getting wet in the first place various methods of waterproofing had been used historically, with some cultures faring more successfully than others. Then, aside from the issue of personal discomfort, there is the matter that soaked fabric becomes heavier, and this was an immense problem for mariners, not only in regard to their clothing but also to their sails. In an effort to prevent absorption some materials were traditionally painted with a thin layer of tar or wax; however, in 1795 an Arbroath-based sail maker (Francis Webster) successfully applied linseed oil to flax sails. The oiled flax material not only proved to be effective, but was also lighter when wet than wet sailcloth, which had been made of canvas. From there the process was extended to create so called oil-skin clothing.

Canvas, originally made from hemp, was a preferred and durable plain-woven fabric for clothing. It could also be coated with multiple applications of linseed oil to prevent water permeation. The big problem with most waterproof methods was the clothes lacked breathability, making the wearer hot and sweaty.

(Large quantities of flax and cotton canvases were also tarred and used for covering goods on wharves, and docks. We know these as *tar*paulins: a word which alludes in the prefix to the tar application, joined with a derivative of *pall* which means "something that covers, shrouds or conceals." During the 19th century, especially in nautical terminology, it was common to abbreviate the word as *paulin*. Others prefer *tarps*.)

After the introduction of the power loom, which originally was a water-driven device, the fabric *canvas* was made from hemp, flax, jute, cotton, and mixtures of such fibres. [Canvas is said to be etymologically derived from the Latin word for hemp, cannabis.] The material had been put to many uses other than for clothing including making sails, bags, shoes and tents. Naturally, it was being used as well as a base for oil painting.

The power loom was a significant step in regards to progress and to big changes in manufacturing. Previously, all kinds of industry had relied upon power of one form or another: hand-power, i.e. man-power (and woman-power), supplemented by animal-power. Output had further been increased with wind-power and water power; however, subsequently, it was to be the age of steam that magnified both the power available and the uses to which it could be put.

Very young children of *both* genders (it was a binary world then) wore dresses or long shifts, and it was a coming-of-age/ rite-of-passage when boys were suitably toilet-trained that they were "breeched" and dressed in trouser-like leggings. (This information was given at the Museum of Fashion in Bath, Somerset.)

The wardrobes of the poor would have been quite sparse, necessitated as much by the want of space as that of income. It also supposes they had a physical wardrobe: clothes may have been kept in a drawer or hung on hooks or on simple nails. I am fairly confident the poorest – overcrowded, over-populated and packed into small barely affordable accommodation - may not have possessed a change of clothes, and had only the clothes they stood up in. Others would have had work clothes and their "Sunday-best," which would in time ultimately wear down and be used for work. Children inevitably wore hand-me-downs: clothes which passed from one elder sibling down to the next eldest (or biggest), and so on providing clothes and children survived. Naturally the practice is still commonplace, especially but not exclusively amongst larger families where it has more longevity. By contrast, for smaller families the process ends when the youngest/smallest has outgrown the stock. For them it is relatively short-lived. Back in the 19th Century, however, the practice was guaranteed to endure throughout the "fertile" lives of worn-out women. If the wear on the clothes was not irreparable, the articles might even find themselves adorning grandchildren. The wear on the women, however quantifiably incalculable, was nonetheless exhausting and ruinous to their enjoyment or any expectation of a healthy life.

Ordinary working-class women and poor women, like Elizabeth Baxter (nee Bradshaw) were clothed much differently from the middle and upper classes. There were apparently exceptions to this; in keeping with (Coast to Coast Walker) Alfred Wainwright's philosophy that there is no such thing as bad weather, there is only unsuitable clothing, it seems that at least one device transcended class barriers. According to the Bath Museum of fashion quilted petticoats with a middle layer of wool stitched together for warmth were worn by all in 1740s onwards. Generally, though, Elizabeth and her female friends wore more robust materials, far different from the fancier clothes and dresses of their "betters." In the daily garb - rather than the fashion - of their time, the Baxter women and their contemporaries worked and shopped in full length skirts made of wool with aprons of cheap cotton (calico), complete with shawls and soft-cotton "mob" hats. Petticoats may have been worn but I doubt underwear featured to any great degree. Naturally, the well-to-do would force themselves – regularly with the assistance of their maid servant - into whale-boned corsets, stays and the like: shapely, but ghastly and uncomfortable underclothes worn under more luxuriant fabrics.

WOMEN'S SANITARY PRODUCTS

Of course, then there was the monthly matter of the "curse," as many women used to refer to it, which I feel is a subject strangely absent in nearly all history books. Perhaps, it has been viewed as taboo or indelicate or maybe it is indicative of the gender of most historians, but it is woeful that a subject has been ignored which is of importance and interest to at least 50% of the population. Whilst I also have some sympathy with the view that this matter is probably best dealt with by those who know best, I will, nonetheless, make this small reference to it. Incidentally, it is more ably considered by Ruth Goodman who covers this in her work for the series a Victorian Pharmacy. (In this great series Goodman, who lacks the reticence of most male historians, also tackled the subject of condoms which she went on to make using sheep's intestines.)

Other sources of interesting information about historic sanitary/menstrual products and practices are provided by Susanna Ives (see Bibliography) for her book *Frail*: Tidbits on Mid-Victorian Era Menstrual Hygiene. Ives further drew on the 1852 work of Charles Delucena Meigs..

Meigs informed an ignorant male world that mainly as soon as the period/menses "is perceived" women applied a T-bandage. He described it as consisting of a "guard" – a napkin, folded like a cravat, which was "pressed between the legs against the genitalia." (I'm sure 50% of the population didn't need telling, but I include it for general information.) The ends of the guard then being "secured to a string or ribband tied around the body above the hips." Some women also used rudimentary hand-made tampons, but it would not be in Elizabeth Baxter's lifetime that manufactured products would be available at the shop counter or off the shelf.

Incredibly, in the UK all and every such women's sanitary products (WSP's) would still attract tax (Value Added Tax) as if they were luxury items until the year 2021 – and this despite the country having (at that point) had two Prime Ministers who, theoretically at least, identified as women.

The average height and weight of a person (or of any particular segment of the population) is difficult to determine in any given period, and it is especially so for those who lived within 19th century Britain. There are so many variables and factors to take into account, but the greatest problem is the availability of reliable data. Omitting an argument as to what type of *average* would have been possible (mean, median or modal) it is, therefore, imperative to bear those difficulties in mind and maintain appropriate reservations while seeking extant and relevant data.

The great slew of Army records of the later 20th century World Wars contain the vital statistics of massive numbers of participants, drawn from generally a fairly close age-range which makes for tighter data; however, statisticians and researchers of the 19th century do not have the benefit of such universal data. Of course there were wars, some of which - like the European Napoleonic Wars - involved large numbers of men, but I am not aware the Military bothered to physically measure their combatants: they were merely there to do or to die.

Most other record sets are on a much smaller scale to those gathered by a later and theoretically more organised military, which nevertheless more often also still treated their soldiers as mere cannon-fodder. The number of participants involved in any data obviously impacts on the reliability of what may be extrapolated.

Michael Mosley (BBC 16.10.2016 https://www.bbc.co.uk/news/magazine-37654373) reported on one study which compared the different heights of Victorian teenagers, based on their class and their income. The study by John Komlos (2005) was entitled "On English Pygmies and giants: the physical stature of English youth in the late 18th and early 19th centuries." It compared not only the heights of lower and upper-class English youths to one another but also to their European and North American counterparts. It found that young recruits to the Royal Military Academy at Sandhurst – the officer class who were drawn more exclusively from wealthier backgrounds – were amongst the tallest young men in the world at that time. Mosley records these as averaging almost 175cm (5ft 9in), and contrasts these figures with statistics gathered by the Marine Society. The latter was a charity that was set up to provide the Navy with humbler stock associated with ordinary sea-farers: Komlos's study of its list of 16-year-old boys (recruited from the slums) found the boys to average 153cm (5ft ½inches or 60.5") and therefore 22cm (8.6in) shorter than their land-based upper-class. In addition to this the height gap between the rich and poor was the greatest in England, and those poverty-stricken English lads were among the shortest for their age in Europe or North America. This appears to be a fairly rare study as anthropometric information was not often collected.

Later researchers of the 20th and 21st centuries will not have such data problems because the "modern" world collects enormous amounts of details and personal information about almost everyone. Now credit companies/ loan organisations, as well as initiatives driven by the medical profession (aided in the U.K. by its universally available National Health Service) all record data.

Thus, in the 21st century UK our doctors may routinely "measure" patients more frequently and use this information, for example, to determine health indicators: whether someone is underweight/ within acceptable normal and healthy weight ranges / overweight/ or very overweight. NHS Patients may go into their Health Clinic or GP surgery feeling that they or their bloated offspring are merely big-boned, chubby, delightfully plump or just a bit "heavy" only to be surprised to discover they are obese: clinically, critically and/or morbidly obese. Squeezing out through the exit door - possibly clutching a diet sheet - they might also find they need their eyes testing.

Unfortunately, information in regard to the physical metrics of people who lived in the 19th century is sparse, but from that which does exist it may be possible (I would venture) to reasonably infer that the degree of undernourishment suffered by that majority inevitably had impacted negatively upon their growth. It seems obvious (a generally dangerous assumption, I would admit) that they would on average be both somewhat shorter in height and a good deal smaller in weight /stature than their average late-20th century counterparts.

As an aside comment, insurance actuaries have used a simple calculation to determine if an adult was a low or high risk candidate for life insurance: it was a Body Mass Index calculation based on the Quetelet Index. This defined weight (w) in kilograms and height (h) in metres within the relationship, $w/(h^2)$. Thus, the actuaries calculated the result of w/(h2) : if that quotient was between 20 and 25 the person was deemed theoretically unlikely to die prematurely and was therefore insurable (unless other medical conditions were evident or pertained). A result equal to less than 20 implied under-nourishment leading to health problems sooner or later, which sharply increases as the number reduces. Similarly a figure in excess of '25' indicated obesity and associated health problems, again with the dangers increasing dramatically as the excess increases. More than '25' was overweight, but '30' was obese at its smallest degree. This calculation is based on adults, who have passed puberty and settled into a somewhat set biological state. Children, naturally, are not measured in this way entirely.

Modern medical techniques allow for other features and incorporate other statistical tools; but - being a little old fashioned

- I am inclined to suspect the simple actuaries' scale is still a good indicator. I tend to trust the reluctant-to-pay-out money-men in these matters: *cui bono* being a generally reliable determinant.

Data from Victorian times, however, does provide some information. Certain statistics, for example, were found in relation to the height and weight of factory children in 1833 and 1873. These were shown by Rosenbaum. (See Bibliography: Rosenbaum, J. *100 years of heights and weights.*) The samples were from 160 boys and 200 girls (aged 9-12) in 1833, and from 740 boys and from 500 girls (aged 9-11) in 1873. As the 1833 pre-dated the official registration of births, it was accepted that ages were unverifiable exactly, and this was acknowledged. The measurement figures were also representative of those deemed physically fit, and it should be noted that examination of one batch of children in 1873 showed 40% were regarded as unfit, and were rejected from the data. The figures, therefore, seem to be representative of the fittest children available.

Rosenbaum's Table 16, which showed that the mean average height and weight of 11-year-old **factory** children in 1833, indicated:

Girls' height in 1833 128 cm (50.39" 4ft 2 $^4/_{10}$ in)	Girls' weight 21.4kg
Boys' height in 1833 128.3 cm (50.51" 4ft 2 ½ in)	Boys' weight 22.4 kg

The record of measurements in 1873:

Girls' height in 1873 129 cm (50.78" just over 4ft 2¾ in)	Girls' weight 24 kg
Boys' height in 1873 128.8 cm (50.7" just under 4ft 2¾ in)	Boys' weight 24.5kg

The heights show a negligible increase between 1833 and 1873, but even given the slight weight increase these children – who, one should remember, were drawn from the fittest of the factory children – would then and today appear quite emaciated. How, though, do they compare with their modern counterparts?

We have better data for children - we certainly have more of it - and we are also able to factor into our conclusions variations which may affect the apparent "healthiness" of a child other than the simple height/weight ratio. All children naturally grow at different rates, so it is normal for weight and height to vary significantly between kids of the same age. Growth spurts and puberty also take their toll on data. A ten-year-old girl may be said to weigh around 70.5 pounds (31.9 kilograms) ***on average***. However, because of the wide variety of weight and height differences among children of this age girls can weigh anywhere from 53 to 102 lbs and yet apparently still be deemed healthy. Nevertheless, according to current NHS figures about 1 in 5 children in School Reception (age 4-5) are overweight or very overweight, rising to 1 in 3 in year 6 (when aged 10-11). (See Bibliography. National Child Measurement)

AVERAGE HEIGHT AND WEIGHT FOR FEMALE CHILDREN

Age 10	138.4 cm	(54½" or 4ft 6 ½in)	70.5lb	(31.98 kg)
Age 11	144 cm	(56.7" or 4ft 8 ¾")	81.5lb	(36.97 kg)

AVERAGE HEIGHT AND WEIGHT FOR MALE CHILDREN

Age 10	138.4 cm	(54½" or 4ft 6 ½in)	70.5lb	(32 kg)
Age 11	143.5 cm	(56.5" or 4ft 8 ½ in)	75.5lb	(35.6 kg)

(See Bibliography Health Survey)

Incidentally, on average, (again, whatever average that may have been) fully grown men in the impoverished 1850's of

England and Europe are recorded as being just under 5 feet 5 inches (164.96 cms) in height, and the women were around 5 feet 1 inch (155 cms). By 1871-1875 the average height at age 21 of British men was recorded as being 167.05cm (5 feet 5¾ inches). (See: Hatton. Tim,) [4]

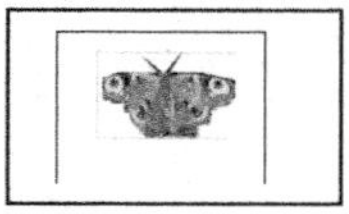

A report in 1907 concluded that many of those joining the army did so as they were out of work, and that most joined for want of food and were in generally poor condition. This want of food was also the best recruiting sergeant in the 19th century.

The Great War, when it came, would find British military leaders alarmed that their soldiers were smaller and markedly undernourished in comparison to their chosen enemies. (Lions, albeit "scrawny" lions, led by donkeys.)

In 1926 it was found that the average soldier, having at least regular food, had put on 7lbs in weight after the first 6 months of service – provided, no doubt, that he hadn't lost a leg or two.

---

4 Being overweight was not a problem for the 19th century poor, and although there is generally sufficient food for UK children in 2023 their diet now contains too much sugar, salt and calories plus additives. Doctors argue these present long-term risks to health, but as the big confection organisations provide financial support to political parties, the latter are reluctant to apply legislative interference - and a greater emphasis is placed instead on self-regulation.

This reflects the general antipathy to - and unwillingness to submit to – regulation which also exists within parliament, the judiciary and the Press. Strangely many of these great untouchables are often heavily in favour of quite draconian regulation of workers' and Trade Unions' activities - because they believe self-regulation does not work.

It was little better for WW2; but by 1971-75 (in preparation for WW3?) and with better health care and nutrition, the average height was reported to have risen to 177.37cm (5ft 10in). [See: Rosenbaum. S., 100 Years of Heights and Weights]

THICKLY INHABITED SOMERS TOWN. SLAVE-MONEY INVESTMENTS. THE SQUEEZE OF CONDITIONS.

In 1841, the Baxters lived in the part of St Pancras designated in the census as district 19. Their actual home was in John's Ct., Somers Town, within the *Hundred of Ossulstone* [5] and in the Borough of Marylebone which was then in the county of Middlesex. The enumerator's schedule for district 19 describes it as being "thickly inhabited," which was not an understatement given that on-going and staggering rise in the population of London which had occurred in recent decades. Taken on the night of the 6th of June 1841, the census gave the total population for England **and** Wales as 18,553,124, (from the National Archives).

In John's Court the enumerator recorded the following Baxter residents: Census return HO 107 685 19 folio 11.

Francis Baxter		40	**Cutler**
Elizabeth	wife	40	
Francis	**son**	**14**	
Thomas	son	10	
Alfred	son	7	
Richard	son	5	
William	son	2	

Whilst I imagine the Baxters were busy throughout the next decade they do not figure officially anywhere for a number of years. The area, though, continued to be a hive of activity and expansion, and before the decade was out Euston's original sheds had been replaced by a Great Hall, and subsequently its two platforms would increase to fifteen platforms.

---

5 A *Hundred* was an ancient administrative division of land in the more southerly counties and elsewhere shires; it was similar to a Wapentake, which were found in old Danish shires of England (York, Lincoln, Leicester, Nottingham, Derby, and Rutland)

Other developments – and more expansions – followed, and in 1846 the standard gauge L&BR amalgamated with the Grand Junction Railway and the Manchester and Birmingham Railway to become the London and North Western Railway (L&NWR). Euston would thus become the southern terminus of services to and through Birmingham, and of trains to Holyhead (and thence to the ferries to Dublin). It was also essentially the West Coast Main Line, running trains to Lime Street in Liverpool, to Piccadilly Station in Manchester, to Waverley Station in Edinburgh and to Glasgow Central.

Incidentally a significant amount of the finance of the railways was derived from slavery and from that compensation paid to the slave-owners. (See: Dr Nick Draper, and Naomi Fowler.) The construction of railways was not always an unmitigated success, and although great fortunes were obtained, on other occasions fortunes were lost. So, people could clean up or be cleaned out by railway investment.

Ordinary people such as the Baxters living in thickly inhabited areas generally found themselves in fairly cramped conditions, which were obviously dictated by what was affordable. The 1841 census like many that followed reveals only scant information and gives no clue as to the physical size of properties or the amount of rooms contained within. In the fairly temporary homes of those in Somers Town, where perhaps there was an expectation that sooner or later railway expansion would swallow them up, it is unlikely the buildings were all that substantial. Many, like those in Agar Town, were built by the occupants themselves and fulfilled their basic need for shelter, but on a 21 year lease. These were single and two storey dwellings. In the wealthier districts of London and even in the richer areas that were local impressive houses were built – with many still surviving – and these were much different, which reflected the ready availability of domestic labour. As Richardson says

(London and its people) the architecture of central London is partly a result of that situation where 5 and 6-storey houses were built "on the assumption that servants would be on hand to overcome their vertical layouts." (Richardson 1995 p324). As outer suburbs developed in the early 20th century, when there were no longer high volumes of servants to call upon, houses there were constructed with much more regard to horizontal planning. At the same time those larger residences in London would be relinquished by their owners and tenants as unmanageable; then the social status of the property went into decline and individual rooms began to be let out.

Back in the early 19th century it was humbler housing stock that was the modest shelter of the working poor and ordinary families. In the four dwellings that comprised Johns Court there were 28 people, identified with 8 different surnames. Reports have it that even in larger premises most rooms were fully occupied to the extent that it would not be uncommon for whole families to be found living in one room. Nowadays we describe places as HMO's – houses of multi-occupancy – but in the crush of reduced supply and increasing demand for accommodation in 19th century Somers Town single people, often unrelated, were often found sharing – and not just rooms, but beds; these, though, would at least be same-sex co-habitants. In later times with more shift working this desperate trend led to hot-bedding where the day-worker's bed was taken over by the night-worker and so on in cyclical fashion. Sometimes this was the diktat of a landlord, while at others it was a voluntary option for people who were really struggling financially. Sadly, this practice still occurs.

IMPRESSMENT

Press-gangs were still operating in the years of the stonemason's infancy, and while the practice largely died out around 1830 its spectre would remain in the public psyche for generations to come. Impressment, as the process was called, had been the notorious method by which the Royal Navy had recruited sailors. In its most benign form a happy land-lubber was surreptitiously slipped a King's shilling in his beer: the act of acceptance of payment (by virtue of having swallowed it) was thus said to have satisfied the law that a contract had been made. Of course the drunken new recruit would wake up aboard ship (merrily?) heading for foreign waters. That, at least is the popular sanitised version. In reality a group of thugs/recruiters would come ashore and hit about the head any chosen candidate who showed a reluctance to serve or an inability to run away quick enough. Dragged, carried or otherwise persuaded with violence they were thenceforward a member of the Senior Service.

Apropos the romantic version, tankards with glass bottoms were made in apparent attempt to thwart "the Press-Gang." I doubt a body could have appealed to their better nature and a sore head would soon have come about.

We might now say such a clump was "in the offing"- it being likely to happen – whereas in 19th century sea-jargon, the offing referred to that part of the sea which was closer to the horizon, and therefore a distant prospect.

DRINKING TANKARD LAST DROP

Drinking tankards were made with glass bottoms purportedly to frustrate the dodgy practice of slipping a drunk a shilling. One such tankard has a gallows etched into it with a drawing of a dead man hanging. The inscription reads: "The last drop."

THE SMELLS OF LONDON

The noses of first-time visitors to London must have gone into over-drive. Supposing a country-person had found his way to Somers Town – not that here was too different from many other locations and neighbourhoods – he would have been in for a pong-fest. It exuded the panoply of urban fragrances: of life in an industrial, densely populated metropolis. These emanated from the gasworks, tanneries, vinegar manufactories, slaughter-houses, open-sewers, bake-houses, dung-heaps/cesspits, beer-brewers, tallow-makers, soap-makers, glue-makers, the smell of rot and decay, of pigs and animals alive and dead, of markets, vegetables and fish, of the unique effluvial olfactory treat of the river, mixed with the occasional sweet yet acrid waft of death and combined with the no-less fragrant smell of the living: the unwashed bodies, sweat-soaked clothes (heightened when dampness had not been overcome), the noisome scents of people, urine, faeces and sweat vomit. Peter Ackroyd describes this heady brew as the intimate yet cloying smell of human life (Ackroyd P., London, A Concise Biography, Vintage. 2012 p321) In the same piece he mentions a mid-19th century traveller, who commented on his visit to Agar Town where he found "the stench of a rainy morning is enough to knock down a bullock." Other areas boasted their own unique whiffs: lime-kilns, fish-markets, herring smoke-houses, white-lead factories, confectioners etc. I recall hearing Carpenter's Road, now the heart of the Olympic Park development, described quite fairly in the 1970's as the street of a thousand smells.

You have to wonder whether or not any in the metropolis could distinguish pollen enough to have then had hay-fever. I wonder, too, how over-riding or noticeable those bodily smells were to those subject to such whiffy immersion. In current times there is no excuse, but in the early 19th century there were few facilities and a reduced access to clean water. Different times.

ABLUTION, BATHING.

In all such over-crowded conditions these residents and lodgers would have struggled with regards to anything that might resemble modern standards or expectations of ablution. Few houses then (anywhere) had bathrooms; nor indeed did they have many other facilities, which most people these days would regard as essential, such as washing machines and driers etc. A certain degree of personal ablution was no doubt carried out but to what extent is another unanswerable question; I believe, though, it was an aspect connected with gradual social change.

In the general absence of domestic facilities there were moves to make provision for public facilities; however it was not until 1846 that campaigners for the installation of municipal-baths actually saw some success locally. With the help of the Bishop of London and Acts of Parliament in 1846 and 1847 the Washhouse-for-the-Million movement led to the first public-baths and washhouses being opened. One such facility opened in St. Pancras in 1846, and according to Nick Higham, it attracted 280,000 bathers in the first two years, with over 90,000 using them to do their laundry. (See The Mercenary River. P191). This seems to indicate that given appropriate facilities people were quite keen to use them.

The public-baths and washhouses contained cast-iron baths, and featured ceramic tiles and marble surfaces, which may have provided employment for locals. As it transpired by 1847 our younger Francis Baxter (the later stonemason) had become – or was least describing himself as – a marble polisher. I believe polishing marble is a very skilled task, and is perhaps preparatory to the fuller accomplishments expected of a stonemason. It is possible also that his services and skills were used in the marble features which were constructed in the washhouses. (A stonemason's work is later described: see "Appendix".)

Francis was then living at No. 15 Marson Street (still close to John's Court and Brill Place). Marson Street is long gone, and is also lost beneath the current British Library; however, Brill Place – while unrecognisable from its Victorian form – can still be found just north of the Library, close to St. Pancras International station, London.

It would seem that Baxters' neighbours here in Brill Place included a Middlesex man (from Harrow-and-Weald): George Gates. He had, in all likelihood, also come to the area for work, with his wife Hannah and at least some of their family. In 1841 their eldest child at home was **Caroline Gates** who was recorded as a 15-year old (although her baptism shows she was born 9th December 1824) so it would appear she was actually 16. Perhaps the Baxters and Gates families were known to each other or maybe young Francis and Caroline had only met fairly recently, but whatever, romance had certainly blossomed by 1847 and the twenty-two year-old bride, Miss Gates, married her *Mr Right* on the sixth day of that September.

Marriage Acts

A marriage certificate was then still a fairly new notion as they had only been in use for 10 years. Francis and Caroline's marriage lines, as they were known, showed the groom as being 23 years old, which may have been stretching it bearing in mind he had been recorded as 14 just 6 years previously. However, even if he was only 20 the marriage would nevertheless have been legal since, in compliance with Hardwicke's (Prevention of Clandestine) Marriage Act 1754, his father obviously did not object: Francis senior – the cutler - being in attendance was on hand to raise objections if he had had any.

Those under the age of 21 had to have parental consent if they married by licence which permitted a marriage to take place without the normal due notice. It might be issued for those in a hurry and was valid for church or for a civil ceremony wedding in a register office, although some time-restrictions still applied. Alternatively, there was marriage by "banns" (where the intention to marry had to be publicly announced and read out every Sunday for three weeks prior to the proposed wedding in order for any objections to be raised). Marriages there of anyone under 21 were valid as long as the parent of the minor did not actually forbid the banns.

Only marriages which complied with Hardwicke's Act were legal: they applied to Anglican couples, and the only exceptions were for Jews and Quakers. Catholic marriages were not recognised under the law, which also affected atheists, Muslims, Hindus and members of any other religious body. If they wished to have legal rights the marriages had to be performed in an Anglican Church. Pragmatically many did so, and Roman Catholics were advised to marry first in an RC church and then go for another ceremony in an Anglican church. A priest was said to have recommended this because "almost every day when the wife of an Irish labourer was deserted by her husband, she was not able to get redress." (See: Bibliography. Chadwick. Owen,) The restrictions on non-Anglicans had been removed in 1836.

[The minimum age for those marrying in the UK fluctuated throughout the 19th and 20th century settling on 16 for both bride and groom provided it had parental permission; but in response to child protection and prevention of forced marriages, it was raised in April 2022 to 18 years of age.] (See Bibliography Independent and The Marriage and Civil Partnership (Minimum Age) Act 2022)

Naturally – and particularly then - a change of marital status between two locals was unlikely to make them relocate and, with work still practically on their doorstep, accordingly they decided to set up their home together within their own neighbourhood. What, though, I wonder, would *home* have looked like?

Despite a preponderance of food banks and increasing child poverty in the Great Britain of the 2020's, I suspect that if one were to look around most homes currently these would nonetheless still be replete with material goods; and I imagine a typical inventory of possessions would be quite sizeable. (If you have moved house recently you will certainly have a better idea of all that you have – both its diversity and its enormity. Such is the paraphernalia and clutter of the modern home: certainly it is of mine.)

In this regard, you may have mirrors, paintings, ornaments, books, armchairs, settees/sofas, carpets, solid-flooring/tiles. curtains, blinds etc. Of course, as is often the case, such things as these would have been available in the 1800's but these were mainly only affordable to a wealthier minority of people. Ours is indeed a material world.

Whilst wealth certainly increases accessibility to new technologies, it cannot buy what has not been invented. There were still things, objects and appliances which were thus then unavailable to all. For example, most people now in Great Britain would regard equipment and appliances (like televisions, radios, fridges, freezers, microwaves, toasters, washing machines, steam irons, computers and so on) as commonplace and probably even consider these items as basic essentials; these, though, were definitely not available to people living in the same era as the Baxters.

Not only had they not been invented but the operating force of all these appliances, *electricity,* had not yet been harnessed as a power source; and like a proverbial horse and cart that power had to come before those subsequent inventions.

Futuristic advancements in the early decades of the 21st century have transformed *some* homes so that currently they not only have lighting, televisions, audio systems, plus electrically driven blinds/curtains and heating controls but in some cases these can ***all*** be voice-activated. Heating for the Baxters would have been a coal fire, which took a great deal of physical work to light, to combust and to maintain the flame. Central heating systems as we know them did not exist in any building, although certain systems were present in occasional and rare circumstances. This would not change until the late 20th century.

In your home you may have some photographs of family members on display, but this type of image creation was in its infancy in the 1830's and 1840's and it would be decades before "having a photograph taken" became a viable proposition for anyone. (Even then, it would not have been cheap, although by 1877 the stonemason or his daughters were able to afford to have their photos taken. See Index: Victorian sisters.)

In 2021 some information sources estimate that almost 90% of the UK adult population had a smart phone – a device for telecommunication using computer programs and platforms, which ALL incorporate camera, photographic and audio/video recording and editing technologies.

We now take all these things for granted. The range and diversity of those inventions have also led us to alter the way in which we shop. This is not just because of the revolution that is our capacity to browse and to "buy on-line," rather it is more basically because we are able to store foods both temporarily in refrigerators and - for longer periods - in freezers; in 19th century Great Britain, however, food was not regularly stored, for most of it was perishable, and thus it was bought and had to be consumed within a day or two at most. Some foods were of course preserved by pickling or by other means of curing. Tinned or canned food was also still a novelty introduced by Dorkin and Hall, who had opened a cannery in England in 1813, which for a long time supplied merely army rations, before later expanding to a wider domestic market.

I wonder what the homes of our Baxters were really like and what possessions they actually had: did they have soft furnishings, did they own books? I doubt their inventory amounted to much, and I suspect that moving their possessions from one home to another was unlikely to have involved a pantechnicon. Indeed it would more probably have required just the use of a hand-cart.

I believe every home would have had pots and pans and rudimentary kitchenware, and on the positive side it is likely the Baxters had better cutlery than most, bearing in mind that Dad was a cutler – a maker of sharps, of knives etc as well as surgical equipment. Plates and linen were also prized possessions in those times, to the extent that these would feature as valued items which were often specified bequests in Last Wills and Testaments. Similarly mentioned in Wills were carpets, rugs and other floor coverings; so none were commonplace objects. (Cupboards, by the way, before they had doors were originally boards for resting or hanging cups on.)

In the absence of electricity, illumination was brought to them instead by means of candlelight and oil lamps. Ordinary people like the Baxters probably had a table, since this was the surface where all food preparation and other household work was carried out, and I would imagine they at least had three-legged stools, a bench or some form of hard chairs to sit on. Note: an itch is an itch no matter what century a person lives in; similarly there are other universal irritations: for example, on an uneven floor surface (of which there were plenty) four-legged Victorian stools would have wobbled and rocked as equally annoyingly then as they would now; so 3 legs good, 4 legs bad. Armchairs and cosy seats were for the more affluent and more settled members of the population.

Open-fires heated the homes, and with pots suspended above them (or sometimes along with *ranges*) these were the means by which water was boiled and food was cooked. Where in previous times the fuel had been wood, demand for this type of fuel - coupled with clearance for pastures etc - had led to many of the great British forests disappearing: now coal – king coal, but dirty coal - was the fuel. The smoke and the grime deposits from every household and from all the new industries changed both the atmosphere and the complexion of the capital.

It would be unlikely for anyone other than the middle-classes and the well-to-do to have wall-coverings such as wall-paper. In all probability the walls would have been distempered or lime-washed. The main constituent of soft distemper was *whiting,* which was made from washed and finely-ground chalk. This was then loosely bound with water-soluble glue which was usually made from animal bones, horns or skin. The common alternative to distemper, Lime-wash, used lime derived from limestone or chalk. This was then 'burnt' in a kiln to form quick-lime (calcium oxide). This substance is apparently highly reactive: when water is added the solution begins to boil violently, producing material called calcium hydroxide aka 'slaked lime.' Further dilutions of this slaked-lime with water rendered the thin paint called lime-wash which could then be applied with a brush. Lime-wash having slight antiseptic properties also made it a little more desirable as it prevented mould and discouraged insects and vermin.

Lead paints, which would later be banned as being injurious to health, were then mostly and widely used on joinery and metalwork but were also found on exterior walls. (They would also be used to decorate toys – available even for teething toddlers - for another hundred years.)

The bed-chambers of 19th century wealthy people may have had 4-poster beds with canopies and curtains /bed-hangings, but the cribs of the poor were much meaner affairs. Families snuggled down together with many bodies sharing the same bed: top and tailing (with bodies resting alternately with their heads at the head-board and the next at the footboard) being the most efficient arrangement. Mattresses were made of organic material: horsehair, and sometimes cow-hair or wool, but otherwise straw was used. Those who could afford both would put the straw mattress under the horsehair one to protect it from the wooden frame or the iron bedstead.

Floor covering such as mats and carpets would probably have been found in middle-class and higher status homes, while rough matting was more likely the floor covering (if they had any) of the less-well-off bedecking their houses/rooms and homes. Linoleum, invented in 1861, gradually found its way into more homes as the cost became more affordable.

Glass windows were very different then and both their range and function were restricted by the technology available. It wasn't possible to make large sheets of glass and so windows were made up of groups of smaller panes. (Until 1851 the maximum size of a pane was approximately 4 feet by 10 inches; this was achieved by Chance Brothers of Smethwick for the Crystal Palace of the Great Exhibition.) Gradually, vertically moving sash windows (double hung) had replaced outward-opening hinged-windows (casements), particularly as houses in the cities and towns had been built ever closer together. Windows, as in the upper floors of houses in alleyways and small streets, was apt to collide with those of their neighbours' opposite.

Houses also absolutely leaked heat – they had no insulation and both the cold and chill winds cut through every abode, so they were probably far from comfortable in winter times. I don't doubt that where they had the means they would have had the sense to block up whatever draughts they could and as best as they could – these may have been different and perhaps more primitive times but commonsense is not necessarily a spectacular evolutionary leap peculiar to the 21st century. Solid window shutters were available in some houses, which provided another internal layer of material against the wind and chill. Some houses, although by no means all that many, had outside shutters instead. I do not recall seeing any evidence of both situated in the same place. And of course there was no double or triple glazing or smart-glass/photovoltaic technology which has begun to appear in this the early part of the 21st century.

There were moves in that mid-19th century to present the wonders of the age: the gizmos, gadgets, machinery and technologies that were available to the rich and to those in business, agriculture and industry. The Great Exhibition of the Works of Industry of All Nations held in 1851 in Hyde Park (and sponsored by the carbonated mineral water/ soft drinks company Schweppes) was organised by Prince Albert, and others. It was meant to represent the first world trades fair, and it provided a platform to showcase British expertise, our scientific and technological prowess and all the various products of our advanced society. It successfully showed off our latest and greatest stunning inventions while just down the road and all around a substantial proportion of the population subsisted with many living in abject squalor, with some enduring a pitiful existence in the workhouse while others starved to death in the street.

The Exhibition lasted for just over five months and attracted over 6 million visitors. (See Bib: Historic UK Ben

Johnson) When the entrance fee was dropped such that the working class might more be able to afford it, the deal was only on a normal working day, which seems unlikely to have drawn many there: to lose a day's wage and pay would have been quite some undertaking. I wonder whence the 6 million came.

A MATTER OF CONVENIENCE

Among the great exhibits within the Crystal Palace was an installation of public toilets, the Retiring Rooms, in which sanitary engineer George Jennings installed his "Monkey Closet" flushing lavatory. Middle-class housing design thereafter would increasingly recommend these as a feature, especially where the new sewer systems were being connected, but toilets for the greater part of the population were and would remain quite primitive.

According to Long there were pissoirs in the street, but I hardly think many were as glamorous or decorative as the one in Carey St/Star Yard. (cf Hidden City David Long 2011 History Press) It would not be for another three or four decades that public lavatories – "houses of office" – that were fitted with penny-coin-operated locks, were first established by British local authorities. (This gave rise to the oft repeated piece of graffiti, "Here I lie all broken-hearted. Paid a penny... and only farted." Inflation and then cut-backs would mainly disappear from the public urban landscape and "Public Conveniences" became a thing of the past. Strangely the need to urinate and defecate has not gone away.)

Toilets, lavatories, water closets and other arrangements in the home are considered a little more fully later in this text, as is the onerous task of washing clothes, including the equipment that was involved and available at the time, because in the first place it presumes the presence of water. Ditto in regards to ablution because it compels us to consider water sources.

One essential domestic item, therefore, would have been a bucket, which was variously made from wood, metal or even leather. Every household indeed would have had buckets, and note this is buckets *plural* – since one or more would be required for obtaining "clean" water, while others were necessary for slops of every kind. As there was no closed sewer system in London there were few toilets as we would know them, and thus slops which included human waste were deposited or tossed into the middle of the street or into cess-pits. Often, the waste contents of buckets or chamber pots would be emptied directly out of upper floor windows, with a warning cry, it is said, of "gardyloo." I have heard this reference often attributed to people living in Edinburgh, which seems at odds since the phrase is meant to derive from the French 'Gardez l'eau!' meaning 'watch the water.' Since the natural consequence of being shouted at directly (and from above) particularly in a foreign language might cause a person to look up, one can only speculate as to the caller's intention. Frequently described as dour, I wonder instead if some Scots possess a peculiar sense of humour.

Latrine-type holes and spaces were designated close to both individual and collective abodes, so shovels were also part of normal household wares.

The more affluent homes boasted an "addition" which could be a small toilet-room abutted to a top room at the back of the house. This garderobe or "privvy" was corbelled onto the house and contained a seat with a hole, which was positioned high above the dumping ground or water. Jimmy Stamp, who describes himself as a writer, researcher and recovering architect, termed the garderobe almost poetically in the Smithsonian Magazine (20.06.2014) as an architectural polyp. He also quoted the historian Dan Snow, who noted: "The name garderobe - which translates as guarding one's robes - is thought to come from hanging your clothes in the toilet shaft, so that the ammonia from the urine would kill the fleas." [6] In urban settings away from a river it was positioned above a slope to the cess-pit or cess-pool, such that the fall of descending excrement would be broken on its path into these privvy vaults. Castles and old fortresses had a similar device, where everyone perched or "parked" above a hill or slope leading into a trough.

The cess-pits and holes which were added to daily would inevitably fill up and had to be emptied and carted off to somewhere else... perhaps to where the people and the locale were more "deserving." This was a task - an imperative job - carried out by Nightmen, so-called because the work was not allowed to be done before midnight.

Despite the downsides of many facets of daily life and insanitary conditions, it was a time when not much was wasted. In the late 20th and early 21st century we have had to re-learn all manner of recycling but the people of the 19th century not only generated less rubbish and waste, but they found uses for the detritus and natural waste they created. Excrement found its way into horticultural and agricultural purposes, becoming fertiliser. The other natural waste, concentrated urine, was liberated from the "facilities" and sold on to tradesmen such as tanners in the leather trade. [7]

---

6 Cf Jimmy Stamp's great article at https://www.smithsonianmag.com /history/turrets-toilets-partial-history-throne-room-180951788 and also Dan Snow's Filthy Cities from Tuesday 5 April 2012 BBC

7 The smell of a tannery and of a tanner is, as they say, not to be sniffed at – literally. It is overwhelming. An acknowledgement of this is historical because even in Biblical times a woman was allowed to divorce her husband if he was a tanner and she found the stench intolerable.

Sewers, such as they were, discharged into the rivers from whence many people obtained their water supplies. The cleanliness of water from many sources was therefore always dubious, often being polluted and prone to carrying and transmitting disease.

In general, with unsafe water and infestations of mice, rats and fleas, poorer peoples' housing conditions in Somers Town and elsewhere were perfect breeding grounds for disease.

As stated earlier, bathrooms were rare; and even Buckingham Palace did not have a bathroom when Victoria came to the throne. (Higham. Nick, 2022 pg 188) The rich were not necessarily any keener on cleanliness than the poor, despite the former having servants to assist and to carry out all the exertions required by the process of moving quantities of water and of heating it, etc. The acts of washing – bodily ablutions - were probably carried out mainly at a wash-stand (a small table) with a washing bowl and a jug of heated water. Written records, in both fiction books and diaries, including those of good old Pepys, often remark that it was only on a daily basis that hands and faces were washed, but little else of the body received any attention. Much less frequently, and perhaps weekly, the working class family might wash themselves one after the other in a tin bath, almost certainly using the same water. The wealthy had hip-baths, which were more up-right sitting vessels: they also had someone else to heat and carry the water, *and* to empty it after. "Butler" sinks (without taps), tin baths and "coppers" (boiling tubs) were used to wash clothes.

The Baxters' clothes, like those of the Queen's and all her subjects, were washed using a scrubbing brush, soap and a washboard. I don't imagine the Queen would have been all that familiar with a washboard.

For some oblique reason the content of this piece brings to mind Spike Milligan, who went on stage and appeared to read out an advert from a newspaper:

"Mattress for Sale. Comfortable. A bargain for £10. Slight smell of urine."

Left: a mangle: feeding washed clothes and sheets etc in between the two rollers and turning the handle squeezed water out to assist in the drying process.

Right: A tub and a larger tin bath hanging up on a wall.

Mangles, tubs and tin baths were part of my normal experience living in the 1950's/1960's. The first two were rendered obsolete by a spin-dryer. There was no room (or money) for a washing machine as well.

Above: A rudimentary washing machine: turning the tee handle inside the fluted tub caused the six legs to agitate the washing.

Above: washboards and a bucket in a shallow type of butler sink

RUNNING WATER 1850'S

The term "running water" may now be a vague anachronism, familiar to few but the elderly in Britain and virtually unheard of because of the general availability of a supply of fresh water to UK households. War-torn countries, such as currently Ukraine, Syria, Yemen, Ethipoia etc will certainly have a better understanding of being deprived of it, while in other places it is weaponised. In modern developed societies at peace all households expect the facility of constant water availability without giving the wonder of it a passing thought; and this is especially so irrespective of what floor they live on – be they in a basement or on the 50th floor of an apartment block. Nowadays we turn on a tap, or open a fawcett as Americans might say, and miraculously there is a flow of water: we think nothing of it, and yet during the 19th century this was still relatively a novel facility.

In the generation between the births of Francis Baxter the cutler in 1797 and his son the stonemason in around 1827 their family home and that of their neighbours' were unlikely to have had a piped supply of fresh clean water to domestic taps within their households; and the water where it was supplied varied greatly in quality. Furthermore it was not available "on demand."

Of course, the wealthier inhabitants could and did pay private companies to pipe water direct to their houses and to their cisterns for their exclusive use: a great many may nevertheless still only had service to the lowest floor. It fell to the servants to transport it within the house especially as there was insufficient pressure to get it to upper floors. Some larger buildings, or company premises, had their own wells, which were not available to the public. (The Pearl Assurance Company had one at their premises at 252 High Holborn, near the Kingsway, when they occupied it from 1914 until 1989. It is now Rosewood London, formerly Chancery Court, and is at the rear of the Sir John Soanes Museum.)

Naturally, the poor and less well-off did not enjoy the same privilege or access to private water supply.

Also, in the squeeze of the burgeoning urban environment landlords rented out their properties into multi-occupancy abodes, where it was not uncommon for entire poor families to inhabit a single room. In such circumstances landlords paid water companies for a water supply, and recouped this from their tenant. These residents would have shared any other facility provided within (and usually more often it was without, i.e. out side) the property, and were no doubt charged inclusively with the rent for that luxury.

THE DEVELOPMENT OF LONDON AND ITS WATER SUPPLY

Water, naturally, has always been essential to life, to living beings and creatures, to horticulture and to agriculture. It has always been key to the establishment of communities, which of necessity developed around sources of water: rivers, lakes, streams, springs and wells.

Successful development was also dependent upon the quality of the water. Incidentally, one criterium that the Roman hydraulic engineer Vitruvius set for determining the safety of drinking water (in the 1st century BC) was to look at the condition and health of those living closest to its source. The Romans were not merely ingenious: they also often just had great common sense.

Di-hydrogen monoxide or H_2O or just plain old water, however, was not used in the 19th century as frequently and particularly not as casually as we use it in the UK today. I dare say if we had to carry it in a bucket for half a mile we would take more care of it and adopt a more frugal attitude to it and to its use.

We now expect each and every property to be supplied with this vital utility, and - theoretically - regulation to ensure it remains clean and uncontaminated means it is potable (safe to drink), and in addition we are able to use it for cooking. It is also routinely used to wash our bodies our clothes and for general cleaning.

Fashions and habits change, particularly so in regards to the incidence of bathing. This is perhaps exemplified in the oft repeated remark attributed to Queen Elizabeth I, who is reported to have said she had "a bath once a month... whether she needed to or no." This attitude to ablution was far from uncommon and persisted for centuries after the Virgin Queen had departed the earthly and earthy state. (Perhaps this reveals a clue as to the sovereign's chaste adjective...) [8]

SO WHAT WERE THE SOURCES OF WATER?

The geology of London had enabled wells to be dug; and while sometimes these were shallow, they could apparently also be in excess of 100-foot deep, an undertaking that certainly demands commitment. Digging any well to whatever depth is essentially an infrastructure project; and all such endeavours require at least two things: funding (for resources/tools/labour etc) and land. Whether these wells were on public or private land they were assuredly on someone's land, which begs questions initially in regard to authorisation and construction, to the financing thereof, and then as to how the public would subsequently be able to access the facility. Personal experience of

---

8 {https://www. historyextra. com/period /tudor/ strange} Elizabeth's immediate successor, James I (of England) (and VI of Scotland) apparently never bathed, and hardly ever indulged in any personal hygiene of any kind – he must have been a real treat, especially for his more intimate contacts.

the human condition would tend me to suspect the man who dug the well – or more likely the man who paid the man to dig the well – wanted something in return: and the cynic in me doubts hearty thanks would have sufficed. Perhaps it was kudos or power – the power to withdraw the right of access (still a powerful weapon as is evidenced, though not often reported upon in Palestine) – or a tool to pacify or defuse desperation. Or, perhaps these were just acts of pure philanthropy! Maybe, or maybe not.

It seems that the major sources of water for Londoners - mainly the rivers of London - were being besmirched by people dumping waste in them, and that this was a process long recognised as compromising the quality if not the safety of the water. Tanners, butchers and other trades as well as people's natural waste had all contributed to the contamination; and it was a problem which seemed inexorable. In response to the acknowledged need for fresh water to be brought into the City plans had been initiated as far back as 1236. It was Henry III who in the 21st year of his reign had ordered or agreed the tapping of a supply from the then town of Teybourne which was just west of modern day Bond Street underground station. The contract was awarded to Gilbert de Sandford who was granted the liberty to run the supply through conduits of lead pipe (see Ackroyd 2006 pg 88) "for the good of the realm, the profit of the city and for the poor to drink" (Apparently, according to Stow, free of charge!.).

Perhaps this last point referencing the poor and no fee was a sop or perhaps they had little facility to meter or oversee the water sufficiently because it appears to be a surprisingly benevolent provision, and quite out of keeping with the normal treatment of the poor: especially so considering labour costs and the price of pipes associated with such a project. Whatever, more than seven centuries ago, water was sourced from Teybourne at Marylebone (St "Mary on the bourne") Lane where the Tyburn river ran. The procurement brought fresh water from there into the City at West Cheap which is now known as Cheapside. It would appear from the path of the original *conduit* that it crossed the river Fleet; the pipes fed the first cistern of lead, castellated with stone, in the city which was called the Great Conduit.

Stow (reprinted 1956) indicates it was funded by "common council." I believe this is a reference to an ancient body which still exists as the primary decision making body of what is now the City of London Corporation, the municipal governing body of the actual City of London rather than that of any greater geographical or political entity.

Of course people in successful business and wealthy people are able to demand and afford the best of all that is available. This encouraged further private companies to form and to compete in the supply of water to individual premises and to house-owners who were to be charged directly. Other sources for the general public remained the brooks, bournes, springs, fountains and pools etc: these included those which were augmented with conduits and cisterns that were variously built by good and charitable citizens (some listed by Stow, 1956 pg 18) or otherwise by charges of the commonality through taxes or levies.

The general increase in population naturally led to a proliferation of extraction points for water. Even in 1598 John Stow had noted that across the city, in almost every street or lane, there were "divers(e) fair wells and fresh springs." (ibid Stow, pg12) Pumps would be placed above these, and later stand-pipes connected to pipes and conduits would also be installed. In this manner simple demand would continue to be met throughout the coming centuries in the newer developing areas such as in Somers Town.

Not all the water sources were part of a network, but there were clusters of outlets such as the wells and springs. It seems these waters in this part of London where the Baxters would later live emanated from aquifers – fed by groundwater over days, years and millennia - which were in close proximity to the River Fleet. In fact according to Stow the River Fleet had been referred to as the river of wells in the time of both Edward I and of William the Conqueror. The description is apt since along and adjacent to its route there were numerous wells including Pancras Well which Cunningham (1849 pg 173) says, quoting Hone's Every Day book (i. 323), was in the garden of a private house near Old St Pancras churchyard. Heading south-east there was St Chad's Well in Chad's Row, Grays Inn Lane, near Battlebridge, whose "miraculous water" was described (Ibid pg 45) as "aperient" and "was some years ago quaffed by the bilious and other invalids." Further south there was Bagnigge Wells in Cold Bath Fields which was adjudged a kind of minor Vauxhall (Gardens), a place of public entertainment "much frequented formerly by the lower sort of tradesmen." It had opened in 1767, in consequence of the discovery of two mineral springs, one chalybeate – containing iron salts - and the other cathartic (according to Lyson's Environs, iii.381). I am assuming it was the latter in the sense of emotional, spiritual and psychological purification rather than a purgative effect on the bowels which I dare say might be unwelcome. A drawing in 1780 shows some rather more well-attired ladies at Bagnigge Wells Tea Gardens, and describes it as an elegantly finished place."In one of the rooms there is a good organ, regularly played every afternoon, Sundays excepted." (Susannah Ives Nov 22, 2022, Late Georgian Tea Gardens) By 1794 it seems the well was built over (Cunningham p223) and a House of Correction opened. There was also Sadler's Wells, Black Mary's Hole and the Clerk's Well in Ray Street, where "the water of which is sweet, clear and salubrious," according to Fitzstephen [Cunningham 1849 pg 211). Its location was further described as on the right hand side of a lane going from Clerkenwell to Hockley in the Hole. The Clerk's well (ibid pg 212) was shown to have been enclosed by the owner of the property, Mr Cross, a brewer, and access was through an old watch house. It was said formerly to have had an iron railing and brass cocks which were since cut off.

This list is not exhaustive, but finally there was, of course, Bride's well.

The river Fleet itself, along with the other London rivers, continued to be under increasing threat. This did not escape the attention of the 16th century surveyor Stow who commented that as the city had grown in the centuries following the Norman conquest, the "incroachment (sic) for buildings and the number of citizens (having) mightily increased" had impacted negatively on all London's rivers, and on the Fleet in particular. Each stage in this general process of continuing "sore" decay brought more pressure to bear upon the authorities, such as they were, to seek sweet water from further afield. Ongoing projects then necessitated more pipes and conduits; it should be noted that the term conduit seems to be used interchangeably for pipe and for the cisterns (and even the pumps) the pipes fed.

The growing demand for a direct water supply to wealthier homes and businesses was a financial opportunity: it was both an expensive and a potentially very lucrative endeavour. There had been smaller companies in the field before Hugh Myddleton's New River Company (NRC) began operating in 1613, but his was particularly successful. Using bored-out elm trunks as conduit-pipes, superb engineering skills and topographical knowledge it relied upon gravity and a well-planned gradient to deliver the water. Without any of the problems of a pressure system the New River water flowed gently from Hertfordshire into the metropolis, and within the areas it covered it managed to maintain a fairly consistent supply. It had low running costs and required a relatively small number of people to keep the route and the water clear – and to check to make sure only fee-payers were drawing water off. The New River overcame the problem of shifting water from a lower level to a higher plane by using "inverted" siphoning, which I was informed of by Nick Higham. (I had often wondered how the New River managed to rise from Petherton Road, up Wallace Road and into the open New River Walk at Douglas Road, Canonbury, in Islington.) I do not know of the NRC's involvement in the Somers Town area.

Other companies *pumped* water from the low point of the Thames *up* into the surrounding London basin, but this was a costly procedure, and the water quality was far from good. Various methods were used: for example, water-wheels driven by the tidal flow were used for centuries and continued to provide the power for large waterworks well into the 19th century. An ingenious device in the late 16th century had been installed in the Thames beneath Old London Bridge: this took the form of an *under-shot* water wheel that used the tide to pump water. The church next to Old London Bridge, St Magnus the Martyr, was part of marketing ploy by one Peter Morris/Morrice who had contrived the device. In a public demonstration it successfully pumped water *over the church's steeple*! That impressive stunt led to Morris winning the right to supply water to the City, gaining an unprecedented (and unsurpassed) contract scheduled for a duration of 500 years! The subsequent demolition of the Old Bridge rendered the mechanism defunct, but by agreement the family gained shares in new companies by way of compensation. Other pumping methods would include that used by the York Buildings Waterworks of London, which operated from 1691 and employed a horse-drawn wheel to pump water from the Thames. The story of London's water, and the machinations of the water-suppliers, is superbly dealt with in Nick Higham's (2022) "The Mercenary River," which is a great and fascinating read.

While wealthier people were able to afford a direct supply the urban poor had to resort to local wells or to the water supply from a pump or a stand-pipe on a street-corner, in a court or an alley adjoining where they lived. The stand-pipes and the public water pumps – "the parish pumps" which were provided by and maintained at the expense of the parish - served them relatively well. These may or may not have been nearby; but, be they close, in-house or distant, getting water and getting it to where it was crucially needed would always involve a great deal of lugging heavy buckets and containers.

Water was carried then from these to smaller cisterns, tanks or butts within or attached to the properties, which were used and shared by the tenants. Water-carriers were employed to do the lugging for the well-to-do, but I suspect ordinary people lugged their own. I wonder how getting the water actually operated: there must have been queues of people with kids in tow and all carrying a bucket or water bottles.

Water could indeed be obtained from a local piped source but it was not available 24/7: it was only turned on within set hours by a person employed by the water-supplier and known as a turn-cock. Indeed the cocks were not necessarily turned on every day.

With few people in early 19th century London having much access to water that could be deemed as fit for drinking, most of the Baxters' contemporaries in the towns and districts of the city generally trusted their senses (their eyes and noses) to determine what was safe. Their experience of poor quality water consequently would lead the more discerning to usually opt for the safer option of drinking alcohol.

Despite innovations and improvements to supply lines, progress towards creating a more universal and comprehensive water (and sewerage) system was relatively slow. In the meantime, however, it was the age of steam-driven engines, which had initially been developed to meet the need to pump water from mines, that changed things forever. In the 18th and 19th century there had been an evolution from low-pressure gravity flow, and from wheeled machines like water mills to higher-pressure systems so that steam-power began to win favour. (In time, of course, electricity would be harnessed, but that prospect was part of a far-off future.)

The advent and harnessing of steam-power which first occurred in Britain would enable water to be pumped more efficiently from the rivers. This, however, was a costly exercise for both provider and for the user, and it seems many locals persistently still relied upon wells, springs and rivers as fixed sources of water supply.

As London developed, water supply companies increased their service to individual housing, charging the house-owner, who no doubt included that consideration within the cost of the rent to his tenants. The increased water service also enabled the installation of more Parish pumps and of stand-pipes in the streets, for which the Parish and vestry paid from monies received via the Rate system.

Many drinking fountains were installed in the 19th century, often at the behest and cost thereto of some generous benefactor, whose names were prominently etched into the structure. These may have been philanthropic but they were also monuments to their munificence. (I am unable to recall any such edifice being identified as an anonymous gift.) From 1859 the Metropolitan Drinking Fountain Association erected hundreds of fountains across the city as well as drinking troughs for horses and cattle.

Clean water and its source were almost inextricably linked to used water, to soiled water and to sewage, but whilst the problem was long recognised there was no joined-up thinking or concerted overall plan to deal with the problem. Instead and to make matters worse, in 1847, London's Metropolitan Commission of Sewers ordered that all cesspits should be closed and that house drains should connect to sewers and empty into the Thames. [See Ackroyd (2000)] Whether this actually precipitated the cholera epidemics, which ensued and killed thousands of Londoners in 1849, and in the early 1850's, is only slightly more difficult to assert in all cases, but it most certainly did not help. It did, though, definitely increase the foulness of the Thames; and so it was that after the hot summer of 1858 when the Great Stink from the Thames had so virulently got up the noses of Westminster Parliamentarians, the government were forced to act. The commissioner for the Metropolitan Board of Works Joseph Bazalgette had a solution – albeit a colossally expensive one - which the government didn't like, but holding their noses to the smell and to the cost they eventually agreed to his plans and passed an enabling act to revolutionise London's sewerage system. Finally, the development of water supplies, of filtration and sewerage systems took off in earnest and is well-documented.

It is somewhat ironic that our "advanced" civilisation had merely managed to produce simple wells, and had benefitted - without effort or much intelligence - from natural water-springs; and our greatest achievement seems to have been the conduits. At a time, however, centuries before Christ allegedly walked upon the water, and while the natives of these isles lived in mud-huts and probably gawped at those springs as wonders of the world, in far-away lands people without much visible water had solved the problems of supply. Iranians or Persians, around 500-700 BC had invented qanats.... a system of subterranean hand-dug channels that delivered potable water by gravity over vast distances. These man-made structures not only moved great and constant volumes of water [*and* avoided the problem of evaporation] but they also managed to supply cool air to buildings and to ice-houses ***in the desert*** [by virtue of the Bernoulli affect]. The irony, of course, is the promotion of some weird right-wing notions of Western superiority over middle-Eastern societies, which is often used to deride (Iran/Iraq) as uncivilised and primitive.

RIVER WATER

There are said to be thirteen rivers that entered the Thames in the *London County Council area.* Most of these London rivers are now subterranean watercourses, which discharge through conduits into the Thames and are only noticeable at low tide. Some of those lost and culverted rivers are occasionally still visible, although not necessarily recognisable: the Westbourne at Sloane Square and the Tyburn at Baker Street, for example, are encased in pipes which can be seen in those underground stations.

The great survivor north of the Thames is the river Lea/Lee, which originates in the Chiltern Hills, Bedfordshire. It is 68 km long and flows south-east through Hertfordshire, along the Essex border and into Greater London. Meeting the River Thames at Bow Creek, it is the most eastern of those 13 rivers, although the River Roding which is outside the area under review is further east.

THE FLEET. HAZARDOUS WATERS NEAR AND FAR.

It was the river Fleet, however, that was the most important river in terms of the Baxter's location north of the Thames in Somers Town. In the 18th century the Fleet had meandered down from its sources in the hills of Hampstead and

Highgate, and wound its way through Kentish Town Road (once known as Water Lane) behind the Castle Tea Rooms, across a meadow to Camden Town, then on west of Agar Town, passed St Pancras (Old) Church to Somers Town. Its fresh water course ran on from there through Battlebridge, along the Fleet Valley towards Holborn, Farringdon Street and on to Blackfriars and down to the Thames. It was therefore the main drainage for Hampstead and Highgate, and for all those towns along its path going south.

In Canaletto's time - and Samuel Scott's (1702-72) - the accumulated water of the Fleet was so great that it was 100 yards wide as it entered the Thames. Creeping decline, nevertheless, was inexorable without regulation, and there were references to the river's general besmirchment in its lower section being noted as far back as the 16th Century: Nick Higham (the Mercenary River, 2022. Headline Publishing Group, pg 25,) wrote, "It had even then become a notorious repository for the noxious effluvia of tanneries, slaughter-houses and Smithfield livestock market, along with domestic privies." A heady description. He further drew on Ben Johnson references in *On the Famous Voyage,* a journey along the Fleet Ditch, which emphasised its contents of "floating turds, dead cats, over-hanging privies" and to its "all encompassing stench." (See Higham's Footnote 16 Ch 1 re Ben Johnson's remarks (from Ben Johnson: Poems. Routledge and Kegan Paul 1971 p69-75.)

Increasingly through the late 18th century and the early 19th the Fleet was also becoming the dumping site for all manner of rubbish and effluent, such that it progressively declined – if that is not an oxymoron – and became more of a major sewer than a river: the fate of most of London's rivers.

The development of the Regent's Canal area led to the section of river between Camden and King's Cross being culverted (bricked in and over) and thus it was incrementally buried in the 1810-1820 period. There are tales of the Poet Shelley wooing

Mary Wollstonecraft and sailing toy boats under its bridges by St. Pancras churchyard, so I imagine this romantic episode occurred before it was culverted there.

Perhaps this is a fine detail or a small inconvenience for a romantic but at the time of wooing young Mary, the poet was rather inconveniently already married to Harriet Westbrook. That may have been problematic, but what should have been a trifle more awkward, to say the least, was that in 1816 Shelley's estranged wife Harriet drowned herself in the Serpentine. Now you might think this event would have occasioned a heightened sense of propriety on his part, but, no, just two weeks later the sensitive poet married the Wollstonecraft girl. I doubt many find that altogether endearing. He was undoubtedly both a troubled and a talented soul: apart from the poetry, he also supported unpopular causes such as Catholic emancipation, an independent Ireland and stopping the oppression of the poor. Whilst his work and life was revolutionary and racy, he also advocated passive, non-violent resistance (see his T*he Masque of Anarchy).* He further antagonised the authorities and the establishment with his publicly avowed atheism. So, he was both troubled and the cause of trouble for the establishment.

It seems water was Shelley's nemesis, because he himself would drown in 1822. The establishment's attitude to the news was typified in the Tory newspaper, The Daily Courant. Unable to contain themselves or even to resist kicking a dead man, in the report of his drowning it was suggested that "now he knows whether God exists or no," a remark which only makes sense if Gods and/or an afterlife actually exist. (See: Blunden. Edmund, 1965)

Jonson's work *On the Famous Voyage* (along the Fleet) contains some indelicate or earthy comments such as: "Arses were heard to croak, instead of frogs;".... "Alas, they will beshite us....." He described the "shore of farts, but late departed," and further wondered "How dare your dainty nostrils (in so hot a season, when every clerk eats artichokes, and peason, laxative lettuce, and such windy meat) 'tempt such a passage? When each privy's seat is filled with buttock? And the walls do sweat urine, and plasters?"

Jonson's waggish piece or moral satire has attracted diverse criticism. This is discussed by Andrew McRae who includes a comment by Algernon Charles Swinburne:

"Coprology," Swinburne snootily suggested, "should be left to the Frenchmen..."

The river Fleet downstream from Camden would incrementally go underground until in the 1870's when it was incorporated into Joseph Bazalgette's subterranean interceptor sewer construction. The Fleet at that point had been fully integrated into the London Main Drainage network.

So, mostly throughout the Baxters' time in Somers Town the River Fleet had been culverted and covered in with tunnels. This sounds quite simple, but it completely understates the construction. The Fleet is now contained within vast elaborate structures and within impressive chambers which divert it and its foul content down to the Thames. (http://www. adeadendstreet.co.uk /2014/11 /river-fleet-cso-london.html contains great images of this amazing watercourse/sewer.)

The Fleet may be viewed - partially at least - in Highgate and Hampstead, but it is mainly now just part of the covered sewer system. There is, though, still a point down in Clerkenwell where it remains audible: there is drain-hole outside the Coach and Horses pub in Ray Street at the foot of Eyre St Hill where you can hear the flow of the buried river. I declined to test if it was detectable by smell: like former U.S. President Bill Clinton I did not inhale.

During the 18th and 19th centuries the the Fleet also became renowned for huge infestations of rats, whose size probably grew with each re-telling of every encounter. Rat-catchers abounded, and whilst people did not want vermin later some rodents indeed do have their champions. Uncommon they may be but "enthusiasts" became intent on promoting rodents both as pets and exhibition animals, forming clubs and competitions for those purposes. (The London and Southern Counties Mouse and Rat club formed in 1915 and the National Fancy Rat Society formed in 1976 are still extant).

A post-script in regards to the Fleet. That 100 yard wide River Fleet of Canaletto's time has now been reduced to a pathetic outfall - a meagre discharge - into the Thames under Blackfriars Bridge. The best view of it from a land position is often cited as from Blackfriars Pier. The not-so delightful outfall may have been the last thing the papal banker Roberto Calvi saw - assuming he was conscious at the time he was said to have hanged himself. Having fled to London he was found hanging under the bridge in 1982: an apparent but seriously dubious suicide.

All things considered, that is pollution, decline, sewage, it was unlikely that the locals of early 19th century Somers Town took their water from the Fleet. The fresh water brought in by Myddleton's New River being both east and north of them, was possibly out of range geographically – I also wonder if it was within the price range of many of the locals. Instead other options would have been to draw water from those local wells, and carry it home with some people being able to afford water-carriers for the task. Perhaps these sources were supplemented by cisterns, butts or tanks which caught rainwater; in time and increasingly stand-pipes and water-pumps would become available to the public throughout developing areas.

A typical water-pump. This one at Sally Lunn's in Bath.

I think it safe to assume that great monetary fortunes did not form part of the Baxters' experience. Cleaning-up for them was limited to more basic domestic and bodily situations: to cleaning their homes, their clothes and to ablution.

The Victorians, like many of their British predecessors, took a different view both of personal hygiene and of their general experience with water. Perhaps this was born out of the difficulty of drying themselves sufficiently in a climate not then renowned for hot weather, and of a propensity for catching their death "of a cold." Getting wet was a serious matter.

The indications are that immersion in water or bathing was not widespread almost two centuries ago. Some people did attend spas, which were available in a few places. These, however, were used for their supposed therapeutic qualities, rather than for hygiene purposes. Furthermore, whenever participating individuals are mentioned, their names seem to indicate that spas were largely the preserve of the upper echelons of society. These bathers would have enjoyed the support and ministrations of servants being on hand to assist them. I cannot imagine the spas were accessible to the hoi polloi – at least not at the same time as the wealthier members of the community.

Unfortunately there is not enough information - at least that I have been able to find - in regards to swimming (whether for exercise, competition/sport or for the pure enjoyment of the activity). One can only wonder how prevalent it may have been for people to chance a dip in rivers, ponds, lakes or in the sea, and how many people were actually able to swim.

Current figures suggest 88% of people in England are able to swim, although the level of proficiency is wide-ranging. Only three-quarters of these "swimmers" believe they could swim the 25 metres that the national curriculum requires Primary School children to do unaided. Age also impacts on these statistics with 20% of those 65+ saying they could not swim. [See Abigail Axe-Browne]

The history of purpose-built pools is a little confusing but whilst some were constructed both in the 18th century and in the early 19th century these were usually private. The first dedicated swimming pool in England about which records still survive was an open-air bath known as the 'Pearless Pool, - behind what was the St Luke's Workhouse and Asylum. This was purportedly purpose-built and opened in **1743**. It is also known as Peerless Pond, being apparently a corruption of perilous, which may infer how dangerous the activity was viewed. Cleveland Pools, built in 1815 on the banks of the River Avon in Bath, is the UK's oldest public lido, but it should be noted that being "public" did not necessarily mean the general public could afford to use them.

There are always some people who cannot resist the lure of water (cf the winter/New Year bathers in the Serpentine) and doubtlessly some Londoners must have swam in local ponds - such as Hampstead or Highgate ponds - and in lakes and rivers where the pollution was not too obvious or advanced; and while this would continue, changes were in process that would offer other opportunities. At the forefront of change was the construction in 1828 of the first municipal swimming pool in England, the St George's Baths, Liverpool which was a salt-water pool; from then on municipal authorities began to build affordable swimming facilities across the country. Initially, it had been private companies which had provided facilities but municipal development began to flourish especially after changes in legislation, most notably the Baths and Washhouses Act, 1846. Aside from being a response to health, hygiene and disease concerns these moves were assisted by the religious concepts of "Cleanliness being close to Godliness" and by "healthy bodies, healthy minds" notions. Vice troubled Church and Government; and all told it must have kept many people up at night and for strangely quite different reasons.

In "Splashing in the Serpentine" (See Bibliography) the writer comments that swimming in England was once practised by only a few individuals – and these were nearly always men, and yet from the 1830s onwards it had developed into an activity engaged in by millions of people with more women being included. Pools were segregated, and men certainly swam nude, probably from a lack of swimming costumes as much as a lack of money to buy them. From just-about-getting-your-feet-wet paddling in the ocean, rivers and lakes it soon developed into a range of disciplines that would go on to encompass not merely recreational swimming, but competitive swimming and other aquatic sports such as diving, synchronized swimming and water polo. Proficiency was also encouraged in the field of aquatic life-saving. Costumes may have been required in competitions, but segregation and nude swimming nevertheless continued and was still not uncommon in the early 1960's.

Swimming in the Victorian period would be given another boost when Shropshire-man Captain Matthew Webb became the first recorded person to swim the English Channel, covering a distance of around 40 miles in a little over 21 hours in 1875.

A FORM OF ADDRESS. DOORS WITHOUT NUMBERS.

In Victorian times you could walk out of the door and be lost forever if you were so-minded. Technology and the widespread coverage of surveillance devices from closed circuit television to street-door-bells have made such disappearance extremely difficult if not virtually impossible. We are - or can be - tracked from our movements, our phones and from unavoidable financial transactions. The places where we do things and where we are to be found are identifiable and locatable. GPS, the Global Positioning System, which is owned and controlled by the US government can now pin-point or locate a radio or satellite transmitted position almost anywhere on the planet and this is accurate to generally within a few metres. The US military and other agencies have demonstrated its capability with devastating effect: a man sitting in a wheelchair in Damascus can be blown up by a person controlling and guiding a weapon while sitting in Langley, Virginia. Those are some of the means by which we can be located, but how ordinary people find other people and places is a different matter.

Actual addresses for locations have been refined with various schemes and other techniques. Computerisation in the 2020's has also given us a facility called "what3words," where every 3 metre square of the world has been assigned a unique combination of three words. We also have postal codes to identify a cluster of houses or homes within a place. (The American equivalent, the zip code, is an acronym for the USA's zone improvement plans). These codes have narrowed down the error for normal and benign location-finding and have greatly facilitated delivery systems and postal services. The very idea that a property could be identified by its position according to a centralised format is relatively new. Furthermore the idea that a property could be identified by anything other than by a name or by the local knowledge of who lived there is also not an ancient concept.

The practice of numbering houses and properties took a long time to become embedded. Its adoption in the UK had been a slow process; and it was far from universally or uniformly applied. It is first recorded at the beginning of the 18th century: Porter (See Porter. Roy p126) states that the *New View of London* reported in 1708 that "at Prescott Street, Goodman's Fields, the houses are distinguished by numbers." Mostly, important premises or businesses had signs: the sign of the black horse or the sign of the Turk's Head etc. The numbering of houses, though still erratic, would gradually become more popular in the late 18th / early 19th century. Recall, if you will, that the Duke of Wellington's home - Apsley House – was known as No.1 London: a suitably impressive address for the Iron Duke.

House-numbering did not become standardised in any way until after 1855 with the passing of the Metropolitan Management Act. Before that, the Postal Museum's website indicates, addresses were very idiosyncratic and far from definite, such that a letter might be addressed to

> *'To my sister Jean, Up the Canongate, Down a Close, Edinburgh. She has a wooden leg.'* *(see postal museum.)*

From 1857 house numbering and street names began to be more systematically regulated and altered. In the same year London was divided into ten postal districts: EC (East Central), WC (West Central), N, NE, E, NW, SE, S, SW and W. The S and NE sectors were later abolished.

To improve efficiency in 1917 postal districts were then further divided into sub-districts each identified by a number appended to the area. The number 1 was assigned to area in which the district head office was located, with other numbers allocated alphabetically by delivery office, e.g. N2 (**Ea**st Finchley delivery office), N3 (**Finc**hley delivery office), N4 (**Fins**bury Park delivery office) etc. Accordingly in the E-district: E1 was **A**ldgate, E2 **Be**thnal Green, E3 **Bo**w, E4 **Ch**ingford, E5 **Cl**apton, E6 **Ea**st Ham, E7 **Fo**rest Gate, E8 **Ha**ckney, E9 **Ho**merton, E10 **Le**yton etc.

Post codes were a feature of the 1960's and 70's while zip codes came much later.

FRANCIS BAXTER'S FRONT DOOR. KEY-LESS. LETTER-BOX FREE.

You may occasionally hear people say, "In the old days, you could go out without locking your door." Well, of course, they are right because the people they are talking about (in those good old days in living memory) didn't have anything worth stealing. They didn't need to lock anything up. Most of those who had a lock on their door had a cheap lock, and they generally had a key on a bit of string which hung through the letter-box. The lock was there to keep out stray dogs, and furthermore a great many people had latches, which flipped open or dropped shut. Rich and wealthy people are more likely to have had locks. *They* had something – many things, in fact – worth stealing.

That, however, relates to times in "living memory." In the early part of the 19th century Francis Baxter's external front door probably looked a good deal different to a modern door. Certainly it would not have been made of Upvc or of some composite material: it would have been made of wood, which I would allow is still a common material.

Francis's door may just have had a latch, rather than a lock, in which case he would not have had or needed a key. I wonder did ordinary working class and poor people usually have experience of door locks? An incidental reference from Dickens' Dombey and Son tells of Good Mrs Brown in Agar Town opening her door with a key which may lead us to think it was not uncommon: on the other hand her thieving ilk would not have welcomed anyone idly looking in on her. The rich, however, and the wealthy and the well-to-do may have had a lock but may not have needed to carry a key. They more probably had servants and or doormen to open the door in the daytime, with doors secured at night-times with shoot-bolts plus an iron bar, which slotted across the door into brackets on the door jambs. Windows were shuttered on the inside and secured with similar bars.

Most doors, as previously mentioned, would not have had a number. It would also not have had a letterbox – at least not before 1840. At that point, no houses had - not even those of the rich! Again, the wealthy would have had servants to receive any goods or communication. No one had mail or post delivered in the way with which we are now familiar. There were no postmen or post-women. There was also no junk mail, pizza menus or flyers to be pushed through the door. In regards to such "input" it appears that at least some small things were better then: the good old days indeed.

The entrance to all common and uncommon abodes may have had some door furniture such as handles and possibly a door knocker. Door-bells, as we might describe them, were not attached to doors, and instead visitors pulled a mechanical component which was linked to a bell by a metal wire that operated the clapper and rang the bell. The entrance also had one other item which was essential. Since roads and streets were mainly rough ways without tarmac and paving stones all pedestrians collected soil (and mud in wet weather) on their footwear. Any visitor and anyone entering a house would therefore have been required to use a simple piece of metalwork which was outside the door - on the step, if there was one – or that was otherwise set into the wall or railings: a mud-scraper for shoes and boots.

WRITING AND POSTING A LETTER (POSTAL MUSEUM HISTORY)

The Royal Mail began as a postage system founded by Henry VIII in 1516. For most of its history, the Royal Mail was a public service, which operated as a government department or public corporation. It delivered the "post," an abbreviated term derived from the initial instruction which, before the invention of postage stamps, was written on the letter or card: "post-haste." In other words the communication was to be delivered as soon as possible. The service, apparently, was first made available to the public by King Charles I, and the General Post Office was created during the restoration by his son Charles II.

The first mail coach was a stage coach service operated by independent contractors to carry usually long-distance mail on behalf of the Royal Mail/Post Office. The service began in 1784 and ran between Bristol and London. The recipient had to pay the cost. The first mail train, a travelling post office, ran in 1830 on the Liverpool and Manchester Railway.

The service and the postal system were inherently inefficient, and it was Rowland Hill, an English teacher and social reformer, who came up with a revolutionary concept which changed the system such that it could flourish. It was Hill who put forward reforms to the postal system, which required senders to pre-pay the cost of postage. In order to certify it had been paid the first adhesive postage stamp, the Penny Black, was affixed to the communication. This began in 1840.

From that point it became easier to send letters and cards. Envelopes were not regularly used, and instead the letter or its outside page was folded, stuck or sealed. Letters, of course, were handwritten.

Now that recipients no longer needed to pay for the delivery they were no longer required to be physically present when the post was delivered. In draughty ill-fitting entrances the mail could simply be slid under the door, but increasingly in better houses and premises a new solution was found: the day of the letter-box as a piece of street-door furniture was at hand.

A NOTE ON PROGRESS:

Following the Postal Services Act 2011 a majority of the shares in Royal Mail were floated on the London Stock Exchange in 2013. The then Tory government initially retained a 30% stake in Royal Mail, but being the party of business (monkey business, that is) it sold the country's remaining shares in 2015. It has been monkeying around with the economy disastrously ever since, while managing to enrich their financial backers.

LETTER-WRITING. A CLERK'S PEN

19th century office workers, known as clerks then, naturally had to be literate and fairly numerate to satisfy the books of and for their employers. They also had to be neat writers. At the time when the Baxters were in the Somers Town area there was no such thing as a ball-point pen (otherwise known as a biro), and there were relatively few fountain pens. The latter which contained an ink reservoir or fountain were a fairly modern invention, despite Samuel Pepys referring to one such device in the 17th century. An English patent had been taken out on a fountain pen in 1809, but it would take decades before technologies evolved to produce a suitable and efficient unit commercially. [9]

Instead, the clerks filled in their accounts and ledgers using a quill pen which they dipped in ink. This was the common writing implement for clerks and for anyone wishing to communicate whether it be a private letter, a business correspondence, a message, greeting or invitation.

The quills were made from the moulted flight feathers of birds. Larger lettering usually required an expensive feather from a large bird, such as a swan. (Note, by pure coincidence, a female swan is called a pen.) Otherwise, and also as an alternative to swan's moultings, feathers were obtained from geese as well as crows, eagles, owls, hawks and turkeys.

The hollow shaft of the feather had to be cured to harden it, and the end had to be carved into a nib using a small pocket knife. This knife was used for thinning and pointing the feather quills. The Latin word for feather, by the way, is penna.

Thus, for these combined reasons, the small pocket knife is known to us as a pen-knife.

---

9 In 1888 a Harvard lawyer, John Loud, invented the first ball-point pen, but as they say "it was nothing write home about ... and also nothing to shout about." Without commercial backing or promotion Loud's invention largely fell on deaf ears and the patent lapsed. It was not until 1931 that Lazlo Biro managed to go into production with an early version, which was later modified and became the ubiquitous writing implement of the late 20th century.

Whilst life was hard - and probably relentlessly hard and without much hope - I can't imagine that people did not manage to find some fun in life. Where, though, did they manage to find it and what was the nature of that distraction or entertainment? We don't all like the same things, a truism at any time; so we can't imagine what particular people favoured: we can only consider what was possibly available to them in the 19th century. Later distractions such as cinemas, games-rooms, bowling alleys, games and betting apps etc were not available to them, but there were still diverse activities, events and goings-on which may have drawn them away from their everyday boring normality.

Hangings, whilst popular (at least with the crowd, if not the condemned), were not quite frequent enough. Single executions or group executions may have provided betting opportunities within the spectators - such is the invention of the compulsive gambler. Also infrequent were fairs, such as Bartholomew's Fair held on his feast day 24th August, its eve and day after, which promised the antics of performers of all types and which for many centuries attracted huge crowds. By 1849, though, Cunningham p59 described it as a real nuisance with scarce a vestige of antiquity or utility about it. Not a fan, then.

Of course, everyday distractions were venues such as pubs and beer-houses, but even then drinking habits may also have varied.

Naturally, for anyone with any disposable income – and even for those who didn't, but who desperately craved some distraction – there were pubs, beer-houses, halls, theatres, fairs and other places of entertainment. Male pursuits of a more direct, earthy or personal nature were indulged by some in stew-houses (brothels for the heterosexuals) and in Molly-houses (for the homosexual). I have not found any references to such facilities for those with Lesbian preferences, nor of any trans-gender or sex.

Other entertainments – for, perhaps, a different audience and possibly with wider appeal - included the spectacle of baiting a variety of tethered animals by aggressively cultivated canines. Unfortunate animals included bears, boars, badgers and bullocks who were usually attacked by mastiffs and dogs, whose breeds have, as a result of these pursuits, been prefixed with the word "bull:" hence bull mastiffs and bulldogs.

Cock fighting was another low "sport" which again is remembered in the name of places such as Cockpit Yard, WC1. It was also popular in Somers Town and in Hockley in the Hole amongst many other venues. The latter, near Clerkenwell Green, was not just a piece of open ground but a definite venue; and whilst I do not know the extent of its building it did have a stage and a gallery. It was described by Cunningham as a kind of Bear Garden, celebrated for bear-baiting and also for trials of skill (1849, P383). Such trials had long been played out in the Hole: there were wrestling and bare knuckle bouts which provided a great betting opportunity for gamblers and for the bet-takers. The events were not restricted to male contestants, and Cunningham gives an example of one particular personal challenge between two women in 1722 when Elizabeth Wilkinson of Clerkenwell invited Hannah Hyfield to box with her for a prize of 3 guineas: a good purse and worth fighting for! Hyfield apparently relished the challenge and agreed the terms of the bout, which was to be fought with both women holding a half crown in each hand, and would finish when one dropped her money. This condition somehow allowed them to get around the normal rules of such combat, whereby an opponent having been knocked down was permitted a set time to get up and return to the centre of the ring, there to toe the line (a naval reference) where a mark was scratched. In the event of not being able to do so the fighter was not "up to scratch" and so was declared the loser. Instead of toe-to-toe slugging and trading punches the women's match promised a rowdier and more fluid spectacle, with both fighters publicly committed to giving and desiring no quarter from the other. It was, in essence apparently - and not just to sell tickets - a real grudge match.

So, the Hole and other places of entertainment contained pugs and pugilists of every shape, size and sex. In 1835 the Cruelty to Animals Act would ban the baiting of beasts and cock-fighting but such sports were not easily given up whatever the Law said. Consequently the Act did not end them entirely, but instead drove them underground where they still fester and occasionally burst forth into the public consciousness.

TEA GARDENS

Tea Gardens also provided entertainment and refreshment, although, I suspect these were more often frequented by the middling classes. There were tea gardens at Bagnigge Wells, Chalk Farm, the Adam and Eve, White Conduit House, Hornsey Wood, the Yorkshire Stingo in Lissom Grove and Highbury Barn.

The White Conduit House was also renowned for its loaves as well as its diversity. Ives quotes The Book of Days by Robert Chambers, "On week-days, it was a kind of minor Vauxhall, with singing and fire-works on great occasions; the ascent of a balloon crowded the gardens, and collected thousands of persons in the fields around. It was usual for London 'roughs' to assemble in large numbers in these fields for foot ball play on Easter Monday; occasionally the fun was diversified by Irish faction fights." There was an Adam and Eve Tea Garden said to be in St. Pancras; however, there was one so-named in Tottenham Court Road near St Giles. The St Pancras one was described as "a pleasant distance from town, where is an excellent bowling green, and a regular company meet in summer, in the afternoon, to play at bowls and trap-ball. According to Ives it was a very good room for parties and to dine and drink tea. She also mentions the Sluice House, which was apparently "good for eel-pies, excellent teas and hot rolls." Ives writes an interesting blog.

Fairs

Fairs were periodic events which always brought with them a range of chancers, prancers (dancers) and all manner of other performers, entertainments and vendors. Bartholomew Fair was originally something of an exposition for drapers and clothiers, being a cloth fair, attested still by a street there called Cloth Fair. Any agglomeration of people tends to pull in a bigger crowd and creates an opportunity to make money: people want to sell, people want to buy or else are there to be convinced they want whatever is being sold from goods and commodities to food and entertainments. It becomes self-propelling – a place becomes "popular" and other people go there because it is popular, which in turn adds to its reputation as a place to go to, and so on until some other place comes into vogue.

So Bartholomew Fair inevitably lured a variety of other chancers, who in turn attracted more crowds. Even after it ceased to operate as a cloth fair, which occurred in Elizabethan times, the tradition continued by virtue of its diverse entertainments. The place of those departed drapers and clothiers was taken up with showmen exhibiting "monsters, motions, drolls and rarities." (Cunningham (1849) pg 56) "Puncheletto and his popets," i.e. Punch and Judy puppet shows, were a favourite of the crowd. The Fair was open to those with stamina – from 10 a.m. until 10 in the evening. (Ackroyd 2012 pg 123)

The Lord Mayor used to get involved, apparently by custom first stopping at Newgate on his way to the Fair, where he would avail himself of a free cool tankard of wine spiced with nutmeg and sugar. This practice was stopped at the close of the 17th century following a fateful incident. The Mayor, Sir John Shorter, had upon receiving his freebie, supped and then closed the lid of his tankard with such an over-enthusiastic flourish that it startled his horse. This caused it to bolt and throw his Lordship. Drinking, as they say, may harm your health – which proved to be the case for the Mayor... who it seems was fatally injured. Free-loading does not usually end so well.

Ben Jonson's book *Bartholomew Fair* recounts many of the treats and joys on offer and references the "old" amusements of wrestling, motions, puppets, operas, tight-rope walkers (cf Blondin) dancers, dwarves, monsters and wild beast and ballad singers.

Museums

The wealthy and well connected had few doors closed to them for their idle amusements. On occasion such clientele could indulge their curiosities and trot off to the Royal College of Surgeons museum in Lincoln's Inn Fields which contained some interesting anatomical specimens: the complete skeleton of 8 ft 4" Charles Byrne, who died in 1783, and the right hand of a fellow Irish giant Patrick Cotter, who had waved goodbye to the mortal world in 1802. He was 8ft 7½". For balance, as it were, it also displayed the left hand of the French 7ft 4" giant, M. Louis. Then on the other end of the height spectrum there was the 20-inch skeleton of the Sicilian dwarf, Caroline Crachami. Here, visiting gawkers could also view conjoined twins, plus a grotesque lump of foetus in feotu i.e. the parasitic twin of erstwhile twins, which had formed in (or had been enveloped by) the sibling's body. Teratoma or parasitic twin it nevertheless drew people to it.

These were in the Abnormal Structures department of the college and open to the Fellows and Members and their guests/visitors. These would not have been open to the likes of the Baxters.

Also, and previously available for private viewing at his home, there was the embalmed body of eccentric dentist Martin Van Butchell's first wife. She had been preserved at his request (Cunningham 1849, p230) – I wonder if that was some kind of message for his second wife...? Elizabeth Garnett (11 August 2020) of the Museum of London writes that following Martin's death in 1814 the remains were offered to the Board of Curators of the Royal College of Surgeons by his son. It did not specify the relationship of the son to the lady in the jar but hopefully the remains were not those of his departed mother.

The lady's preserved body was apparently put on display in the Hunterian Museum in London. Garnett states that her embalming was not totally enduring and that deterioration had become evident such that a visitor in 1857 had remarked that the remains then were 'shrunken' and 'hideous.' A sad observation, but at least one inescapable feature stood out for the visitor: the occupant of that bell-jar still sported a 'remarkably fine set of teeth.' Perhaps this was a final shining testament to her husband's dentistry skills. Modern scientific techniques may have opined on the matter, but a fire, which was caused by a bombing raid in May 1941, destroyed Mrs van Butchell's remains - together with a large part of the museum's collection.

The specimens, with the possible exception of Mrs Van Butchell, were mainly of lower class individuals and being no one of importance, it provoked no ethical outcry.

A sign in a pub, the Windmill, in Lambeth High Street offered advice and treatment for stress. The sign, pasted to the brick wall said, "Bang head here."

Head-bangers and head-cases in the past were committed to institutions, such as Bedlam – a name and a term that has passed into the general vocabulary. Bedlam was itself a corruption of the word Bethlehem, but it was neither a spiritually uplifting place nor a kindly psychiatric hospital where those in control understood and treated mental illness. It was just a last resort lock-up where sufferers were condemned to live out their tormented days. Little was then known of mental illness, of brain disease, depression or of the effects of trauma. It was pure incarceration, but it did, though, perform another role.

Bedlam and other asylums were also sources of entertainment. For those with the necessary bribe or entrance fee they could either passively observe or aggressively bait the lunatics as was their wont. Back in 1753 two pennies (2d) bought the ticket for those wishing to make "sport and diversion of the miserable inhabitants." (Cunningham 1849, p84) One visitor reports that over a hundred people were doing the same, so that was about a £1 in the venal gaoler's pocket – a nice little earner. Cunningham suggests that until the beginning of the 19th C such exhibition was open to the public; I imagine a little private enterprise nevertheless kept it available afterwards for a suitable price: indeed it may well have been one of the sights that visitors to London would have had on their bucket list. The asylums were not entirely without care or humanity since the worst afflicted inmates were kept in cells lined and floored with cork and Indian rubber. Perhaps, these had been jilted lovers driven mad with jealousy while the somewhat less heart-stricken on the outside were also susceptible to being caught on the rebound in a different manner.

Certain amusements had passed into history such as the ducking ponds and the practice of mounting severed heads on railings and spikes. By 1837 the pillory had also been abolished. Over time "do-gooder spoil-sports" - as perverts and right-wingers often call libertarians with a humane streak - would get these and public executions either stopped or removed from the public space. Now the abusive term is "woke," but it's the same type of people using the taunt.

There was also demand for wax-work exhibits: long before Madame Tussauds ("two-swords" in the London vernacular) a Mrs Salmon satisfied that need at her premises near the Horn Tavern, Fleet Street.

TIGHT-ROPE WALKERS

Tight-rope walkers were popular with the crowds. They appeared at fairs, such as Bartholomew Fair, and at other circuses. Some were singularly notable: Jean-François Gravelet, who was born in France in 1824, became internationally famous as Blondin. In 1859 he had crossed the gorge below Niagara Falls on a 335 metres-long tightrope which was suspended 49 metres above the water. It seems that nothing was ever enough for long enough with insatiable crowds who always wanted more. Having achieved this he was compelled to greater variations and extensions to the feat; so he did it while blindfolded, and then in a sack or pushing a wheelbarrow. The crowd always wanted more so he did it on stilts and then while riding a bike. Always, though, novelty had to be found so he rode a bicycle across the Niagara gorge while carrying his manager on his back – that man earned his 10% that day. On other occasions he devised to carry a small oven stopping midway to cook an omelette.

It seems these antics were part of the showman's life, and the need to keep adding a little to the routine had a long-history. Ackroyd (2012 pg120) mentions Scaramouch - a rope-walker, many years before Blondin - who completed his walk pushing a wheelbarrow with two kids and a dog inside – and a duck on his head. All, it seems, were ever striving for more ridiculous things to please the crowd.

Michael Ray at (britannica.com /biography/Blondin.) *s*tates that in 1861 Blondin appeared in London at the Crystal Palace, "turning somersaults on stilts on a rope stretched across the central transept, 170 feet (52 metres) above the floor." He gave his final performance at Belfast in 1896, aged 72. He is buried in London at Kensal Green.

Francis Baxter the elder, previously of Ratcliff and late of Somers Town, was a cutler: a maker of cutlery and other sharps, such as swords, cutlasses, knives, pocket-knives, pen-knives, scissors, scythes and surgical instruments like scalpels... and razors. Of course, there was always a local need, but the development of new processes would increasingly go on to affect the local tradesmen and craftsman wherever he was situated. Technical advances and the scale of production (because of large industry and mechanisation), particularly at home, and the advent of competition from abroad also impacted.

The Cutler's Company, which oversaw the trade, had received its first Royal Charter from Henry V in 1416, and is therefore one of the most ancient of the City of London's livery companies. The Company declare its origins are to be found amongst the cutlers who were working in the medieval city of London in the vicinity of Cheapside, where great cutler (and jewellery) firms were still to be found up until the 1960's.

After the Napoleonic Wars, the Battle of Waterloo, plus sundry other belligerent interventions and the Crimean War, the art and means of warfare swiftly developed, such that guns and artillery came to the fore. Increasingly, though not entirely, there was less reliance on swords which led to a decline in the cutler's trade (and the near demise of the sword-making craft). Sharps in the form of knives were still – and ever more will be - required for hand-to-hand combat and silent killing.

In line with tradition the function of a trade guild is to protect the interests of its members; and thus, with change and adaption required, the order of the day demanded a suitable response from the Cutler's Company, who promptly directed its attention to the surgical instrument trade – and initiated apprenticeships therein.

This protected their members' immediate welfare, and over time shifted the emphasis of the trade from warfare to surgical implements, to cutlery and other domestic wares such as razors and scissors. Accordingly, it seems that Francis Baxter the elder would and did shift increasingly into the surgical implement and appliance trade.

Francis, who had been born in 1797, had of necessity therefore adapted to changes in a supply market which was rapidly becoming industrialised – and he would be recorded and shown variously as a cutler or (more often latterly) also as a surgical truss maker. It is impossible to determine how hard life may have been for him and his family, although we can safely assume he would have some tough times. Hopefully, during those changes which were forced upon him and others, he had some good times; life, though, rarely ends well, and whatever he would die in 1872 in the workhouse.

Interestingly, perhaps, Francis died without ever being acquainted with the safety razor – a device which would finish a great amount of his otherwise surviving trade. The safety razor – a one-sided blade - would not be invented until 8 years after his death when it was first introduced into the United States in 1880. It would also take another 15 years before Mr King C Gillette came up with the idea of a disposable, double-edged razor blade. It then took another 6 years to develop that idea into production.

The old-style razor, familiar to Francis Baxter senior, was beloved of professional barbers – Sweeney Todd, included, if we accept his existence. It may even have been favoured by the few men who preferred tidy beards or a clean-shaven look. Of course, the fashion, which was more one of utility, was to have a beard. The blades, when skilfully stropped on leather to produce their keenest edge, were so sharp they could easily slice a jugular without too much effort, and thus they gained the obvious name of *cut-throat razors.* It was not, therefore, uncommon for this device to be used by those unfortunates who, for whatever reason, felt they could no longer go on with the daily struggle. Suicide, though, was against the law.

Naturally, the authorities couldn't prosecute a successful slasher, but a botched attempt allowed them to inflict the unfortunate with not just a prison sentence but also hard-labour – just to add to his troubles. In times where life was regarded in the majority of cases as cheap the authorities and the Church frowned upon suicide. The latter saw it as sinful, while the authorities, I can only imagine, may have considered that it deprived them of the person's use: they certainly felt no responsibility for the person's welfare. Suicide in their eyes was otherwise ascribed to insanity. There was little or no concept of depression, no sympathy for utter hopelessness or understanding of mental illness, and all responses were less than sensitive.

Hopefully, those tormented desperate survivors found some relief or distraction somewhere – if not in drugs or alcohol then maybe in just a simple quiet smoke.

SMOKING

Is smoking a recreation activity or a distraction or just a habit? It may be all three. It may be a comfort or a form of relief, it may be enjoyable, it may be an addiction, but it is not an amusement.

However, on a day-to-day hour-by-hour basis I believe it was a common leisure practice for both men and women to smoke clay pipes - such instruments as are commonly still found strewn along the Thames' riverbanks by modern "mudlark" enthusiasts. The exhibit below, though found elsewhere, is in the Somers Town Museum.

Clay Pipes,
Found in basement of the
old Nisa stores on Chalton Street

and below at the Beccles' Museum.

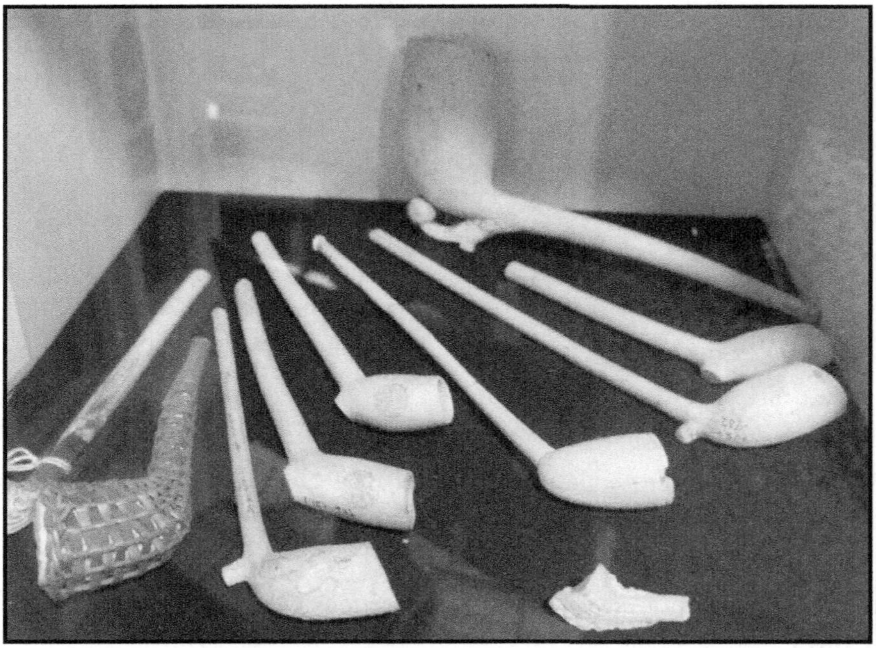

Cigarettes, the popular convenience smoke of the 20th century, were not common in the early 19th. Dickens (in Bleak House) had mentioned Spaniards walking about with their "small cigars," which possibly confirmed Goya's 1777 portrayal of a cigarette smoker in his painting La Cometa (the Kite). Hand-rolled and tailor-made units were reliant upon the material available to encase the tobacco. Cigarettes began to become more popular in Britain after the Crimean War where our soldiers had observed the Ottomans smoking tobacco apparently wrapped in strips of newspaper - and the fashion had been copied. Whilst Philip Morris had in fact opened a shop in London's Bond Street in 1847, where he began selling rolled cigarettes, consumption did not pick up significantly until after the 1880's. Of course, the fashion and the habit of smoking cigarettes, aptly described as "coffin nails," would grow in epidemic proportions, and despite the nick-name people were mainly oblivious to the associated catastrophic health hazards.

In the meantime, whilst some chose to chew tobacco, for most of the 19th century in Britain, pipe-smoking was the common method of using it; this medium meant that the smokers also required pipe-knives and tools to clean and clear their pipes. More work for the cutler.

Of course, London was not the only centre of the cutler trade; for example, Sheffield had become famous for steel and implements and it was where silver-plating first occurred. The discovery of the process of creating Old Sheffield Plate, which fused silver to copper sheets and made this type of silverware far more affordable, obviously expanded the consumer base. Sheffield consolidated its success with the Huntsman's crucible steel process, developed in the 1740's, which allowed steel to be poured into moulds that could make anything.

As the production of silver and plated items increased it prompted the opening of the Sheffield Assay Office in 1773, which reduced the amount of silver goods that had to be taken to London to be hall-marked. (It is said that this also affected the trade of the Highwayman, reducing his potential bounty. Proper Highwaymen nevertheless abounded in the late 18th and early 19th century but foot-pads – "muggers" – also roamed the streets and alleyways looking for wealthy or middle-class victims.)

After the 1840's electro-plating became a more common method of silver plating metal items. Developed in Birmingham by Elkington's this process effectively knocked out and replaced Old Sheffield Plate as a manufacturing method – even in Sheffield. Whilst being synonymous with steel (stainless or otherwise) for more than a century, the actual largest manufacturing centre at the time, however, was in London where trade continued to be controlled by the Worshipful Company of Cutlers.

Competition continued and would remain a cut-throat business.

Is a man who kills himself sane, or insane? This was a question which determined 19th century reaction and attitudes to his suicide. Whatever untreatable disease or unbearable poverty people might be suffering and despite starving to death (or being cannon-fodder in pointless wars), life was held to be God-given and sacrosanct. There was no acceptable notion of what we now would term as depression, nor was there any sympathetic regard that a life could be so hopeless and miserable that a perfectly lucid man would not see the rationality of ceasing to endure its unrelenting hardships.

Suicide was considered in two ways. The dead person could only be mad or a felon. Suicide was either the result of insanity or it was the result of a deliberate sane action. If the latter was true it was first an offence against God and secondly, more secularly, it was viewed as an attempt to escape not just a lamentable life but to avoid justice and or the consequences of debt. If the person was sane it was declared an act of "Self-murder"/ a "felo de se" (a felon of himself).

It had to be established at the Coroner's Inquest whether or not the person was sane. In the event that sanity was determined the deceased was denied a Christian burial - and instead would be carried to a crossroads in the dead of night and dumped in a hole or pit. In true Gothic style then a wooden stake would be hammered through the heart of the corpse pinning it in place. Quicklime was then often added.

There were to be no clergy or obvious mourners on hand, and no prayers offered. Gruesome certainly; and it could be described as wantonly unnecessary, if you ignore that they were really making a point. And the matter did not end there. The deceased's family were stripped of their belongings and his assets, which were forfeited... to the Crown (of course. Who else?)

In the 19th and 20th centuries the institutions of religions universally declared suicide "a mortal sin" and did it with the same fervour then as some people now disapprove so vehemently of abortion. I appreciate that opinions on abortion vary for many reasons: my own view is that I believe a woman should have the right to decide what happens to her body entirely.

I would note, though, that of those righteous souls who historically and currently maintain that life is sacred, there appears to be almost none who are prepared to help or offer financial assistance to those under pressure. Content to prevent abortion/termination of the pregnancy it would seem they are mostly then indifferent to the welfare of the living. Their view – if their inaction is taken at face value – is that children can live in misery and whole families can suffer while they display not the least inclination to provide any assistance to an over-burdened under-nourished family. Pregnancy as a result of rape does not move them either. It is all "God's will," they spit ... as they walk away.

The U.S. has just changed its laws on abortion, ostensibly because of the sanctity of life, but it nevertheless allows practically anyone (or any white person) to buy a Kalashnikov to murder children at will.... "Guns don't kill people," they chuckle. ?

Near to where Francis Baxter the cutler had been born (St George's in the East) there occurred the eponymous Ratcliffe Highway murders which were attacks on two separate families – the Marr and Williamson families. The two attacks which occurred twelve days apart in December 1811 claimed seven fatalities. The main suspect in the slayings, named as John Williams aka John Murphy, committed suicide before he could be put on trial. On 28th December he had used his scarf to hang himself in his cell.

With the legal and Coroner proceedings done his body was brought out on a cart, which for the further entertainment of the crowd also displayed the murder implements: a pen maul, a ripping chisel and an iron crowbar. The cart stopped outside the home of the late Mr Marr's family and then proceeded on to St George's Turnpike, where the New Road of Ratcliffe [now Commercial Road] is intersected by Cannon Street Road. The procession was also said to have stopped for ten minutes in front of The King's Arms, where the coachman reportedly whipped the dead man three times across the face. [Take that, you swine! ?] Honour satisfied or pointless outrage vented, perhaps, but the rather theatrical action also has the whiff of both the mindless mob and a certain amount of playing to the gallery about it. With the assault and the insult hardly likely to have unduly distressed the deceased culprit, the remains of John Williams were afterwards tumbled out of the cart into a six-feet deep hole, whereupon someone hammered a stake through his heart. Such, at any rate, was the report of Thomas De Quincey.

They took these things very seriously then and took no chances where evil might be concerned or may have been abroad: the stake was apparently meant to keep the restless soul from wandering, while the disposal at a crossroads was meant to confuse whatever ghost or devil might arise from the grave. In a further act of grossly primitive and pointless activity the grave was said to also have been deliberately made too small for the body, so that the murderer (incredibly) would feel uncomfortable even in death. They appear to have seriously mistrusted death as being the end of sensate feeling. As a final stinger quicklime was added and the pit covered over.

(There is a report that in August 1886, a gas company began to excavate a trench where Cannon Street Road and Cable Street cross at St George's in the East where Williams had been buried. The workers were said to have accidentally unearthed a skeleton, reportedly buried upside down and with the remains of the wooden stake through its torso. The landlord of the local pub, the Crown and Dolphin, is said to have retained the skull as a souvenir, although its current whereabouts is unknown.)

Forfeiture of goods, assets and property continued up until 1822, when finally it seems there was some recognition of the financial blow this was to a bereaved family. "The suicide of an adult male could reduce his survivors to pauperism." (See: MacDonald, Murphy and Holt)

Suicide, though, whilst a crime in England and Wales, was apparently not a crime in Scotland – perhaps another sign of Scotland's greater judicial/ legal maturity.

Crossroad burial was officially abolished the following year by Act of Parliament of 1823; it has been suggested that this was encouraged when George IV's carriage was held up near what is now Victoria Station by a crowd of spectators at the burial of Abel Griffiths, who had committed suicide. (How inconvenient for the bloated King....) Others claim that the suicide the previous year of the Foreign Secretary Viscount Castlereagh had an effect on how suicide was viewed, although I think this is unlikely since he was far from popular: the public is said to have resented Castlereagh's part in the unpleasant and shabby divorce of George IV and Queen Caroline. He was also tarnished by the passing of the Six Acts, which among other things aimed to suppress any meetings for the purpose of radical reform. If that wasn't enough he was also hated for the Peterloo Massacre, and was referenced in Shelley's poem *The Masque of Anarchy,*

> I met Murder on the way –
> He had a mask like Castlereagh –
> Very smooth he looked, yet grim;
> Seven bloodhounds followed him.
> All were fat; and well they might
> Be in admirable plight,
> For one by one, and two by two,
> He tossed them human hearts to chew
> Which from his wide cloak he drew.

The authorities struggled with Castlereagh's suicide. He was a high-ranking person in the government and was, after all Lord and Marquis Londonderry, Viscount Castlereagh — architect of the Grand Alliance, the person who shaped post-Napoleonic Europe, Foreign Secretary, and leader of the House of Commons: to declare him insane would have impugned the government and its recent decisions. On the other hand to declare him sane would require him to be buried at the crossroads.

They opted for a sort of fudge which described a disease of the mind with late and recent experiences of delusions caused by the disease. Under the influence of the disease he had struck at himself, and unwittingly perhaps had "hit his carotid artery" rather than specifically had *cut his own throat.* (Such subtle distinction, allowed Byron - in a pithy critique in his preface to cantos VI-VIII of *Don Juan* - to describe His Lordship as "an elegant lunatic"). The ruling was that the act had caused him thus to destroy himself. In effect a sort of unintentional, disease-driven death. It was their intention to bury him in Westminster Abbey but this provoked a furore, by advocates of crossroads burial, by Castlereagh's opponents and especially by radicals such as Byron. They did bury him there, but saw it fit and prudent to tone down the excesses of pageant usual for a State funeral.

Of course the treatment of Castlereagh had contrasted so wildly and publicly with that of Griffiths that the authorities were finally compelled to equalise matters and to alter its position. The passage of the 1823 law made it illegal for coroners to issue a warrant for burial of a felo-de-se in a public highway. Social attitudes slowly change, and opinion varied as to abolition of crossroads' burials, staunch advocates of keeping the status quo held that the disgrace of such crossroads burials was a deterrent to suicide. Other objectors to abolition felt compelled by their long-ingrained superstitions; and whilst the law was changed, nevertheless the church remained defiant: those who had committed suicide were only permitted to be buried in un-consecrated land – and the procedure was to take place within 24 hours, at night and with no accompanying ceremony allowed.

Although attempted suicide was prosecuted increasingly less, it was still punishable as a crime in England and Wales even until after the second half of the 20th century. In the 1950's the Conservative Home Secretary, "Rab" (R. A.) Butler felt "there is no evidence that an alteration would be universally acceptable to public opinion." However, in the environs of Somers Town (and elsewhere) there was dissension to Rab's view, and on 27 February 1958 the St Pancras-North Labour MP Kenneth Robinson tabled a motion contending that suicide should cease to be a criminal offence. Within days 150 MPs had signed it, and it was finally repealed three years later in 1961.

FOOTBALL.

Football, in some guise or other, has always been played. The object to be kicked has varied to whatever was available so that sometimes it may have been an inflated pig's bladder, while elsewhere the head of a rival soldier has sufficed. Fun is fun, and boys will be boys... And lately, girls will be girls with the modern game being both open to and enthusiastically taken up by female players.

The beautiful game was not, though, as ubiquitous as it is in modern times with daily televised coverage (probably) in the majority of pubs and bars globally. It is now a multi-billion-pound business with internationally recognised star-performers: players earning in excess of a half-a-million-a-week. In early Victorian England it was barely a sport: it did not exist in any form of organisation. There were no leagues and not even stadia (huge or small) to visit to watch live matches. Mostly, for the Baxters and their ilk – if they were so inclined - it was a fairly robust kick-about on even rougher ground.

It was not until the second half of the 19th century that *Association football* (more commonly known as soccer – from an abbreviation of the word association to as***soc*** - or just simply as "football") was popularised, and universal rules applied. These rules established that a game was played between two teams of 11 players using a spherical ball, and there was a goal at either end. (The modern game now allows for substitutes to also take part.) It is currently said to be played by approximately 250 million players in over 200 countries and dependencies, making it the world's most popular sport to date. (Anglers might disagree…)

The world's oldest football competition, the FA Cup, was founded by the footballer and cricketer Charles W. Alcock, and has been contested by English teams since 1872. England is also home to the world's first football league, which was founded in Birmingham in 1888 by Aston Villa director William McGregor.

The original format contained 12 clubs from the Midlands and Northern England.

During the 1850s, many clubs unconnected to schools or universities were formed throughout the English-speaking world, to play various forms of football. As the game increased in popularity employees got together and played against rival firms and companies from other towns.

Somers Town did not have a football club, and the London clubs that joined the Football Association were not nearby. The Club which is now closest to Somers Town, the Arsenal, was a South London Club until 1913. It had been formed as "Dial Square FC" by a group of munitions workers who worked in that square within the Royal Arsenal in Woolwich.

Up in Yorkshire, Sheffield, that other home of steel and of sharps, boasted two football teams, Sheffield United (whose team's nickname is "the blades.") and Sheffield Wednesday ("the Owls"). The Blades formed in 1889, and the Owls, who originally played on Wednesdays, were formed in 1867. Their football ground is in the district of Owlerton.

Even though the FA was founded and clubs were deemed professional they were barely recognisable as professional institutions. It was to all intents and purposes very much an amateur endeavour and largely remained so until the middle of the 20th century, when the truly professional game began to emerge, commercialism and sponsorships took over and it became a global enterprise. Thenceforward the game was neatly controlled and administered by ever corrupt bodies with limitless capacity for greed. In 2022 FIFA lowered the ethical bar to a level hitherto undreamt of where only billions of banknotes in single file had sufficient headroom.

For most of its existence in the English Football leagues teams and individual players relied upon the services and ministrations of bucket-and-sponge men. In the event that a player was temporarily incapacitated he would be doused with cold water and mopped with the sponge until he was revived enough to continue. Concussion? Brain damage? Cold water sorted it all. Torn ligament? Fracture? “Run it off!” Such is what passed for medical attention in the days before the emergence at the end of the 20th century of top-class athletes who now require (and deserve) high-grade medically-trained professionals, masseuses, physiotherapists and doctors: all with an armoury of tools, equipment, hydro-pools, and oxygen enriched rooms. All such marvellous things are now rightly available for those at the top of the game, but meanwhile in the lower leagues and amateur divisions the players languish as their forebears did when medical attention was condensed into the form of a primitive bucket and the simple sponge.

Other games were played such as bowls, skittles and all sorts of card games.

On the earlier list of materials which were used to make Victorian buckets, you may have noticed that *plastic* did not feature. Now whilst the term plastic originally was just an adjective which meant "pliable and easily shaped" today it is also used as a noun: "it is made of plastic." As we currently describe them such items - which have varying degrees of flexibility - have been created from man-made (synthetic) materials. All the different forms of such "plastic" goods, however, are more correctly variations within a group called "polymers."

In the mid-19th century there were no man-made polymers, but there were a great many polymers to be found in nature. Polymers (meaning "of many parts") are distinguished because their physical construction contains long chains of molecules. Cellulose is a natural polymer, which is abundantly found in the cell walls of plants. It is the molecular structure of cellulose that makes plants flexible and capable of bending in the wind.

The story behind man-made polymers originated as a result of the coincidence of the growing popularity of the game of billiards and of a shortage of ivory which was used to make billiard balls.

The shortage of natural ivory – and a 10 grand (Ten thousand dollars) offer to anyone who could find a substitute – led John Wesley Hyatt in 1869 to conduct a series of experiments. Hyatt used cellulose - derived from cotton fibre - and treated it with camphor which successfully resulted in the creation of the first synthetic polymer (i.e. a man-made plastic). His process could be used to create products that could not only be moulded into any shape, but could also be made to imitate natural substances like horn, linen, tortoiseshell – and ivory.

From then on the craze for billiards went on unimpeded, and Billiard Halls galore opened up everywhere. Billiard tables appeared in public houses and in working men's clubs, such as the Mildmay Radical club in Newington Green, Hackney. They were also employed in Temperance Halls such as in Mare Street, where people could then play without the temptation of the demon drink. Alcoholism and temperance were big issues in the 19th century.

From those billiard-ball beginnings (and the desire to tinkle the *ivories* of piano keys) scientists learned how to make many synthetic polymers, but it wasn't until 1907 that Leo Baekeland invented the first fully synthetic plastic. His product, Bakelite, which contained no molecules found in nature, was durable, heat resistant and a good insulator. It could also be shaped or moulded into almost anything and was ideally suited for mechanical mass production.

No longer constrained to make synthetic polymers from natural substances like cellulose, industries began using the plentiful carbon atoms provided by petroleum and other fossil fuels. The new processes expanded the synthetic range and allowed other substitutes to be created such as Nylon, invented by Wallace Carothers in the 1930's as a synthetic silk. Of course this was used for tooth brushes but as hosiery it also would adorn millions of legs. (It was also used during the war for parachutes and other objects.) https://www.sciencehistory.org/the-history-and-future-of-plastics

===========

So, the Victorians had synthetic billiard balls but had to make do with their metal, wooden and leather buckets.

I suspect that almost every country, in the name of raising revenue for whatever essential or spurious reasons, demands payments of taxes. The word tax, for example, implicitly suggests burden or strain; under the hegemony of Capitalism we have been further conditioned by both the ruling classes' and the employers' innate aversion to paying taxes: they do not regard taxes as a just duty of society, a moral necessity or as money which could well be spent to enable everyone to live decently. Those do not fall within the range of their desire or their philosophy: they see tax at the least as something to be avoided – why else would they pay so much to huge Accountancy firms?

You may also have noted that I opted - perhaps subconsciously - for the word "demands" in reference to tax payments: it is after all a fairly aggressive term and a loaded description which implies something devoid of volition. Demand always has a negative connotation. "Demand," according to employers' organisations (and to the Press comprised of journalists sympathetic to their philosophy), is what a trade union does: these combinations of workers do not, apparently, "offer" to hire their labour or services at a rate which offsets higher costs or in return for better conditions or indeed in return for enriching their employers. The public are told that "they demand." One can only imagine what sort of parents those employers make? When normal / common / ordinary people feed their children, they do so not to meet demands but in order for their offspring to thrive and to grow. Normal people do not do feed their children meagrely or reluctantly.

Governments, though, need money. Theoretically they do not have money: they hold and use money which has been earned by the general population. In a society where the Government has sold off most of what the country (i.e. its occupants) had materially owned, it is no longer able to benefit from the spoils of ownership and from the production derived from that asset. Therefore, Government needs the country's citizens/residents to contribute to and further replenish the Public Purse. This they do by taxation, by compulsory contributions from the majority (working under a Pay As You Earn system) and from others by different contrivances which may or may not be subject to negotiation of some kind.

Tax may be associated with incomes, gains, inheritance, investment and profits as well as attaching to a diverse range of objects, entertainments, goods, vitals and services. Parliament from time to time has historically imposed various taxes upon *luxuries* such as heat and light, which took the form of the hearth tax (based on the number of hearths in the home), and similarly by a window tax.

Original taxation came in the form of tithes which were paid to the established church by individuals within each Parish. As ecclesiastical and secular laws scratched each other's backs tithing became part of the Clergy's right in regard to church ownership of property or land. In time this would allow that right to levy the tithe to be bought and sold, leased or mortgaged, or assigned to others. At the time of the dissolution of the monasteries and the Reformation the monks' and the Church's lands and property were either taken by the Crown and the King's new reformed Church or were given or sold to favourites of the Crown. Tithes associated with that ownership became the personal property of the new owners, or lay impropriators. Otherwise the new established church continued to extract the tithe.

The tithe represented one tenth of the value derived from three activities for which payment was required:

1) *Predial* tithes were the products of crop husbandry - such as grain, woodland, and vegetables
2) *Mixed* tithes were the products of animal husbandry - such as cattle, calves, milk, lambs and wool
3) *Personal* tithes were the profits of a person's labour which would include fishing, milling or labouring.

It was paid in kind with the collected 10% of crops gathered and stored in tithe barns, and with monies paid to the church representative. The payments were meant to support the church, the churchmen (the Clergy) and to allow them to help the poor: it also fabulously enriched the Church; a fact not lost on Henry VIII.

All were subject to the tithe charge. Householders were liable to pay tithes unless the property they owned or occupied was specifically exempted due to some long standing custom or association with the parish. (See: British History: Tithes) As the tithe was calculated also on rents I imagine the householder incorporated the tithe within the charge he imposed on the tenant/occupier or those who dwelt on the property.

Tithes were still in force at the time when Francis Baxter and his pre-Victorian ilk were living in Somers Town. By that period, the early 19th century, tithe payment in kind was becoming increasingly an out-of-date practice. The ONS describes the payment of tithes per se as having become "unpopular, against a background of industrialisation, religious dissent and agricultural depression." Changes, though, were afoot (cf the 1836 Tithe Commutation Act, which required tithes in kind to be converted to more convenient monetary payments called tithe rent charges). It was not quite the end of tithing, but it was a practice which needed to make way.

Governments did not exist as we know them, and it was only at the inception of greater centralised control and of the theoretical shift of power to Parliament that the need for different types of taxation had to be found.

The reality was that the "rich", a minority, were reluctant to pay anything, and it was the rich who were in Parliament. Finance and revenue were needed and someone would have to pay. The problem was that the majority of the people were poor or relatively poor: whilst there were more of them, it was not possible to impose the burden of taxation on these ordinary people because they were already barely subsisting on paltry wages. Their income may also have been affected by deductions for "bed and board" and perhaps for livery. The solution could have been to pay the majority more, but as the incumbents of Parliament were rich, land-owners and employers this was an unpalatable notion. It remains so. (Cf the resistance to the implementation of the Minimum Living Wage, and similarly thereafter to increases to it.)

In the face of social unrest and as a response to an on-going existential threat the establishment of the UK had gradually contrived a very slow and controlled evolution into an apparently reasonable and more civilised nation. The roots of that change can be traced back centuries, but at every stage there was a price to be paid – by someone, and it wasn't going to be paid by those in power or by those with money.

Tricks of taxation, i.e. in regards to avoidance, had to be developed and were refined over time to prevent it falling proportionately or otherwise on those who had wealth, and instead – as in the view of President Donald J Trump – it had to be paid by the suckers, who were the poor majority. See footnote overleaf.

10

Currently, in mature, civilised and socially aware countries the mass of the population – its decent citizens - accept income-tax and other forms of direct taxation, as well as indirect taxations on goods and services, as part of the cost of enjoying the fruits of a theoretically benign and caring society. They merely require honesty and transparency in how it is raised and how it is spent: most people seeking a wage rise are not crying out to pay less tax. This notion of direct income tax is, however, only a relatively recent invention.

There were always levies which were raised to pay for wars, but - in general - taxation (at least from the 18th and 19th centuries) took the form of indirect taxation with vast amounts being raised by excise taxes. Indeed the Excise men still have more power than the Police in regards as to what they can do in all matters. Excise was put on everything: beer, malt, salt, spirits, wine, soap, coal, glass, leather, silk, cotton, lace, tea, coffee and tobacco etc. It hit all the consumer goods which the poor consumed or used, and it did so disproportionately - as it always does. If, for example, it costs £200 to feed a family and the poor family only earns £300 then that food bill is a much bigger burden than it would be on a rich family earning £3000. That tax on goods etc (coupled with the odd and occasional hearth, window or poll tax and excluding the tithe system) was roughly the extent of

---

10 (He didn't pay tax, he said, because he was "smart;" not like most of those dumb-asses who voted for him. No, he wasn't that type of sucker.... For some reason the word parasite comes to mind....) There is a term for that sad and peculiar condition where working-class and poor people vote for billionaires like Trump in the belief that those enormously rich, entitled people will improve the lives of the poor: it is called "self-harm."

personal taxation until William Pitt thought up the idea of direct taxation in the form of an income tax.

Pitt had initially imposed it in 1799 to pay for war with revolutionary France and then for the Napoleonic Wars. It then went out of favour until Robert Peel re-introduced it, whereupon from 1842 it became a permanent method of raising money. It was, however, not aimed at the poor in the 19th Century, largely because - as alluded to earlier - you can't get blood out of a stone...

I cannot determine how tithe payments may have affected Francis Baxter and his ilk, but I doubt they were great contributors to the HMRC, the Inland Revenue, or to its 19th century equivalent. In turn, they were not great beneficiaries of any welfare system. (They might as well have been poor people living in America today.)

999 ? SERVICES ?

At that time, the country did not have centralised services (except perhaps in regard to the army and Navy). The state supplied few if any of the services that we in the UK today hold as vital necessities: it had no public fire brigades, or national police force, and no ambulance services etc.

It did not have a Health service, nor an education system, and it did not provide any scheme for pensions or social care. [11]

---

[11] Individual businesses and some building occupiers paid private insurance companies who then provided a fire service for subscribers; so if you hadn't subscribed.... Of course after the Great Fire of London in 1666 there was less of an appetite for wooden buildings which led to an increase in brick and stone constructions. There were still fires but the danger of them spreading wildly was reduced. A municipal service was only formed in London in 1865.

Road tolls paid for roads, and there were levies raised for different required revenues as and when required; so, altogether there wasn't a great need to raise money by universal and regular taxation.

Indirect taxation was generally acceptable but there was great opposition – from those who naturally had money - to income tax, apparently on the *principle,* (an unusual term) that disclosure of personal income represented an unacceptable governmental intrusion into private matters: it was, therefore, deemed to be a potential threat to personal liberty (or to the personal liberty at least of those who had money).

Occasionally the British (and some foreign) governments dreamt up an unusual scheme to raise revenue: one such was that already mentioned window tax; it had long been applied and consisted of both a flat rate plus a variable rate based on the number of windows in a house: having eight windows would incur additional tax in 1825. Houses from the period can still be seen to have bricked-up window-spaces which enabled the owners to avoid the tax; it was repealed in 1851. (In *The Wealth of Nations,* Adam Smith observed that the window tax was relatively inoffensive because its assessment did not require the assessor to enter the residence - a building's windows could be counted from the outside, with no invasion of privacy.)

A NOTE IN REGARDS TO ROADS

It should be remembered that there were neither trains, cars or lorries nor motorways when the stonemason was born; and that the road system up until the late 18th century was a mere collection of historically trodden muddy tracks, drover's trails, Roman routes and dirt-packed King's highways.

So, post-Roman road-making was in its infancy in those earlier decades of the 19th century, although advances were being made, particularly in France. It may be fair to say that some of the ideas of Trésaguet – the great French pioneer of road-engineering – had filtered through to the (also great) "British" engineer Thomas Telford (1757–1834). [12]

Of course, the latter was actually Scottish, and I am (tongue-in-cheek) merely following a trend of the English media in the field of international sports. Such a trend was particularly noticeable in 20th century football matches, when reported nationalities were subject to certain conditions. For example, the English media would consistently report a win by a Scottish team or individual in an international competition as a "British victory," while a loss would be dismissed and branded a "Scottish defeat." (Oh, the games people play....)

The unbelievably talented Scot brought many improvements to road-building in Britain, with his constructions benefitting from his insistence on proper drainage. He maintained that drainage was vital to the continued integrity of the fabric of roads. Alongside Telford and drainage-pioneer John Metcalf, there was also the undoubtedly famous John Loudon Macadam (1756-1836) who reduced the material (and therefore the cost) of construction, by introducing smaller stones and a reliance on more level roads which utilised cambers for drainage.

---

[12] This now renowned Scottish civil engineer was responsible for many road and canal projects in Shropshire, which was later recognised when the new town of Telford was named after him. He also built harbours, bridges and tunnels, and had input to Portsmouth Docks, being also involved in renovations to Somerset House, to castles, prisons and churches. Apparently such was his reputation as a prolific designer/engineer of highways and related bridges that Telford was dubbed *The Colossus of Roads* (a neat pun on the Colossus of Rhodes)

Whilst the maintenance and construction of roads fell then to Turnpike Trusts, who administered and levied tolls, there was no concerted national plan. It was Macadam who advocated effective road maintenance and that the management and control of this should reside within a central road authority with trained and salaried professional officials (which it was hoped might discourage corruption). It was a noble thought, but this does seem to be a very strange, rare and peculiar incidence of Scottish naivety...

THE STREET ORDERLY BOY

One job associated with roads in the 19th century was that of "*the street-orderly*", whose job it was to keep the streets orderly, i.e. clear of the ordure of horses.

They would chase behind and between horses and carts, hurriedly scooping up the horse shit before other horses trod in it and before the wheels of the carts ground it into a greasy smudge both in and on the surface of the road.

It was a very precarious occupation, with a very real danger of being run over by the horse-drawn traffic. I imagine the droppings were recycled, as were those of pure-finders (dog-shit collectors), whose find was sold on to tanneries.

Other scavenging jobs included river bank mudlarks, and bone-grubbers who hunted for bones which they sold on to bone mills to make soap and other products. Toshers, though, worked the sewers with nets, panning for lost valuables, coins and nails. One can only wonder at what they retrieved; like anglers did they boast "I caught one THIS big..." ?

It may be that as toshers worked with and in "shit" that the name became associated with inferior work, such that a poor redecoration/paint job is said to have been toshed over.

A statue, erected in 1943 in Paddington Street Gardens, Marylebone, by Italian sculptor Donato Barcaglia, unusually commemorates the activity and the service these Street-Orderly boys rendered.

What medical help was available to Francis Baxter? After the dissolution of the monasteries ordinary people who were ill had no great organisation to go to; they had to resort to apothecaries, herbalists, barber-surgeons, "doctors" and (later) to workhouse infirmaries. Medical science was – and is – ever an on-going enterprise, having both to learn and sometimes un-learn; and some practitioners, treatments or remedies were better than others.

Standard practice for Doctors' – for their cures, procedures, interventions and treatments - was then driven by a mixture of ancient and current ideas that mixed largely European philosophy with physiology. These had developed from a rationale which was based on the belief of the existence and relevance of four *humours* in the body. Humour in this instance was derived from the Latin for liquid/fluid/moisture and referred to blood, phlegm, black bile and yellow bile (choler). These humours affected the temperament such that a person with an imbalance of black bile might be described as melancholic (cf melancholy = melan [black] + khole [bile]). Another might be phlegmatic if they were lethargic due to the consistency of their phlegm, etc. Thus the quartet were required to be in balance if a person was to be healthy and therefore any imbalance could manifest itself in a variety of complaints or diseases – from pneumonia, fever, colds, chest infections, sore throats or swellings to just about anything. All could be treated by suitable intervention. Venesection – blood-letting – addressed one of the humours; and because the doctor exuded confidence and perhaps because desperate patients believed - or wanted to believe – both in the doctor and in the procedure, they sometimes appeared to get better. Success - a placebo effect – was attributed to the doctor's skills and to the efficacy of the treatment, whilst failure was probably God's will.

Charles II (1630– 1685), for example, was bled following a stroke: he may have had hope, but despite its therapeutic intent even placebos have their limits.

A couple of millennia ago Hippocrates himself swore by bloodletting, and he was a man known for his oaths; and the practice had continued to find favour with patients, doctors and barber-surgeons in the Georgian and Victorian eras. In regard to its prevalence J R Coll (2014) mentions Sir William Hale-White (1857–1949), who in April 1927 lectured the audience at the Royal Society of Medicine (London) and reminded them that in 1840 a doctor had been charged with malpractice for failing to bleed a patient with pneumonia.

In the mid-nineteenth century, though, the effectiveness of blood-letting had been convincingly challenged (especially for treating diseases such as pneumonia) by Pierre Louis (1787–1872) – who is considered to be the first to use medical statistics - and John Hughes Bennett (1812–1875); and yet while there was a great decline in blood-letting from the latter half of the 19th century it nevertheless was not wholly abandoned. Indeed, as J R Coll asserts, "medical conservatism ensured the practice continued well into the twentieth century. As late as 1942, a famous medical textbook [by Sir William Osler (1849–1919)] (still) considered bloodletting (to be an) appropriate treatment for pneumonia." Coll's communication to retired Haematologist DP Thomas on the demise of blood-letting makes for an interesting read.

It is a common enough problem: when we accommodate an idea – when we believe something – it gets set within our minds as being true, valid or accurate. Once it has taken hold such is its grip that it remains immune to enlightenment and is frequently implacable. (It is a little like the idea that Brexit would change things for the better.) The delusion is not just something which affects ordinary people - be they intelligent or otherwise – we are all susceptible to the charms of an idea which may have sustained us and our prejudices – and doctors are as capable as the next person of falling into its trap.

Blood-letting was sometimes combined with purging: both very popular practices in the 19th century when the Baxters were living in Somers Town. Blistering, or vesiculation, was another diabolical technique in the physicians' armoury of tools to combat disease and ailments of the body, the brain or mind: it was certainly favoured as a treatment for insanity and neural afflictions. The procedure used a substance in the form of an ointment or paste which was applied to the skin. This paste was usually composed of cantharides (often obtained from blister beetles) and a mixture of ingredients which were also stimulants or irritants. Applied to a small area or all over the body the paste produced blisters, which when sizeable enough would be snipped or otherwise opened, thereby releasing the bad or excessive humour. (Ridiculous, perhaps, but no laughing matter....)

It was only in the late 18th-century, just a matter of a few decades before the Baxters moved to Somers Town, that all three techniques had been inflicted upon George III: the poor chap was at the mercy of no less than five of the country's most eminent doctors, "specialists" who were the crème de la crème. As Emma Shepley, RCP senior curator reports (28th March 2014) these top-guns had viewed the efforts of the King's most recent doctor, Francis Willis (1718–1807) rather critically. The cosy coterie regarded him as 'little better than a quack.' Pot and kettle come to mind. Nevertheless, the collective brains of these physicians of the Royal College opted first for a benign action: urine analysis. Ok you might think they were only taking the p... but then they intervened a little more dramatically and prescribed purgatives "including rhubarb, castor oil, senna, the highly toxic antimony, extract of gentian and emetic tartar." This must have had a catastrophic effect simultaneously on the King's stomach and bowels. One can only assume they stood well back. For good measure – probably a belt and braces procedure – they then subjected the monarch, in Shepley's apposite words, "to a brutal regime of bloodletting and blistering." God bless medical science and experts! Little wonder he was mad!

Incidentally Shepley reports that recent research has established beyond doubt that the widely held theory that he had porphyria is incorrect. According to Professor Timothy Peters and specialists at St George's Hospital, London, the King probably suffered from 'recurrent bipolar disorder, with at least three episodes of acute mania, chronic mania and possible dementia." So, blood-letting for bipolar disorder and or dementia wasn't likely to be effective!

Two things which relate to blood-letting have survived into the 21st century: the barber's pole and The Lancet journal. For centuries blood-letting was usually carried out by a barber-surgeon and the barber's pole, which is still exhibited outside their shops in High Streets up and down the land, is significantly red and white: the red standing for blood, the white for bandages or the tourniquet and, according to Coll, "the pole itself, for the stick grasped by the patient to assist in dilating the arm veins." The practice involved various instruments from simple syringes or lancets (scalpels), to fancy fleams and, of course, a catching bowl. So, the other historical reminder of the practice is indeed obvious in the title of the journal of the British Medical Association, The Lancet, which surely attests to its close association with what was considered an indispensable item of medical equipment for doctors.

Leeches were also then used fairly extensively, but in time this fell out of favour. Science ruled it ridiculous, but science being a process is never the end of a story... and the use of the leech has been resurgent of late in the field of plastic surgery and in the reattachment of severed digits.

No Welfare State for the Victorians

In that great age of advancement which was the Victorian period it was still hell for the ordinary and generally poor people of Britain. Poverty was rife, and people lived with the threats of starvation or the Workhouse, and with the promise of death in the shabbiness of their poor homes, in the gutter or in the Workhouse Infirmary. The National Health Service and the Welfare State (which were introduced in 1947 post-World War II Britain) were still a long way off; but the seeds of those fantastic institutions had been sown centuries before, and strangely the machinations of the Victorian and the Workhouse system helped to keep the growth going. Not that the people of the Victorian age would ever be aware of any potential for future benefit.

Unwittingly, it was a long line of legislation - successively designed to limit the movement and wages of workers and to deal with beggars - which all incrementally led to wealthier people becoming more responsible for their local poor. Having drawn a net around the lower orders they found that they too were caught within it. Of course, the Russian revolution, the Great War and the broken promises of a land fit for heroes, followed by the Great Depression and another World War all helped to increase the existential threat to the wealthy; but it was the cumulative effect these and of that early legislation which unexpectedly created a state of affairs that only a welfare state could cure – pro tem, that is, until they could find a better way to control the poor.

It all started, though, a long time ago.

The long road to a Welfare State

From our vantage point in time it is difficult to comprehend the realities of the oppressions that shaped the lives of ordinary people and their families who lived in the 19th century in the UK, and who were far from having a Welfare State. We can, however, get a sense of it if we consider the incidental historical information which can be elicited from the incremental legislation, the various Factory Acts and Poor Laws. The details of these all help to shed light on the conditions the Victorian plebs endured (rather than enjoyed). Surprisingly even plagues and epidemics played their part in the process. The nets which the ruling class spread to prevent free movement and to restrict the bargaining power of the ordinary worker would eventually ensnare those who had tightened the net. In controlling the working poor and the destitute, the rate-paying class bound themselves with responsibilities they were ultimately reluctant to finance and certainly did not wish to afford.

Patriquin (2007 p217) noted the example of a dearth of ratepayers in Aberdare, Wales, where in 1820 that industrialising parish had 3400 inhabitants but only 150 rate-payers, and these were mainly small farmers. Of course, this was an unsustainable ratio where many rate-payers were subject to levies of 15%. Across the country rates were subsequently applied to incorporate lower grades on the property scale, but these provoked requests for relief and exemptions, which were mainly granted. The poor just were not in a position to contribute; and the process continued with the numbers of the poor ever increasing.

My interpretation is that it wasn't altruism which gave us the Welfare State. It was that slow, incremental process of succeeding events and of the responses of the ruling classes to these whose unintentional consequences inexorably led to the creation of a system that would provide accessible health-care and pensions universally throughout the UK population.

The Black Death (1348-50) had led to a great shortage of workers, and in order to prevent the survivors from benefitting from the natural law of supply and demand (by taking their labour elsewhere to a higher payer), the King (and his henchmen) imposed controls of wages. The Ordnance of Labourers 1349 was an early incomes and prices policy, designed to stop *"grasping"* labourers offering to supply their labour and services in exchange for a better rate of pay. It also tried to thwart the more desperate landowners' attempts to seduce those available workers to toil for them for a higher wage. It seems these servants

"...seeing the necessity of masters, and great scarcity of servants, will not serve unless they may receive excessive wages, and some rather willing to beg in idleness, than by labour to get their living."

It neatly conflated the workers' request to offer their labour at a suitable rate with a preference to beg if it was not granted. It did not state whom it was possible for them to beg from....

The ordnance was not held to be a huge success although various sources state that most wages did not in effect apparently rise post-plague. Of course, whatever the reality, the perception that it was failing led to the Statute of Labourers drawn up by Edward III *"and by the assent of the prelates, earls, barons and others of his council, against the malice of servants."* ("Malice," indeed and claimed with such arrogance! No value judgements there then...)

The statute set a maximum wage for labourers, which was to be commensurate with wages paid before the Black Death, specifically in 1346/47, the 20th year of Edward III's reign. (He had got the top job at aged 14, in 1327 – so I wonder what he knew about hard work?.) Whilst it was an offence to ask for - or to offer - higher wages, punitive measures were naturally only enforced against workers and not employers. The Act also mandated that able-bodied men and women should work and imposed harsh penalties for those who remained idle, although how they would have lived "idle" is beyond me.

The Statute of Cambridge in 1388 imposed strict terms and limitations on the movement of the worker and of beggars. Ordinary people had to have permission to leave their Parish or to have proof of guaranteed employment elsewhere. If they were found away from their Parish without the allowed permissions/testimonials they could be placed in the stocks until some surety was found; or they could be transported back, with the cost of that transportation charged to the home parish, who then sought compensation or retribution. To stop the spread of wandering beggars it decreed that the "impotent poor" were to remain in the towns in which they were living or in the towns where they were born. While restricting these movements each county "Hundred" was made responsible for relieving its own impotent poor; i.e. those who, because of age or infirmity, were incapable of work.

Taking the long view this was a degree of progress because it was the start of a distinction being made in regards to the impotent poor and the idle poor. The impotent poor were now to be licensed by their betters and allowed to beg. The new law did not provide relief or care but merely afforded them the right to beg at the discretion of the public.

It must be said that by 1530/40 - with the dissolution of the monasteries, which had formerly given alms - begging became more difficult. Gradually there was an acknowledgement that someone had to fund the "impotent" and more 'deserving poor' who could not work, and the finances would have to come from those that had the means.

From 1530/31 the idle poor, now classified as sturdy beggars, were subject to increasing punishment. Merely "putting them in the stocks" had gradually given way to more aggressive treatment: they were to be whipped and then confined to their place of birth. The children of the poor were put to service or put into apprenticeships.

Laws continued to be passed to deal with the problem and to punish sturdy vagabonds and beggars. If a person outside of their Parish was found without what was adjudged "sufficient" money on their person they could be and were imprisoned for vagrancy. Within our language we might lightly describe someone as "branded" as a coward or as a vagrant, but the reality was that by 1547 vagrants caught begging or a migrant worker found without means or proof of income could be, and was often, literally branded with a burning hot iron impressing a V-shaped scar upon the forehead. They could then be enslaved for 2 years or **executed** if it was a repeat offence. This was actually repealed after three years, but something had to be done to address the problem.

These terms and restrictions laid down by various legislations which had historically kept wages down and controlled labour, increasingly tied the worker and beggar to his old Parish, but it further meant that the Parish therefore also had some responsibility for keeping him. Alms for the poor and basic infirmaries had once been provided by the monastic orders, but now the Poor Laws required the Parish to take up more of the slack.

Labour shortages due to mortality from epidemic disease continued to play its part in shaping the path to increased responsibility. The shortage - coupled with inflation, poverty, and general social disorder - led Queen Elizabeth I to enact the Statute of Artificers 1562. It again sought to fix prices and empowered justices to fix wage rates for virtually all classes of workmen. It also increased the restrictions to the workers' freedom of movement by compelling them to seek permission to move from one employer to another. In addition to this it regulated who could claim to be a particular tradesman, and controlled the growth of skilled workmen by imposing compulsory seven-year apprenticeships.

The Act for the Relief of the Poor 1597 established both "Overseers of the Poor" and a complete code of poor relief to be applied at local level. It again controlled the workers and reinforced their permitted areas of operation and thereby enclosed and fixed the responsibilities of the parish.

The Poor Law Relief Act, popularly known as the Old Poor Law, was passed in 1601 and made three distinctions of how the poor were to be regarded: it decreed that the *impotent poor* i.e. people who were unable to work mainly because they were "lame, impotent, old or blind, were to be cared for in alms-house or a poorhouse." On the other hand, they decided there was the *able-bodied poor*, who were to be set to work in a house of industry. The third category comprised *the idle poor* and vagrants, who were to be whipped and sent to a house of correction or even to prison. The system's administrative unit was the parish. It was not a centralised government policy but the law actually made individual parishes responsible for Poor Law legislation.

The Settlement Acts (Poor Relief Act 1662) sought to establish the home (settled) parish to which a person belonged; it therefore clarified which parish would be responsible for him should he become in need of Poor Relief (whereupon he was declared to be "chargeable" to the parish poor rates). If a man left his settled parish to move elsewhere, he had to have a settlement certificate, which guaranteed the host parish that should he become in need of poor relief then his removal costs (back to his home) would be paid for by his home parish. As this would involve both poor relief **and** transportation costs home parishes were reluctant to issue such certificates. Poor relief was proving to be a drain on the resources of the wealthy.

The 1723 Workhouse Test Act compelled almost all those seeking to receive poor relief to enter a workhouse and undertake a set amount of work. It was intended to prevent irresponsible claims on a parish's poor rate.

So, the Workhouse system developed [13] but of course the system and the service had to be paid for; and whilst the wages of those picking oakum and beating hemp in the workhouse were meagre, their sold-at-a-higher-rate output did not always self-finance the system. Then there was the ever present problem of the sick and infirm: that burden fell on the parish, which meant that it fell on the wealthier inhabitants of the parish because the provision of poor relief was paid for out of the "poor-rate," which was a tax on property levied on the middle and upper classes in each parish. [14] Obviously the poor had no property, and did not – and could not – contribute to the poor-rate. The wealthy begrudged paying the rate and suspected they were paying the poor to be lazy and avoid work.

Now a great work ethic is a much lauded quality, and hard work in particular is often and usually advocated - although mainly by those who don't do much physical work. ("Hard work never killed anyone" and "Arbeit macht frei" comes to mind....) Such ethics demanded that even children were required to work long hours. In the new factories of the late 18th/early 19th

---

13 600 parish workhouses were constructed between 1723 and 1750.

14 It was collected under both the Old Poor Law and the New Poor Law, and was only absorbed into the general-rate local taxation in the 1920s. The tax continues currently in the form of Council Tax, which is now levied for other local services.

centuries, which had grown up as a result of industrialisation and mechanisation, children were not only working extremely long hours but were being used in many dangerous situations. As factories had not existed before there were no laws which related to the running of factories, nor to the safety of workers.

Various and multiple Factory Acts gradually changed some of the conditions of workers, and provisions made for child workers also strangely impacted on conditions for them in workhouses, specifically in regards to education.

The use of child labour increased, and the children were often misused and abused. They worked extremely long hours and could be severely punished for any mistakes: lateness, for example, incurred loss of wages, a disproportionate fine or deduction and possibly a beating. Children worked on dangerous and unguarded machinery; exhaustion and tiredness led to many accidents and frequently caused serious injuries to these young workers. [15] Deaths and mutilation by machinery occurred and gradually this scandal came to be acknowledged. All effected societal change albeit in very small steps.

The Cotton Mills and Factories Act 1819 addressed the issue of very young workers who were under 9 years of age. It stated that no children under 9 were to be employed in factories and that children aged 9–16 years were henceforward limited to 12 hours' work per day. These limitations and restrictions only applied within factories and did not apply in silk mills or elsewhere. (This Act regulated the maximum hours children were to be worked: adults were compelled to work longer.) [16]

---

[15] Mechanical guarding around many pieces of equipment and machines would not be enforced until the late 1970's in most industrial settings.

[16] I wonder how you might feel about your children and grandchildren working at such ages and for such long hours

However, whilst I doubt parents then even contemplated their children not being required to work, I wonder if they may actually have disliked the interference and the imposition of restrictions: their children's wages were simply needed – if they were not essential - to help feed the family in toto. Primarily they didn't know any different and the notion of children not working had never been part of their experience; and vitally they were faced with the same hard reality which still occurs in the so-called 3rd world: it was a matter of survival for the family unit.

Althorp's Act 1833 mandated lunch breaks and also set limits on the hours children could work. It also required factory owners in the textile industry to provide 2 hours schooling a day for its child workers. (This sounds altruistic but in reality it was to be paid for by a deduction of a penny in the shilling – 8.5% from the children's wages.) Ordinary people did not get anything for nothing in the 19th century.

The cost of the relief for the poor continued to rise, and a new Poor Law in 1834 was introduced in the hope that it would both reduce the cost of looking after the poor *and* take beggars off the streets. Its aim was also to "encourage poor people to work hard to support themselves," which seems a reasonable aim - providing the hard work actually was rewarded with a decent living wage. (It rarely does.) It created a nationwide and universal system with parishes grouped into unions, and it required each union to build a workhouse if they did not already have one.

The Act stipulated that except in special circumstances, poor people could now *only* get help if they were prepared to leave their homes and go into a workhouse - although I imagine if they couldn't have afforded the rent they would have been out on the street pretty quick anyway. (I wonder what implications this had for whatever few possessions they might have had...)

In order to assuage the complaints of the rate-payers (that they were financing the laziness of others), the conditions inside the workhouse were deliberately harsh, so that only those who desperately needed help would ask for it. Paupers had to abide by strict rules and regulations or suffer the consequences. The inmates' heads were shaved – not wittingly to degrade them but to cut down on the infestations of head-lice - and families were separated: men from women, and adults from children!

In such circumstances the Act ensured that the poor were provided with shelter and that they were clothed and fed. They were given rough uniform to wear, and the diet, whilst mostly sufficient enough, was monotonous and mean. Such was the base standard but even these conditions and provisions were subject to abuse by the Masters, Matrons and administrators of the workhouse. [17] In return, and whilst this supposed munificent service was variable, nevertheless all workhouse paupers *including children* (but excluding the sick) were consistently still required to work, and that work was generally hard and unpleasant.

Under the 1834 Poor Law Amendment Act, the Poor Law union were required to provide at least 3 hours a day of schooling for workhouse children, who were to be taught the 3r's plus, of course, a good dose of Christian principles (i.e. do as you are told, know your place, keep your mouth shut, abide by the 10 commandments – except when those in control – the monarch and aristocrats, the government and the Church - tell you otherwise: in those circumstances it would become ok to steal and kill "for King and Country" as long as the spoils were handed over. All

---

[17] Overseers of the poor were replaced by boards of guardians in 1834 as a result of the Poor Law Amendment Act; despite this some were retained in some places and used to collect the poor-rate.

instruction and other moral lessons was to make them fit for service, to train them in the "habits of usefulness, industry and virtue"... and importantly to make them less likely later to need poor relief: in other words it was to reduce the long-term burden on the Poor Law system and the local tax-payer.

Of course, others would still debate whether pauper children should even be taught basic literacy, with one group (the Guardians of the Bedford Union) suggesting that perhaps those paupers could be taught to read (instructions, presumably) but not to write. What a corker! The matter was apparently settled by the Parish Apprentices Act of 1844 which decreed all pauper apprentices were required to be able at least to read and to write their own names.

See: Workouses.org.uk/education/workouses.shtml. Read anything by Peter Higginbotham, who is prolific in his research on Workhouses.

WORK IN THE WORKHOUSE

The National Archives hold anti-Poor Law posters, which describe examples of the work required in the poorhouse/workhouse such as "beating hemp" and "picking oakum." They record the former work as being worse than breaking stones – another form of work and punishment common to prisons and the workhouse. Beating hemp involved first the softening of old maritime hemp rope or rigging by beating it repeatedly with a mallet to remove encrusted tar. This "junk" was then cut into 2 foot lengths. The thicker strands (lays) of the rope then had to be untwisted by bare hands into separate individual sections, which had to be rolled backwards and forwards over the knees or thighs using the palms of hands until the tangled mesh loosened. All of this was extremely tough on the hands and fingers, which caused sores, blisters and bleeding even to hands well-used to rough work. The rope could be further unravelled by putting it in the bend of a hook and sawing it, thereby removing more tar and grating the fibres apart. Inmates were required to pick set amounts of junk (by weight) every day. Sometimes picking involved the use of a nail or a spike, but more often workhouses, prisons and houses of correction preferred the picking to be done by hand. (Entering a workhouse was also known as going on the spike for now obvious reasons.) Once the fibres had been picked out individually, the final product, oakum, was sold back to ship and boat builders. It would then be mixed with tar to become caulking, which was used to plug any gaps between the timber boards of a wooden vessel – and for the deck planking of iron and steel ships - and thereby make them water-tight. The term *money for old rope*, meant to describe a means of getting money from something apparently worthless, had its roots in this activity. It is sometimes now used rather perversely to imply getting easy money... I wonder what workhouse inmates and Victorian prisoners would have made of that suggestion.

The posters also reveal other details about the conditions and regulations: so many lashes of the whip for taking longer than 10 minutes to eat, withdrawal of food for going out of the workhouse yard, and lashes and confinement for being disobedient. One Poor Law poster comments that the bodies of children were sold to the surgeons (for research/dissection) at the hospital on a weekly basis. [18]

---

18 Details extracted from the National Archives, HO 44/27/2. Also Hogarth depicted such work in his Harlot's Progress. The inmates beat hemp to pay for their keep and to profit the warder, who threatens them with his cane. One person is standing with their hands trapped in the stocks above head height: above a sign says, "Better to work, than stand idle."

The poor, who had no say in the matter and manner of relief provision, were at the mercy of the system and could only rely (for any improvement and representation) on the good intentions of a few philanthropists.

Paupers, the working-poor and all workers hated and feared the threat of the workhouse; and it was a threat that could become a reality at any time if a worker became unemployed, sick or had been injured and become unable to work. Increasingly, workhouses contained not just the poor but orphans, the old, the sick, the disabled and the insane. It seemed to punish people who were poor through no fault of their own. (The resentment and fear of that system were deep-seated and persisted long after it had been dismantled. Even in the 1960's I found those feelings were still very raw to some of my older aunts and uncles!)

Richard Oastler, who was known as the Factory King, was against the new Poor Law and called the workhouses 'Prisons for the Poor.' One scandal of abuse of inmates and misuse of funds occurred at the infamous Andover Workhouse in Hampshire. Headlines reported that half-starved inmates were found eating the rotting flesh from bones. In response to this and other scandals the government introduced stricter rules for those who ran the workhouses and they also set up a system of regular inspections. The inmates, though, continued everywhere to be at the mercy of unscrupulous masters and matrons who could still treat the poor with contempt and abuse the rules.

Such was the prevailing conditions of our Victorian ancestors and of those who, living in Somers Town – just a mile from the Mother of Parliaments - were at the epicentre of the greatest empire the world has ever known.

Incidentally, it wasn't until the end of the Victorian age in 1901 that the minimum age for workers in all industries was raised to 12 years.

A poor and harsh existence would continue throughout ordinary people's lives, and it would not be until after most of Francis Baxter's children were dead that anything much would change for the better. They would not see all men and women enfranchised with the right "to vote," would not benefit from Trade union representation and would not enjoy improved standards in living and working conditions. They would not live to enjoy the liberation (from fear of sickness and want) that came with the introduction of the National Health Service and the Welfare State in the 20th century.

The Ordnance of Labourers 1349 distorted the positions of workers, but nevertheless the claims they were grasping and idle (pot and kettle again come to mind) have been echoed down the centuries. Naturally it would be naïve to expect the ranks of vested interest within government to ever be wholly – some would say even partially - truthful. This has always been so, but arrant mendacity has probably never been quite so overt as in the daily business of Boris Johnson's morally bankrupt administration (23.07.2019 – 05.09.2022) which was as corrupt as it was deficient in integrity. (And the gaggle that have been his immediate successors within his party have sadly proved little better.)

Unfortunately those qualities were lauded by the majority of his political party, by members of Parliament and financial backers who – whilst historically I have disagreed with them profoundly - I have hitherto held to be otherwise fairly honourable. Previously Tories could be divided into those who displayed honesty and a genuine commitment to public service, and the remainder who nevertheless and at least pretended to observe and abide by some limits while feathering their nests.

Sadly Johnson et al's antics also appeared not to unduly ruffle an amoral and largely apolitical electorate, who have generally become distrusting of all politicians and yet allowed them to remain in office. In the end, though, it was the Tory party's survival – good old self-interest - and a relatively insignificant straw that broke the camel's back. Relatively insignificant, that is, in comparison to all the other scandalous chicanery which also culminated in unnecessary loss of life.

Dorothy Hartley in her epic book, Food in England, noted the effect of trades upon workers' diets and the flavourings they used, craved and required.

She noted that iron-workers, whose daily toil was carried out in the searing heat of the furnaces, learnt much about light beers – and about strengthening ales and liquors. She also reported that lime-workers were issued with extra grease and butter as emollients to save their skins – and prevent their eyelids rotting - which she said caused them to develop a compensating taste for vinegar and milk. People who worked with various chemicals such as painters (and I imagine plumbers – all being lead users cf *plumbum*) found their diet and cooking needed extra salt and acid flavourings. Apparently, field workers who sweated in the dry harvest fields were given free barley water (which is slightly acidic) and well-salted oat porridge to counteract the dehydration.

I doubt that pre-global warming it got that hot in Scotland, but perhaps the Scots were just working excessively hard. It would account for their seeming preference for salt on porridge, rather than sugar.

Not that it affected their health necessarily, but she said that leather workers became so "impregnated with the tannin from the oak and willow bark used in the dressing of hides, that their bodies did not decay after death, but shrivelled and dried up like old leather sacks." (1954 p233)

Hartley comments fascinatingly on the different methods of cooking that leant themselves to the nature of the work, such that a forester cooked on a wood fire, and a plank steak came from that specialism of craft cooking. Seek out her book. It is worth it.

DIET

Rich and poor have always eaten quite differently in regards to quantity, quality and variety: the children of rich Victorians obviously ate much better than the poorer children. With a greater variety of foods they thrived and grew, while poor families with fewer options and a restricted diet tended to be malnourished and develop scurvy and rickets.

It was not only income, however, that influenced what was bought. A family's immediate environment also contributed to determining their diet and people ate what was available and affordable or what was locally abundant.

Strangely dietary surveys (See Sage 1997) showed that the poor labouring population who lived in isolated rural areas of England (and as far afield as mainland Scotland and in the west of Ireland and on peripheral British islands) actually enjoyed the most nutritious diets of similar labourers elsewhere. The remoteness and the not easily worked terrain of these regions helped. These had not been subject to the forces of capitalism in quite the same way that other areas were: the enclosure of most common fields had shifted farming towards a capitalist approach whose focus had increased the general efficiency of agriculture. The change, however, also altered the balance of the farming system where it then coalesced into (see Braudel 1992, and Patriquin 2007 p26) a social class triad of landowner, capitalist-tenant and wage-labourer. Agricultural workers had been turned into paid labourers with many now employed on a seasonal basis and reliant – as they were not hitherto - on a cash economy for their housing, food and clothing. In time the poverty of their situation drove many away from the land and into urban areas where although jobs were more plentiful, sometimes more regular and sometimes better paid, their conditions and their diet suffered.

Traditionally in the country and in less densely packed villages and towns people had eaten what they could grow or what could be hunted or caught locally. Of course there were many restrictions placed upon those who unlike the landowners did not own the fish, the fowl or the flesh (be it deer, lamb, hare or lowly rabbit). (An amazing statistic in 2023 is that still only a paltry 8% of land is available to be legally accessed by common people – and if that is shocking the figure for rivers it is only a mere 3%! See Caroline Lucas)

Throughout Britain, though and with the exception of those more nutritious areas, as reported by Sage, bread was the staple component of the diet. It accompanied every meal if it was not the major feature of the meal.

When affordable, though, there were plenty of seasonal fresh vegetables from indigenous and local crops to be found in the markets, including cabbage, carrots, leeks, onions and turnips: all were used in stews and soups, which ranged in consistency - depending on meat or wheat/oatmeal content - from gruel to potage to a thick frumenty (which was more of a porridge). Wild alexanders, a type of celery-like flavouring, were more in use then but seem little known now. Some vegetables and fruits had found their way into the diet whilst being comparatively new to Britain like broccoli (from around 1700) and tomatoes (1750). Peas and runner beans were summer foods. Native fruits included acorns, apples, sloes, brambles, wild currants, blackberries, cranberries, haws, hazel-nuts, hips, purple plums, raspberries, wood strawberries, (and other berries from elder, heather, holly and roan), and beech-mast. Dandelions and nettles also had their uses within soups (and herbal remedies). Honey was also as ever a brilliant food, a sweetener and also used to make a sweet alcoholic drink called mead. On the other hand, those foods which had to be transported or imported would be more expensive, and whilst there was no consideration or notion of carbon foot-prints (most goods being brought in by sailing ships) these foods were often beyond the pockets of the poorer sections of society. The invention of the railways and steam ships allowed more foods to be transported and greater variety was available across many areas.

The cheapest vegetables were onions, which were widely used being variously cooked, used in soups and stews or made into gravy. Only slightly more expensive than onions was watercress, which is high in iron and fibre. As it was in season from April to February both its availability and its price made it a popular daily choice. Ordinary poor working class people regularly ate it for breakfast with bread and dripping.

Nearly everyone preferred meat, but the poor ate less and the poorest ate next to none. Meat might only feature in the Somers Town diet on a Sunday, whereas at other times – but not every day - a tiny piece of meat, fat or bones was used to add flavour to soups and broths. Pork was the most common form of flesh with the poor able only to afford the cheapest cuts: slowly cooked shin and cheek were popular cuts.

I have not seen much mention of chicken in the records. It seems they were kept for their eggs rather than for their meat, and were only eaten when the hen's laying days were over. I suspect it may have been a more costly animal then than we have become used to in these current days of intensive farming and dreadful battery farms. There was no notion at that time of such awful concentration and barbaric containment so also there was no concept of free range/free roaming chickens as we know it.

Chickens and chicken meat is just now described as chicken, an all embracing term, but in the Victorian age (and in the

1960's) there were still distinctions which included such as pullets (young hens who were not yet laying) and capons (castrated cocks). Hens begin laying when the hen is between 16 to 24 weeks old depending on breed: they are kept until 72 weeks old. (The meat chicken (Broiler) can be slaughtered anywhere from 28 days to 81 days old. (Laura Bridgerman https://the humane league.org.uk /article/broiler-chickens Feb 11th 2021) The higher range applies if they are organic. The RSPCA report that most birds reach their slaughter weight of 2.2kg in 35 days, but in the UK, the typical slaughter age is 42 days. Due to their accelerated growth these are not adult birds and factory-farmed birds are still just chicks when they are killed. To underline this point, formerly the average carcass would have to have its legs cracked to allow sinews to be pulled out, a process made obsolete by the slaughter of the underdeveloped birds of today.

Fowl for ordinary folk would also naturally include pigeons and many other birds.

Coastal regions and seaside towns and villages obviously had a diet rich in fish with cod and haddock being the most popular white fish. Plaice, herring and sprats also featured. Seaside people and city-folk in the capital were also partial to eels, crabs, oysters and other shellfish. Cockles, mussels, whelks and oysters were sold by street vendors on stalls and barrows, and these are credited with feeding many of London's poor throughout the Victorian period. Eels could be served hot or cold (where they were jellied) which were particularly favourable to the London palate. These eels were first cooked in a broth, which when cooled set into the jelly-like substance that encased the chopped eels.

Bread was vitally important to the Victorian poor. It featured in most meals, and was often the major portion of the meal. If they knew no other prayer or hymn I imagine the Baxter's of Somers Town knew the Lord's Prayer, a doxology which contains the spiritual and desperate physical plea: "give us our daily bread." The Lord's Prayer, also called the Our Father, or the Pater Noster, appears in two forms (Matthew 6:9-13 and Luke 11:1-4) in the New Testament. Of course it is subject to variation and it depends upon which version of which Bible you care to read as to the one the average Christian may know. The church of England Portsmouth and Winchester diocese states the following is the traditional Anglican version, which incidentally is the one I was taught. It may also well be the version that would have tripped off the tongues of Baxter's old and young. (There appears no great consistency as to usage being exclusively applied within Roman Catholic or Anglo-Catholic (Protestant) churches.)

"Our Father who art in heaven,
hallowed be thy name.
Thy kingdom come.
Thy will be done
on earth, as it is in heaven.
Give us this day our daily bread,
and forgive us our trespasses,
as we forgive those who trespass against us,
and lead us not into temptation,
but deliver us from evil.
For thine is the kingdom, the power,
and the glory,
for ever and ever. Amen.

For many poor people across Britain, it was white bread made from bolted wheat flour which made their daily bread that was the staple component of their diet. Whole-wheat flour on the other hand is flour that is ground from the whole grain and contains all the constituents of the wheat kernels. When stone-ground the wheat grains were crushed, which made it a coarser, less refined grain. In this process the three parts of the wheat grain (the bran for fibre and b-vitamins, the germ for B- and E-vitamins and the endosperm for starch, carbohydrate and protein) are all crushed together and never separated. Bolted flour, though, is whole grain flour with the coarsest bran particles (about 80% of the bran) sifted out which makes it a compromise between whole grain and all purpose white flour. The end product in that period, according to the Victorian Web, was the *quartern loaf*: it was made with exactly 3.5 pounds (56oz) (or 1/4 stone) of wheat flour, and its finished weight was approximately 4⅓ pounds. Thus, two quartern loaves of finished bread weighed the same as the larger gallon loaf which previously used to be the common size.

The great problem for people in the Victorian age was a lack of regulations.

REGULATION

There will always be those who see regulations and minimum standards as impedances to the easy profit of unrestrained activity, of abasement, of adulteration, of unsafe working conditions, and other dodgy money-saving practices. They deliberately conflate regulation with nit-picking nanny-state-ism, to avoid impediments to their rapacity. Their message is fed to others who suck up this nonsense. The drip-feeding is successfully accomplished through the organs of media owned and supported by similarly-minded tycoons. It is persistent and not easily overcome: it was more recently the real driving force for those heading the Leave campaign in the 2016 Brexit vote.

No class of people are wholly good or wholly bad, and there are thieves and crooks at every level. Poverty does not make crooks of people, it just makes them desperate, and only relatively few resort to illegality even when they are most desperate. Those who succumb are not usually wildly brilliant at it, and their endeavours are generally small scale. The most successful crooks, of course, have always inhabited – and continue to inhabit – castles.... and more often boardrooms; they tend only to be desperately greedy. However, in the 19th century there were also sub-sets throughout the hierarchy of production who were particularly and increasingly reckless in regards to the health and the safety of the public. Unfortunately, nowadays, people have been cynically conditioned by those pervading forces of self-interest (like those leading Brexiteers) to respond negatively to the conjunction of those two notions: "health" and "safety." Those who scoff, though, tend to carp when their own flesh and blood have an avoidable accident. I wonder how they would feel, though, if they or their children were being poisoned in the name of greed and profit?

ADULTERATION

Of course, some people adulterated the food they supplied because like their customers they were also desperate to survive.

Unfortunately, some of these 19th century crooks were taking chances with the lives of the public and Victorians suffered from widespread adulteration of their foodstuffs. It was so widespread amongst a great many suppliers and purveyors of foods that it attracted the attention of Arthur Hill Hassall, a physician and scientist with an interest in microscopic. His input, produced in the Lancet medical journal, led to a campaign and battle against food adulteration. *Death in the loaf*, an article by Annie Gray (2016), reveals that there were habitual dilutions of milk and beer, and also that potato and other starches were used to bulk out products like bread and pies; all of which cheated their customers but did not directly harm them. Alum, though, and chalk were also added to bread which, in an age of malnutrition (and with the population's over-reliance on bread), was not exactly beneficial to their health. Of course you may argue that chalk contains calcium which is good for teeth and bones, but alum? This chemical compound was only added to whiten the bread, but it is an astringent which inhibits the absorption of nutrients: this increased the incidence and the degree of dehydrating diarrhoea, which was likely to be devastating and possibly fatal.

To compound a bad practice adulteration could be done by anyone in the bread chain, by the millers or by the bakers: all of whom were often feeling the pinch financially and might feel the need to squeeze a bit more out of their take. Those dependent upon bread (and especially small children who ate it with milk another product vulnerable to adulteration) could be in for a tough time. The threat was exacerbated when *both* the miller and the baker were adulterating the basic ingredient and the product.

It was a problem which particularly affected the less wealthy sections of society. Millers did not sell their flour direct to ordinary people because individual families needed less flour (a matter of scale) and because the poorer classes almost certainly had neither the space to store flour nor perhaps an oven in which to bake. Instead, the miller mainly sold his flour to bakers; but he could also sell to wealthier households, which comprised large families, room to store more bulky provisions plus a good number of servants. They were also likely to have their own cooks... and an oven. Furthermore, having a better general diet, wealthier families did not suffer from either malnourishment or under-nourishment. So, whether or not they bought bread from the baker or flour from the miller, the adulteration of bread affected the wealthy less – and the less-wealthy more.

With more awareness fuelling debate and demands for something to be done, the government at first fell back on a reliance on market forces: you know the sort of tripe, people "will realise the difference in quality" etc "and will make an informed choice." The problem was two-fold. *All* the food was adulterated; and the price of items drove the poorest people to the cheapest and therefore probably to the most adulterated products.

Hassall's campaign sought to alter government opinion, and in the 1850s, his analyses of London foods found not a single loaf of bread tested was alum-free. Furthermore, plaster of Paris, potatoes and sawdust could all also be found in bread. There were no regulations then in regards to food information, labelling and listing of ingredients. Hassall's findings in those *happy* (?) regulation-free/ non-nanny-state days increasingly revealed levels of tampering and dodgy additives, which eventually could not be ignored.

Gray (12.01.2016) indicates that the results precipitated the Food Adulteration Act (1860) which provided some funding for authorities who wanted to test foods or bring prosecutions; the Act, however, apparently achieved little or nothing, and it would take a further generation before other legislation became effective. It seems by then the food-suppliers and purveyors changed track and started to promote their products instead as having been proven negative for adulterants. Gray asserts that loose products such as tea began to be sold in sealed packets "with a clear maker's mark as a brand of quality."

Market forces, **with** regulation, enforcement and information available to the consumer, apparently can work.

STALE BREAD

In researching bread I have come across accounts which I do not recall ever featuring in my history lessons at school. Of course, one can't be taught everything but it is a great pity I think that many may have missed out on information surrounding the Stale Bread Act of 1801. At the time there were the Napoleonic Wars and failures of crops and reduced imports there was a shortage of wheat. The Act sought to address the problem. "Let them eat cake" ? No, not quite.

The government, it seems, appreciated that bread was the staple of the vast majority of the population's diet. Given its prevalence the government were faced with a tricky problem as to how they could persuade or convince the public to eat less of it – especially when no substitute or additional food was available to or affordable for the masses. Some bright, and probably fat, spark realised that warm fresh breed is nice to eat; it also makes you want to eat more of it. Stale bread, on the other hand, is not so nice, not so tempting to have more and – an especial bonus – it fills the stomach more: it is said, up to 20% more. The strategy seemed a total win-win for the government, whose fat-cats saw warm, fresh bread consumption rather more as an indulgence for greedy poor people. So, in an effort to reduce demand they passed the Act which decreed that bakers had to keep their breed for 24 hours after it was baked before they were allowed to sell it to their hungry customers.

There is a similarity between this situation and that of the problem of bread adulteration: again, the poor did not generally have indoor ovens and were not able to bake their own bread. In addition to this, even if they had had the space for an oven, and even if they could have afforded one, they would still have needed fuel to heat it; and the system of "enclosure" had rendered them less able to gather wood. Town and city people, especially, now had to buy all their food and, therefore, they also had to buy their bread. It was the main component of most of their meals.

The Act soon proved to be a disaster: it was unworkable, unpopular, and largely unenforceable and most of all it was dangerous to the stability that the wealthy and well-fed enjoyed. Consequently, and before very long, the government re-thought the idea, and promptly dumped the Act.

Bad ideas - and especially bad un-thought-out ideas - tend to make for bad solutions, but strangely they tend nevertheless to be cyclical. As someone once said, "those who do not learn their history are condemned to repeat it." A similar trick to the Stale Bread Act – although with a 12-hour gap between baking and selling - was tried during WW1 when similar problems were facing a similarly unsympathetic government. It did not last long. I wonder when another administration will again suddenly light upon the brilliance of such a scheme. Over to you Prime Minister...

THE WORKHOUSE MENU: A TEMPLATE

As Norman Davies said (2007 pg82) "reconstructing the past is rather like translating poetry, it can be done but never exactly." Different sources, for example, may give different and contradicting information; both may be accurate, but may also be subject to variation because one area did things differently to another. In regards to bread some sources report the Victorians used stone-ground flour for their bread while others, a majority it would seem, say generally they preferred a white loaf. How much of it they ate and what is consisted of is another question.

In regards to the very poor we may get a better idea from Workhouse dietary recommendations. Indeed, the main constituent was bread. In 1835 the Poor Law Commissioners issued six dietary tables as examples. Men in the Union Workhouse Abingdon in 1836, for instance, were allocated 7oz (women 5oz) of bread for breakfast, along with 2 pints of gruel made from water and oatmeal or sometimes from flour and oatmeal. Sometimes they may instead have had broth which was made from the boiling of dinner meat with a few onions or turnips. Soup, in turn (and an occasional alternative), was broth thickened with barley rice or oatmeal. Dinner on 3 days comprised cooked meat with vegetables (5oz total, one day, with 4oz on the remaining days) On the days where no meat and vegetables three times a week with 2 pints of soup every other day. One day-a-week it was bread and cheese, which must have made a boring dietary experience since supper every evening was also 7oz/5oz bread and 2oz/1½ oz of cheese. This was a basis for recommended levels: I do not know if it was a minimum. However, Patriquin (2007 pg145) suggests that the "food, clothing and shelter provided by these (workhouses) institutions was comparable to that obtained by the poorest labourers on the outside" – and occasionally they were even better! The amounts and variety were of course subject to corruption and abuse by those in control, as in the Andover scandal. (see Higginbotham The Workhouse Cookbook 2009 ISBN 978 0 7524 4730 8.) The workhouse diet was also supplemented with pints of beer or tea. Most inmates drank beer mainly and sometimes light beer, while girls and small children drank milk and water.

Rare Obesity

There are few examples of morbid obesity– and assuming they were not well-to-do or aristocratic gluttons these people usually earned a living as freak show exhibits. They may have been metabolically unhealthy and suffered from a medical condition; some claimed, as did Daniel Lambert, to only drink water and to eat in moderation. There is a portrait of the unfortunate Lambert in the Wellcome collection where the dedication describes him as weighing "almost forty stone." It also states that he was the son of a Leicester gaoler and he had been born in 1791, whereas the Newarke Houses Museum gives his year of birth 1770. (They celebrated Daniel Lambert Day in 2020, and his clothes and chair are on display there – so, no longer a freak show. There is also a Daniel Lambert Society). At the time of his death aged 39 he weighed 335Kg (52 stone 11 pounds). Wellcome suggests his girth measured 9 feet 4 inches. His Society reminds us that he had other interests – he wasn't just a fat lump who did nothing – and that he also had great knowledge of breeding dogs and cockerels.

Whatever he suffered from there was little help then in the 19th century: a fat chance of any dietary education, psychological or bariatric interventions.

ROOM FOR FOOD

Space in a working-class home was usually limited and mostly overcrowded. There wasn't much if any room for things to be stored: they weren't keeping family heirlooms or bric-a-brac. There weren't even the conveniences a modern family might expect such as fridges, which had not been invented as a domestic appliance and was still a long way from being one an ordinary family might be able to afford.

The storage of any food was limited because there wasn't the facility. Ordinary people did not have great storage cupboards or kitchen units – mostly they didn't have kitchens.

A modern store cupboard/unit will contain amongst many things tinned or canned food. Tins of food, however, only began to become available after the 1860's and while the canned product was generally of cheap quality, it was also certainly cheaper than fresh products, particularly meat. Before the era of refrigeration, food was preserved by smoking, drying, pickling and by salting.

The inability to store food also affected people's eating behaviour. If they had a range or a fire, and if they could afford fuel, they would have cooked economically, eking out meals in the form of soups and stews. Bacon was quick to cook or could be thrown into the pot, while at other times bread and bone-soup was not an unusual repast. All food tended to be mainly eaten on the day of purchase or almost immediately. This was particularly obvious since the general Victorian diet – and that of anyone who is struggling at whatever time – acutely reflected income: it often contained which quite simply was cheaper than meat. When they couldn't afford fish, it was vegetable-based; potatoes, for example, could be cooked (and eaten) conveniently in their jackets.

Sometimes they just ate cold simple fayre: the ubiquitous bread, which dominated the diet of the poor, and cheese. This also would not have been uncommon for most Victorian slum-dwellers, few of whom according to Michael Mosley (BBC) would have had ovens or even cooking utensils. (Naturally the one is rather superfluous without the other, but he further added that many didn't own plates or spoons either.) At other times in the urban environment, and when they had money, they may have resorted to buying from food vendors who offered culinary snacks or delights from shops, carts and stalls. Pies from bakers, sausages from stalls and nuts were also to be found roasting on street braziers.

It was hard work earning enough money to afford a diet necessary to maintain a worker, especially considering the calories needed for the amount of physical work most jobs demanded

All towns and villages then boasted many craftsmen and women: people who made things, who fixed, fitted and mended all manner of goods, tools and equipment. Most of their skills were also required on farms, and the different and often interdependent tradesmen were usually hired locally.

Trees were chopped down and taken to saw-mills where the sawyer processed the trunks, boughs and branches into wooden planks, posts and other shapes for other wood-workers to further fashion. Woodworkers included: carvers and carpenters for the construction of buildings, fences and gates; joiners made furniture; others made wooden bowls and utensils. Then there were coopers (barrel-makers) who used a mixture of skills, while the wooden-clog maker sometimes relied upon the blacksmith to add metal tips. The blacksmith would forge tools, bars, hooks, horseshoes and other metalwork. Coach-makers used a range of skills involving many different materials (including wood, metal and upholstery). Wheelwrights made cart wheels and wagons. Skinners and tanners worked in the process of animal hides for clothing and leather goods, from which Saddlers, made saddles, bags and harnesses and the cordwainer made shoes. Hat makers, straw bonnet makers, glove makers, tailors, seamsters and seamstresses and many many others were all engaged in making something: making some physical, practical, useful and sometimes beautiful product.

(It would, of course, be William Morris who advised that the harmony of these features should dictate or exclude the presence of an object in your home.) Everything was concerned with the art and skills of "making" – of manufacture, especially in its original sense of being hand-made. It is a far cry from the current state of affairs where the UK makes very little of anything, except money for those already wealthy.

Also in that 18th/19th century environment there were watermills and windmills all driving machinery to produce, shape or process materials and even to create flour for bread. All played their part in Victorian town, village and farm life.

LAND USE

Up until 1750 Britain was largely self sufficient with food, but later it became seduced by the flavours of different imported goods – tea, coffee, sugar, tobacco, rum, cinnamon, olive oil, and pepper. Change would come, especially as it inevitably does as a result of the increase in population.

Whilst at the start of Victoria's reign more than half the population of Great Britain worked in the countryside, it is easy to think that the land was used mainly for agriculture and food production, but in the pre-industrial period domestic agriculture did not specialize on food production. Instead, land was also required to supply other needs: forests and trees were needed for wood, vital for fuel and construction. This was also supplemented with turf for fuel purposes. Domestic agricultural production of energy, however, was replaced almost entirely by the coal industry by the 1860s.

Sheep and pigs were still reared for all their potential uses: wool, sheepskin and leather for clothing and bags as well as for food. Fat in the form of tallow was needed for candles, grease and soap. Flax was used in clothing, while oats and hay were needed to feed work-horses who pulled ploughs and drove transport. Clapped out horses were killed and used amongst other things to make glue – it is said, that unlike those dastardly French we did not eat the meat. I wonder. Cannibalism works if you are hungry enough, so I doubt many of the starving or otherwise would say nay (or neigh) to a horse steak.

Agricultural Revolution: Change in Weight and Fat Content in Animals and Links to Angina Pectoris

The agricultural strip system had been contrived to affect a fairness of distribution, but it suffered from certain inefficiencies. Combining and reorganising the parcels of land into consolidated fields with hedgerows changed the state of things for the better – would that they had stopped there. Pre enclosure, animals roamed and grazed or foraged where they could: cows on the common land and in forests, deer in woodlands, pigs in the woods, etc. Of course without limits to their roaming they were also free to associate sexually, which meant there was no chance of selective breeding to improve characteristics of the stock.

Animal husbandry, (breeding and feeding techniques) and newer forms of land management and enclosure produced farm animals that matured at earlier ages. Whilst they could not alter gestation they found they could produce bigger animals, sometimes of a gross nature. Thus the overall effect of the new methods and breeding techniques meant that all the animals were both fatter and fattier.

These methods and the change from oxen being used as a draught animal – being put out by Clydesdale Horses – meant the availability of meat increased at a time when the population of the country was increasing. (The furlong length remained unaltered despite - before standardised measurements - being tied to the connection with oxen: a furlong, derived from 'a furrow long', was the distance that could be ploughed by an ox in a day, such that an acre (one furlong by one chain) was that which could be ploughed by 8 oxen)

The change in husbandry also increased the weight and numbers of other animals (pigs, sheep and poultry [hens, ducks and geese] etc) who were sent for slaughter. Fussell noted that during the eighteenth century there was close to a threefold increase in the weight of cows and calves, and of sheep and lambs sold in London's central meat market at Smithfield. (E Fussell and Constance Goodman, 1930)

Dairy cattle increased in size, an effect which was multiplied by the cross breeding of Guernsey cows with Devon Bulls. Milk yields doubled, leading to an increase in the production of cheese, butter and cream. These more solid forms were also easier to transport, especially given the more efficient distribution systems: even before the railways' massive impact, better roads, canal networks and coastal trade had all bolstered the amount of animals and products coming to market. In addition to the bulking up of all animals going for slaughter and of greater dairy produce, egg production also increased.

Britain led the way in agricultural changes, implementing these five decades ahead of European rivals. As mentioned these changes had led to the emergence of fatter and more-fatty animals, which research has shown had knock-on health effects. It has been noted that roughly it is this 50-year interval that separates the emergence of angina pectoris in England from its first manifestation in any other country on the European mainland. (Fisher. H A L, 1946 pg 777.)

At the beginning of the Victorian age, and indeed throughout the 19th and most of the 20th century, people probably had a different perspective on sex and procreation. They almost certainly regarded these not just as inextricably linked (as they are) but the latter being the inevitable consequence of the former.

In this millennium and in this culture couples tend to plan pregnancies. Such responsible people are increasingly likely to have waited until they were more able to withstand the additional seismic financial shock to a household budget before embarking on that reproductive endeavour. Of course, in the exercise of any plan there are moments which may appear to threaten its progress: while illness may thwart it (and death will kill it), such things as false alarms/late periods can be the cause of a certain panic. We are disposed to believe that getting pregnant is as easy as hanging a pair of trousers on the back of a chair and that as sure as night follows day there will be a baby at the end of it. For with planning, modern care, better nutrition, cleaner environments, healthcare and welfare what could go wrong? Ah, as Robert Burns famously counselled ("To a Mouse"): "The best laid schemes o' mice an' men ... gang aft a-gley."

Family-planners are often shocked when subsequently they fail to conceive at the drop of a hat or indeed of a pair of undergarments. They are similarly devastated when they learn from traumatic personal experience that even with modern healthcare, with ante-natal monitoring and awareness of all the issues – the do's and don'ts of producing a healthy baby - that about 1 in 4 pregnancies still do not go to full term. (I wonder if that is – or if that will be - taught in our 21st century schools?)

Back in the 1840's, though, couples had no need for official statistics to enlighten them; "God's will," or no, they – and particularly the women - were resigned to a grim cycle. They were only too aware of miscarriage, of still-birth and also of the deaths of mothers from puerperal fever: events which were subsequent to the seemingly inevitable occasion of perpetual conception. Thus, and given the absence of efficient practical (and chemical) contraception, there was almost no notion or means of guaranteed family planning beyond abstinence/chastity. Of course, some did use ad hoc diaphragms and home-made condoms, while some relied upon unreliable timings/"safe-periods" and coitus interruptus. All that notwithstanding, pregnancies generally soon followed (if they did not pre-cede) marriage. In 1847 Caroline and Francis Baxter the stonemason, along with all *newly-wed's* expected to be expecting babies; and so it happened – and with fingers crossed they hoped and probably prayed their Baxter family unit would indeed increase, survive and thrive.

The cycle of relentless pregnancy, confinement and birth (and often miscarriage or death) was the lot of rich and poor alike. Even Queens were not exempt from the vagaries of reproduction; for example, the young Queen Victoria, who at that point had been married seven years and seven months, had already given birth to five children and was pregnant with her sixth. (Over the course of seventeen years she would give birth to nine children, who all survived to adulthood.) She had a successful run, unlike one of her predecessors, Queen Anne. In a similar, though earlier, time period (from 1684 until 1700) Queen Anne had been pregnant at least eighteen times! That desperately blighted woman had miscarried 8 times and given birth to 5 stillborn children! If that wasn't torment enough for her, matters got even worse: of her five live-born children, four had died before reaching the age of two. Queen Anne's sole surviving child, the Duke of Gloucester, died at the age of eleven in 1700.

They say she drank excessively. I couldn't blame her.

Of course, the arrival of other mouths to feed does not and certainly did not then carry the same financial burden across the social classes. Indeed, the further you get from being poor or waged the more immune you become from such concerns as to whether you have sufficient money to feed and shelter your family. The fortunes of Queens are ever unlikely to be financially affected enough for them to be concerned about the cost of living; but for others..... In 1847 there was also a Banking crisis, known as "the great panic," which did rattle a few wealthier cages.

Now, I cannot imagine our stonemason had ever seen the inside of a bank (as a customer, at least), as those institutions were then definitely not for the ordinary working person, however talented or skilled they may have been; and so I would also assume that for a very short time Francis Baxter had something in common with a monarch: *he* had no immediate cause to panic.

It seems, though, that interest rates had been rising for some time: a situation which usually made it an attractive proposition for wealthy and well-to-do investors to put their money into government bonds. (This was a counter-inflation device or scheme, from which big government projects were funded, but where dividends were guaranteed. Of course the dividends were not spectacularly excessive, and certainly not in comparison to other speculative – and therefore more precarious - ventures, but they were safe.) However, the apparent success and seemingly bountiful profits of the railways had become somewhat irresistible and had driven salivating investors to plough their money into railway schemes.

You might have thought the British government would have wished to control this, but that same government was made up of rich and powerful men who also wanted to get their noses in the trough. It was in their personal interest to encourage an official British government policy of 'laissez-faire,' (a system of almost total non-regulation) which in the field of railways naturally gave free rein to all manner of thieves and sharks. Thus, within this free-for-all, and with no effective checks on the financial viability of constructing a railway line, corruption thrived. As Nobel Laureate Bob Dylan said, "Money doesn't talk. It swears!" (1965. It's All right Ma (I'm only bleeding))

The apparent promise of big dividends drove the share prices up, which created more demand, thus driving the prices up further and so on until... of course, reality finally struck: with fraudsters siphoning off money–and/or with naive estimations of the cost of construction projects – came the inevitable situation where there simply was not enough left in the "pot."

So, some railway lines could not be completed (for the want of further injections of finance from sources that were already depleted); and then other lines, which had been finished, proved not to be commercially viable and yielded insufficient returns. In order to honour and fulfil their contracts some of those recklessly grasping shareholders found themselves caught between a rock and a hard place: should they try to protect what they had already spent by investing more money? The term "throwing good money after bad..." springs to my mind as it indeed may have sprung to their minds. This was a huge dilemma for them since there was a good likelihood they would never be able to recoup their outlay let alone make a profit. There was nothing left but to desperately try to cut their losses by selling their interests (i.e. their shares and their commitment) which then led to a rush to sell; and share prices plummeted. Companies, investments and banks collapsed, and in that dog-eat-dog world the smaller railways companies were bought up cheaply by larger ones etc., for whom the top-up investment was a relatively inexpensive price for the bargain of the finished product. Such is the world of business, capitalism and greed.

I expect the Baxters, like most of the population (who were not as we might currently say "stakeholders") were oblivious to the "plight" of rich speculators. Nevertheless, those ordinary folk at the bottom of the heap would inevitably experience the effects of the fall-out of slump, recession and inflation.

Revolution, Slaughter and Re-charting Maps

The banking crisis was not the only problem in that period: there was also much political unrest – with considerable upheaval throughout Europe, including Great Britain, and in the Americas.

It was a very different world then, and countries and states as we know them did not necessarily exist within current political arrangements. For example, California, Texas and a great big chunk of other territory were part of Mexico right up until that year of 1847 when they were lost to the United States. Even closer to home the European "Map" was different, too; but were our Baxters (and the other ordinary people of Somers Town) aware of the shifting sands of nations? Did they, for example, know of the struggles by Mazzini and Garibaldi to create a unified Italy from the ragbag of separate kingdoms which then prevailed in that landmass?

Perhaps if the Baxters had seen maps of Europe, then the countries they would have observed would also have been very different from those to be found on one more current. Geo-political maps are always subject to change – sometimes drastically; and their maps would have contained a massive country called Prussia, which spanned parts of what are now

Germany, Poland and Russia. In the mid-19th century the lands we know as Germany were not even a unified entity: the country we may take for granted was a creation of the 1870's. Yes, incredibly that country whose efforts to expand caused two World Wars in the 20th century did not even exist when the Baxters were in Somers Town. And thus, treaties are made and broken –and apparently solid political-unions collapse, and maps are re-drawn.

Indeed, in the 20th century Yugoslavia, the USSR and essentially Palestine all disappeared; the map of the EC continues to be amended and the wider map of Europe may well also change again in the light of the 2022 war in Ukraine: nothing is certain, and who knows, given the political climate in North America perhaps, in the not too distant future a map of that continent may not show a United States as it is familiar to people of the early 21st century. Instead it may portray the fruits of fragmentation with different unions emergent. [19]

NATIVE AMERICANS: THE TRAIL OF TEARS

What did our Baxters - and most of their contemporaries' - know of the world beyond our shores? What was the level of their education and the extent of their knowledge? What news found its way to Somers Town from within England – let alone from around the world? In the "Information-age" of the 21st century it seems that if someone farts in Manchester, it is immediately heard about in Montreal and within parsecs a goat herder in Mongolia will get a whiff of it, but not so then.... surely.... ?

They certainly lacked the immediacy of modern communications, but did news still trickle through? Did our

---

19 Perhaps California will become an independent and separate country?

Baxters and their ilk know anything about North American antics, which included the brutal removals of native aboriginal Americans from their ancestral home-lands during the 1830's and throughout the Victorian period? Removals, that is, which followed theft, barbarity and genocide. Were there any official reports or did news come by word of mouth? Would official reports have bothered with discussion of why those removals were necessary? I doubt natives from anywhere then were important enough to even be considered news-worthy. The 20th century and its only slightly more demanding public are used to having odious actions, doused in fragrant excuses, wafted under their noses: security, being a much favoured old chestnut, is oft cited to excuse all manner of atrocity.

In the 19th century, though, those re-locations whether reported or not happened to become especially pressing when the natives' ancestral lands were found to contain gold. It is an integral part of the American dream, to stumble upon someone else's gold (or oil) and decide it would be nice to have...

The golden land held by indigenous tribes in the south eastern states was thus mightily required (while the tribes' presence definitely was *not*): and sharing may be what primary school children do at morning assembly, but it does not apply where gold is concerned. The tribes were forcibly removed to an alien area west of the Mississippi River, which had been designated as *Indian Territory:* gold-free Indian-territory. Who in Europe, by whatever course of communication, knew of these forced displacements of around 60,000 indigenous people? Who had heard of their struggles along what has become known as the Trail of Tears, where members of the Cherokee, the Muscogee (aka Creek), the Seminole, Chickasaw and Choctaw nations died of starvation while en route to their new "home"?

Naturally this was only one instance of oppression in what could be – if one chose to record them – an almost endless litany of universal inhumanity; and you might wonder, especially when few people then anywhere around the globe had any "rights," why this example may have had any particular significance. It is, of course, mentioned for a reason which will become apparent subsequently.

Whilst we may be lured or enticed into thinking that our modern world has changed enormously, it might be prudent to take a step back.

In many ways the change is purely superficial, and what is presented to us as evidence of our humane civilised society often does not stand up to scrutiny. When the sanitised headlines have faded different realities emerge. Most country's interventions then become barely indistinguishable from just overt exercises in "Might is Right" where black-gold (oil) and now rare-earth materials are there for the taking. (Cf the Iraq War, the Libyan regime change etc. Ukraine/the Donetsk Oblast? Taiwan??) We may officially decry the actions of others, such as the invasion of Ukraine by Russia, but our country and its allies still have plenty of recent blood on their own hands – blood more often spilt on behalf of oil magnates and multinational companies and corporations than to protect the vulnerable. Bosnia may be a rare example of apparent altruism, but I wonder if this opinion will hold up in the future when classified documents eventually are safely released. The adjective "safely", that is, refers to a time when all the beneficiaries and enthusiastic proponents involved are safely dead and beyond being held to account.

So we may not be able to adequately gauge foreign policies of more recent and current governments, but history has shown that vested interest and greed operated ruthlessly throughout the 19th and 20th centuries. The actions of Britain's leaders in the Great Brutal Empire on which the sun never set are right to be condemned, but they weren't on their own. Greed has no particular nationality, no borders or boundaries.

The division of lands into states and countries were especially artificial in the continent of Africa. There, straight lines still abound on maps: the historical result of the late 19th century "race for Africa" where borders were cut imperially through culturally, religiously and ethnically homogenous communities. France, Italy, Germany, Belgium, Holland Spain, Portugal and Britain were amongst those vying for big slices of African land and resources. Of course, the ramifications of those unnatural geographic divisions – those scars of empire-builders - still cause problems and wars.

The lines were the only thing straight about the people who designed this situation for their own ends, for the profits which continue to be wrought and for the monies that are still diverted from the natural population. Lengthy occupation, the harvesting of resources and the plunder of heritage may in the end prove to be temporary in the grander scheme of things, but maltreatment of the weak, in varying degrees of barbarity, is an on-going problem. It has not been confined to one continent.

However, before a nation can export its own terror it must be secure at home, and Britain's population had been subdued. If its people were not content to live under the cosh, they didn't show it very often. They appear to have also bought into the might of England as a super-power and were primed to swallow the "**we** are the great British Empire" con hook, line and sinker. Perhaps they felt they were still doing better than others. Remarkably that sentiment still lives on in many inexplicably proud quarters of the country. Proud and down-trodden... yet still - weirdly - optimistic and sometimes positive...

For some reason, this reminds me of the comedian, Jeff Innocent, a Newham resident, who observed that in a recent survey Newham had been voted the 29th happiest borough out of 30 London boroughs. Generously, he said, "It's those poor sods in Brent I feel sorry for..."

Nevertheless, in the 19th century, and great Empires apart, and all the while, Britons in a prosperous motherland were living in pretty dire conditions.

THE RISE IN URBAN POPULATION

In 1841 the Baxters were living in Somers Town which was described as being "thickly inhabited." That area was not alone in such density: all towns and cities had succumbed to the great influx of populations from country areas. Some of those people were attracted to the availability of jobs in the industrialised centres while a great many were driven by forces beyond their control. High on the list of those forces was the process of "enclosure" which over time increasingly ended the traditional rights of country folk to have access to common land formerly held in the open field system.

With enclosure they no longer had rights to use that land, by which the livelihoods and household economies of small-holders and landless labourers subsisted and their survival depended. The shrinkage of land which they had access to had been a long process, sometimes with slow incremental change and sometimes it was a brutally rapid progression as was occasioned by greater enclosure.

Rights that had been won in the 13th century were eroded particularly during the 16th, and this was on-going such that by the 19th most of the unenclosed commons were large rough pastures in difficult if not inaccessible terrain. They survived on the high ground of Northern England, as well as on the Fens, but only relatively few small parcels of common land were left in lowland settings and these included many village greens across England and Wales. Enclosure and the advent of farm machinery led to different farming practices, which increased production enough to impact on the need for labour. Suddenly, many workers were surplus to agricultural requirements.

So, enclosure was not only one of the causes of the agricultural revolution but it was also a major factor in the migration of labour from rural areas into industrial and urban settings.

One source describes the methods by which enclosure of common land was accomplished: the ground rights and all common rights could simply be bought at a price beyond the pockets of the landless, but which was less than what the value of the land grew to afterwards. Alternatively the law was used to cause or compel enclosure, (such as by parliamentary enclosure) which was "sometimes accompanied by force, resistance, and bloodshed." It "remains among the most controversial areas of agricultural and economic history in England." [20]

The people of England and Britain were allowed a very limited liberty during the preceding centuries and throughout the Victorian era; they had been subjugated by outright brutality, with a complicit church, and by laws which protected the wealthy and powerful.

In order to understand the exodus from the land into the towns and cities it is necessary to know how the political and social system of the country and the countryside operated, and how it had developed.

---

[20] https://courses.lumenlearning.com/suny-hccc-worldhistory2/chapter/the-enclosure-act/

FEUDALISM

The dominant social system in medieval Europe, known to us as feudalism, was a spectacularly *anti-social* system operated by a hierarchy of thugs. At the top of the pile was the boss of bosses - the gang-leader or the leading gangster: the King, and his family. This *capo di tutti capi* in England ran a brutal organisation which efficiently controlled all levels within society by fear, terror and intimidation and by the laws he made. (In time in England this gang would style themselves as *the Crown*.)

While the gangland family had its own lands it allowed the next strata beneath them to also hold lands according to some conditions and maybe for some other consideration - what mobsters of today might call a slice of the action. These were their henchmen who are known historically as the nobility, and they were assured they would be able to operate their own rackets and would not be molested as long as they provided military back-up when the King required it (for example, when he desired to threaten or kill some insurrectionists at home or when he went stealing abroad). In this way favour was bestowed downwards through a chain, while a proportion of wealth in money, goods and services returned steadily up the chain.

Thus, the nobles controlled and sub-let lands to lower grade tenants, known as vassals, who in turn controlled those beneath them - the peasants (described as villeins or serfs) at the bottom of the pile. The peasants were obliged to live on their lord's land and were compelled to pay him homage, to give him both their labour and a share of the produce they had reared or cultivated. (I imagine one might have to possess an extraordinary level of gullibility to imagine the peasant enjoyed the lion's share.) The peasant rendered all these services notionally in exchange for "military protection": today such a scheme would rather more simply be called a protection racket.

Other conditions prevailed, for example: a male peasant wishing to marry also had to pay merchet to his lord– this was a fine or a tax which had to be paid for the privilege of his consent. Merchets were variously said to "compensate" the lord for the loss of a female worker's output, while other sources interpret it as payment for the droit du signeur to be waived.

(The droit du signeur was reputedly the right of the lord to rape a peasant's bride on the wedding night. The official church also had a finger in that pie: it was said to have prohibited sex / consummation of the marriage on the first night, unless an "indulgence" was paid which could waive the prohibition. Kings, Lords and churchmen... nice people?)

Magna Carta. Really?

Feudalism and this state of affairs all trundled on nicely for those at the top except for the bump in the road which was Magna Carta, signed on the 15th of June 1215. Taught in British schools as being the great day for the freedom and liberty of Englishmen it more accurately was a deal forced on the King by the nobles to cut them – the earls and barons – a bigger slice of the cake.

In order to avert a civil war with his own barons he signed the Charter, which declared that from then on all men were equal under the law – even the King! Well, if you believe that was ever likely then leave some biscuits out for Father Christmas and leave a note to ask him to say hello to the Tooth Fairy...

Magna Carta was originally known as the Articles of the Barons, and it specifically related only to "free" men – essentially the barons and noblemen themselves: not to those lower orders. It has also been judged that "... what happened in 1215 was that the kingdom turned around and told the king to obey his own rules." [21]

According to the New Yorker magazine, the single thing that most Americans were likely to remember about Magna Carta from their High School History class was that Oliver Cromwell supposedly called it "Magna Farta." It added that he also called the Petition of Right (1628) the "Petition of Shite." [22]

COMMON LAND AND THE CHARTER OF THE FORESTS

In contrast to Magna Carta, the Charter of the Forest of 1217, asserted the rights of those without property, the rights of the commoners, and of the "commons." It was probably more important and of greater significance to the ordinary person than the much lauded Magna Carta. [23]

All Acts of Parliament and legislation tend to be unreadable to those whom the law mostly affects... and I am not convinced that is just a coincidence, but then again that might just be my suspicious class-paranoia at work. Unsurprisingly I found even transcriptions of the actual Charter similarly difficult.

---

[21] David Carpenter, a professor of medieval history at King's College, London, explains in "Magna Carta" (Penguin Classics) reported in the New Yorker by Jill Lepore. April 13, 2015

[22] Ibid. (By Jill Lepore April 13, 2015) That petition had been sent by the English Parliament to King Charles I seeking sought recognition of four principles: no taxation without the consent of Parliament, no imprisonment without cause, no quartering of soldiers on subjects, and no martial law in peacetime.

[23] The Charter of the Forest apparently has the distinction of having been on the statute books for longer than any other piece of legislation. It was repealed 754 years later, in 1971, by a Tory government. Of course.

The Act itself is full of arcane terminology, as well as containing words which are seemingly familiar but whose meaning differs in varying degrees from modern interpretations. For example, we currently take the simple word "*Forest*" as referring to an ecosystem where trees are the dominant life-form among both plant and animal systems: all thriving in a series of complex organic relationships. (Or maybe you just think: trees...) You might also assume that earlier bods could just have wandered into a forest and enjoyed some of the fruits within, or had been able to trap a rabbit or perhaps even to catch a fish for their meal; however, those rights were strictly controlled, with severe penalties for transgression. To understand those, it is necessary to fully comprehend the terminology of the time.

In those earlier times, *Forest*, was a specification not just of the land in an enclosed area, it also referred to the flora and fauna within, and to all rights associated with them. One specific meaning was that some thug-buddy of the King was allowed - by the monarch- exclusive rights to everything in the Forest. The land within might also be designated to be the thugs' own private hunting lands, separate from those of the King, and those areas would be called *chases,* thus cf. Cannock Chase. *Forest*, therefore, referred both to those animals, which might be kept or hunted in the chase (such as fallow deer, roe deer, fox, marten etc.) as well as to the greenery (*vert*) upon which they fed (such as the leaves, the berries, the fruit, nuts and fungi). "*Forest*" also referred to large areas known as *commons* that further included heath land, grassland and wetlands, and which were or could be productive of food, or could provide grazing and other resources. It was, therefore, quite an extensive and all-encompassing term, and its roots dated back to 1066, when William the Conqueror not only distributed parts of the *commons* to his bunch of marauding bandits but also scooped up large tracts for himself and turned them into 'royal forests.' These "*Royal Forests*" i.e. those hunting preserves owned by the King, took up one-third of all the land. Whilst people lived in settlements around the forest and used the land for grazing their animals and growing crops they were restricted as to what they could do there, on the common land and within the forests.

The Charter restored the area classified as "forest" to that of Henry II's time and protected common pasture in the forest for all those "accustomed to it." It thus achieved a reversal, which forced the then current monarch to recognise the right of free men to pursue their livelihoods in forests. It had considered all the conditions that applied to areas of forest and to the commons, which covered esoteric terms such as: *pasturage,* (the right to pasture animals viz to let sheep graze there); *"pannage"* (the feeding of pigs off the land) and *agistment* (which refers to the care of cattle and horses for money that included their grazing). Within its scope also was *turbary* (the cutting of turf and the right to take peat for fuel), as well as *estover*: the collection of wood to be used for heating or making fires to cook upon. It further encompassed even the cuttings from trees which had been coppiced and *pollarded,* i.e. cut back to encourage the growth of new, straight stems. (Forest owners were jealous of every part of the *forest* and of all the cuttings which could be utilised in any way, including them being used to make wooden hurdles - frameworks of interwoven branches that were usually used for enclosing land or livestock. The saying "they wouldn't give you the drippings of their noses" comes to mind.) The Charter also referred to the right to dig and use clay, which might be used to make pots and utensils or for housing and shelter. The rights considered also the right to fish, the right to water, and even the right to pick fruit and take honey.

The Charter seems to allow free men certain rights, but still under condition. It also limited the action and penalties for going into the forests and for using the resources there, such that a transgressor no longer was liable to execution or mutilation, but instead could be fined or imprisoned. Certain classes were allowed to take some resources as long as they blew a horn to alert foresters and verderers they were present and so doing. Other conditions applied to the animals owned by common people/ ordinary visitors, such as their dogs, pigs, and sheep. Dogs could be taken into the forest, but they had to have claws removed to prevent them being able to be used to hunt *venison* (this term did not just mean deer, but any meat from any animal). At the heart of the Charter is the concept of the ***commons*** and the need to protect them and to compensate commoners for their loss.

Reports suggest that for hundreds of years this Charter, being more applicable to the peasants, had to be read out in every church in England four times a year. Thus it restored to the common man some real rights, privileges and protections against the encroaching abuses of an avaricious aristocracy, but I imagine the purpose of a quarterly reading was to remind the congregation of what they were (and were not) allowed to do and to re-state the penalties for transgression. I do not believe Magna Carta, which dealt with the rights of the robber class of earls and barons, ever featured in a Sunday reading. (Even the notion of Magna Carta, and its' supposed importance, was only taken up centuries later.)

Of course the Charter has been under constant threat for centuries. For example, Henry VIII confiscated ten million acres of land largely for himself, but he also dished them out to his favourites – as his closest henchmen were known. Importantly, Guy Standing [24] notes that their descendants still possess

---

24 6th November 2017 OPENDEMOCRACY

hundreds of thousands of acres. This source also asserts that the Enclosures Act of 1845 was another huge land-grab.

Meanwhile, the commons have continued to attract the eyes of asset-strippers and have been further eroded: the commons also included the 400,000 acres of land that were hived off by Margaret Thatcher when she gave the waterways to private companies in 1989. [25]

CONTROL IN THE 19TH CENTURY

Now, of course, feudalism and its subsequent intricacies and later manifestations directly affected the lives of Francis Baxter's ancestors; but the accumulated machinations of the forces of control (the monarchy, the aristocrats, the Church, nobility and landed gentry) would continue to play their part in the lives of Francis Baxter and his common ilk (and of their descendants). The Baxters may have walked the streets of Somers Town oblivious to that history, but they still did so nevertheless in the shadow of a well-honed if slightly less overt tyranny. [26]

It has to be admitted that the system has been admirably and carefully controlled; and whilst feudalism in England

---

25 Guy Standing produces some interesting information. He states that in the 110 years between 1760 and 1870, a land-owning elite instituted over 4,000 Acts of Parliament, which managed to confiscate seven million acres of commons. He said, "It is no exaggeration to say that the land ownership structure of Britain today is the result of organised theft."

26 The system now is even more refined. It affects a sophisticated air of tolerance, while keeping everything under surveillance: free-speech is allowed – as long as no action is taken or promoted which might actually threaten to change anything. Cf Emma Goldman, Tony Benn

apparently ended in centuries long gone by the racket has always bent with the times and has continued to endure successfully.

Reform

Change has been the drip-drip of gradual refinements which were necessary for Crown and nobility (seated and housed in parliaments) to maintain control. Those adaptive measures, which had been needed to ensure survival of the system, are always lauded as representing the deliverance of greater freedom and liberty. The false implication is ever that these would be freedoms to be enjoyed by the ordinary populace. Such a measure was the first Reform Act of 1830 which merely and only slightly broadened the electorate. Nevertheless most 19th century Britons had no representative government and still had very few rights. This was the normality faced by the Baxters and their class of ordinary common people.

However, whilst arrant feudalism was apparently dead in Britain, medieval attitudes persisted in other countries where similar practices, such as serfdom, continued to be inflicted upon the majority of their population. Serfdom differed from direct slavery in that individual people were not exactly slaves (who could be bought or sold *individually*), but they were instead an integral part of property or land: in this way they were part of the parcel, and remained with the land no matter who it was sold to. Of course, the serf had no right to leave their situation.... (and it was said that wasn't slavery! Perhaps they were enslaved prisoners...)

Serfdom was not only, as you might suspect, applied in far off China, but it lived on in Russia, Hungary, Romania, Austria and even in the home-state of Queen Victoria's Consort (Prince Albert): in Saxe-Coburg-Gotha.

The Napoleonic Code

Alongside the schema of control the force of European history was also at work. First there was the French Revolution, and then there was Napoleon...

The British have always hated the French, and have been encouraged to do so (and still are today overtly in the tabloid press and slightly more craftily in the broadsheets.) The powers that be particularly hated Napoleon, although quite how he would have adversely affected the mass of the English population is something quite beyond me.

Those in control especially hated the Napoleonic Code which aimed to regularise a universal civil code of laws, rights and responsibilities that granted freedoms, liberties and equalities that were applicable to every man, no matter what their class or rank. Vested interests don't like such things because codification and reform tends to encroach upon their privileges and rackets. They sell "regulation" as an interference: it is "just so much red tape" which stops them making money, for example by preventing them selling contaminated goods for human consumption... or perhaps getting rid of that red tape might allow workers and your children (not their offspring) to work in dangerous conditions....

Absolute power

Throughout the 18th and 19th centuries there were also *absolute monarchs*, as the Tsars were in Russia. These tyrants held unchallengeable absolute power and could imprison or execute anyone without trial and on a whim: the victims could have been revolutionaries or simply someone who had displeased the monarch. It may also have been because they were related to such a miscreant and they were, therefore, abused or killed as an example and as a warning. Such absolute powers did not then exist in Great Britain, and we did have rights under the Habeus Corpus Act, which theoretically prevented imprisonment without trial. This, however, has always been suspended whenever it has become inconvenient to the ruling class. [Habeus Corpus, like the Human Rights Act continues to be presented by the right wing again as merely "red tape" holding "everyone" (i.e. them) back.]

It was also only in the 1830's and 40's that the death penalty was removed here as punishment for over 100 offences, such as theft of goods valued at more than a shilling, poaching, stealing a sheep and many more minor offences. (There is a small section on this called Capital Punishment and the Bloody Code.)

So naturally whilst the State had eased back on what crimes or misdemeanours they might execute someone for committing, it still held great punitive powers against those ordinary people, especially workers who wanted to improve their conditions.

After the French revolution the British government (and most European governments) were on hyper alert for signs of rebellion and subversion. They saw and feared the latter in the formation of Trade Unions. Of course, at the time such organisations were termed as "combinations" of workers, and the government had promptly passed Acts of Parliament in 1799 and 1800 which apparently made such combinations illegal.

Combinations were actually already illegal under both common law and statute; in fact, most anti-union prosecutions which took place relied on those longer established legal restraints (such as breach of contract, the 1563 Statute of Artificers - punishing unfinished work – and under the common law). Of course, when all else fails they had their favourite act of last resort: the old catch-all chestnut of "conspiracy." It has been noted that the Combination Acts were thus nothing exceptional, but instead were intended to simplify and speed up prosecution by summary trial.

While the Acts also banned combinations of employers as well, in practice they were used only against workers. A sop for the workers was that the 1800 Act prohibited employers from acting as magistrates in cases involving their own trade, which would have been a piss-take too far and could have led to greater unrest. It is interesting that they were sufficiently aware of this.

The Acts of 1799-1880 were instigated by William Wilberforce – so, the apparent hero abolitionist was not such a wonderful guy... His plan was carried through and the Act led to a ban on all combinations, and restricted what workers could do: it became illegal for them to "combine" or join together in an effort to offer their labour at a higher rate or for them to try to better their working conditions. They could neither encourage anyone to stop working nor refuse to work with others. They also were not permitted to attend meetings or collect funds for illegal purposes. (Illegal meant anything to do with being a trade union.)

The aspirations of the ordinary working man continued to be thwarted, whilst those of the ordinary working woman did not even feature... By the means at their disposal the government and employers were able to induce a climate of fear among workers and of confidence among employers. Regardless of the actual number of prosecutions under the acts, the threat of being individually targeted or prosecuted was very real for a worker whether or not legal action was ever taken. [27] In 1824, though, and due to the efforts of Francis Place and Joseph Hume, the Acts were repealed; however, jubilation, if such was felt, was premature: the State was not quite prepared to just roll over and instead another Combination Act (1825) then restricted the right to withdraw labour not only in the furtherance of seeking better remuneration but also of trying to prevent wage reductions.

In addition trade-union organizers could still be prosecuted under older laws as was evidenced by the plight of the Tolpuddle Martyrs. In 1834 six agricultural labourers from the village of Tolpuddle in Dorset had formed a trade union lodge and sworn an oath of loyalty to this group, which allowed the authorities to prosecute them under an Act of 1797 that forbade "unlawful oaths." They were sentenced to seven years' transportation. Although unions were no longer illegal, and the Tolpuddle men had sought only to resist a reduction in wages, the government were fearful of rural unrest, which had elsewhere led to rick-burning and machine-breaking: the tactics of Captain Swing and of the Luddites.

---

27 The same principle applies when police employ snatch-squads to pluck out individuals from groups of demonstrators: it disrupts the collective element.

Captain Swing may or may not have been an actual person, but his spectre embodied a proactive movement which employed hit and run guerrilla tactics against employers and farm owners. The Swing Riots of 1830 in southern and eastern England centred on breaking threshing machines and was an agricultural variant of the Luddite threat. Whilst Ludd may have been a real person, in popular culture a focal fictional persona was created around him: for one side he was a rallying figure and for the other he was a Bogeyman and an excuse for draconian responses. The creation, Ned Ludd, was considered responsible for the widespread actions carried out by aggrieved workers who operated against industry, factories and mills, mainly attacking and destroying machines in the midlands and in the north of England. So, spectres of 'King' Lud(d) and Captain Swing both served mutual purposes. [28]

The resulting harsh sentence meted out to the men of Tolpuddle managed to provoke petitions and mass demonstrations and two years later the six were pardoned. Many other workers were transported in that time, but the Tolpuddle Martyrs continue to steal the headlines.

---

[28] Real or fictional, a central character allows governments and employers opportunities to undermine, to smear, to falsely accuse the individual of corruption and illegality, to try to create a distance between leader and follower. Those tactics are regularly employed: with just enough success against Arthur Scargill of the NUM and other Union leaders; whereas, frustratingly for the government, an unaffiliated Mick Lynch of the RMT does not present as a credible target. The unruffled personification of reasonableness he presents as merely following the instructions and mandate of his members and has steadfastly refused to appear to be rabble-rousing. It must be infuriating for them. It is unlikely, however, the powers that be will be content to let that situation continue without some chicanery being invoked.

[29]

Ordinary people at the beginning of the 19th century had no rights and no way to change or improve their circumstances, but as the aforementioned actions and protests indicate this did not mean they all happily complied. There were rumblings of discontent. Events such as the French Revolution had shaken the tree and everyone had noticed: monarchies throughout Europe, governments, rulers and the barons all woke up to new possibilities and as to how these might threaten their positions. The lower orders were, though, gradually becoming driven by desperation more than by any ideological dream, but either impetus still posed a threat to the established order and discontent and unrest had to be dealt with one way or another.

The political instability was seeded by many causes: hunger and famine, high food prices and low wages coupled with the advent of industrialisation; these were compounded by the invention of new technologies and processes. All these factors in turn further reduced wages and created unemployment, which fuelled more poverty and hunger.

The production of textiles for example, was scaled up as a result of these inventions into a full-blown textile industry during the 18th century. The irrevocable change began in 1733 with John Kay's *flying shuttle*, which enabled cloth to be woven faster, and allowed the process to later be mechanised. Refinements of water-powered systems and then the introduction of steam power coupled with improvements in iron foundry processes further drove cloth production away from the simple cottage-industry of

---

[29] In fact, two of my maternal grandmother's kin had been caught up in the Swing Riots of the 1830's and had been sentenced to death for machine-breaking. This was Isaac and John Mann from Andover: their death sentences were, though, commuted to transportation to Australia.

mainly individual workers. Subsequent inventions such as Hargreaves' Spinning Jenny (1764), Arkwright's water frame (1769) and Crompton's Spinning Mule increased the size of the plant and henceforward the operations needed to be incorporated and housed in the new mills and manufactories. The efficiencies achieved destroyed the livelihoods of the individual skilled artisan. Each change and new invention like the power looms meant that textiles could be produced both faster and cheaper because the machines could now be operated by less-skilled, low-wage labourers. (Intricacies of pattern were also made possible by Jacquard's "programmable" loom.) The mills would go on to employ huge numbers of men, women and children. And all were relatively low paid. Similar innovations and improvements also occurred within farming and agriculture, which resulted in greater mechanisation that impacted on employment and wages.

All these factors led to growing, albeit slow-burning industrial and agricultural unrest in Britain.

In the same way that I was taught in economics at school that an acceptable level of unemployment was 500,000 people – a figure far more acceptable to those in employment than to those without work - poverty is similarly more generally tolerable for those not in want. Desperate poverty, though, has a potential to inspire insurrection, a state which the wealthier, who have the most to lose, naturally find threatening. Normal reaction to any stirrings in Francis Baxter's time was usually extremely harsh but they were now more wary.

The discontent which had culminated in revolution in France led those with wealth and power to a new-found appreciation of a need for some change and reform. Whilst they didn't want change and reform, they were even less keen on the alternative. They would implement some change, but only to the degree that any threat could still be controlled. Of course, this was easier for them than for the Bourbon aristocrats and monarchy because firstly they were not as recklessly stupid as them, and secondly they had learned from their mistakes. As history and current affairs show, they were also helped because the English are far more malleable and used to being contained than their French counterparts. They would give a little, but only as much as made very little actual difference.

CHARTISM

This was a period when the Chartists were at their most active in calling for constitutional change and reform. Whilst they organised mass petitions and demonstrations they were not successful in the short-term. The six reforms identified by the Chartists to make the political system more democratic were initially successfully resisted, but eventually and after the Stonemason was dead – in case you were inclined to think it happened overnight or within decades - five would be adopted. 1: A vote for every man, aged twenty-one years and above, with the proviso they were of sound mind, and not undergoing punishment for a crime. 2: Votes to be cast in a secret ballot to protect the elector. 3: The removal of property qualification for Members of Parliament (MPs), to allow the constituencies to return the man of their choice irrespective of his wealth. 4: Payment of MP's, to enable persons of modest means to leave or interrupt their livelihood to attend to the interests of the nation. 5: The division of constituencies into more equal sizes, and thus doing away with rotten boroughs. [30]

---

[30] Those eventually were achieved. They had also called for Annual Parliamentary elections, in which I am glad they were not successful. I don't think I could stand being lied to that consistently.

The Chartists were not alone: there were also other new ideas and political ideologies emerging: calls for greater liberty, for rights and equalities. These, though, were not a serious threat to the wealthy and to those in control and nor would they be as long as power was wielded ruthlessly and carefully. They had learnt from some of the mistakes of the Bourbons, and managed their situation very much better.

The extent of the general population's political awareness or how much of the bigger picture was known to the ordinary man and woman in the early to mid-19th century is unknowable. Their access to information and to broad and lengthy formal education was nothing like we in the UK currently enjoy or is apparently available. Not that this access and provision has created much discernable astuteness or awareness in the public at large in the 20th and 21st centuries.

Some might feel this is an immense testament to the malign efficacy of media which is mostly influenced and controlled by vested interest.

Prior to widespread literacy and to the revolution in printing technologies which facilitated the easy availability of newspapers and books, information was passed by pamphlets, leaflets and by word of mouth. General information, including gossip of course, was conveyed mostly in conversations and spread, as it were, along the grapevine; but there were also *town criers*, men officially employed to literally declare important news and cry out announcements to the people of the town. As many people could not read or write, these men were historically authorised to deliver government and royal Proclamations, and to give information about local by-laws, market days and events. At a suitably busy time the Town Crier would appear at a prominent public place which was usually the market square or a busy corner; he would then ring a hand-bell to gain the public's attention whilst loudly calling out, "Oyez, Oyez, Oyez," before making his announcements. The word "Oyez" means "hear ye." ([31])

---

31 Amongst the organised amusement and entertainment offered at Butlin's Holiday Camps' post WW2 they included a competition for the best Town Crier. This light-hearted relief survived at least into the 1960's and 70's.

Butlin's customers were the post-War (WWII) working class, and the camps provided music, dancing, variety shows and games for all their families. They also ran beauty contests for younger single ladies and Glamorous Granny competitions for older women. In addition there were talent contests, fancy dress contests, yard-of-ale drinking contests and other sporting competitions such as: for football matches, snooker, table-tennis, lawn tennis, and darts for adults. It provided many activities, amusements and contests also for children. Cheap package holidays abroad (and in sunnier climes) led to a big decline in this type of holiday/entertainment.

Also known as the Bellman the Town Crier had other duties, which included attending public hangings to read out the order of execution: why the person was being hanged. It was said (See Ellen Castelow) he would also help to cut down the deceased. Inevitably, as other means of communication came to the fore, the role would mainly fade into the mist of time but their presence is still to be found at different ceremonials, fetes and village events. The City of Chester currently employs the last remaining official Town Crier, although these days he (or she) only assists in the execution of communication duties. Traditionally the Crier wears boots, breeches, a bright distinctive coat and a tricorn hat.

At the start of the 19th century, the highest-circulation newspaper in the United Kingdom was the Morning Post, which sold around 4,000 copies per day. By 1850, though, sales of *The Times* were around 40,000 per day nationally which was about 80% of the entire daily newspaper market. The well-to-do and middle classes may have taken a daily newspaper, but these publications were not especially cheap – they also incurred a specific Newspaper Tax; consequently their target audience was not the ordinary people. While the literacy rates of the general populace were low, you may wonder would even the literate ordinary person have splashed out money - for mere news – when precious funds were needed to put enough food on the family table? (Newspapers then carried little news on its front page, which instead included many diverse individual adverts: you had to buy it to open it for the news. Some 21st century newspapers are now operated by media moguls and their corporations to foghorn their own brand of self-interest and politics, and to influence democracy and politics. They fund, where necessary, individual politicians or whole political parties, and derive income from charging its advertisers to promote their wares and services. They are free to the public, but given modern information streams you might ask would they be able to actually "sell" some of those free newspapers now?)

It was common then for establishments like hotels and inns to provide newspapers for their clientele to read, although I doubt their clientele would have often included the poor working man.

Even given access to wider news – both national and international – I wonder would much of it have interested (or been felt to concern) the average working man and woman. What news would have been important to them? They surely weren't holding their breath for someone to ameliorate their poor circumstances: little or no relief was on its way to them in this life – and they knew it. They endured.

This is not a particular slight on those Victorians, for indeed in this 21st century people can still be extremely insular and both reluctant and resistant to the charms of broader education: you can take a horse to water (to the well of knowledge and information, perhaps) but you can't make him drink.

THAT WAS THEN. WHAT ABOUT NOW ?

On a note about awareness, education and knowledge I do not know how the British would currently do if tested. I suspect we may be a little better than our backwoods/backward American cousins but then again.... one never knows.

The National Geographic–Roper 2002 Global Geographic Literacy Survey interviewed 3000 18-24 year olds from the US, Britain, Sweden and France. It found that:

> *About 11% of the surveyed Americans couldn't even locate the U.S. on a map. (The GREATEST NATION ON EARTH?) The Pacific Ocean's location was also a mystery to 29 % of them.*

Almost one-third of those young U.S. citizens polled said that the U.S. population was between one billion and two billion; 20 years later, and with growth, the actual number is still only around 330 million people.

In 2003 a US Strategic Task Force on Education Abroad concluded that the US "has a serious deficit in global competence" and that "geographic ignorance is so deep and widespread that it may constitute a national security threat." (Wider ignorance was surely evidenced in the January 2021 attack on the Capitol.)

They say that travel broadens the mind. In 1994 only 10% of US citizens were recorded as owning a passport. Whilst the number is currently about 40% the increase did not arise from any sudden overwhelming urge to explore the world; it was fuelled by terror attacks, which shocked a country more used to dishing them out than to receiving them. The increase was in part the result of the 9/11 experience which led to restrictions in regards to travel: these made it necessary to have a passport to go across the land borders to visit Canada and Mexico. Not to go to Europe ... wherever that may be.

THIRSTING... FOR KNOWLEDGE?

What the common people of the Victorian age did drink, though, became of great concern to many of the shakers and movers of their time.

In fact the morals of the general public in this neck of Christendom tended to excite sections of elite society and the governing classes, who were not especially renowned themselves for self-control. Nevertheless, the perceived physical and moral health of the common people led to various legislation aimed at improvement of the lower orders. Ordinary people needed to be distracted from drunkenness and debauchery apparently, and the generally well-meaning temperance movement was very vocal and active in their attempts to get people away from drinking emporiums and other morally low dens of iniquity. Increased drunkenness was held to lead to more crime, more prostitution and other social ills and temptations: the vices of intoxication, as J S Buckingham, MP and supporter of temperance, put it. (Others might have agreed that whilst this would be beneficial to the lower classes per se, it might also make it easier for them to be controlled.)

It was suggested that their free time could be better spent in more sober activities, for example in educating themselves; and since the poor and ordinary folk like the Baxters could ill-afford to purchase newspapers and books the notion of Public Lending Libraries began to grow.

Libraries

Libraries, Reading rooms and wider education had been advocated by the great social reformer, Francis Place. He had joined the London Corresponding Society, which was a federation of reading and debating clubs that encouraged the participation of working men (such as artisans, tradesmen, and shopkeepers). Place started the London Working-men's Association, which was targeted at skilled workers rather than the mass of unskilled and factory labourers. It was also a foundational organisation of the Chartist movement, and Place associated with many of the leading philosophers, theorists and reformers of the day (such as William Godwin, John Stuart Mill, Robert Owen, Jeremy Bentham, Joseph Hume, Rowland Detrosier and scholar and economist Thomas Malthus). He also lobbied successfully for the 1824 repeal of the Combination Act, which helped early Trade Unionism.

The Public Libraries Act of 1850, which was introduced by William Ewart, gave local boroughs the power to establish free public libraries. This allowed municipal boroughs in England and Wales to establish public library facilities and staffing using funds raised from the rates. This, however, was capped at a maximum of half a penny in the pound and it did not allow them to buy books and other materials under the same provision. (See Historic England)

When the first purpose-made library was built in 1857 in Norwich many others may have been anticipated, but just a dribble of additions would be created before Elementary Education Act was enacted in 1870. This Act was the first real attempt by the state to achieve a level of universal literacy in England, and it may have further encouraged the growth of public libraries. A big boost came in the 1880's when philanthropists like Andrew Carnegie began to have an impact with vast endowments of their wealth. (Newspapers would later become available in Public Libraries.)

It would eventually lead to the creation of a national network which continues to provide universal free access to information and literature.

(In the early 21st century - as paper books have given way to computerised information sources - these buildings currently also house computer terminals and hold audio/ video records of music, literature and film. They are now often designated not as Libraries but as Ideas Rooms or Ideas Spaces.) [32]

---

32 Ewart also advocated the blue plaque system of linking houses with their former notable residents. His statue is in the Liverpool Oratory, his portrait in the National Portrait Gallery, and his blue plaque outside his former home which is now the Hampton Library in Richmond upon Thames.

Literacy 1800-1870

The absence of a national education system meant that it would always be difficult to assess the levels of literacy within the country. Lloyd (2007) states that, "as late as the 1850s, approximately half of all children in England and Wales attended no school - (other than Sunday school). Day schools were not as popular as Sunday schools for working-class children, as they charged fees and operated during the week." Economic necessity compelled poor families to send their children to work, rather than to school. In addition to this the average length of attendance was only around three years so even those attendees were unlikely to achieve significant level of educational attainment.

The declared rates of literacy elsewhere were estimations based upon examinations of church records for marriages, and were extrapolated from the number of brides and grooms who either signed their name or left their mark. It was unreliable since those able to sign did not necessarily have skill much beyond that: they had learned how to form their own name, but could they actually read a page from the Bible or from a newspaper? There are suggestions, though, that people who were not necessarily capable of physically writing did in fact read. This was because it was apparently usual in the eighteenth century for reading to be taught before writing. The need to write was not as important in the main as the need to read; consequently, even if you could read or write or not, X marked the spot and was sufficient to signify acknowledgement and agreement. While their writing skills may have been confined to a simple signature, this ability often was an indicator that the person could read.

Subsequent examinations of those parish registers nevertheless have shown a trend towards greater literacy: whilst in 1800 illiteracy was *"measured"* in England and Wales at around 40 percent of males and 60 percent of females, by 1840 an improvement had been noted: one third of all grooms and half of all brides were then deemed illiterate by virtue that they appeared not to be able to sign their names at marriage. By 1870, the findings were said to indicate that only 20% of men and 25% of women were then illiterate. What literature we might ask did those potential readers have access to? A bible - if they possessed one?

Of course, positive moves had been made to improve literacy amongst the population. The motive for these is debateable: it could be argued that as the franchise was extended and more people could vote it became ever more pressing that they cast their vote in a way which suited the ruling classes. Others declare that the development of public education grew in parallel to reform legislation and in response to the growing needs of an industrialised and commercial society, where increasingly records and ledgers had to be kept. I suspect both are true.

The shift away from an agrarian to an industrial, manufacturing and commercial economy in particular had exposed the level of the deficiency in literacy. This had highlighted the potential impact on the country and to its coffers: a good deal of the workforce was not fit for purpose as they were adjudged to be in rival economies. Subsequently schooling became more widely promoted with an emphasis placed on simply learning to read and write with some basic numeracy skills.

While there remained no unified education system, there were some activities and services provided by the Church and by some independent schools who charged fees. Of course the poor were both reluctant and mainly unable to pay, and I imagine their reluctance would have been less if their income had been more. Gradually, though, more and more children were compelled to attend school, but they were still not entirely free to their parents.

In 1870, the Forster Elementary Education Act established partially state-funded Board Schools to provide primary education in areas where existing provisions were inadequate, but they still charged a fee, which many poor families could not pay. Alternative solutions came in the form of makeshift schools such as ragged and dame schools. By 1880, additional legislation stated that compulsory attendance at school ceased to be a matter for local option. Children now had to attend school between the ages of 5 and 10, with only some seasonal exceptions granted in agricultural areas. (There is a statue of William Edward Forster in the grounds of Victoria Embankment Gardens.)

In 1891, the Free Education Act provided for the state payment of school fees up to ten shillings per week. This was to help poor children attend school. By 1893 the school leaving age was raised first to 11, and then later again to 13. In 1897, the Voluntary Schools Act provided grants to public elementary schools not funded by school boards, which were typically Church schools. At the close of the 19th century illiteracy rates for both sexes are said to have dropped to around 3 percent. (Lloyd 2007)

The Church of England, which for good reason, has widely been known as the Tory Party at Prayer, delivered a scriptural and mainly right-wing education stripped of any of Christ's socialistic tendencies or doctrines. The purpose of the education provided was to promote compliance and to maintain the existing order. It discouraged students from thinking for themselves – and was little short of pure indoctrination.

Thus, religion and tightly regulated education worked in concert and were both very efficient at socially and politically controlling the greater part of the population, whilst allowing a certain class of individuals almost an absolute free rein.

NAME-CALLING: SWEET CAROLINE

Newly married in 1847 Francis Baxter the-stonemason and Caroline Gates may or may not have been oblivious to what was happening beyond their Camden horizons, but they certainly could not be unaware of all the hustle and bustle of railway expansions and of the building projects they were living amongst.

They were now located at 12 Phoenix Place where their family soon grew: baby Francis Baxter (the third) was born on June 10th 1848, and was probably named traditionally after his father or his paternal grandfather.

To be frank, all these Franks and/or Francis's can get quite confusing, if not very tedious; names, though, also follow trends. Historically, biblical names have been very popular and featured large, but then there are also names which become *fashionable* - and that – despite what you might be inclined to think - is not just a problem peculiar to the present day. Brooklyn's and Beyonce's may currently abound, but in fact some names gained popularity through celebrity or star appeal even back in those days. In the first half of the 19th century the name Caroline was connected very much to celebrated popular figures. For example, Francis's younger brother Thomas (aged 20) was a confectioner, who had apparently gone sweet on a Caroline Collier[33]; and so at this point Francis the Stonemason and his brother, Thomas, now both had wives then styled by the name of Caroline Baxter – another opportunity to confuse records.

Of course this was a coincidence, but whilst the name *Caroline* might also later be or become a family name within the Gates and Collier families, it had nevertheless been the name of the Prince Regent's wife, whom the public had far greater affection for than the Prince himself.

"QUEEN" CAROLINE

The Prince Regent apparently found his Caroline neither sweet nor fragrant; indeed *he* found her short, fat and not only ugly, but - more significantly - a good deal shy of a bar of soap! Although the most redeeming quality with which he was still rather taken was that parliament was poised to settle his considerable debts IF he married her and produced an heir.

One can only imagine their wedding night. Did he view his bride in a similar fashion to the way in which Marilyn Monroe's character (in the film Gentlemen Prefer Blondes) imagined her multi-millionaire admirer. When Monroe's *Lorelei Lee* casts her eyes upon her not-so-bonny beau – a distinctly tubby old diamond-mine owner - she envisions her true heart's desire:

---

33 *Family history information: The couple were married at St Jude's in October 1849, Whitechapel*

suddenly on screen his head transforms into a huge spinning diamond! Well, they say that money can be a powerful aphrodisiac to the greedy and the needy alike.... I wonder. Perhaps the Regent just held his nose, or blocked it with scented plugs.

Howsoever it was perpetrated the nuptial matters and the conjugal deed were accomplished: its doubtless brevity was nonetheless a successful action, and the Prince Regent's seed proved to be less indolent than the Prince himself. Caroline became pregnant with Princess Charlotte, and the Prince - having hit the jackpot pay-out and with no further need to reprise his one-off "wham, bam and thank-you ma'am" - dropped poor Caroline as quick as he would have done if he had been handed a dosser's sock for a handkerchief. She was shunned both publicly and privately, and was excluded from the court from 1811.

Nevertheless, she – Caroline of Brunswick – had remained a popular person with the general British public. They sympathised with her, especially in respect to the abominable manner in which she had been consistently treated by the future King whom they widely regarded as loathsome. For example, he had not only vindictively restricted her access to her daughter, but had also launched investigations – *Delicate Investigations* as they were called – on the assumption of her adultery. (This would be something the Jews call chutzpah, and its brazen cheek was not lost on a public who were aware of his own flagrant infidelities). For her own part Caroline later joked to friends that she had indeed committed adultery once — with the husband of Mrs Fitz-Herbert. [Mrs F had been a long term "companion" of the King, and indeed at some point had actually entered into a marriage with him, although this had been ruled invalid.]

Caroline had received widespread support; unbeknownst to her this included Jane Austen who, in a private letter to a Martha Lloyd, wrote: "Poor woman, I shall support her as long as I can, because she *is* a woman and because I hate her husband."

Austen, though, did express some reservations about comments Caroline's made in a letter to the Hampshire Chronicle in 1813, wherein she (then Princess of Wales) had maintained an "affection for her husband." Possibly the comment was pragmatic and just part of her public relations' initiative.

Whilst the Prince Regent had made every effort to ditch her as wife and would-be Queen, he was officially and legally unable to do so; and by the time that he became King George IV in 1820 all he could spitefully do was to bar her from his coronation.

All things considered, in the eyes of the so-called London mob, the Prince Regent stank a good deal more than she did, and the name "Caroline" would be a favoured moniker assigned to many new-born daughters. Incidentally, Caroline was only Queen for a short time: she died just 18 months after the King had acceded to the throne.

The name, admittedly, had also previously been popularised with the accession of a previous Queen (and Regent) to King George II: Caroline of Brandenburg-Ansbach. It was also the name of their daughter, Princess Caroline, and was, therefore, a name of established celebrity and regal appeal.

FAMINE, AND FAR-OFF RELIEF

While in 1847 our Baxters were possibly eking out a poor-ish existence in Somers Town amongst the metropolitan masses of working-poor, an agricultural blight ruined potato crops in many countries. The potato may have been a staple in Ireland, but reactions to the crop failure by the land-owners led unnecessarily to a catastrophic famine there, which resulted in the deaths of one million people! A further one million fled their homeland. There are reports that the pathogen, which caused the blight of the potato, had its origin in Mesoamerica (Mexico and south down to Costa Rica) and was transmitted via northern America. [34] Some Irish people nevertheless - and unknowing of the blight's origins - went west to America, while others found their way to England, particularly to Liverpool and London.

The influx impacted significantly on the locals: on both jobs and accommodation. Starving migrants came to neighbourhoods (like that of the Baxters) seeking food and work; and of course the nature of the work they sought was both manual and menial: the very same employment which was the bread and butter of the poor English working classes. It is important to note *they didn't come to do the jobs the English didn't want to do.* In order, though, to secure a job – even a one-day employment – migrants desperately (and understandably) were compelled by their poverty to "volunteer" to work for less money than was on offer to the locals: this became a daily race to the bottom. It was manna from heaven for employers.

If the situational penny hasn't dropped, this effective undercutting of the wages reduced the earnings' potential of the home-bred poor: understandably this did not overly endear the migrants to those similarly desperate locals. Without a Welfare State then, it was a scrawny-mangy-dog-eat-scrawny-mangy-dog situation, which suited those above the dog pit very well.

The impact also affected housing: while wages went down, the cost of renting went up. Rooms became more expensive, with whole families living in (i.e. squeezing into) a single room. I have

---

34 Perversely this seems like ecological revenge for the 16th century gift of European corporeal pestilence – we gave them measles, smallpox and venereal disease which wiped out an estimated 90% of their population; perhaps, in return they gave Europe the potato blight.

read of two families sharing one room, but I haven't come across this or seen it indicated on any census – yet. (Either way, this certainly wasn't the comfortable "down-sizing" of the early 21st century middle-classes.)

From this period, where desperate people competed for ever-smaller scraps and for inferior accommodation, the seeds of discontent and prejudice were laid down in both the English and the Irish camps. The Irish seemingly blamed "the English," apparently *in toto* (not "the British," and nor even specifically the UK&I government) for their poverty and their starvation. Oral tradition has transmitted the feelings, animosity and accusations down through generations and – in my experience – deep-held resentment is often still never too far from the surface. Unfortunately misplaced grudges always allow the real culprits to go unhindered.

Perhaps you were surprised by the use of the term, UK&I, for the oft described *British* government of the 1840's; but it had in fact been the government of the United Kingdom of Great Britain **and Ireland** since 1801. The parliament may have been in England, but England like Scotland had already been subsumed into the Kingdom of Great Britain for almost a century before Ireland joined that union. (The Kingdom of Great Britain – unifying Scotland and England – occurred in 1707. Wales which had been conquered in 1282 was completely annexed by England from 1542.)

The famine certainly did not receive sympathetic attention from the Great Britain-and-Ireland government, who couldn't give a fig about the poor – be they English or Irish, Scots, Welsh, Hindus or whoever you may care to choose – as long as the starving did not affect the comforts, positions, incomes and assets of the upper and ruling classes. They – the government of the UK&I, NOT *the English* – ignored pleas for help, for assistance and for changes in policies.

The problems of the starving and jobless in Ireland were made even worse by the actions of their landlords, who also evicted them from their homes because they could not pay their rent. Daniel O'Connell and others suggested that if Ireland had had a domestic Parliament, it would have implemented alternative polices, which would have provided solutions to the starvation and poverty. It was said (rightly) that the poor would not starve if the abundant crops raised in Ireland had been kept for the people of Ireland {instead of being exported for the profits of foreign (Anglo-Irish) landlords}. O'Connell et al also advocated a programme of public works to provide employment which without question would have helped.

Another fervent Irish patriot, John Mitchel, owner and editor of the news journal *The United Irishman*, espoused more vocal and direct opinions: he said that British actions during the famine (and their treatment of the Irish) had been a deliberate effort to murder the Irish. Later, in 1861, he would write, "The Almighty, indeed, sent the potato blight, but the English created the Famine," a narrow view which has sadly persisted.

Mitchel was wrong that *the English* created the famine, although it was certainly the ruling class in England who were responsible for the policies which undoubtedly caused mass starvation. Many of the big names of the day within the UK&I government held lands in Ireland and it was they in particular who refused remedies and ameliorations which would have been beneficial to the starving. They were not just dis-inclined to act, they were vocal in their opposition because "relief" would also have been detrimental to their Lordship's own financial interests.

There were also shootings of some landlords, which provoked calls for armed responses. One of those calling for these was Lord Clarendon, who nevertheless believed that the landlords themselves were mostly responsible for the tragedy in the first place. He apparently said, "It is quite true that landlords in

England would not like to be shot like hares and partridges ... but neither does any landlord in England turn out fifty persons at once and burn their houses over their heads, giving them no provision for the future."

Relief for the starving Irish instead came from unusual sources. The marvellous Quakers gave their usual unconditional support, which contrasted with the usual partisan strictures which the Catholic and Protestant religions demanded in return for help. “Pray to our brand of God, and we will give you food!” Pray... and then contribute to the coffers. Pray... and pay.

Large sums of money were donated by charities, although how it was distributed to the poor is a little uncertain; the first foreign campaign in December 1845 included the Boston Repeal Association and the Catholic Church. The Irish Diaspora also contributed, and apparently almost £14,000 came from India where money raised included contributions by Irish soldiers, who were raking in money by terrorising the Indian peasants there on behalf of the East India Company.

The truly amazing thing that happened then was that the native-American/aboriginal Choctaw tribe had somehow heard about the Irish famine; and in a fantastic display of empathy for a country and a people so far away, they made a contribution to the relief fund.

Mitchel was definitely a pro-Irish Nationalist, but as is the complicated way of potential heroes, he was also an advocate of negro slavery and was against the emancipation of the Jews. If that hasn’t raised some suspicions Mitchel further urged capital punishment for crimes such as burglary, forgery and robbery. (Definitely not a poster-boy - as far as I am concerned.)

As Baxter numbers increased in the 1840's so, too, around them the railway companies continued their individual expansions - with the Great Northern Railway (GNR) developing their London terminus in the area (around King's Cross) between 1849 and 1852. The GNR, by the way, had purchased land for the station to the south of the canal, and also land to the north for its goods station and steam locomotive depot. [35] Thus, at this time, and within a radius of just over one mile, there were now three railway termini: Paddington, Euston and Kings Cross. [36]

During the period of the development of Kings Cross Station the stonemason's next child was born. Having failed to christen their first-born, Francis and Caroline decided to baptise their two boys together, and duly went to St Pancras Old Church on the 24th of January 1850. [37]

Walking through the churchyard they may well have browsed a few names on the gravestones, perhaps scanning the names for divine inspiration. (I wonder if their glances flitted upon the names of William Godwin or of Sir John Soanes' whose memorials were there.) But, no, they had probably already set their minds on a name for their son. Of course, *he* could have been named after a King (or indeed a Saint) but their baby George Baxter was in all likelihood just traditionally named after Caroline's dad, George Gates.

---

[35] The first temporary passenger station opened in 1850 in Maiden Lane (now York Way) to the north of the canal. This station was used until King's Cross station opened in 1852 as the London hub of the GNR.

[36] London had 7 all told: these three, and London Bridge and Waterloo to the south, with Shoreditch and Fenchurch Street to the east.

[37] Information about St Pancras Old Church is included later in this text.

Strangely, the baptisms of their boys Francis and George ([38]) coincided with that of an Eliza Baxter, who was also recorded as the child of Francis and Caroline. [39] However, this is certainly dubious because the date of birth given for Eliza shows her as born on October 3rd in 1843! Now as this is four years prior to the stonemason's marriage, it would have made Caroline 17-ish and our stonemason 15 at the time of conception. The record is historically a primary source – authentic/original and written at the time and in the moment – and poignantly the detail is not inconceivable, but it is an anomaly: a small strand of confusing information which is not unusual, but commonsense or at least a wariness must always stop us from seizing upon every suggestion or declaration as Gospel.

Fortunately, the birth certificate of Eliza Baxter (born indeed on the 3rd October 1843 at No.5 Edwards Place, Old Street Road) records her mother as *Elizabeth* Baxter nee Bradshaw and confirms the child was the *cutler's* daughter and not the stonemason's. Kids, it seems, often stayed with relatives.

Therefore, indisputably, and despite the record, the Eliza - who was baptised with the toddler Francis and his baby brother George - actually was the stonemason's sister!

38 *Family history information: baby George was born on Dec 28th 1849*

39 *Family history information: IGI CO 47935 - 8560 Subsequently, in the 1851 census, Eliza would be recorded aged 7, living at Pancras Walk with Elizabeth and Francis the Cutler.*

All in all, the local population around Somers Town (which included our cutler, our stonemason and a heap of related labourers plus their wives and growing families) were beavering away at the epicentre of colossal infrastructure projects.

Development, however, was not entirely limited to industrial and transport expansion, and by the end of 1850s, the construction of residential buildings was also well advanced. Steady and on-going development continued on the western side of King's Cross with the terraces and squares of Somers Town. The middle-classes and the more genteel inhabitants had by then largely decamped and the remaining properties were now occupied to the brim by railway and industrial workers. Apparently an area between Somers Town and the Goods Yard was even leased to workmen to build their own homes, with the consequence that the area quickly became associated with poor quality ramshackle dwellings.

Subsequently, though, more housing was knocked down in the railway expansions in order to create space for the tracks, terminus and goods yards; and by the mid-19th century and onwards it became more difficult for all workers (including railway workers) to find decent affordable housing and shelter close to their place of work.

The Baxters and their contemporaries would have been surrounded by the noise and bustle of these developments as well as being hemmed in on all sides by them. They would have all been affected by the work and by the effect on housing. Overcrowding and increasingly poor conditions went hand-in-hand with the so-called "progress."

Somers Town, which had originally been part of the medieval parish of St. Pancras, was named after one Charlie Cocks, 1st Baron Somers. Cocks had represented Reigate in Parliament and had risen in the noble pecking order. He was made a baron and in 1784 took the dormant title of John Somers, his great-uncle, who as Lord Chancellor under William III had been granted the land here. So, Charlie Cocks had become 1st Baron Somers. His son would rise further becoming Earl Somers and Viscount Eastnor, the latter being a reference to the Cocks' ancestral seat at Eastnor Castle in Herefordshire. [40]

In time Somers Town became part of the Borough of Marylebone and then of St Pancras, before eventually that Borough was extended and renamed as the London Borough of Camden. That, though, is jumping too far ahead and Somers Town, at the time when the Baxters lived there, was in the grip of change: progress, if you like. Of course, perceptions of change are always time-relative, and change (for example, in the case concerning levels of immigration) is thus often more palatable when it is gradual.

However, back in the 1830's and 40's there wasn't much that was gradual about the change when fourteen acres of Somers

---

40 *Until the second decade of the 21st century there was a pub called the Eastnor Castle in Chalton Street, Somers Town. An old-fashioned establishment it was very welcoming to ordinary people; in fact, my cousin Tracey Titley and I enjoyed quite a few pints there in that most convivial atmosphere. Sadly, being a traditional and therefore anachronistic local, it could not survive the strain of modern demographics and the apparent insatiable desire and unfathomable demand for soul-less gastro-bars: like thousands of ordinary English pubs without sufficient patronage it closed forever in about 2015.*

Town land was taken by the Midland railway. The area – no longer the bucolic acres of the 18th century – had become covered with dwellings occupied mainly (perhaps at this stage almost exclusively) by densely packed poor families, often with whole families living in one room. In time, such land appropriation meant that whole swathes of this local population were to be driven out of their old homes to make way for the railway.

It wasn't just that land was needed for a couple of tracks to be laid: into this small area - within a space of just thirty years - would be shoe-horned three huge and adjacent mainline railway termini, i.e. Euston (1838), Kings Cross (1852) and a little later St Pancras in 1868. Naturally, whilst this would create work it also destroyed the housing stock needed by those local workers. To compound matters it also reduced the availability of land for building homes. The displaced families, which may have included Baxters and Gates, were now euphemistically "free to seek new or different accommodation opportunities.... elsewhere." Many migrated a little further north to Kentish Town, Camden Town and Gospel Oak.

By the year of the Great Exhibition, 1851, Francis was now shown as working as a stonemason and was apparently living at No.11 Little Camden Street with his brood. The most recent addition to the family at the time of the census was 1-month-old Eliza – yes, Eliza, another repeat name to add to the list! [41]

---

41 Family history information: Eliza was born on February 20th 1851. In addition for the benefit of other family history researchers I would point out there were other couples called Francis and Elizabeth Baxter. One such was a Norfolk-born floor cloth printer and his Yorkshire wife who lived in St George the Martyr, Newington, in Lambeth. This couple were both born circa 1824/6.

So the stonemason's family now numbered five (parents and 3 kids: Francis, George and baby Eliza). They also had five lodgers, although I do not know whether or not this generated an income for stonemason Francis. I somehow doubt it because they seem to have moved around a bit – perhaps they were hopping from house to house as a large part of the local population did – all dancing to the tune of displacement as the railway gorged upon the area. Or maybe it was for other reasons.

Whatever the housing situation was like, more babies came: William Baxter, named after Francis's brother, arrived in 1852, just fourteen months after Caroline's last confinement. She did not have much of a break then either as she would give birth to Martha Baxter 17 months later in 1853. Three kids born in 2 ½ years – and 5 kids altogether within 63 months! Between almost continuous pregnancies, breast-feeding nippers, washing cloth nappies and looking after toddlers – as well as all the other washing, cooking and cleaning – it is hardly surprising that a great many women in Caroline's time didn't make old bones. [42]

I suspect the whole family might turn out for regular Sunday Church services then, such was the strength of religion; and its popularity is perhaps indicated by the size of the churches that were being built and particularly by the number of pews installed on the basis of the expected congregation. In those days I wonder how common it was for anyone to be absent from a baptism. (There was no TV or very many other distractions.) It also occurs to me to wonder, what time of day baptisms were conducted because the next Baxter baptism took place on a

---

[42] *Family history information: Francis Baxter (the third) was born on June 10th 1848;* George was born on Dec 28th 1849; *Eliza was born on February 20th 1851; William was born on the 26th of April 1852 and Martha on 30th September 1853*

normal work day: Thursday, the 20th of October 1853, when Eliza, William and Martha went to the font. Incidentally, it appears the Baxters were back in Marson Street.

St Pancras Old Church

The baptisms of the three younger Baxter children were again performed at St Pancras Old Church (SPOC), which nestled alongside the River Fleet (since covered and flowing underground). Bits of the SPOC graveyard it seems have always fallen prey to the lust for railway expansion, with the Midland Railway taking a bite in the 1850's and Eurostar more recently. Whilst many graves were lost or relocated in the 19th century at least the grave and memorial of Sir John Soanes and wife has managed to survive. The memorial, by the way, was the inspiration for Giles Gilbert Scott's design for the original red telephone boxes/kiosks.

It is said that Miss Mary Godwin and her Dad, William, often visited the grave, here, of her mother, Mary Wollstonecraft; and also that the graveyard is where Miss Godwin secretly met Percy Bysshe Shelley before their elopement to France. In time her father would be laid to rest in peace here in the old churchyard with his wife. It would not be, though, a lasting peace or a permanent rest for this renowned couple because, in accordance with the death wishes and instructions of their daughter Mary Shelley (the erstwhile Miss Godwin), their bodies were exhumed in 1851. Then they were re-united and all removed to the Shelley family tomb in the church of St Peter's in Bournemouth.

As a footnote to the famed feminist, during her lifetime Wollstonecraft had apparently an "intense friendship" with Frances Blood. Now I do not know (or care) if this reported intensity was a euphemism for a lesbian affair, but I can say Mary's friend had a truly awful or unfortunate name. You see, as is the way with the women called Frances, their name is commonly changed. This occurs with men called James, who become Jim, and Charlottes who become "Lotties". There are numerous examples. Frances in turn changes to "Fanny." And I don't know of many London women who would wish to be called "Fanny Blood." It is just a thought.

SWIFT BURIAL

Now all of the aforementioned illustrious departed were adults, but should we need to be reminded, these were times of premature death and high infant mortality; and only four months after the three Baxter kids were baptised this latest baby, Martha, had died. I believe she may have been the four-month old child buried in St Giles in the Fields on the 5th of February 1854. [43]

The burial was certainly swift – perhaps they were more efficient then and managed to conform to burial within three days or maybe the cause of death had been an infectious disease. However, as no one else in that Baxter family seems to have been infected or died then maybe it was just a matter of efficiency.

---

[43] *Family history information: The death is registered as in Pancras, 1854 Jan-March Vol. 1b, page 89. The burial notice seems to indicate her abode was Saville St, so that may be a discrepancy I cannot account for at this moment.*

Demise and bereavements apart, there was and is nothing else for survivors to do but get on with life.

Whilst people of the 19th century are reputed to have been religious they tended also to be superstitious. They may have thrown spilt salt over their shoulders, declined to open an umbrella indoors or saw a potential ill omen in putting new shoes on the table, but I can only imagine that stonemason Francis and Caroline's superstitions were limited. Far from being superstitious and rather keener instead to preserve an exclusive memory, I do have to admit I still would not have "tempted providence," as they perhaps did, when just 8 months later on Oct 11th 1854 they had another baby girl... and called *her* Martha!

To set this very individual and personal event into a wider historic context, Martha's birth in October 1854 was just ten days before Florence Nightingale (and a staff of 38 nurses) set off for the "Crimea."

THE CRIMEA; AND FLORRIE TO THE FORE

The Crimean conflict would make Florence Nightingale – the Lady of the Lamp - an international celebrity, and in true popular style this would cause a flurry of Florries at baptismal fonts all over the country. In no time at all, Florences abounded! The name, Florence, had not been popular or in any way common (in England at least) before Nightingale gained fame in the Crimea. Indeed, like many of the children of rich movie stars and renowned footballers, Miss Nightingale had got her name by virtue of where she had been conceived: Florence, Italy.

When Nightingale arrived in the Crimea she had been appalled at the British losses through disease and the insanitary conditions in the Military Hospitals, and she made great efforts to improve the conditions there. Her subsequent reports led to a Royal Commission into Military Hospitals. The War at this point had already lasted a year: twelve months where Britain, France and Turkey had pitted their leaders' brains and their men's heroic brawn against their Russian counterparts. Instead of covering Britain in glory the sorry exercise would serve to highlight the woeful deficiencies of the British "brains" and their deplorable management of the brawn.

No better example was evident than on the 25th of October – when Martha Baxter was just a fortnight old – Lord Cardigan led the ill-fated and infamous *Charge of the Light Brigade* at the Battle of Balaclava. News of this did not find its way back to Britain until the Times reported it on November 13th 1854.

Of course, the charge had been immortalised in Tennyson's poem, and many people know at least these few words:

> *".... onward, onward rode the six hundred,*
> *into the valley of death rode the six hundred."*

Back in London, and just four days after the news of Crimean debacle/Herculean bravery had broke, I suspect the Baxters adopted a more leisurely pace: they certainly didn't charge off to St Pancras Parish Church. More likely they just strolled up there on November 17th 1854 to have Martha (Mk II) baptised.

Here, they recorded Canterbury Place as their home, which would not change for some years; and here they were cheek by jowl with the great gasometers of St Pancras.

It would seem that the stonemason's 2-year old son William passed away also around this time. Births, though, like Deaths, were nevertheless a continuous feature of everyday life in those days before adequate contraception became available.

In 1854 there was a severe outbreak of cholera in Soho, just down the road from Somers Town. It killed 616 people locally, and it became famous as it was this outbreak that led physician John Snow to conclude that germ-contaminated water was the source of cholera. Previously it was thought to be an air-borne "miasma." Snow traced the source to a water pump in Broadwick Street, had the handle removed and made history.

At the same time as our Baxter families were increasing in size the Railway companies were also growing and expanding, and they all required both skilled and unskilled men. Labourers, masons and stonemasons were in much demand.

I have no idea whether the Baxters or their contemporaries knew or cared about the bigger picture or about anything other than on a domestic scale, nor what their exposure was to news and national and international affairs. I doubt it was much: there was no TV, radio or internet then, and no tabloids for the common man and woman to ponder. So, perhaps they were as unaware of the railway companies' predicament as they may have been that ideas and technologies (such as standard versus broad gauge rail design) were competing for supremacy. Maybe they knew, but just took the view that regardless of the competition there would ultimately be a "winner," and the winner would still be almost certain to require labour. To the Baxter's I imagine it was barely detectable background noise.

For the present then the basic design incompatibility of those different gauges continued to prevent an efficient *National* railway network: journeys had to be interrupted to allow passengers to change trains dependent on the suitability of the prevailing track gauge. Standard gauge slowly emerged as the favoured design, but change could not be made overnight; the problem required a quick fix, and so in the interim refinements were made to Brunel's track. A third rail was fitted, which henceforth allowed standard gauge trains to also operate on Brunel's routes. This augmentation began in 1854.

Big Thinkers: Telford, Brunel, Stephenson

Unfortunately the absence of a "Big Plan" always comes to haunt piece-meal projects, and the railways were all independent, unconnected and funded privately. Governments seem reluctant to commit to really big schemes – perhaps there wasn't enough public funds; perhaps, joint public and private investment did not appear to be a viable option? Was the risk too great for private investors? Big schemes and projects demand excessive finance and have a longer time-table for pay-off and returns, which does not always suit an impatient investor. Either way, it seems to be commonplace that big thinkers' joined-up ideas tend to lose out to reticence and to the lure of more immediate profits. As the Americans might say, the "quick-Buck is master."

Of course, there were big-thinkers in the late 18th and early 19th centuries; and, whether or not all their schemes were taken up in that period of the Industrial Revolution, Great Britain did have a good share of brains, drive and ambition. George Stephenson was known as the Father of the Railways, and his contribution cannot be underestimated, but there were three others in particular who stood out: Thomas Telford, Isambard Kingdom Brunel and George's son Robert Stephenson. The two unremarkable Francis Baxters (elder cutler and younger stonemason) lived in their time.

Thomas Telford had been the son of a shepherd and was also apprenticed to a stonemason; you might say he built his own stepping stones because he flourished in many enterprises and fields. Telford was also a poet, and friend of Robert Southey, who later became Poet Laureate. [44]

Telford would go on to build harbours (one at Whitstable), many churches, bridges (reportedly in their hundreds but apparently 40 bridges in Shropshire alone), and the first major suspension bridge (the Menai) in 1826. He built St Katharine docks in London, as well as tunnels, roads and canals. Among other structures, this involved the spectacular Pontcysyllte Aqueduct over the River Dee in the Vale of Llangollen and the Caledonian Canal before he died aged 77 in 1834. This left the

---

[44] Robert Southey who had been 15 at the time of the fairly recent French Revolution was then fervent in his commitment to political reform. It was strengthened when he read William Godwin's "Political Justice," and Godwin's assertion that most social ills were a product of the extremes of poverty and privilege. Southey and Samuel Taylor Coleridge, who married sisters, came up with the idea of "Pantisocracy," or "equal rule of all." This was to be a communal, society based on the egalitarian principles of the French Revolution. Their idea was to create a settlement in America where everyone could live in harmonious brotherhood.

way clear for other big-thinking prodigiously prolific young bucks like Brunel and Stephenson. Of course they would only last another generation and so were also soon to pass.

In their span, though, they achieved colossal works. Brunel had built dockyards, the Great Western Railway (GWR), a series of steamships which included the first propeller-driven and transatlantic steamships {including the SS Great Britain}, and numerous important bridges and tunnels. He designed Paddington Station and the Clifton Suspension Bridge, although there were arguably subsequent and not minor modifications to that design before it was actually completed. He had worked on the first tunnel under a navigable river (the Thames, no less). It is fair to say his designs were major contributions and they revolutionised both public transport and modern engineering; and he was only 53 when, already ill with Bright's disease, he died after a stroke on September the 5th 1859.

Stephenson had worked and built projects in the UK, South America, Europe, Norway and Egypt. He was a mining engineer in Columbia, then returned to Britain and designed the steam locomotive the Rocket, which he ran in the Rainhills' Trials of 1829, and won. [45] He was Chief Engineer for the London and Birmingham Railway Company, and designed and built the original Britannia Bridge over the Menai Straits in 1850.

---

45 At the inauguration of the Liverpool and Manchester Railway in 1830 notaries included the Duke of Wellington (then Prime Minister) and William Huskisson MP, who all travelled on board one of the inaugural trains. At one point Huskisson, who reputedly liked a drink, had stepped off the train for what purpose is only open to conjecture. Whatever it was his plan was ill-timed, for he was immediately run down by the Rocket coming along the other line. Carried away, he died of his injuries soon after.

Apparently the two great engineers were friends as well as rivals, and shared the same heavy-smoking and hard-drinking habits; and, like Brunel, Stephenson also had Bright's disease. He died just 5 weeks after Brunel, and aged only 55.

Brunel, Stephenson and Telford were giants of construction, design and engineering, but I wonder whether - had they lived in more modern times - most of them would have been given the chance to do what they did. Telford had been a stonemason not a civil engineer, but being an amateur did not exclude him from diversifying and achieving. All three crossed occupational lines which I believe modern systems would now prevent.

I am not sure where the worlds of architecture, design and engineering currently overlap or meet, and it seems for some the line is more than blurred. I have read that modern engineering and architecture has been melded into Ove Arup's view of Total Architecture, which I understand advocates great collaborations, for example, as would be required in the work of planning, designing and building a whole capital city. Such a project happened when the construction of Brasília was undertaken in February 1957; it was led by an urban planner and Brazilian architect, Lucio Costa, by architect Oscar Niemeyer and by landscape designer Roberto Burle Marx. A triumph of collaboration.

The stonemason and his family meanwhile were no doubt hard at it work-wise, and also without any uncertainty the Baxter family grew. The next baby, Caroline, arrived on the 11th of November in the winter of 1856. (So, now, we have three Caroline Baxters.)

Just four days later (at St Leonard's) a Caroline Baxter witnessed the marriage of Alfred Baxter to one Phoebe Collier. Who did this signature belong to? Alfred, the stonemason's brother, was a confectioner (like their brother Thomas) and the bride was in fact Thomas's wife's sister. Thus in all likelihood the signature probably was that of his wife, Caroline Baxter (nee Collier). [46]

Thirteen days later on the 28th of November 1856 baby Caroline, daughter of the stonemason was christened; but that Christmas was sadly to be her only Yuletide. She died in the summer, before she was one year old.

Now, in the nine years of their marriage thus far Caroline Baxter nee Gates had given birth to seven children, three of whom had died (a Martha, a William and a Caroline). The survivors were Francis, George, Eliza and the second Martha. I don't know if that percentage loss of children was the norm (it may even have been less than average), but you still have to think that those circumstances must have been "challenging."

Perhaps they needed a drink.

---

[46] *Family history information: two Baxter brothers married two Collier sisters. In time this trend would repeat, with two of Francis Baxter's daughters marrying two Titley brothers. And the trend would not stop there because the stonemason would have two grandsons (Titley brothers again) who married two Logan sisters!*

There were plenty of venues in London: from gin palaces to beer houses, refreshment rooms, music halls, theatres, dram shops, public houses, private clubs, and oyster bars. The "evils of drink" led some people to support the temperance movement. In 1869 the government sought to take more control, invoking regulation and bringing in licensing. Medical, health and social concerns were raised, with Liberals tending towards pro-temperance (enforced abstinence) while Conservatives supported the brewers, producers, retailers and consumers.

New technology meant beers could be mass produced and the speed of delivery by railway enabled different beers and ales to be happily transported throughout the country before they went off; and the public were apparently lapping it up a little too liberally and riotously for some.

The 1869 Wine and Refreshment Houses Act was designed to promote more civilised boozing, and to encourage wine drinking etc. (I have always found that a strange notion since I seem to have encountered more people "out of their head" on wine than on beer.) Public drunkenness was seen as a lack of moral fibre, a source of financial ruin and as the root of crime and deviancy; although, on the other hand and batting for the other side, at one point some doctors opined that alcohol was therapeutic (obviously the kind of clinician a drinker would wish to consult).

The problem of alcohol abuse – as it is currently termed - had been recognised for over a century, with moves made to counter it as far back as 1729, and by a series of parliamentary Acts up until 1751.

Gin had been popularised, promoted and encouraged after the accession of William of Orange – which then saw restrictions made and higher taxes put on the import of *French* brandy (the produce of the foe). It was first brought in from William's homeland in the Netherlands. "Gin," being an alcoholic distillation of grain infused with juniper berries, was a contraction of its former name, genever: an English word derived from the Latin for juniper. Its distillation also helped our grain trade. Despite sometimes temporarily diluting the misery of the poverty-stricken, its unregulated use caused many social problems.

I am not sure of the strength of the spirits then but I am quite certain that sobriety could not have been aided by the custom of selling spirits in large measures – such as by the pint! That is 568 millilitres – more than half a litre in your glass! - if you are not familiar with old imperial measurements. No wonder it was called "Mother's ruin." *Gin Lane*, a print by Hogarth depicting the terrible lives of such drinkers, was produced in support of the 1751 Gin Act. That print accompanied another, wherein Hogarth contrasted the miserable state of those embroiled in the gin craze with the apparent jolliness of those enjoying the fruits of industry, prosperity and health on *Beer Street*.

Further attempts at control by regulation and changes to legislation continued to be made. 1818 would see a slightly different approach with other legal efforts made to end the larger brewers' monopoly of tied houses. It was felt that these business concerns not only provided overpriced and poor quality beer, but they also sold relatively cheap spirits like gin, whose consumption was widely regarded as being responsible for much of the unwanted and anti-social behaviour. The Beer Act of 1830 essentially deregulated beer sales and allowed everyone and anyone to sell beer. It was hoped this would break the power of the brewers, make beer cheaper and that this would wean the public off the ruinous spirits.

In time, the Beer Act failed to weaken the brewers' position, but continued industrialisation and urbanisation plus the various subsequent alcohol laws did change the culture of the Great Britain that our Baxters were living in.

Naturally in later times much smaller quantities prevailed, and these also give us a clue to the further complexities of our then imperial weights and measures systems. In the pre-metric United Kingdom of Great Britain and Northern Ireland fluids, such as alcohol, were sold in pints, or sub-divisions of pints or in fluid ounces. Beer was sold generally by the pint and the half pint, while spirits were sold by a measure known as a nip; and a nip of gin, for example, was a particular fraction of a now defunct imperial measurement known as a gill. The exact fraction depended on where in the UK&NI it was sold and it could be ¼, $^{1}/_{5}$ or $^{1}/_{6}$ of a gill.

Measure for measure Liquid

Explicitly a gill was a quarter of an imperial pint, and since a pint was 20 fluid ounces, a gill was therefore equal to 5 fluid ounces. A spirit bottle, certainly in the 1960's, held 1⅓ pints or 26 and ⅔ fluid ounces: this is 5 and $^{2}/_{6}$th gills which were dispensed to the consumer in $^{1}/_{6}$th of a gill measures. This meant that there were 32 measures to a bottle. Converting to metric, one fluid ounce is equal to 28.41ml. – so a $^{1}/_{6}$ of a gill nip was equal to (5/6 of 28.41 =) 23.67 ml. Trying to take all this in, and without having drunk a drop, I wonder if your head is spinning... just a little?

Now those bottles, as containers, did not immediately need to be changed when the metric system was adopted in the UK. The same sized 26.67 oz bottles could hold 26.3963 imperial fluid ounces with a little room to spare, thus accommodating 75 ml.

Currently, spirits are sold generally in 25 millilitres measures, with some drinks being dispensed in 35ml measures.

Therefore, a 700ml (70cl) bottle holds 28 x 25 ml nips (or twenty 35ml nips) depending on the size of the optic dispenser.

I think, dear reader, that you and I may have had it up to the gills with imperial measurements. If anyone thought the metric system was difficult in any way, surely it is time to think again. It is superior by far!

LICENSING HOURS:

The Alehouse Act of 1828 and the Beer-house Act of 1830 saw the introduction of licensing for the sale of beer. It did not set restrictions on the time that beer could be sold. This largely remained within the gift of the licensee until the Great War, when pubs were forced to close for a 2½ hours in the afternoon. No further changes were made until 1988.

In Charles Booth's survey in the last decades of the 19th century his surveyor, Mr Duckworth, and the local Police Inspector, Flanagan, interviewed a pub manager, Mr Cox. The latter provided some interesting information (see index, sections within: Booth's survey, and see Geometry in Action) and he also reported making payments to the local police. He said he paid 1/- (a shilling)a-week "call-money" for the beat copper to knock-up the bar servant just before 6a.m., in time for opening at 7 a.m. His pub at Shoreditch opened at 5.30 a.m.

This would indicate a laissez-faire attitude to licensing hours, which probably altered from pub to pub and from area to area. Market pubs almost certainly catered for the hours (day or night) when they were most likely to have a good footfall of thirsty customers.

TIME, GENTLEMEN. PLEASE. A 20TH CENTURY CRY.

Licensing hours were a big feature of life in the 20th century. At the beginning of the 1900's opening and closing hours were very fluid, and it was only (if that is the right word) the Great War and the need to keep munitions workers out of the pub (or to encourage them to return to work) that fixed hours were introduced. Naturally these restrictions, brought in as part of the Defence of the Realm Act (DORA), did not apply to Private clubs with memberships, to "Gentlemen's Clubs" and to the then most exclusive of all male clubs: the Houses of Parliament, where they could - and still can - drink all day and night.

Licensing hours were revised in the Licensing Act 1988, which caused prices to rise to compensate the brewer/ pub-landlord allowing for the alleged increased wages for labour and extra running costs, such as electricity and heating. Naturally the argument that these were already in-built into the price of each and every drink sold did not hold sway: UP the prices went in readiness for all day (11 a.m. to 11 p.m.) trade. When it was realised that people could only spend as much as they could afford from their "disposable" income a great many pubs reverted to shorter hours. "Well, there is no use in being open if there are no customers (or not enough customers to make it worthwhile), is there?" Quite right; but the price per drink noticeably did not go DOWN to what they were previously. In 2003 a new Licensing Act made it legal (from 2005) to sell alcohol 24 hours-a-day where the vendor was licensed to do so. Few, if any, chose to do so.

Our Baxters - in common with the vast majority of the population - seem to have been very unimaginative with naming their children. I often bemoan the current fashion where the unlikeliest of spellings contort even the more un-likeliest of names (Shaday, Sade, Cheyanne, Dwayne, Qwayne, and Dypschtick – perhaps not that one). Alternatively, I could say that to an extent the delightfully dyslexic dim-wits of our day do at least provide more variety.

Our Baxters, though, were extremely traditional and stuck steadfastly to family names, which pop up time and again as nods to favoured and close relatives. Accordingly, the stonemason's next patter of tiny feet in 1857 belonged to baby Thomas Baxter, named after his uncle; and then the day after Francis and Caroline's twelfth wedding anniversary in 1859 Phoebe Baxter (named after her aunt, Alf's wife) was safely delivered at home. She was born at No. 3 Canterbury Place, off Archer Street in Camden Town. On the other side of Pratt St was the St Martin's graveyard, which is now a community garden. [47]

You may wonder at Phoebe's parents' thoughts for this little girl's survival in those times of high infant mortality (especially having already had several visits from that grimmest of grim reapers). Obviously they were not to know that a full eighty-six years would pass before their little darling Phoebe finally shuffled off her mortal coil.

---

[47] Archer Street was renamed Curnock Street (NW1 0LY) and was within the block that was Pratt St, Bayham St, Plender St and Camden St. Another Canterbury Place backed on to the gasworks at the southern end of SPOC, a short walk from Somers Bridge.

Around this time in 1860 the stonemason's brother Richard, a Smith, of Wakefield St. married Elizabeth Holland in St Pancras. (Here, Richard's father's occupation was stated as a cutler.) By 1861, the Baxters appear not to have been the poorest of the poor in urban society, or, if they were, then at least they now lived as a family unit in one house with no lodgers or tenants sharing with them. Perhaps a stonemason's work was well rewarded, and hopefully his pockets were not overstretched either by the further arrival of Joe (Joseph in 1861/2) or even by the birth of Alfred (named after the stonemason's brother…ughhh..) in 1863/4.

BELLE ISLE: NAMED BY SOMEONE WITH A SENSE OF HUMOUR.

Belle Isle was near to Horsfall Basin and perhaps the last vestige of its existence can apparently still be seen by eagle-eyed commuters as the first timing point along the railway line out of Kings Cross Station. James Greenwood, a pioneer of investigative journalism in the mid-1860's and thereafter, gave this direction to locating Belle Isle. First, follow your nose, and then:

"Keep straight along the York-Road, and gradually you will be sensible of leaving civilisation behind you," and there you would have arrived.

He made great use of adjectives such as rank, foul and sickly, which would under the circumstances seem to be fairly mild as warnings of what was to be found. He did, though, warm to his theme, and described that Belle Isle was approached through Pleasant Grove – you have to admit the Victorians were not without wry humour when it came to naming places. Here, Greenwood eloquently noted: "It is hardly too much to say that almost every trade banished from the haunts on men, on account of the villainous smells and dangerous atmosphere it engenders, is represented in Pleasant Grove." He mentions such industries as bone-boilers (where they were made into bone-handles), fat-melters, "chemical works," firework makers, sulphurous Lucifer-match factories, and several extensive dust-yards.

According to Mary Cosh, the area could also boast of a grease works, varnish factories, tripe makers, vinegar works, mustard makers, horse-slaughter-houses and a white-lead factory. To off-set the olfactory treats of these stench factories further, apparently there were also open drains, and yet... somehow in the air there could still be detected the smell of pigs – "kept by many locals alongside their hovels." And, of course, there was the Gasworks. (One can only imagine a candle-lit dinner for two: a couple in an amorous mood seduced into enhancing the ambience by over-boiling some cabbage...)

If all that wasn't enough this area of des res's also had slaughter-houses which despatched hundreds of diseased, lame, broken-down and worn out equines. Released from their sorry existence, they were rendered down, boiled in immense coppers into cat and dog-food, or processed - as their hooves and rears were - to make glue.

Greenwood did further make mention that the pursuit of one of England's finest sports was not lost to the locals. Living in the most unfavourable conditions, with neither facility nor equipment, there is little that would deprive an Englishman of his sport and his heritage: cricket will always out. Here, though, it was not quite the fine game played by gentlemen in their "whites" upon the village greens with the gently bucolic sounds of leather on willow. Here, local boys played between two dust heaps, with wickets fashioned by a pile of old hats, the bat was the leg-stump of an old bedstead and the ball was the head of a kitten. Catch!

[48]

Now, I can only wonder whether this substitute for a ball was an embellishment: either that or they must have had a good supply of kittens' heads because surely one would hardly have lasted an over...

48 James Greenwood had begun writing for his brother's publication from around 1865. At that point the area was becoming a little more developed, and his accounts (such as, "A Night in the Workhouse", 1866) did not sanitise his observations. The realism he portrayed painted a fairly brutal picture of the state of things, and as with all fly-on-the-wall investigations a public outcry ensued – and just as quickly died as they do. His accounts established his reputation as both an investigative journalist and a social commentator. As a journalist, Greenwood used the pseudonyms The Amateur Casual and One of the Crowd. His strategy of going under cover would later be taken up with great effect by Jack London for his People of the Abyss.

By the beginning of the 1860's the Midland Railway (MR) had prospered by bringing coal and iron – and beer from Burton-on-Trent – to and from the capital. Its passenger traffic had also steadily increased, which was both a bonus and a bit of a growing problem. Hitherto, the MR had been making use of parts of the Great Northern Railway lines, but this was on the condition that GNR trains got preference, an arrangement which increasingly meant MR passengers were delayed. Frustrating your customer base is not a good business plan, and it could not be allowed to go on, so finally the decision was taken for the MR to have its own terminus in the capital. The passing of appropriate legislation (the Midland Railway (Extension to London) Bill 1863) meant that a new line would come from Bedford to Moorgate. The Passenger service began operating on the 13th of July 1868. Services into St Pancras started on October 1st, 1868.

During this period, and if the area wasn't busy enough for our Baxters, the Great Metropolitan Underground railway decided to cut and cover a track from Paddington along the New Road (now Marylebone and Euston Roads).

Skirting both the existing termini and the new proposed St Pancras the "Tube" would drive on and extend the link to Farringdon. The 6 kilometre distance covered by the Metropolitan Line – as it became known – was opened in 1863.

These first tube trains were steam engines which caused considerable pollution and must have been quite horrendous, but they were popular due to their speed and efficiency.

In 1863 there were no cars, vans or any motor vehicles, and no buses – except Mr Shillibeer's horse-drawn omnibuses which took the well-heeled from Paddington along the New (Euston) Road and on to the City. There was not even a bicycle (as later generations might know them) – and of course, there were no electric vehicles either. There were a few tricycles but these were rare, and in case you have heard of them, hobby-horses and velocipedes were in existence, but these also were for the very few and for the very rich..... and they did not have pedals. (In fact, it would not be until 1863 that the first *pedal-driven* French bicycle was invented. It changed the world). Other than that personal transport amounted to horseback, pony and trap or some other horse-drawn vehicle.

Skateboards etc had not been invented; and while a version of roller skates were around as a plaything for the rich, they were only suitable for very flat regular surfaces and so were no good for roads, streets and pavements.[49]

I would imagine that our Baxters were not horse-owning people, and that their mode of transport was almost invariably what used to be known as Shanks-pony (i.e. walking or using their own shanks/ legs). Getting anywhere was almost certainly a trudge, but people then restricted themselves to places of work that were within walking distance – or else they moved closer to the source of the work.

---

49 These were the invention of Joseph Merlin, who created the fantastic clockwork Silver Swan. There is a portrait of Merlin in Kenwood House, Hampstead, London; it also houses two examples of his work: a clock and a wheelchair for those who could not walk, which was propelled by the user turning cogged wheels.

The strain of having children, of feeding, clothing and sheltering the living ones (and burying the dead ones) must have weighed heavily on the stonemason; and I can't imagine, either, that life's struggles weren't showing on his wife: Caroline. Although only about thirty-eight years old, she had already had at least ten children... and maybe even more pregnancies!

This was a hundred years before the advent of the contraceptive "Pill" gave women the power to take control of their bodies by using - or not using - birth control. But Caroline Baxter nee Gates was a woman trapped by her time: a slave, therefore, to confinement, childbirth, child rearing, infant mortality and to an unceasing prospect of dying in childbirth. These must have all been pretty efficient at wearing a person out: it must have taken its toll.

Incidentally, ONS UK Birth Summary Tables show that stillbirths in 2012 were 0.4% - less than around 4 in 1000 - while in 1927 (the earliest record) the figure was almost ten times that at 40 per 1000 – and that no doubt was a huge improvement from the 1860's!

Thinking of slaves I am prompted to comment on the 1860's in America – the self-styled land of the free –where the army of the Confederacy was just about to surrender to the so-called abolitionist Union side. Whilst the famous Gettysburg address, delivered by Abraham Lincoln, contained noble thoughts and sentiments, it would still be another hundred years before a black man could ride on the same bus as a white man! It makes you wonder what it would have been like if the Confederacy had won. Of course the Thirteenth Amendment to the United States Constitution, which immediately abolished slavery and involuntary servitude, was supposed to change things but the 13th also held the caveat "except as punishment for a crime." This exception has allowed de facto slavery to continue within the US's privately-run prisons where more than 80% of the prisoners are black or non-white.

Overt legislative and institutional racism in American society nevertheless persisted into the 1960's and 70's, and in some states little has changed since. In the 1970's the term "coloureds" had found favour as a way of describing Afro-Americans – it then being seemingly a little more liberal than calling them negroes or niggers.

The extent of racist attitudes may perhaps be best appreciated by this example from an interview for Rolling Stone magazine. When questioned in 1976 by John Dean about racial equality and civil rights, the U.S. Agriculture Secretary, Earl Butz, clarified his position on the then burning issues. Incredibly he felt it was appropriate to say:

"Coloureds only want three things: first, a tight pussy; second, loose shoes; third, a warm place to shit." An absolutely stellar twat. Mind you, he had to resign; so at least the climate was beginning to change, although by no way fast enough. Even having had an African/American for a President much of the country still seems gripped by ignorance, fear and hatred. Land of the Free?

Marriage. Public Execution. Death. And on To Kentish Town

On the 17th of May 1868, a George Baxter married a local St Pancras girl Esther McIntosh. For some reason they married in Bethnal Green with him describing both himself and his father, Francis Baxter, as masons. Our George (born in December 1849) would have been only 18½, but oddly the groom is there shown as of "full age," which usually implied being above 21 years old or seeking to appear so. This is an anomaly but I still lean in favour that this George is nonetheless the son of our Francis the stonemason. Census records indicate this is reasonable.

I doubt they could afford a honeymoon, but I am sure in that unlikely event their break still would not have lasted long at all. Days of leisure were restricted to the Sabbath, Holy-Days (from which we derive the term *holidays*) and unemployed days. Christmas day and Good Friday were the only other days off work allowed in the 1860's. It would not be until 1871 that the Bank Holidays Act established public holidays (known as bank holidays) and designated four days in England, Wales and Ireland: these were Easter Monday; Whit Monday; the first Monday in August; and Boxing Day/St. Stephen's day on the 26th of December or the next day if this fell on a Sunday. The earliest Good Friday is March 20th. The latest Good Friday may occur is on April 23rd according to the Gregorian calendar.

So wherever they may or may not have gone they would certainly have been back in London nine days later. There, if such entertainment was their thing, they would have been able to witness the last public execution in England.

The decision to conduct execution behind closed doors may have been influenced by the ineptitude of Calcraft the hangman, who had botched the hanging of William Bousfield in 1856. Bousfield had gone through the trap, but had then managed to get his feet back up against the sides of the trap. (see Arnold. C. P196.) A helpful warden cast him off once more, but the reluctant victim managed to get back up again. On the fourth foray into the darkness – and with Calcraft hanging onto his legs – Bousfield was finally despatched, and the spectacle ended for the crowd. A Royal Commission in 1864 would recommend the abolition of public execution, which would be made law in the summer of 1868. Thereby, any shambles would be played out to a more select audience. Public or private, it would not matter to the condemned person who might have other things to occupy them rather than the reaction of an unseemly crowd.

And so it was that at Newgate on 26th of May 1868 Michael Barrett, a Fenian, was the last person to be hanged publicly. He had been found guilty of causing a fatal explosion at the Clerkenwell House of Detention in a botched attempt to free some fellow Irish Republicans. Not that George and Esther Baxter would necessarily have had a good view if they had made it to the scene, because crowds in their thousands had flocked there – many having travelled there on the newly-opened Farringdon Underground Station. The roof of St Sepulchre's church opposite – where they rang the execution bell – contained many spectators. (The Church still has the bell on exhibition.)

In the April of 1871 time also caught up with the stonemason's dad. Francis Baxter, the cutler, sharp maker and surgical implement maker, was 74, when died in the Holborn workhouse. His occupation had been recorded simply as a Truss maker, which he had done for quite some years. I imagine he was not just destitute, but was beyond looking after because his wife Elizabeth (nee Bradshaw) was elsewhere. She was living in Rotherhithe, which was then in Surrey, with their daughter, Eliza Tuckwell, a mariner's wife. [50]

The stonemason's Baxter family had also shifted in 1871. By that year they – like so many of their neighbours - had been pushed out by the relentless railway construction and its consumption of local housing. The trains were then operating on the 13,500 miles of railroad that had already been laid, which would be 2/3rds of the final peak of railway line coverage. The engines were of course steam driven, a form of locomotion which would outlive most if not all of these Baxters.

Francis and Caroline had gone north of Somers Town, and were now living in Frideswide Place, which was (and is) off Islip Street - just behind the new Kentish Town Station. [51] At this time the Baxter's home also housed Francis's youngest brother - 30

---

[50] Elizabeth would survive her cutler hubby by some 11 years, but she too would die in a Workhouse Infirmary, albeit south of the water in St Olave's, Rotherhithe. A great number of people would see out their days in these infirmaries – there were no other hospitals. These places were the nowhere-else-to-go-to final destination (in this world) for the decrepit, for those in their dotage, for the decaying and for many just plain exhausted souls who were glad-to-be-soon-to-be-dead.

[51] The first station was opened by the Midland Railway in 1868 on the extension to its new London terminal at St Pancras. The station is currently served by the High Barnet branch of the London Underground Northern line, and by Thames-link trains on the National Rail Midland Main Line. It is between Camden Town and Tufnell Park on the Northern line, and is also on the main line between West Hampstead and St. Pancras International stations.

year-old William Baxter, a Smith's-labourer, his wife Susannah and their three children.

Despite their move they were all still practically living at the heart of a massive building project, which included not only the construction of the Railways through Camden Town, but also the building of Scott's design for St. Pancras Railway Station. The use there of Nottingham bricks and Ancaster stone for that *'great wedding cake of ornaments,'* as St Pancras was described, must have provided a wealth of work for a stonemason, and the building programme continued to attract workers from far and wide. (Dickens' *Dombey and Son* gives a great description of the excavations and construction of the railways there, if you are minded to seek it out.)

It was a time of record employment. [52] London was booming in terms of work, although I don't know if that translated into good wages or whether the migration of really poor workers from the countryside and from abroad had a depressing effect on the value of the urban wage. Nevertheless, still more labourers, engineers, builders, masons, carpenters, glaziers and many others flocked to the capital to find work. The influx of people seeking work also again impacted on the availability of residential properties, and the subsequent scarcity of housing led to some dire living conditions, a real problem for many of them.

People, though, are pretty resourceful when they are in need of distractions, and where there is a will, they usually find a way. In the case of Francis and Caroline's daughter, Eliza Baxter, her "will" took the form of a "Will"-iam King, a glass cutter/glazier.

---

[52] The ONS report on Long term Trends in UK Employment 1861- 2018 records the highest employment rates were in the years 1872, 1943 and 2018, at 76% of the working age population. See https://www.ons.gov.uk /economy/ nationalaccounts/uksectoraccounts/compendium/economicreview/april2019 / long term trends in uk employment 1861 to2018

The young couple married in June 1873, with both the bride and groom recording their address as FrideswidePlace.

I am not sure of how co-habitation was viewed (not well, I imagine) so perhaps Will King had been lodging there, but couples often gave the same address to avoid the cost of paying for the Banns to be read at two different churches. (Their marriage lines were witnessed by Eliza's sister Martha Baxter, and by Thomas Gates - probably their uncle. As was – and is – the way the Kings had a son, William - soon(-ish) after.

Amongst those flocking to the heaving metropolis was one young Shropshire man, who had left Ironbridge and had come down to London possibly via the "Black Country" to try his hand at whatever came along. He found work as a Labourer, but as it happened he also found himself in demand with the Stonemason's daughter, Martha Baxter. He was another "Will" or he may have been a "Bill" (William Titley, in fact), and he and Martha were married in 1874.

The King photographs were found on www.ancestry.co.uk in the family tree of someone else. I can only assume these were within their family and are the people they are purported to be.

William King 1852 -1887

Eliza Baxter

Francis Baxter's two daughters above (and below) do not look overly or especially poor. They certainly could afford to have their photograph taken. I wonder, though, if these were their own clothes or garments provided by the studio.

Phoebe would start work as a domestic servant (which definitely wasn't great pay), but would eventually become a shop-keeper/ chandler /grocer.

Eliza King nee Baxter

Phoebe Baxter aged 18

Death of Caroline Baxter nee Gates

During the spring of 1876 it appears the stonemason's wife, our Caroline Baxter nee Gates, had begun to suffer with haemorrhaging from the bowel. It was then ascribed to an ulcer of the lower bowel, but perhaps it was bowel cancer. Whatever, she carried on for six months before succumbing on the twenty-second of October. Her death-certificate gives all this information, and states that she died at home at 13 Frideswide Place. In all probability she passed away with her family by her side: her son-in-law, William Titley, is recorded as having been present at the time of her death. Caroline was shown as being only 53.

Caroline was buried in accordance with the law, but the law didn't yet give her the right to be cremated.

Cremation notes

The Cremation Society has a website with some very interesting information in regards to their history and to the path which led to cremation being considered legal.

The Society was created by Sir Henry Thompson, Bart., F.R.C.S., and Surgeon to Queen Victoria. He had done so after a cremating apparatus had attracted his attention. It had been invented by Professor Gorini of Lodi in Italy and Professor Brunetti of Padua, which they had exhibited at the Vienna Exposition in 1873. Thompson thereafter became the first and chief promoter of cremation in England, writing a paper entitled The Treatment of the Body after Death, which was published in January, 1874, two years before Caroline Gates had died.

The website states that Thompson's main reason for supporting cremation was that "it was becoming a necessary sanitary precaution against the propagation of disease among a population daily growing larger in relation to the area it occupied."

Sir Henry Thompson called a meeting of a number of his friends at his house at 35 Wimpole Street in January, 1874, to discuss the idea. Here the Cremation Society of England came into being, with a declaration stating their desire to substitute some mode of disposal which "shall rapidly resolve the body into its component elements, by a process which cannot offend the living, and shall render the remains perfectly innocuous."

The Society first tried to ascertain whether cremation could be legally performed in this country. It also proposed to erect a building (it wasn't yet called a crematorium) for the performance of the rite and bought an acre of freehold land adjoining the cemetery at Woking from the London Necropolis Company. Professor Gorini was invited to supervise the erection of his apparatus.

On 17th March, 1879, the body of a horse was cremated: it was completely and rapidly reduced to ashes, proving that an adult human body could be so reduced in a matter of from one to two hours.

Despite a decade of opposition from the Home Office the cremation of two deceased members of a Captain Hanham's family, (and later of himself) excited much comment in the Press, but the Home Office decided to look the other way. Having decided not to decide it took no action.

The following year, however, an eccentric Doctor (a William Price who also claimed to be a Druid High Priest) attempted to cremate the body of his five months old son. He had already christened the child Jesus Christ so perhaps he was just drawing attention to himself in a boastful way: the child had been born to him at the age of 83. Price was arrested and put on trial at the South Glamorgan Assizes in Cardiff.

In February, 1884, Mr. Justice Stephen delivered his all-important pronouncement that cremation is legal provided no nuisance is caused in the process to others. This was a breakthrough moment.

The Cremation Society, however, realised that it was imperative at this stage to give no cause whatever for criticism and, consequently, they set down conditions which had to be strictly observed before a body would be accepted for cremation at Woking. These conditions were designed to prevent the evidential destruction of a body which might have met death illegally. These continued for many years to be the only form of certification for cremation and they remain substantially the basis of the statutory forms used at the present time! (See: https://www. cremation.org.uk/history-of-cremation-in-the-united-kingdom.)

Mourned and lamented, Caroline Baxter nee Gates may have been, but "life," as they say, "must go on." Eighteen months later, and only in his mid-fifties, our stonemason married a widow ten years younger than himself: Elizabeth Dyde. [53]

The timing and location of his marriage (and subsequent census returns) indicate the likelihood that the stonemason and his brood had left the Somers Town, Camden Town and Kentish Town areas in the latter part of the 1870's. [54]

Francis moved east to Hackney. In fact his brother, Thomas the confectioner was living in Gainsborough Road, near Hackney Wick. This was just around the corner to Clarnico's, on Carpenter's Road, which was then the largest sweet manufacturer in the country, employing 1,500 people. In an article by Sarah Ingrams (see Bibliography) she describes the factory as being "ideally situated for deliveries of sugar on the banks of the River Lee navigation channel." Clarnico's had originally made marmalade and jam, but then its products included mint creams,

---

[53] *Family history information: The wedding took place in St Philips, Dalston, in the first week of June 1878. Elizabeth was also the mother of two young sons: Robert and James Dyde. James would marry Maria Mary Baxter on 4.3.1886. (She was his step-father's niece: Alf Baxter and Phoebe Collier's daughter.) Witnesses: Eliza and Alf.*

[54] *Family History information: The electoral registration for 13 Frideswide Place (21831, St Pancras ward no 3 ref MR/PER/B/028) in 1878 still includes the stonemason so I imagine he moved in that summer.*

liquorice, Chinese Pigtails, coconut-based Toasted Haddocks and "Pig's Head & Carrots." [55]

By 1881 many of those who had originally arrived in Somers Town searching for work had spread their wings a little further. No doubt they were still chasing work, but for some they might be looking for a less densely packed environment. Not that all of them found particularly genteel or salubrious Shangri-La's, but many of the Baxters had nevertheless found new bases. Whilst the stonemason's eldest daughter Eliza King had moved a little west to Hays Court in Soho [56] most of the family had relocated eastwards - particularly to Dalston in Hackney.

---

55 Gainsborough School is still where Thomas lived – I actually taught there occasionally over 120 years later. In another life I also did various contracting work and lift-repairs in Clarnico's in the 1980's. By the way, the factory was knocked down to make way for the 2012 Olympic Park, and it is proposed to call one area of the development "Sweetwater" as a nod to its confectionery links and its proximity to the river. Also the Hackney Hospital/workhouse had a casual ward in Gainsborough Road next to the vinegar brewery in the 1890's.

56 Family History Information: *Eliza was in Soho with her glass cutter husband, William, and their 8 year old son, also William King. It further appears that the stonemason's sibling William Baxter the wheelwright remained in Camden as did his sister Elizabeth Stuart, wife of the paper marbler, who was now living in Arlington St. Aged 76 a widowed Elizabeth Stewart (sic) was admitted to the workhouse in 1897 but didn't die until 1904.*

DALSTON, HACKNEY

The move to Dalston for all the family was again probably due to the availability of work there: not only was the railway expanding east and northwards from the Liverpool Street and Broad Street stations, but also at around this time more residential housing in the borough was being built. Dalston junction was noted to be 9-13 minutes by train to the city.

In 1881 Francis Baxter the stonemason took up residence in Lee Street, near Haggerstone Station (with an e) in Haggerston, which is off Kingsland Road. [57] (Some 16 years later, according to Booth's poverty map, Lee St was said to be a mixture of housing and occupancies with some comfortable and others poor.) It so happens that the Lee Street house was actually registered to a John Baxter, whom I have not found or positively identified. [58] It

---

57 The house in Lee Street was only feet away from the bridge arch of a railway line, which ran parallel to Kingsland Road, up to Dalston Junction. This was known as the Broad Street/North London line and it took travellers from the City at Liverpool Street through to Dalston, and onward through Canonbury and Highbury, and on through what was then suburban London in a huge arc ending at Richmond on the Thames. It was a great trundling, leisurely journey, which my parents took us on as kids when we happily used to visit Richmond and Kew Gardens.

The line was closed I believe as part of Dr. Richard Beeching's reorganisation of the railways in the early 1960's, which also removed about 6,000 miles of route nationally; the line has since been revived in sections, and is now part of the London Overground system.

58 *Family history information: a John Baxter, journeyman cutler, is known to have lived locally. I suspect, therefore, he was some relation to our Francis the cutler.*

was also home to Francis's two youngest sons, Joe and Alf Baxter, who were working as labourers.

The stonemason's daughter, Martha, and her growing family of Titleys, were also local, living in Blomfield Street (alongside the North London line). This street ran from Middleton Road to Forest Road, and crossed Lenthall Road. Lenthall Road was cut short at some time, and the last part of it was instead incorporated into Richmond Road. This part contains the pub (where it was once known as the Swan – where customers also danced - /and is now the Haggerston, where they don't). This was on the corner of the Kingsland Road Waste, which once was a thriving market, but has now all but disappeared.

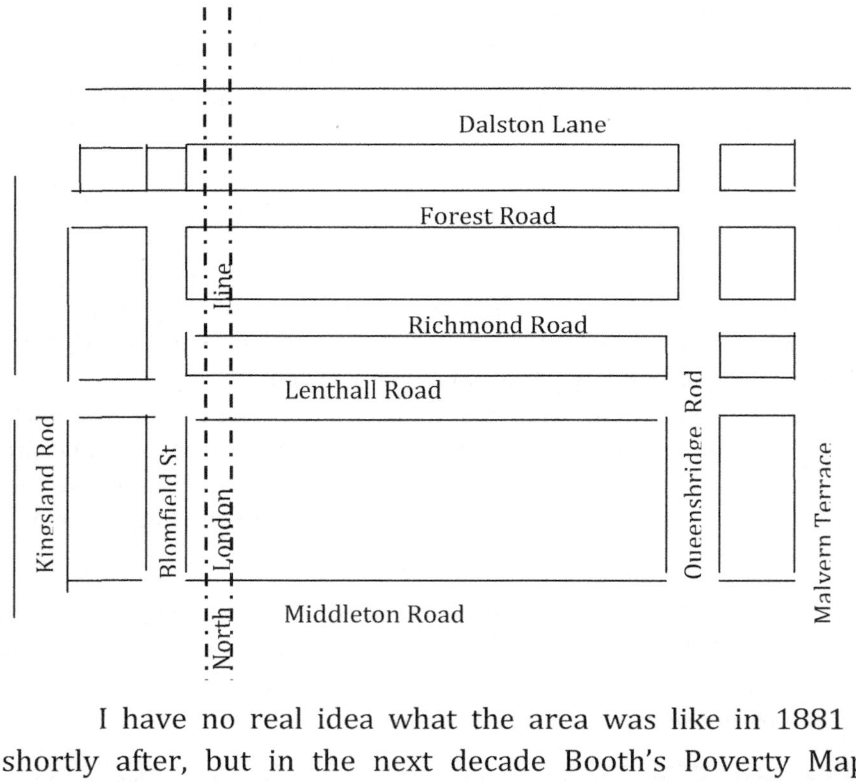

I have no real idea what the area was like in 1881 and shortly after, but in the next decade Booth's Poverty Map of London fills in some gaps – and provides a wealth of diverse information if you should care to seek it out and read the notes.

It seems the Titley's had a boarder: Martha's brother-in-law, another Shropshire lad looking for work, named Francis Titley. (Another Francis!)

The stonemason's youngest daughter, 21 year old Phoebe, had gone into domestic service, and was living within just a mile in a slightly more salubrious part of Hackney at 122 Sandringham Road. So, there were quite a few Baxters in the immediate Dalston area; and apparently the stonemason's son Francis, who had married in the spring of 1883, was also not a stone's throw away in Bethnal Green. [59]

SEX, STAGS AND SHOT-GUNS

So the wedding of the stonemason's son was the latest marriage in the Baxter family, and babies were expected to arrive following on soon-ish after. Now of course in Victorian times there were children born "out of wedlock" but these were stigmatised, as indeed were unmarried couples who were living together "in sin." Local people knew if other locals were married or not, and without marriage lines a single woman living with a man was regarded with disfavour and disapproval. (These

---

[59] *Family history information: In March 1883 the younger Francis (mk III?) married 30 year old Mary Elizabeth Cane there at St James the Great. On his marriage certificate he reported his dad's occupation not as grandly as a stonemason, but instead as a bricklayer. Perhaps this described more accurately what his dad was actually doing at the time: it was certainly something within our stonemason capacity. I believe this Francis may have had a son, called Francis (AGAIN), but I do not think he survived. Also* in late 1882 the stonemason's mum died at St Olave's Workhouse infirmary aged about 84.

attitudes probably continued for another hundred years until the Church's influence began to wane and society began to loosen up.)

In the Victorian period, though, churches were regularly attended: people went literally religiously; and marriages were seen as integral to family life, to sex and to decency. And marriage was "until death do us part." Divorce was not an option for the vast majority of people, although there were loopholes which the rich usually managed to exploit: they had the means to have their marriages "annulled". For most other people trapped in an unhappy marriage their situation - as described almost poetically in its vivacity by Catherine Arnold (2012 p220) - was akin to "being chained to a rotting corpse."

Sex which had not been religiously sanctioned by the church was fornication – and hell-fire and damnation etc. awaited fornicators; therefore, sex was (theoretically) conditional and "morally dependent" upon couples being married. Thankfully, "God" made rebels, too. Nevertheless, and consequently there were a great many marriages, and with all such events other rituals and traditions are followed.

I would imagine the men had some form of "stag night" as the evening before a wedding was called. This celebration or occasion was meant to signify the man's last night of "freedom" before he would "forsake all others" if he had already not done so. This tradition carried on until almost the end of the 20th century when the "night" became stretched into a "stag week-end". Subsequently, these week-ends have been superseded and it may now encompass a fortnight in Fiji.... Twentieth century women also had "hen nights" before the wedding – which sometimes were quite staid... sensible even.... Others, as is the way of all individuals regardless of gender, have been known to be rather raucous, if not downright bawdy occasions; forsaking all others down to the wire, as it were....

Of course, things change and by the turn of the millennium, most "engaged" couples had already set up home with each other before any marriage which may or equally may not have followed.

In my lifetime there has been a huge social shift in attitudes and conventions. Growing up and as a teenager it was taken for granted that if a girl became pregnant then "the culprit" *had* to marry her. It did not matter that they were barely children themselves, were unwilling to marry or whether the two had anything in common other than the pregnancy; the future grandparents tended to unanimously agree that a quick visit to the Church was virtually the only solution. (Of course easy solutions now abound: prevention through contraception, and or the so-called morning-after Pill. Abortion proper was only made legal in 1967, and then only for specific medical reasons: they were difficult to obtain.) So, without the benefit of modern science, proper medical attention and social liberality, the mother-to-be would be forced up the aisle – complete with baby-bump – and dressed in virginal white (despite it raising an eyebrow or two and it eliciting an inevitable few sotto voce scoffs from the congregation). These were known for obvious reasons as shot-gun weddings, and equally obviously not that many of the happy couples, went on to have a happy life, well not at least a happy life *with* each other.

The terminology "culprit" here is deliberate and accurate to both the time and to the perceived status of each within a relationship – which especially ignored any female volition. Polite conversation did not allow of women's needs, wants or desires – not unless they pertained to a washing machine or a new electric iron, apparently.

Young men were quietly expected to sow a few wild oats – or to get their oats – but the idea and any mention of such activity in regards to young women was considered extremely bad form.

By this time the stonemason had seen two sons (Francis and George) and two daughters (Eliza and Martha) married off. The latter (Martha) had been attracted to our Salopian (William) Titley and presently that same chemistry seems to have worked upon her sister Phoebe and his brother Francis Titley. The two, as we now say, became "an item," and subsequently they were married in 1883. [60]

The Titley men of the nineteenth century, having fled the increasing grinding poverty of a Shropshire environment, had thus not only found gainful employment in London, but had also acquired wives as well. Their world had definitely changed, and naturally the inevitable arrival of children would add to the changes.

By the autumn of 1883, both young Mrs Titleys (Phoebe and Martha) were pregnant. In due course Martha gave birth to Clifford **Baxter** Titley on the thirty-first of May 1884, and less than three weeks later Phoebe safely delivered her first child. Now here we may observe another example of tradition defeating imagination: considering that her granddad, her dad, her husband,

---

[60] *Family history information: So, two sisters had married two brothers, (or vice versa, if you prefer) which apparently was not uncommon then. In fact people did not go far to woo: neighbours and near neighbours/locals tended to meet, court and wed. Phoebe and Francis' wedding was witnessed by Phoebe's brother, the stonemason's son, Alf Baxter, and by his girlfriend Alice Brignall, who were both residing in Sandringham Rd. Alf was shown as being at No. 122 – and possibly with Phoebe – while Alice was at No. 154. By the way, Francis and Phoebe would subsequently return the favour when on Christmas day 1885 they were signatories at Alf and Alice's marriage at St. John's Hackney.*

her brother and her nephew were all called Francis, you may have thought that Phoebe (*and* hubby, Francis Titley) might have been tempted to try a fresh or different name for the baby. And of course, you would be wrong! "Francis!" it was. In fact, to be precise they called him Francis Alfred Titley, although thankfully he was known as Alf. (Not that there weren't any other Alf's in the family....) By the way, whilst traditions hold sway and there would be other Clifford Titleys, Martha's baby (Clifford Baxter Titley) sadly died before the year was out. [61]

By now the stonemason was a granddad many times over, and, as is the way of life, there were still more to come. In November 1886 Phoebe and Francis had their second child: Ernest Baxter Titley. So, babies were indeed still coming, albeit along with the high infant mortality rates. All things considered and bearing in mind the prevailing conditions in the Victorian age death was never far away.

---

[61] Martha would end up being delivered of **13** children, though incredibly and devastatingly only **5** survived to adulthood! It appears Phoebe only had 4 children and they all survived. Considering these two sisters married two brothers, who all lived and worked together and probably had the same diet and life styles, one can only assume that Martha and William were just a good deal unluckier than Phoebe and Francis.

Family history information: In 1885 the stonemason's son Joseph Baxter married Clara McBride in Bethnal Green; they were probably living then in Warley Street (which was not too far away from his siblings in Haggerston). Joe was at that point a general house repairer. He would be there for years to come: with Clara's widowed mother in 1891, then while working as a decorator in 1901. The 1911 finds Joe still there, but now he is 49-year old widower, and working as a builder/handyman. It records he had been married for 24 years, was born at St Pancras.

In 1887, Martha and Phoebe's brother-in-law William King died in the Strand registration district. He was only 36; and this left their sister, the stonemason's other daughter Eliza, as a widowed mother of two. Difficult times indeed, and especially with no social welfare net!

HEALTH, AND SAFETY

The list of fatal conditions then stack up to form an awful and perilous prospect: it may not have been helped by the absence of adequate health-care, but even if it had existed it could not have treated numerous diseases. Medical knowledge was advancing, but it was still very limited; and some treatments ranged from the brutally medieval to the plainly "primitive." Illnesses had few known cures and in the main remedies were ineffective.

It should be remembered that many now commonplace drugs – for example penicillin and antibiotics –were not available: in fact they would not be discovered for at least half a century. In addition to this, work on germs - and the notion of sterile environments and anti-septic treatment - was indeed still in its infancy. Then, if we add widespread general malnutrition, insufficient standards of hygiene, insanitary housing and open sewers we find we have quite a toxic stew. There were, though, other horrors awaiting working people.

This was the age when boys were sent up chimneys to clean the soot; and the practice of a Master Sweep setting a small fire beneath the child - as a form of encouragement to work quicker – was common enough for a bye-law to be passed in Middlesex stating that it *should not* be done. Agricultural work, though extremely poorly paid, could at least be said to have afforded the worker the benefit of fresh air. In the urban and industrialised environment (and beneath ground) general conditions were much worse: the demands made by many employers, who gave scant regard to the safety of their employees, verged on scandalously reckless. Sometimes these demands lay their workers open to diseases, like Phosphor Jaw and Black (or Miner's) lung, while in other circumstances and more immediately there were merely high incidences of accidents, injuries and death at work. There would be no such thing, for example, as safety-guards on machinery (that would take another 90+ years): and there were no safety harnesses or personal protective equipment, (which would not become commonplace until the next millennium). The only wonder is there weren't more alcohol abuse and suicides.

PUERPERAL FEVER

Men, women and children were all prone to disease, but childbirth in particular was a real danger spot for the pregnant woman.

Deaths caused by puerperal fever, such as Mary Wollstonecraft's (in 1797), would continue unabated for many years. It would be another fifty years before there was even a chance of progress; and that chance came when Ignaz Semmelweis tried to persuade the medical profession of a connection between hygiene and disease. Sometimes apparently referred to as the "saviour of mothers," Semmelweis had postulated that the practice of antiseptic hand-washing by those attending women in child-birth could drastically reduce the incidence of puerperal fever (and the associated mortality rates). He had noted empirically that women giving birth in the Vienna general hospital, who were attended by (male) doctors, were significantly more likely to develop puerperal fever than those attended by mid-wives in another institution. He had observed that the mid-wives washed their hands regularly as a matter of practice, whilst the doctors did not. His assertion that this practice was the vital difference was not met favourably by the male medical profession. Whilst he advocated using chlorinated lime solutions to cleanse hands etc they steadfastly continued not to wash their hands citing the absence of scientific proof of any connection.

This was not available until the emergence of work on germ theory, where Louis Pasteur considered the spread of disease and proposed that micro-organisms should be prevented from entering the human/animal body. This led Lister to develop antiseptic methods in surgery, and a new era was born where doctors edged a little closer to the doctrine of Hippocratic Corpus: "first, do no harm..."

This was too late, though, for Semmelweis who, suffering rejection and ridicule, was deemed by some colleagues to have gone insane. Against his will he was committed to an asylum where his resistance caused him to be injured, and ironically his wounds led to his death from sepsis. Thus, he would not be vindicated in his life-time.

Of course Doctors were exclusively male at the time, and whilst mid-wives generally attended to childbirth, the men sought to extend control over all areas of medicine. They dictated that, despite the gravitational advantage (and a modicum of less "discomfort") offered by standing, child birth should be conducted / endured IN bed or lying down. The Doctors were keen to cut female midwives out of the Obstetrics equation, which was very likely to have been to protect their own revenue stream.

Note: "Obstetrics" derives from the prefix *ob* (in front of or facing), *stet* (standing) and *trix* (a female); such that obstetrics related historically to the attendance of a female standing in front of the woman giving birth (who was in all probability also standing).

Women were hit by all sorts of ravages: from constant pregnancies, lack of medical care, hard work and poorer wages than even the men's pitiful wage, from bad and dangerous conditions at work as well as a social climate that thought it was fair to beat them harshly and violently. It wasn't a good time to be an ordinary man; it was even less so for the ordinary woman.

MATCH–GIRLS AND A SERIAL KILLER: FEARFUL AND FRIGHTFUL DAYS.

The following year, 1888, was an interesting time in the east end of London with two news stories coming from that then most un-delightful quarter. The first, in July, was the Bryant & May match-girls' strike, whose plight was first reported on by Annie Besant in her ha-penny weekly publication, the Link.

Messrs Bryant and May, it seems, were Quakers, and unusually for adherents of that creed they did not seem overly bothered by the awful conditions which their employees suffered. What did bother them somewhat more was that their employees refused to publicly refute the details of Besant's story. Their subsequent plan to coerce the workforce by dismissing one particular individual backfired, and led to others withdrawing their labour. This rare show of solidarity was effective, and B & M reinstated the individual, but the smell of the blood of success emboldened the match-girls and prompted them to also stick out for changes to their conditions.

At that time the match-makers, who were mostly girls between the ages of 13 and 20, worked either in the factory or were outside-workers toiling under the sweating system. (The latter –being called sweat shops–were not subject to the Factory Acts–nor to much else). It was mostly piece work, although girls under 14 apparently received a wage – of 4 shillings a week! The girls in the factory were subject to fines and to deductions for the cost of materials, like for the cost of glue and the brushes they needed to make Bryant & May's matchboxes. (Similarly, coal miners were charged for the candles they burned while toiling underground, so piss-taking employers in fact abounded.)

The girls were often too poor to afford shoes and worked bare-footed, but a foreman could still fine them for having dirty feet. Other unfair deductions /fines which could be - and were - imposed, included having an untidy workbench, or for merely talking. The girls worked a 10-hour shift, and ate their lunch at their workstation.

Under the terms of the new agreement most of the deductions were abolished, a rudimentary grievance procedure was introduced, and from then on a separate room was to be provided where their food would no longer be contaminated by close contact with flesh-and-bone-destroying phosphorus. With terms agreed, the strike ended. Such were the times and the general working conditions which would not have been unfamiliar to our Baxters and Titleys.

The second news-worthy item that year occurred on September 1st1888 when the body of a poor and desperate woman had been found. She had been a married mother of five, a charwoman and a domestic servant, who had fallen upon hard(er) times – not that there were any easy times for the working class. Her depressed condition, though, had led to her becoming a drunkard with all the attendant problems of alcoholism: she became unable to afford rent, and subsequent rough sleeping and a rougher lifestyle had all contributed to her then succumbing, as many poor souls did, to survival by means of prostitution. Of course, to the newspapers she was just a prostitute, and it was in that capacity that she easily fell prey to her killer. (In very recent times the press have managed to adopt a more neutral *politically correct* tone and refer to those in the oldest profession as "sex-workers," but I imagine historic victims will still continue to be simply labelled "prostitutes".)

This poor Victorian woman had had her throat cut, and her murder was at first linked to two previous homicides in the area; but then as details of Mary Ann "Polly" Nichols' further mutilation emerged, another victim was brutally murdered within one week! The devastating hallmarks of these two recent murders were plainly similar, and now the wider public's attention heightened. These, as you may have guessed, were to be the first two of what was to be the series of gruesome murders in East London, which have come down to posterity as the work of the infamous *Jack the Ripper*. Whilst he may have had other victims, only 5 murders were definitely attributed to the assailant, and these are known as the canonical murders.

The police never solved the crimes or found the culprit, but for some reason the Ripper murders stopped. Naturally, though, no one knew if they had stopped for good or if there were more to come; I would imagine the fear of attack, therefore, lingered –and probably did for years. [62]

---

62 The Coroner for most of the Ripper victims was one Wynne Edwin Baxter, a Sussex man (a Lawyer and a Botanist) whom I suspect was not a relative of our Francis Baxter. W E Baxter died at his home at 170, Church Street, Stoke Newington, in 1920, at the age of 76. Apparently he has a memorial against the east wall of the churchyard of All Saints Church in Lewes.

Incidentally in 1888 there were apparently over 200 common lodging houses in that Whitechapel area, where beds were available on a nightly basis. These "slept" over 8000 desperate people, who if they had four pennies (4d) could have the use of a single bed until maybe a little after dawn. [63]

If a weary soul could not afford that four pence they could pay half-price for a "hang-over": now in case you might think this had something to do with the after-effects of a binge drinking session, this hang-over was a different experience. It referred to a dubious luxury that could be had: for the cost of tuppence an exhausted body was allowed to hang itself over (or drape itself over) a rope which had been stretched across a dormitory. I suspect you would have to be pretty drunk or otherwise wrecked by an exhausting day to derive any ease or any degree of rest from that, let alone any sense of enjoyment..... but still...in its favour, it kept you off a draughty, damp and cold floor.... and out of the rain...**and** perhaps more importantly you were out of the public domain.

There were no shop-doorway sleepers then as there are currently and seemingly everywhere in the UK (and particularly in London – the very "heart and centre" as capitalists proudly boast "of the world's financial institutions"). Neither were there "cardboard cities" – those bleak conglomerations of the destitute which also currently abound within London, below the bridges, at the back of railway stations and under the raised sections of

63 Remember the striking Match-girls? They only earned 4 shillings or 48d per week. At that rate even a week in the doss house would have cost them more than half their wages!

motorways. No; all forms of external rough sleeping were not allowed then. Any person found sleeping rough in a public place, a park, on a bench or in an open space would attract the rougher attention of the police. All such acts of sleeping/resting-from-exhaustion were offences for which the police could and would imprison you. Although, they no longer branded people with a V on their forehead, vagrancy was still alive offence which was prosecuted actively).

Getting on with Life

Fortunately the stonemason always seems to have had enough work or income to have kept a roof over his and his family's heads. They also appear never to have had to resort to the workhouse, so even if they weren't rich they at least were not the most desperate and poorest. Their homes were always to be found where there was work, and therefore they would never inhabit the most genteel sectors of the city; but as Booth's poverty map of London shows, though, even the well-heeled gentle sections still nestled cheek by jowl with some of the poorest sections on a street by street basis. No one was ever geographically far from poverty and degradation.

Less than a couple of miles from the scenes of Jack the Ripper's homicidal activities - and when the murders were still fresh in the minds of all the locals – the stonemason and his family were all going about their business.

Cottage industries and home-working enterprises may well depend on a family all working in the same trade while operating different divisions of labour, but elsewhere, it doesn't do to put all your eggs in one basket.

Whilst the stonemason's Dad had been a cutler – a maker of sharps and blades – and his grandfather had been a bricklayer, he had learnt and knew his own craft. Here was a family who knew and understood the value of diversity, a unit perhaps better able to sustain a slump in one trade as long as others still had work. Thus, Francis's brothers also mainly learnt their own individual trades: William was a wheelwright/tyre-smith, while Richard was a blacksmith, and Alf and Thomas were confectioners and cooks.

Some trades overlapped, and some were to an extent co-dependent. In 1891 his brother, William, aged 50, was still working as a wheelwright/tyre-smith in Clarendon Street back in Somers Town. [64] The term *Wright* comes from an Anglo-Saxon word *"wryhta"*, meaning a worker or shaper of wood. The wheelwright specifically and usually would have been working with three main types of timber because each had qualities and properties which were vital to the construction of a successful wheel. He would have used elm for the nave – the central part or hub of the wheel – because its grain is interwoven, which doesn't split easily. This quality is important when the spokes are driven in as tight as possible, it being imperative to have no movement

---

[64] *Family history information: With wife Susannah, and children Leonard, 20, Alf, 14, Charles, 11, and Alice 8. William and Susannah appear to have survived until at least 1922 when they were still in Leighton Rd.*

between or in joints. William would have used Oak for the spokes which radiate from the nave, because this timber is strong and solid; it doesn't bend or compress. The spokes connect the nave to the outer rim, which is known as the felloe of the wheel. Here the timber from an Ash tree was mostly used because of its flexibility and shock absorption. All that was needed to finish the construction was to fit a tyre.

Now whilst Robert Thompson had patented a pneumatic rubber tyre (one that could be filled with air) in 1847, he failed to develop it. In 1888, though, John Dunlop was more successful, but his design and production did not become widespread until the 20th century. Therefore, in 1891 William Baxter's construction of his wooden wheel needed to be finished off with a solid-iron hoop or tyre, which would have been custom-made by a blacksmith like William's brother, Richard Baxter. The circumference of the iron-tyre was always made slightly smaller than that of the wheel; and in order to fit it around the felloe of the wooden wheel it had to be heated, causing the metal to expand. Then the wheelwright would hammer the tyre while levering it on using his "devils claw." At that point when it was properly aligned it would be quenched in the ducking pond which - upon cooling - shrank the iron-tyre onto the wood, tightening all the wooden joints of the wheel. Unfortunately the days of wooden wheels and the need for a wheelwright were numbered (as are now in the 21st century the days of the pneumatic tyre). Nevertheless William carried on his craft, and appears to have been the last Baxter link to remain within Somers Town. The rest, though, seem to have all moved on.

His sister, Eliza Tuckwell, had gone south of the river some years back when she had married a mariner. There she had looked after their Mum essentially until she died in the St Olave's Workhouse Infirmary in Rotherhithe. Come 1891, though, Eliza was living in Reculver Road, Deptford, with her husband William.

Eliza – if I have the correct one – appears to have died that very year, aged about 48. *(William, Tuckwell, the stonemason's son-in-law died, I believe, in 1901 and their daughter Eliza Elizabeth Tuckwell (b 8.6.1872, according to the 1939 register) was aged 24 when she married 22 year old Amos William James Chandler, a carman in 1896.. In 1901 she would be living just around the corner from her cousin Martha Titley nee Baxter in Haggerston in Acton Street.)*

At that time and not far from the stonemason's children in Hackney, his brother Alf was still boiling sweets. The 57 year old confectioner and his wife Phoebe (nee Collier) were living locally in Stanley Rd off Balls Pond Road, near Boleyn Road and Kingsland Green with two sons: yet another Francis Baxter (a printer's compositor) and Walter. They would shortly move to Dartford in Kent. The other brother-confectioner /cook, Thomas Baxter, and his wife Caroline (nee Collier) are said by sources on MyHeritage as dying 28.6.1895 at 13 Pancras Walk, with Caroline dying in 1884. *(Their daughter, Caroline, born 1864, married Jabez Hewlitt; and worked as a confection packer, living in Osborne Rd H/Wick. She had 15 children by 1911 - of whom 6 died.)*

Meanwhile, the 67-year-old stonemason had left siblings, children and Hackney behind, and had headed off to Essex. He was then living at 90 Collard Road, between Shernhall Street and Wood Street in Walthamstow with Elizabeth (then shown as 57) and her 23 year-old son Robert Dyde (RG12 1356/32). I can only imagine that given his occupation he was a hardy soul who managed to keep going.

Even in my youth most people in their sixties tended to be at least a bit frail, often with wavering quivering voices, and could be mistaken for being knackered in all senses. Things, in that respect, have changed for the better and the elderly generally are looking healthier, fitter and a bit more positively charged. Michael Caine, the actor, recently commented that he had heard that the death of one Old Charlie had been greeted with,

"Well, he was 80! He'd had a good innings!"

Caine, rather indignantly said, "A good innings? I'm 83... and I don't feel like I've come in to bat yet."

The whereabouts or indeed the fate of the stonemason's brother, Richard Baxter, and his wife Susannah is not yet known; a number of people so-named - and within areas where they resided - were recorded as dying between 1881 and 1887, but any of those candidates might have been them. However, the blacksmith/Smith (a worker in metal) was not recorded as being dead on the marriage certificate of his daughter Alice Baxter to William Edward Bush, a canvasser, at St. Mary's Islington on the 15th of September 1891. (Sometimes they omitted to record such details, which may and can mislead a researcher.)

Occupations and livelihoods apart, Francis, meanwhile, was about to become a grandfather again; I wonder, as this would be about his 18th grandchild, whether he had stopped counting. In the summer of 1892 his daughter, Phoebe, duly had her third son: Arthur Ewart Titley (my Grandfather), who was born at 8 Lenthall Road, Dalston.

So, the family increased, but then, as it happens, Alf the confectioner did not get to appreciate the Kent air for long. He died there on January 13th 1893, aged 59 years. [65]

Death was always knocking on the door, and they never knew whose door would be next. Unfortunately for the stonemason, his son, George Baxter, (Phoebe and Martha's second eldest brother), would be getting an early call from the grim reaper. I believe, he was only about 45 year old when he died in 1896 in Bethnal Green.

That third son, born in 1892 to Francis and Phoebe, was Arthur Titley. His middle name, Ewart, strangely does not appear to have ever occurred within either Titley or Baxter families (or any other associated family name); perhaps, instead, it may give a clue to the political affiliation of Francis and Phoebe.

CLUES TO THEIR POLITICS ?

Ewart was the surname of the liberal MP who amongst his other achievements not only removed the death penalty for many offences but had instituted the provision of Public Libraries. Alternatively, the choice of Ewart may have been a nod to the middle name of William Gladstone, four-term Prime Minister, as well as a four-term Chancellor of the Exchequer. Having served in both capacities for 12 years each amid a 60 year parliamentary

---

[65] *Family History information: His gravestone in East Hill, Dartford, also commemorates his wife Phoebe who died 28.9.1925 aged 89; and also their sons Alfred, who died 16.2.1919 aged 57 years. Francis (1865-1908), Charles (1867-1918) and Walter (1869-1919). The whereabouts of their daughter Maria, who was 17 in 1881, is unknown. Incidentally, twins (Charles and Frances a girl) were born to Alf and Phoebe on 26.8.1865, baptised at St Mary's Islington*

career, he was known as the G.O.M. (the Grand Old Man.) He had brought in the Reform Act of 1884, which extended the vote to agricultural labourers and which gave the counties the same franchise as the boroughs—adult male householders and £10 lodgers. It further boosted the total number of men who could vote in parliamentary elections by six million.

Gladstone amazingly apparently supported the London dockers in their strike of 1889. He would later say, "It is a lamentable fact if,... at the close of the nineteenth century, the workhouse is all that can be offered to the industrious labourer at the end of a long and honourable life." *The Times* (12 December 1891), p. 7.

Outside Bow Church – not the one whose bells Cockneys are supposed to be born within the sound of – there is a statue of Gladstone. It was made by Albert Bruce Joy at the behest of match manufacturer, Theodore H Bryant of Bryant and May in 1882, who paid for it.

I don't know how they voted but a Baxter and a Titley were recorded as being in attendance at a local political meeting, which if it does not indicate support does show interest. On the 29th June 1892 a Titley and a Baxter appear listed in the Gazette as present at a meeting in Bay Street, Haggerston, around the corner from Lenthall St. where Francis Titley lived. Perhaps this Titley may have been Francis Titley.

This was before the creation of the Labour Party, and it appears Francis had some involvement with the Radical Club and possibly favoured the Liberal candidate J Fyfe Stewart (an "unsung hero amongst Quaker emancipators). I had heard tell of a family connection to Quakers (the Society of Friends), and although I have found nothing specific this appears to show some Quaker connection or may point at least to sharing certain sympathies with a Friend.

The Hackney Gazette's article initially reported a manifesto being issued by a group of workers, who represented members of the Hackney Radical Club, the Political Council of the Radical Club, the painters' union, the Clickers Union for certain people in the shoe manufacturing trade, the Shoemakers' Society, and the National Union of Boot operatives. (This seems to underline the fact that Hackney was an important centre for shoe and boot-making. In time, Cordwainers' college was set up in Mare Street.) Fyfe Stewart had been interviewed by these local labour leaders who found that he (Liberal candidate) was "earnestly desirous of shortening the hours of labour" and in favour of legislation that would benefit the masses. The article stated he was also strongly opposed to sweating in any form. This referred to the so-called 'sweated' industries, which relied upon home workers: men, women and children who made a product at home. The conditions in homes were not subject to or regulated by the Factory Acts, so that wages, safety and the working environment were beyond control. The products were wide-ranging, but the common factor was that these were desperate workers; people who worked hard, throughout long hours and in poor conditions for very low pay which was only a fraction of the ultimate retail price. They mainly worked for a middleman, who sold the products on to the retailer, making a good profit for himself and for his buyer.

The manifesto appealed to people to support the candidate. Fyfe then attended the Bay Street meeting, which was held in a schoolroom. A vote of confidence in the candidate and the Liberal and Radical programme was enthusiastically carried with only two dissenting voices. (I cannot confirm or deny who were the dissenters but family hearsay would seem to lean towards those two not being a Titley or a Baxter.) The report says that nevertheless Fyfe Stewart's canvassers will have their work cut out for them.

'TIL DEATH (LITERALLY) DO YOU PART. ILLEGITIMACY. WOMEN'S RIGHTS/ACCESS TO CHILDREN. DIVORCE.

Circumstances, attitudes and conditions all change. In my era attitudes to unmarried people, to cohabitation and to children born "out of wedlock" (bastards, no less) had all changed – and dramatically so from when I was a teenager.

Theoretically, at least, there was a sequence to the progress of a couple's relationship: courtship, marriage, copulation, procreation.... Although, naturally, the order was not universally adhered to, and of course, not everyone got married. Regardless of that there were inevitably babies born to single mothers and to co-habiting couples, who did not marry for one reason or another. Some of those who did not marry their current partner were already married, and short of their actual spouse dying they would never get the opportunity to remarry. They could not get a divorce.

They used to say, "When poverty comes in the door, love flies out of the window..." but of course that might not be the only strain on a marriage. Whatever straw it may have been which broke the camel's back, there were desertions, but mostly a great many people lived unhappily together in a crippled relationship. Similarly they had little choice.

Divorce had been nigh on impossible for the vast majority of people at the start of the 19th century, save for the few wealthy people who could afford the expense of a private Act of Parliament. Mid-way through the century some changes were made, but divorce was still not an easy option – such that towards the latter part of Victoria's reign there were only around 300 divorces in total in all of England and Wales for the year of 1890.

A note about co-habitation:

At school in the 1960's I wrote an essay for my English teacher extolling the virtues of co-habitation as opposed to living in holy wedlock/ or following a civil marriage – which would then have been a marriage, that is, between a man and a woman. {There was not even the most infinitely small fraction of a scintilla of a notion then that there might ever be such a thing as a same-sex marriage; same-sex ***sex*** *had only just become legal between consenting adults!} To return to the matter of co-habitation, however.... the teacher snootily commented, "It makes them sound like chickens..." Perhaps I misunderstood him.*

A SMALL OVERVIEW OF SOME DATA

Of course there are knock-on effects of changes in the number of marriages. As *marriage* declined in the late 20th century, the data reflected the trend set by co-habitation with its impact on illegitimacy.

In 1889 ONS data shows that of 885,944 births in England and Wales that only 40,627 were illegitimate. This was just over 4.5%. In 2019 out of 640,370 births the figure had risen to 310,399, almost 48.5% - thus nearly half of all children born in those two countries in that year could anachronistically be considered as "born out of wedlock." The fact of illegitimacy is now rarely if ever mentioned, and stigma no longer attaches in the way it once did – if it even attaches at all.

Social attitudes have also changed. Many couples now would almost insist on living together first before they entered into marriage. They may not be aware of the old adage but they are certainly more careful not to "marry in haste and repent at (their) leisure". They accept now that as a result of changes in Divorce laws -and a growing intolerance to living in a bad relationship –that they will not have to repent for too long. Divorce, like illegitimacy, no longer carries a stigma in civilised, western and cosmopolitan environments. These have all affected the numbers of dissolved marriages, and today ONS data shows that around just over 4 in 10 marriages end in divorce.

It must be recognised, though, that the number of marriages have of late received a boost as a result of cultural differences that attend immigration – where there is a greater expectation of marriage before living together - and from the legalisation of same-sex marriages.

DIVORCE IN THE 19TH CENTURY

Bad marriages, vile, profligate and abusive husbands and insane wives were features of 19th century novels and to an extent they are testaments to the laws as they applied then. The contributions of Jane Austen, George Eliot and Charlotte Bronte all illuminate our understanding of the times and of the conditions that particularly (but not exclusively) affected women.

Marriage traditionally subsumed the rights of a woman, such that her husband not only gained rights to his wife's property, but from that point on she was not permitted to enter into any contract (or apparently even make a Will) without her husband's consent. Any independence was lost.

Women, such as the heroine of George Eliot's Middlemarch, Rosamund, were trapped within abusive and loveless marriages, and had no means of redress or legal way out of the union. Wives were viewed in law as mere chattels: property belonging to their husbands. Any woman trying to escape her situation had to bear - or be liable to - various punitive consequences. For example, in Anne Brontë's novel, The Tenant of Wildfell Hall (set in the reign of George IV when Francis Baxter the stonemason was born) the "tenant," Helen, is forced by circumstances to conceal her real identity. She has to live under an assumed name because by fleeing the marital home, she has broken the law and deprived her husband of his property. Helen has also compounded the offence by taking her child with her, thereby further depriving her spouse of more of his property: their offspring. (If she had left her husband for another man, the latter would be liable for "damages.")

The husband was master; and at the time he could control every aspect of the home and of his wife's life: he was also allowed to prevent his wife from seeing or having any access to their children. She simply had no right to her children.

This situation is evidenced (Margaret Wood 2018) in the actual non-fictional case of Caroline Norton, a writer and social reformer, who had married in 1827. It was her misfortune that in doing so she had thus tied herself to an abusive, dull, lazy and vindictive husband, with whom she disagreed vociferously - and publicly - on politics and many other matters. She was, though, certainly no doormat. It is unlikely he greatly appreciated her forthright manner, but he was also a conniving wretch. He had been a Tory MP until he lost his seat, whereupon he apparently asked his wife to use her influence with the Whig politician, William Lamb, who - as Lord Melbourne - was able to secure him a position which gave him £1000 a year. When he later got into debt it was said he approached Melbourne directly for money; upon being refused Norton went on to accuse him of "alienating his wife's affections," and sued for "criminal conversation" with his wife, which was tantamount to an accusation of committing adultery with her. He also exercised his right to remove his and his wife's children to another house and to bar their mother from any access to them.

In order to obtain a divorce wealthy people could apply through a private Act of Parliament to dissolve the marriage on the grounds of adultery. However, when Norton lost the case against Melbourne, and with the adultery not proven, he was unable to get the marriage dissolved. Stuck with her, he continued to deny Caroline access to her children.

As was the way of things *her* reputation was ruined, and whilst he carried on sponging, nevertheless Caroline campaigned for changes to the rights of mothers and children: she was partially successful, in that the subsequent Custody of Infants Act of 1839 granted mothers the right to petition for custody of children under the age of seven and for access to their children under the age of sixteen. Women did not gain the right of custody nor to access, but now they had the right to petition for them.

Private acts of Parliament continued to be effectively the only way to obtain a divorce for more than the first half of the century, but this was only available to wealthy people - with only about ten private acts for divorce being passed in Parliament each year. It was not until the 1857 Matrimonial Causes Act that a special court system was set up to deal with divorces. While parliamentarians (and their wives) continued to have upper-class liaisons and affairs they were very selective with their views on morality. To discourage "unbridled immorality," which they thought might be occasioned by the lower classes having access to divorce, the Act established just one court in London. Thus, divorce continued to be unavailable to many people throughout England by virtue of being geographically beyond their reach in most cases.

The new Act also set unequal conditions for allowing the divorce: women, as usual, were to have tougher and more difficult grounds than men. Whilst a husband need only prove just one instance of his wife's adultery, a woman could only obtain a divorce if her husband was physically cruel, incestuous, or bestial – and in addition she had to prove repeated instances of adultery.

You might imagine it would be intolerable, but women subjected to that cruelty were also required to remain with the husband or within the marital home until the divorce was obtained! If she left she would forfeit claims for property as well as custody of the children. Her rights to property she had brought into the marriage would also be lost. It would not be until later legislation like the 1870 and the 1882 Married Women's Property Acts and further amendments that married women were granted more control over and rights to their own property.

It was, though, the 1857 Matrimonial Causes Act which allowed the stonemason's niece, the daughter of Richard Baxter and Elizabeth Holland, to go to court in 1896. There, Alice Bush nee Baxter sought a divorce from her boorish husband. It appears she had more than enough grounds.

Alice listed the places they had lived and the duration they had spent there: Malmesbury St, Bow, for 5 months, Alfred St, Bow, for 3 months, Merchant Street for 4 months, and Langthorne Street Stratford until January 1895 when she had been forced to leave as a consequence of his habits, violent ill-treatment of her and his intemperate behaviour. They had two children: 3 year old Ethel Maud Alice Bush and 2 year old William George Bush. Alice cited repeated occasions of physical abuse, of being hit with his fists, of being thrown out into the garden, of her husband's repeated drunkenness and examples of his adulterous antics. And for good measure he had (given her) a venereal disease!

Divorce granted - and well deserved..

(England & Wales Civil Divorce Records 1858-1918 > 1896 >17853-17862> 17854:BUSH)

It was in that year of 1896 that from April 6th until the 15than athletic festival took place in Athens: it was the first modern Olympic Games. These inaugural Games were attended by 280 athletes from 12 countries. I doubt many women will be surprised that the competitors were all male.

It was also in 1896 that the stonemason's daughter, Phoebe Titley nee Baxter, gave birth to Clifford Rolland Titley. So, at that point Francis Titley and his wife, Phoebe, had four sons, who at least appear to have been healthy. [66]

Well, kids, however delightful and entertaining, are always still basically "eating and drinking machines." They also happen to need clothing, cleaning and shelter, and as such they are a drain on resources and the family budget; of course "family planning" (as we know it) was only rudimentary then, and perhaps it was by nature or by effort (restraint/ luck/ whatever) and/ or by choice that this Titley/Baxter unit only had four kids. What is entirely probable, though, is that they had other plans and appear to have harboured some ambitions for future prosperity.

One example of the effort for self-improvement is that I understand Phoebe actually taught herself to read and write, which does signify a certain determination. She must have been a bit of a dynamo, but whether she was THE driving force of her relationship (and whether that matters) I could not say. (Of course the stonemason had to have known how to read and write

[66] Family History information: They would all grow to become not quite Olympians but still very active sportsmen and boxers. No one, though, could know that yet – and even so three of them would nevertheless die relatively young: aged 48, 49 and 53! Such is the matter of life and of death; and who knows what the future holds?

so there must have been some level of literacy within the home of Phoebe's youth; although, bearing in mind the prevailing times, education as it was, and attitudes to women, it may be that the Baxter girls were not taught to read.)

I wonder how the stonemason viewed his offspring in the Hackney area, and what level of personal contact they were all able to maintain with him. I can only think he would have been pleased with their ambition, because as the 19th Century drew to a close, the three family groups of Titleys and Baxters, who had resided at 8 Lenthall Rd (off Queensbridge Road) in 1891, had apparently each embarked on their own enterprises.

It was relatively small-scale, but it showed some degree of aspiration. His son-in-law, Martha's husband William Titley, had set up as a builder, his son Alf Baxter and wife Alice had opened a grocery at 88 Boleyn Road, Dalston, and Phoebe's husband Francis Titley was described as a house decorator. I am not sure who had the enterprising genes, whether it was the Baxters or the Titleys or both, but it would not be long before Phoebe and Francis Titley also became chandlers and grocers: first in Stoke Newington, and then with shops near the Angel Islington and in Hoxton.

Booths' Survey

Perhaps the Dalston area had changed from the 1880's, but I'm not sure whether it was for the good or bad. Whatever, George Duckworth noted for Booth, in Queen Victoria's Diamond Jubilee year of 1897, that Blomfield Street had 2-storied housing (ranked as purple / rather poor) with some prostitutes known to live there.

Blomfield Street was bisected by Lenthall Road with the northern part marked as very poor and its residents as in chronic want, with the southern part slightly better off: that same mixture of comfortable and poor as occurred in Lee St. I don't know on which half the Titleys were living but I doubt they were "in the pink." Duckworth also noted that 2 Lenthall Road was on the corner of Blomfield and contained a dancing-place, which he added was well conducted. The policeman, Inspector James Flanagan, who accompanied him described the inhabitants as "rough."

In London there were and are always pockets of poor and of wealthier people nestling, but I wonder if and how the area had changed between 1881 and 1897? In nearby Wayland Avenue off Sandringham Road and Dalston Lane at that later date there was a Public House which had been closed down for harbouring prostitutes; nevertheless the Pub was said to be very clean and well kept. Opposite was a *refuge for fallen females*: it is described as "a kind of rescue home". Apparently after they have been sufficiently "reclaimed" the superiors of the home found the girls work; unfortunately Flanagan said, "the new employers take advantage of them – knowing their backgrounds – and pay them such low wages they have to revert to prostitution." He also noted that general servants in the area had the reputation of being queer kind of girls. The inspector called it a monstrous shame.

It is difficult to reconcile some of the comments as they can be so contradictory. Despite the rather bleak picture many of the houses were classified as pink or red; a "well-to-do" area according to Duckworth where a sole servant must come with references and does the housework, while the wife of the householder does the cooking.

From Duckworth's notebook: Police and Publicans District 14 West Hackney and S E Islington, and District 15

For those who fail to appreciate the relevance of why they are taught geometry – and are unable to see any beneficial use in their daily life – it seems the Victorian drinker had other ideas.

Mr Duckworth noted an interview with Mr T. Cox, manager of five public houses, on the 10th of November, 1897. The manager said that until recently people had their beer served in pots or jugs, such that the worker who collected empty vessels was called a potman. Commenting on the transition from customers using pots and jugs to an increasing use of glasses (particularly in the better class establishments), which had occurred of late he made the following observation. He suggested that a likely cause was that women working in the pub always had their favourites and gave them nearly a pint for the price of half; as a result other customers became wary. Those who asked for a half-pint to be put in their pint pot were concerned that they might not be getting their full amount. I suspect they may have felt they were possibly being shorted by way of the barmaid's stock adjustment (to conceal and compensate for the largesse she bestowed elsewhere). It seems, according to Mr Cox, that customers brought a little unstated geometry to effect to prevent being shorted: in order to check they resorted to tipping their pot or jug thus :

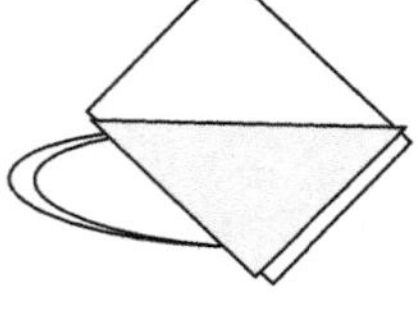

It may then not have been scientifically proven in the first half of the 19th century but the established fact in the eyes and noses of London inhabitants was that water was not clean enough (and almost certainly not safe enough) to drink. This led to beer, port and gin becoming the ubiquitous drinks of choice particularly of those 19th century Londoners. The upside was that they were safe options but the downside was they were alcoholic, which as some might tell you is apparently only good in moderation – whatever that means. (Beer was even part of every child's daily sustenance ration in the Workhouse until the 20th C).

Beer – in its role as the lesser of evils – was indeed seen as preferable to the other alcoholic alternatives, but the Victorians nevertheless had many concerns about the general lack of sobriety and the possible social unrest that it potentially threatened. This led to the creation of a big temperance movement, and advocates of abstinence were keen to find and promote other beverages.

Coffee had long been a contender. Pieter van der Broecke or Bröcke, a Dutch trader (1585-1640), is recorded as having tasted a hot and black drink (coffee) when he visited the port of Mocha, in Yemen. Broecke's portrait by Frans Hals is in Kenwood House, where visitors are told – possibly erroneously – that he was responsible for bringing coffee to our part of Europe. Perhaps he was one trading vehicle, but it was a Greek named Pasqua Roseé who became London's first coffee vendor, selling Turkish coffee from a stall on Cornhill in 1652. The habit and the trade grew, such that there had been a proliferation of coffee houses in the 18th century, and these had spawned an alternative meeting place to the taverns and alehouses. Charging a one-penny admission fee the coffee houses in Oxford were said to provide a forum where there was a culture of discussion and intellectual discourse, which led them to become known as "penny universities." (Perhaps the absence of alcohol and the presence of more sober individuals encouraged discussion of matters which might otherwise have resulted in some unseemly or dangerous brawl?) The popularity of both coffee and coffee-houses continued to rise.

Coffee's origins were in Ethiopia/Somalia and its usage had spread throughout the Muslim world; it was apparently brought to eastern and mid-Europe by the Ottoman Empire, and it was that Turkish connection that was most evident in London. As the levels of literacy were low it was common for pubs, tailors, drapers and all manner of businesses to have pictorial signs hanging up outside their premises. In this way Coffee houses were symbolised by a man in a Turkish turban: a sign that became known as the Turk's Head. The product had been described as "bitter Mohammedan gruel" which does not sound that appealing, but according to Dr Matthew Green (2013) the number of coffee houses in London then surpassed all other cities (in the western world) except Constantinople. [67]

These became places to exchange news but it was predominantly a manly pursuit, and in time coffee usage went into decline, and the fashion for tea drinking – which had an appeal for men *and* women – picked up. Tea was much easier to make – it simply needed just the addition of boiling water. It required no

---

67 Dr Green (2016). The Hoxton Square Coffeehouse was apparently renowned for its inquisitions of the insane: a suspected madman would be tied up and wheeled into the coffee-room where a jury of coffee-drinkers would observe, prod and interrogate the unfortunate object of their attention. Then they would vote on whether to incarcerate the accused in one of the local madhouses. Sounds like great sport – unless you were the one tied up.

roasting or grinding etc.: it was quick and easy money. Tea was, though, quite political.

All governments keep a keen eye on whatever the public spends its money on, so that by the imposition of taxes the public's pleasures are turned into new and very profitable revenue streams. This strategy had, after all, led to the "Boston Tea Party" which culminated in the American War of Independence. Control was lost there, but Empires and imperialists are as relentless as they are ruthless: driven by monumental greed not much will stand in their way, and they soon found other opportunities for their avarice and desire for acquisition.

By the start of the 19th century, the import trade in goods produced in China (such as tea, silks and porcelain) was extremely lucrative for British merchants. Well, that should have been good, but there was a problem : the Chinese would not buy British products in return . (In any trade deal the notion - at least–of reciprocity is paramount! .... Particularly for the weakest partner.) The Chinese, though, were steadfast in not wanting to "exchange" their tea for British goods, and insisted on payment in silver; and as a result large amounts of silver were leaving Britain.

Now at this time there was a truly ruthless organisation, which would in today's terms make the combined mafias, triads and south American cartels look like kindergarten amateurs. This organisation ran its own shipping lines (a veritable navy) and had its own armies to enforce its will upon any unwilling entities. It was called the East India Company, (EIC) and during the early to mid-19th century, it was said to be responsible for half the world's trade. Farrington, A (2002). Controlled by merchants in the city of London it operated under licence from the monarch, thereby enriching both. With regal snouts in the money trough, it was thuggery, theft, exploitation and murder by Royal Appointment! John O'Farrell, (2007 page 247) commenting on the actions of the

Company, described it as the paramilitary wing of the London Stock Exchange.

In order to find another way into the Chinese market and to recoup that silver the EIC and other British merchants began to illegally export Indian opium into China. We normally call this smuggling – unless it is being done by us, our friends and our financial backers (where "us" and "our" do not pertain to ordinary working men and women and their families). This trade also relied upon a demand for payment in silver; the proceeds were then used to buy tea and other goods, and by 1839, opium sales to China paid for the entire tea trade– according to the National Army War museum.

The trade of opium obviously resulted in much addiction (indeed that is the very point of the trade); and it had a devastating effect on the Chinese people and on the country's economy. The Chinese had actually accepted that opium had certain health benefits but they were only too aware of the negative impact of addiction. By 1840 there were said to be 10 million Chinese opium addicts: I do not know how this was quantified, nor whether it related to a specific area, but even allowing for a huge population that is an enormous number of people "using" at a rate quicker than could be earned. And, of course, illegal trade does nothing for official revenues: for taxation and for the type of statistics that economists view when they consider the "balance of trade." Such matters, though, did not concern those involved with the East India Company.

It might be interesting to see who thrived within the East India Company, and what other institutions it created and particularly which individuals it enriched - and whose current "respectable" wealth and property derived from that lawless thuggery?

The Chinese attempted to stop the trade, seizing shipments and destroying them, which certainly alarmed the greedy narcotics dealers and their friends in the UK&I government. This upset led to what became known as the Opium War (or First China War), but we should remember that its roots firmly lay in that trade dispute between the British and the Chinese Qing Dynasty which involved both opium ***and*** tea.

At the end of that war China was forced to cede Hong Kong, to pay big fines and to give preferential treatment to the British (such as is now termed *favoured nation status.*) The 2nd war would force the Chinese to make opium import legal: so that henceforward the merchants of the City of London could deal and trade opium to their hearts content!

So deals were done, but you don't build empires by sticking to a deal or keeping your word – and you must always keep an eye on the future. With that forward-looking strategy in mind the powers that be also decided that their reliance upon China for tea was not a guaranteed long-term option – they wisely didn't take it for granted. They also realised that tea could be grown successfully in the climates of India and Ceylon, which by way of being another bonus were not as far away as China was to the centre of the British Empire. In common with all the enterprises of the much lauded British Empire the tea trade was based on an imperialist cut-throat economic agenda.

Tea in the domestic setting was often kept under lock and key in robust caddies in the wealthier homes of England and was, therefore, a luxury item; but as usage increased the price went down and it became more available to a wider consumer base.

Naturally, there was a rush to get supplies here: the quickest ships could get to the market first before the slower ships were able to flood the market. (This was the age where speed very much meant money, and Tea Clippers, ships like the Cutty Sark, were the darlings of the tea shipping trade.)

Initially the tea was taken in its bitter form, but gradually milk and sugar were added to kill bitterness. Now as a non-alcoholic beverage it was able to be marketed as a respectable drink.

Tables were set up in the streets, and ordinary workers were now able to imbibe a safe and refreshing drink. Employers and the rulers of society liked the sobriety of tea, and since it was apparently non-addictive, and was only made with boiled water, it was an easy form of social control. The availability of a non-alcoholic drink was also music to the ears of Methodists and others who favoured and advocated abstinence from alcohol.

Of course, the ingredients of the good old English cup of tea also had their own back story. The availability of sugar had been made possible by the slave trade and the sugar plantations in the West Indies and the Americas, and they are all well known facts. Milk had its own tale. It had previously been supplied by local London dairies which had their own cows and land; but with land being bought up for other purposes the demand soon outstripped local supply. Also the supply problem was now able to be solved by the new railway system which suddenly made it possible for milk to be brought in from country areas. The speed of delivery again meant milk could now be sold in more distant markets before it went off.

All of these factors led to more tea being drank, and also to a demand for the paraphernalia of tea usage: tea services, including tea pots, milk jugs and sugar bowls. Again these had been the preserve of the rich, but then in the 1840's Josiah Wedgewood expanded his output at his Staffordshire Etruria factory. Now his tea sets were aimed at a much wider market, and in time, and from then on, ordinary families – perhaps like the Baxters – began to see these ceramics as an essential part of the home equipment.

WALTHAMSTOW.

By 1901 the stonemason had left Dalston and had relocated again: here we find him in St Mary's Parish in far off Walthamstow, then in Essex.

This area to the north-east of what was then London had also seen a great deal of house-building (as testified to by the age of the properties there – with most streets laid out – and residences being built – between 1880 and 1910). This was a natural overflow response to the rapid increase in the capital's population, but it would still be sixty-four years before London "expanded" and incorporated Walthamstow. (Indeed there are still people in Walthamstow who talk about "going up London." Similarly people still say Romford Essex, when that association also actually ceased in 1965! It is Romford Havering.)

Until then Essex began, as it were, or at least one of its western boundaries was marked, at Lea Bridge Road on the east side of the river Lea, opposite where the Prince of Wales pub was situated. {In an astonishing act of prognostication (of 21st century trends), Prince Charles' marriage to Lady Diana Spencer effected a change of gender to the premises; and it was thereafter known as the Princess of Wales.}

At the turn of the 20th century, though, in Walthamstow there were also many local industries, some larger than others, but they did include the workshop in Grosvenor Park East, off Hoe Street, where the first British car was made. The Bremer Car can still be viewed at the Vestry House museum. When Francis lived in the area every type of trade or service that a community needed was present.

There were many little cottage industries tucked in between and behind houses, off alleyways and side-turnings in Walthamstow, which even in the 1970's still surprised me with the breadth of the enterprises that were then hanging on against the tide of mass production, and just about managing to survive. They would succumb eventually, but strangely in the early 21st century there has been a slight revival of artisan workshops and industry. In that mid-period of the 1970's, though, until the 90's when I lived there, on each corner of my street there was a butcher, a baker, a green grocer and a general shop. In Queens Road there were allotments, a cemetery, three pubs, a fish and chip shop, a barber shop, a newsagent, an undertakers and a vast coal yard (which stretched alongside the railway between Queens Rd and Boundary Rd.) Behind houses there were upholsterers, carpenters, joiners, garage mechanics and steel fabricators, amongst many other trades and small industry. I imagine such shops and facilities were there when the Baxters were in the area. (After his time, large industry would arrive in the area, with for example Hawker Siddeley, an aircraft parts and transformer manufacturer. Hawker Siddeley is now long gone, as indeed are many other things. A change of demographics meant the pubs all closed, and many Asian dress shops opened.)

I do not think Francis the stonemason just went there for the fresh Essex air and the easy life since he was recorded as still being occupied in his craft and was further described as a "worker." Now it depends how you view this level of industry, but I would add, however, that he was now reported as being seventy-six years old with probably upwards of seventy years hard graft under his belt! So good luck to him, or..... heaven help the poor old sod.

So at the time of Queen Victoria's death and the accession of Edward VII, Francis the stonemason was living in three rooms at number 90 Collard Rd just off Shernhall Street with 67 year-old Elizabeth, who thankfully was not shown as a worker. *Census 1901: RG13 1628 f123 Pg11*

His son, Thomas, was an engine driver who was also living locally in Gosport Road (in November 1902), with his wife

Maryann or Marion Wharton. It was there that their son Charles was born. All things must pass. [68]

It seems that Francis Baxter the stonemason outlived his younger second wife too, and in his old age he eventually went to live with his son Francis Baxter junior, who was a railway porter/ticket collector and his wife Mary Elizabeth Baxter nee Cane. Anyway, the old man was a devout coffin-dodger and he also saw his son off, with Junior dying aged 57 in 1906. (The registration district was West Ham, which could confuse anyone familiar with the areas but this district then covered parts of Stratford, Leytonstone, Leyton and Walthamstow.) At that point the stonemason was eighty-odd and would trundle on to the ripe old age of eighty-eight, which can be great if you have wit, health and resources.

---

[68] *Family history information: The engine driver and his family would move on to Limehouse/Stepney until about 1908 when they moved to Sutton in Surrey. They had 6 children: Richard (1900-1905), Hilda (1901- possibly married a man named Haynes?), Francis (1903-?9 born Stepney), Charles Alfred (1902-1977 and Catherine Victoria Baxter (1908-1998) A daughter Matilda born 1910 or 1911 was baptised in 1915 after her dad, Thomas the engine driver – not the Tank Engine – had died. Catherine Victoria Baxter married William Dalgarno in December 1940, and died in December 1998.*

It's entirely probable that our old stonemason Francis and Elizabeth's move to that area led to the introduction of Walthamstow to his Titley descendants: Francis and Phoebe would own or occupy property there in the 1920's (also in Gosport Road), and then I think their sons Alf and Clifford Titley and their wives (Logan sisters) would later also have shops in and off Queens Road in the 1950's. I believe their son Ernie's wife's family (Norris) also had a shop there

An Overview of the Stonemason's life.

Having lived at 88 Major Road, in Leyton/Stratford, Francis was eventually taken into the Union Workhouse in Leytonstone, where he died on March the 10th, 1911. (In 2021 the building has been incorporated into a Tesco's supermarket near the Green Man roundabout, Leytonstone.)

Apparently and sadly he was a touch over-ripe – for the stated cause of his death was senile decay. Now the term *Senile decay* may have been the description of physical decrepitude and or of disability, but I suspect it was probably some dementia, which was then far from sympathetically treated – being much less understood than it is now. Whatever, I hope the longevity and the decay may cause you to reflect that it's not the length or quantity of life which is really important, but it is the quality of life that matters.

Francis Baxter the stonemason and his wife Caroline Gates had at least 11 children, eight of whom survived to adulthood. The fertility of these offspring was wildly variable, and whilst they had at least 25 grandchildren, less than half survived. The stonemason and Caroline definitely laid down the foundations of potentially a considerable dynasty. Life, though, has a way of impacting on immensity and tends to level it out: some people, like his daughter Martha Titley (wife of William), had 13 kids – and only five survived – while others had many less. Others may have had one or even none.

Changes and Innovations, including a Police Force

The stonemason's life coincided with the reigns of 5 monarchs, including the not inconsiderable nigh-on 64-year stint of Queen Victoria. It is certainly hard to imagine both the way things actually were when he was born and the breadth of changes that he saw in his lifetime. These encompassed changes that were made to the environment and to the landscape – the constructions, the building and infrastructure programmes. There were also fabulous technological advancements, innovations and new inventions that were wonders of the age in which he lived, and yet which are the very fabric of much of the normality we mainly just take for granted.

Francis the stonemason would witness those great changes, seeing at first hand the revolution in modes of transport: from a time when horse-driven travel dominated all the means of movement which were faster than man's own natural locomotion. He saw the early days of steam trains, the invention of underground railways, of penny-farthings and bicycles, of motorised cars and vehicles. He may have wondered whether anything else was possible but then he was still alive when man overcame the hurdle of direct flight in a heavier-than-air vehicle (an aircraft). Indeed, it is even possible he may have seen an aircraft fly because it was only locally – on Walthamstow-Marshes – that in 1909 A V Roe became the first Englishman to fly a British-made airplane. [69]

All these incredible transportation advancements occurred essentially in the stonemason's lifetime. In London he would also see fantastic technological achievements like the introduction of gas lighting in homes, as well as the revolution in sanitation which

---

69 It was a tri-plane. Roe and his brother Humphrey became rich(er) when they founded the successful Avro aircraft manufacturing company in 1910. High-flying Humphrey was interestingly and unusually a supporter of birth control and wanted to fund a clinic for the purpose. In the course of trying to achieve this he met (and went on to marry) Marie Stopes, who had just written "Married Love". He funded the publication and with the aid of his wife they opened the first birth control clinic in 1921 at 61, Marlborough Road in Holloway, North London.

was the construction of the great sewer by Joseph Bazalgette. He was among that first generation to experience the different and wondrous applications of the new-found energy source: electricity.

Of course in his work as a stonemason he may have often used his muscle and rope-block-and-tackle to lift heavy stones, but he would live to see the invention of true lifting machines, electric driven cranes, hoists and Lifts (elevators). I cannot say whether or not he actually made use of the new telecommunication devices that were invented in his lifetime (the telegraph and the telephone), but I imagine he may have heard music being played on a phonograph. (He must, surely, somewhere in the last four decades of his life, have experienced the thrill of "listening."Edison, after all, had invented the device – to reproduce *captured* sound on record – in 1877, when Francis had only been about 50 years of age.) Unfortunately the stonemason wouldn't quite live long enough to hear radio broadcasting.

The streets and the environment he knew had all undergone change as did other areas of daily life within his 88 year span. There were also then *new* institutions whose familiarity to us now could easily lead us to erroneously assume they have always been there. For example, when he was a lad there was no official police force – there were thief-takers and the Watch etc., but there was no organisation that was linked directly to the state for the general purpose of what we might regard as even rudimentary policing. The prototype Metropolitan Police in London was formed when Francis was an infant, but the top-hatted Bow Street Runners would still continue to operate until he was about twelve years old. It is difficult to imagine a society without some form of police presence or availability – even granted that they were effectively formed not to serve the public but to protect the rich and wealthy from the public or from a good section of it.

It is also hard to envisage any town or city without other uniformed officialdom such as those individuals who were once known as "traffic wardens." (Naturally, and in due course, the latter will soon be superseded totally by some form of universal camera surveillance... And perhaps drones will patrol or survey the streets? I believe that is called progress, but I can't help feeling it is a fast-track to a loss of both liberty and of the freedom to be "lost" to the eyes of State.)

In addition to the absence of official personnel there was then very little, if any, "street-furniture" barring the occasional signpost. There were, though, gas-lights in some of the streets of London from when he was a lad, but not street lights as we might know them. There were - rather weirdly - a few street gas-lights which used the methane gas from the sewers, such as the one last relic which remains at the back of the Savoy Hotel in Carting Lane. There were also no purely mechanical street items such as pavement/crash barriers, information signs or bus-stops; and of course there was nothing which would rely upon electricity such as traffic lights, pedestrian crossings, illuminated traffic signs, speed cameras, red-light cameras, pollution detectors etc. There were not even road markings or parking bays. (I am assuming parking meters will soon disappear entirely.)

Also absent or non-existent in Francis's day were one-way streets, dual carriageways and motorways, and some streets, roads and bridges still had turnpikes and tolls; and whilst they very nearly almost disappeared totally, tolls in recent years have been re-introduced to pay for bridges, tunnels and some stretches of motorway, as well as for access to city centres.

In Francis's time the now traditional English cup-of-tea, which has become synonymous with Englishness, was in its infancy with tea drinking merely a new fad.

Unlike his grandfather, the stonemason was of a generation who, thanks to the invention of photography, was now able to capture real life images of himself and his kin. Unfortunately, if there were or are photographs of him, no images of him have found their way down to me.

Perhaps these words will suffice to give you a sense, if not of him, then at least of the bigger picture.

THE COMING OF DEMOCRACY AND LIMITED EDUCATION

It was within the stonemason's life that the notion of democracy was adjusted slightly to better the illusion that it could reflect the will of the people, and that ordinary people could change the governing political party: in fact it was in his lifetime that the electorate increased from approximately 5% to 30% of adults.

The early and very gradual steps that ultimately would lead to full emancipation and universal suffrage were set in pace curiously by the efforts at self-preservation of the rich. They hoped the limited extension of the franchise – the right to vote – would encourage the poor to forsake revolution. In this way they sought to ensure their own safety and to protect their position and privilege; and they hoped that the right amount of controlled education would educate the masses just enough to both quell them and for them subsequently to vote "wisely." It had also been seen that the wider provision of education in Prussia had been instrumental in recent 1870's Prussian successes (in business, in mercantile and military operations), and the rich hoped it would impact positively here.

Of course, this "wisdom" the education inculcated did largely preserve the status quo as intended; nonetheless, it was still a significant shift. There had been some private schools and other institutions before, but it wasn't until Francis was in his forties - when the first Elementary Education Act was brought in – that children from the age of 5 to 12 years old were universally entitled (in Britain) to education.

A couple of years later Francis also saw the introduction of the Secret Ballot Act 1872, which managed to be passed despite opposition that secrecy pandered to the unmanly and cowardly. There is apparently some connection between The Elementary Education Act 1870, which was commonly known as Forster's Education Act and the Secret Ballot Act. William Forster, a former Quaker, had introduced the former and he was also a leading advocate of the secret ballot, and supported its introduction by Edward Leatham. The first secret ballot was used on 15 August 1872 to re-elect Hugh Childers as MP for Pontefract.

The original ballot box, which was sealed in wax with a liquorice stamp, is held at Pontefract museum. Liquorice being a local confection is the chief ingredient of Pontefract cakes, which are incidentally about the size of 3 Victorian bronze farthings stuck together (and a little less thick than one 2022 pound coin).

Opportunity for the Fit... but still the Workhouse

So, Francis saw a great many improvements to the system and to the infrastructure of both London and the country, but I wonder how many of these actually positively impacted – and to what extent – upon his daily life or in fact ameliorated the conditions in general. The flush toilet, though, must have been a bonus – *if* he ever had one.

There, of course, must have been some opportunity waiting to be seized by the strong, the fit, the brave and the wily, otherwise the entrepreneurial force which motivated some of his offspring would not have been able to break through into the retail sector of provision-shops, etc.

On the credit side in the book of life's accounts he did not live to see the devastation of the two World Wars of the 20th century, and he missed the Spanish flu epidemic and the depression. I wonder how different an experience he would have found the latter considering the harsh conditions that prevailed throughout his life.

Back to the debit side he would not live to see the creation of a Welfare State and free health-care, nor would he ever be able to enjoy the potential benefits of a pension. In their absence he would know only the daily struggle to survive where at any time injury, illness, unemployment or just old age might tip the fragile balance between a hard existence and life and/or death in the Workhouse. He knew the constant threat of grinding poverty and imminent destitution, and his lot was not improved by the complete lack of employment rights and of human rights.

He was not a slave; he was - it was true - a free man, and in this way he and his fellow Englishmen had, and could enjoy their "white privilege" that is now oft spoken of: the freedom to starve to death in the street or to die in the workhouse – which he did.

I have no idea how this reflects upon Francis Baxter the Stonemason, but I would add a small footnote to this. He was buried in Manor Park Cemetery, Forest Gate, on the 20th of March 1911. I found the reference for the burial, which showed he was in Grave 570, contained in Square 43, which currently forms part of the LG9 section of the graveyard. This grave appears to have been a common or pauper's grave, and has long since been ploughed up, so there was nothing there when I visited it in 2001.

And that struck me as somewhat ironic: the stonemason, having worked with marble and stone until he was apparently over eighty years old, seems to have been buried without even a headstone!

ALL IN A DASH. FRANCIS BAXTER 1823 - 1911

When I look at that date "1823 – 1911," I am reminded of the stark fact that as someone once said, "It's all there in the dash. A whole life is in that dash!"

The dash that was the life of Francis Baxter began in the reign of George IV and ended in the reign of George V, encompassing five Monarchs in total and a considerable span of 88 years.

Now for some forty of those years Francis lived in and around Somers Town, Pancras and areas on the periphery of King's Cross, which is something I mention simply because coincidentally it is said that the latter district was actually named after George IV or at least with him in mind.

It had previously been known as Battlebridge, but that was before a statue of the King was erected there.

KING'S CROSS: HOW IT GOT ITS NAME

The King, George IV, who had been the Prince Regent, had lived the life – as we would say now – of a playboy: constant rounds of wine, women and song... and anything else that might have occurred to him or his pals and hangers-on. The Prince had clung to such hedonism, but inevitably it had taken its toll: as they say, "the years had been kind to him... It was the days and nights that did all the damage..." Yes, as youth slipped away, his life of dissipation had not improved his appearance and in cruel recompense had increased his bulk: there was even more ugliness to contend with and spread across a bigger frame. He was no longer a slim handsome young Prince, just a privileged frog with an excess of corpulence and vanity.

One of the Prince's closest friends had been the dandy, Beau Brummel, a chap famous for his stylish trend-setting sartorial elegance and for his entertaining company. At some time, though, their friendly relationship had broken down and soured beyond restitution. Now, the soon-to-be new King not only cut Brummel from his circle, but also publicly snubbed his witty former friend. Revenge, they say, is a dish best served cold.

On one occasion the decidedly portly George had been out walking with a mutual acquaintance of his and Brummell's when their path coincidentally crossed that of the dandy. No doubt an awkward moment for the third party caught in the middle, especially when George, still intent on shunning his erstwhile pal, again pointedly ignored Brummel. In passing, however, the snubbed dandy enquired loudly of their mutual acquaintance, "Who's your fat friend?" Marvellous.

Of course, the arrow stung mightily the vanity of the man-who-would-be-King, but sadly the reaction of the friend has been lost to posterity. I would have liked to have seen it. Unfortunately that same vanity, self-delusion and/or plain arrogance would subsequently render the King apparently unaware that a sculptor might ever portray him, shall we say "warts and all."

With dignitaries and 'adoring' crowds assembled at Battlebridge, along the New Road by St Pancras, George turned up oblivious to his fate. Awaiting further glorification of being immortalised in stone, and with high expectation of the usual flattery he was accordingly unprepared for the level of realism: George was aghast when the statue was unveiled. Mortified by his evident flabby likeness, he was literally both flabbergasted and livid about its very public presentation.

Quaintly described in 1909 as a ridiculous statue, (perhaps in its meaning that it ridiculed him,) it was said to be the cross he had to bear. Hence it - and subsequently the area - became known as the King's Cross.

Well, that is one version. The other, as stated earlier, is that King's Cross is merely a contraction or abbreviation of the term "the King's Crossroads." I somehow prefer the image of a disgruntled fatty, yoked to the heavy cart of his vanity...

GAUGING AFFLUENCE AND POVERTY

Times change. Fat – that is being fat - is now a political issue: obesity is a current crisis, an epidemic which affects mainly poor people. Its origins are found in poor diet, food additives and education, and as such the wealthier in 21st century society tend to be obesity-free, mainly presenting leaner images: they have money, a comfortable life and they want to live forever. Fatness never before afflicted the poor, and in by-gone days was more likely to be observed in the upper classes.

Art galleries, stately homes and palaces abound with paintings and portraits of aristocrats, royals and the rich elite. These images speak to us across time and as intended allow us to see the opulence of the rich in their fine clothes with evidence of their importance and wealth incorporated within the images. Portraits were essentially statements of wealth. Occasionally, these privileged people are obese, but it is safe to say that those few probably represented the only people in the 19th century who could be said to have been digging their graves with their teeth. Fat or thin, though, these were all undoubtedly wealthy people. The only depictions of ordinary people were the portrayals of their servants, who were usually displayed also in fine clothes to emphasise the wealth of the patron. Other than those few examples of richly adorned servants it is rare to find images of ordinary people – certainly in an urban setting - in their normal and daily attire: the rich who commissioned paintings were unlikely to display the poverty which attached to the system that otherwise enriched them.

Of course it is difficult – if not impossible – to gauge accurately just how poor any particular Victorian might have been. Being "Well-off" is relatively easy to assess because in that age someone so favourably positioned would have employed and housed servants, and the greater the number of servants would be a fair indicator of greater levels of wealth. At the other end of the scale, naturally, when a family was found to be in the Workhouse you wouldn't be sticking your neck out too far to assert they were poor to the level of destitution. It is not, however, so cut and dried with people who did not have servants and were not in the Workhouse: people who were mainly hard at work, whatever the pay amounted to.

In an attempt to refute claims in the mid-1880's that ¼ of Londoners lived in poverty the shipbuilder-cum-social geographer Charles Booth embarked on research which led to a piece of social history called the *"poverty map of London."* To Booth's surprise the research revealed the number in poverty was actually closer to just over 1/3rd.

His researchers did, however, distinguish districts of the "very poor" from those where the residents were in "casual (work and lived in) chronic want." Using colour coding on his maps Booth classified the merely poor (light-blue) where the income for a moderate family was 18 shillings to 21 shillings per week, which in today's currency is 90 – 105 pence per week. He did not put a figure on those he classified as very poor (dark blue); and he probably felt he was unable to quantify the earnings of the lowest class at the bottom (shown in black). You were suitably and literally *"in the pink"* if you were fairly comfortable with good ordinary earnings.

Moral judgement. Imperfect. Class-ridden

His survey provided an indicator of poverty levels, but his definitions and analysis were more hierarchically based upon social class and status. The categories Booth assigned to poorer areas were explicit and selective, especially in regards to what he regarded as the moral characteristics and behaviours of that lowest class. He was seemingly happy to label these as "vicious, semi-criminal" classes, but notably did not comment either upon the industry or the ethics of those inhabitants of the wealthier areas. (Perhaps it just didn't occur to him to label those as "idle-rich," or as "avaricious" or "prodigiously-exploitative.")

A Servant's lot

Naturally, Booth's endeavour was a general survey and those areas which were designated as *well-to-do* and wealthy could not reflect the lot of the many servants there, who may indeed have had shelter and food, but who nevertheless had no longer-term security.

{I wonder if servants' wages - after deductions for bed, board and livery –allowed them to put aside enough or at the least anything in order to save for a future beyond servitude. What was life like for a servant living under the constant threat that the relative comfort of their present situation depended precariously day-by-day upon their acquiescence and subservience? What was the pressure like knowing that it also depended on whether they had sufficiently demonstrated industrious efficiency while keeping (and never forgetting) their place in the social order?

A servant's security, therefore, was dependent upon satisfying the whims of their employers. Any move they might wish to have made was also further dependent on an employers' permission, on being allowed to go and thereby obtaining a suitable reference; and without a good reference there was no chance of future employment in service. Altogether an extraordinary amount of threat and pressure to live under.

POVERTY: A CLEARER VIEW

Even at that time, many had written and commented on the situation of the ordinary majority. Many also campaigned for social justice, for the betterment of general conditions and pay for workers; and they particularly raised concerns for the working-poor and for the infirm. Perhaps, though, those concerned commentators had a clearer view of poverty than some of us may have in the present day, where living in better circumstances and more comfortable surroundings may still disguise underlying poverty.

Our 21st century UK society – even with the benefit of the Welfare State –currently displays a false affluence, such that material possessions are often conflated as indicators that someone is not poor. The vast majority of the population may now have a television, a computer, washing machine/driers, carpets and curtains, but they may still be one of the approximately 2.5 million people in the United Kingdom who used a food-bank in 2020/21. [70] The year may have been twenty-twenty, but our vision still isn't.

---

[70] This was over 600 thousand more than the previous year. The number of food-bank users has increased in every year since 2008/09, when they were used by just under 26 thousand. (See: D. Clark, 2021)

WAS THE STONEMASON POOR, AND HOW POOR IS POOR....?

So what was – and is – poverty? How can you assess it or grade it? Where is the line that is crossed between being a bit hard-up to actually suffering real hardship? Various metrics are currently used but given the scant information available I find it is virtually impossible to determine how my ancestor – the stonemason – may have been "doing." There are indicators from which certain things might be inferred, but most are rather indefinite.

I suspect, though, that Francis Baxter the stonemason may indeed have fared a little better than some others (including many of my other ancestors) for the simple reason that the "workhouse" only apparently swallowed him up at the end of his lifetime.

POVERTY LINES AND THE SEAT OF EMPIRE

Whilst there are different gradations of poverty which may attach to individuals and families they all make for a less than comfortable life. Of course, abject poverty is the ground zero and involves the scarcity or absence of basic food, clean water, health, shelter, education and information. We regularly find such conditions in war-torn zones, where people naturally tend to struggle just to live, and where they often endure a high incidence of infant mortality especially from otherwise preventable diseases. Such *was* the poverty, though, described by Jack London when he visited London in 1902 to investigate the plight of the poor.

In his book *People of the Abyss* he was appalled that poverty was widespread in this capital city, and especially that it attended not just the idle and infirm but even those who were working hard. (As if working hard was ever synonymous with success and a comfortable life....) Mr London found the flagrancy of their pitiable lot all the more disturbing since it resided openly and cheek by jowl with great wealth. To make matters even worse he was sensitive to the fact that this state of affairs existed at the very seat of what the prevailing leaders of the country had the temerity to call "the greatest empire the world has ever known." Indeed the sun never set on the British Empire, but only very few basked in the glow. [71] People who had fled rural poverty and its peculiar attendant problems often found that migration into towns and cities deposited them in the different situation of urban poverty: akin to travelling from the frying pan to the fire.

Measuring poverty is always difficult because there are so many types of it (from relative to situational and generational), but there are also problems with setting the criteria for measurement. (See Appendix) Mean averages which occur in many Victorian studies are probably the most inaccurate.

We must be wary - pinch of salt at the ready - of *mean* averages. It would be more informative to look at the *modes* of income at different times, i.e., the most common amount paid. Even then there would be a need to factor in whether or not their wages were subject to other deductions and charges for materials, use of equipment, fines, the cost of rent, food and clothing/livery, all of which occurred and were imposed on the 19th century worker.

---

71 To add insult to injury, those who lived in the inglorious shade would be "envied" – and, later, they and their descendants would even be harangued and castigated (by others and their kin) "for living high on the hog, while *THEY* starved." Unfortunately, both the envious and accusers were taking it personally, and did not know they weren't *special*. They were ignorant to the fact that their common social class was treated with similar contempt no matter where they resided in the empire. Sadly, many of those in the motherland felt they were in some way superior to those other foreigners: the capacity for incredible self-delusion. Prejudices, though, become ingrained and are very hard to change.

Income may have been positively affected by the provision of "benefits" or negatively by the influence of the seasons on employment. Farm labourers in the 1880s were reported to have taken home around 15 shillings a week – for the weeks they worked! However, out of season they were not required, and when the weather was too bad to work they also just weren't paid at all.

A servant, however, of the Victorian age might earn very little per annum, but theoretically would have all of his or her living expenses covered. They would, in addition, be employed for the entire year whereas an hourly-paid agricultural labourer was at the mercy of both the seasons and of the weather.

Bruce Rosen (see after) wrote: "A Match-woman in the East End of London, in the 1880's would, as we have seen, be likely to have earned from 6–12 shillings (i.e. 30-60p) a week." (The younger women were paid much less.) Even were one of these women fortunate enough to be employed throughout the year, her annual income, at best (that is at the highest rate), would only be around £30! A bank clerk, a shopkeeper or a street-seller would be doing well to bring home a pound a week, and thus approximately £50 per year.

Some indication of the level of wages in the latter years of Victoria's reign Rosen refers to A. L. Bowley(1900), but there are caveats because (Bowley 1899 p555) "of fluctuations in summer/winter earnings for bricklayers, labourers etc.," – and certainly for all those working outside. Agricultural labourers, for example earned different rates in different seasons, with some work paid by the task and others by a fluctuating daily rate. Given all the above details it is extremely difficult to estimate true wages, and even then there is the no small matter of what an amount could buy or pay for.

Another interesting source you might wish to consult is Frederick Morton Eden's *The State of the Poor,* which was published in 3 volumes in 1797, roughly at the time the stonemason's dad was born. It covers a great deal of ground between the amounts of wages which were theoretically earned by the worker and the stoppages/deductions made by unscrupulous employers for the supply of light, of tools or materials etc., necessary for the employee to carry out the work. These conditions were to last for many years.

It may be interesting to make a comparison and to put yourself in the position of that Victorian worker... especially if you have a negative view of trade unions.

IMAGINE YOUR EMPLOYER CHARGES YOU FOR THE WORK YOU DO...

***Imagine** you are working for your employer, perhaps in the city and perhaps in a huge office block. Your office is on the 18th floor, it is winter. You do your work diligently and faithfully for the pre-agreed salary and at the end of the week or month you find you have not received all your wages.*

In fact your employer has made certain deductions. These are not anything to do with any form of taxation, insurance or pension scheme. You find he has charged you for using the lift to get to the office. He has also charged you for the use of his computer, and for the ink and paper used by you to print out the documentation he or she needs you to produce. You are also charged for the electricity used by the computer, and for that used to provide the lighting and for the heating or the air-conditioning. Not only are these charges levied but they bear no relation to the actual cost involved: the charges are dictated by the employer and are calculated at any rate he chooses to charge. In fact you may owe him so much you cannot afford to pay your other bills for rent or food. Your kindly employer then lends you the money you need to survive, and charges you an exorbitant rate of interest. You are now in debt bondage.

Of course the abuse has been updated to make them relevant to your world but all these type of charges were legal (and normal) for employers to impose on their workers when Francis Baxter was living in Somers Town. (And then radical politicians, libertarians and those apparently nasty Trade Unions (that people are taught to despise) came along and fought to stop those kindly practices of those employers. I bet you wished you lived then – or maybe you wish you were an employer then...)

For a long time employers had the power and the legal right to do those type of things. The employer could even pay their employees in different currency or formats - as they did under what was known as the *truck systems*.

These were also known as company stores, where instead of paying the worker in coins of the realm they were given tokens which the worker could exchange within the company store for goods. Of course workers were forced to take goods at their master's valuation, and naturally those goods were over-priced/highly-inflated which further depleted the value of the workers' wage. The store might – and usually did - provide everything from food to tools, and from clothing to lodging/housing; and as the tokens were often insufficient for the workers' total needs this also commonly led to debt bondage. This was particularly prevalent in manufacturing industries, but the system was also present in many trades and occupations.

Francis Baxter was fortunate enough to live through times when social reformers and Trade Unions sought and managed to get rid of such wheedling chicanery, abuses and mean crookedness. During his lifetime he would see the introduction of the Truck Acts, which were vital steps in that endeavour.

The Truck Acts, the name given to the legislations that outlawed truck systems, were first introduced in 1831 when the practice was made illegal in many trades. In 1887 it was extended to cover nearly all manual workers of England. The Acts established the obligation of uniformly paying the whole wages in cash: specifically in the current coin of the realm.

MONEY IS ONLY RELEVANT AS TO WHAT IT CAN ACTUALLY BUY

Of course an amount of money, say £1000, is meaningless unless it is related to what it can purchase. In 1972 £10,000 would buy a house in most parts of London – that seems so little in regards to modern prices that you might wonder, why didn't people buy a handful? The answer is that one was all a buyer could afford, and usually they were stretched to pay for that: if you needed a mortgage (which most people did) it would still take 25 years to pay off, given the interest rates. Only then could you rightly declare you had *bought* it: a common mistake most people made while still "buying" was to make that assertion on the false assumption of ownership, only for quite a number of them to have their houses re-possessed by the mortgage company.

In the 1970's also the so-called "average" person in Russia was said to earn something like £40 per month, which was considered by the UK population as rubbish, derisory and pitiable wages. (Our capitalist government advertised this as proof positive that the grass was not greener elsewhere in a planned economy. However, they failed to mention that the citizens of Russia lived in house and flats where the rent had not been increased for 50 years – not since 1927!)

Furthermore in the depression between WW1 and WW2 it was said the Germans needed to take a wheelbarrow full of money to the bakers to purchase bread – such was the hyper-inflation and value of the Deutschmark. The same distinctions - of what one unit of any currency will buy - need to be applied across the spectrum to the cost of food, clothing, shelter, heat, fuel and the cost of travel.

A pound, a dollar, a Euro, or whatever unit of currency, are each only as good as what it can buy – and this is also dependent upon the moment in time (when you have it) and specific to location (where you have it). A million units won't feed you on a desert island; a billion won't warm you in the Arctic (unless you burn it...). At least, though, thanks to the Truck Acts people had to be paid in legal tender.

VICTORIAN RENT

An *average* cost of rent for accommodation in any era is impossible to calculate because there are so many variables: locality, domestic facilities (such as bathrooms/ showers/ W.C.'s {water closets} and utility machines), size of premises, aspect, proximity to transport /entertainment/recreational facilities etc. In regards to the Victorian era the issue is further complicated because the period spanned more than six decades. But honing it down to the very poor it might be interesting to have a few examples of the rent, which might have been paid in London.

Take one particular family of seven – two parents and five children – who were paying a weekly rent of 5 shillings and 9d (about 28½ pence) in September 1880 for their accommodation in Peabody Buildings, Stamford Street. This wasn't a whole house. The wife in that particular household, "Polly" Nichols, would go on to be the first victim of Jack the Ripper.

Annie Chapman, the second victim, resided in a Lodging House at Dorset Street from June 1888, and paid 8d (3⅓ pence) a night for a double bed. Perhaps she paid by the night, but weekly the rent came to 4 shillings and 6 pence (or 22½ pence) for a bed.

According to Paul Begg (*Jack the Ripper: The Facts,* also *The Definitive History*) and Philip Sugden, the last victim - Mary Jane

Kelly - lived in a single twelve-foot square room, with a bed, three tables and a chair. There was a small tin bath – and no doubt a *goesunder* beneath the bed. Two irregularly sized windows faced the yard, in which the dustbin and the water tap serving the property were located. The weekly rent for this room, according to Sugden (*The Complete History of Jack the Ripper*) was 4s 6d (or 22½ pence). How much, I wonder, did she or the other victims need to earn to pay for their rent of such less-than-luxurious shelter? Mary and the other residents occupying the twenty-odd "apartments"/rooms shared the outside water tap/pump and the toilet facilities, which amounted to three privies at the back of the courtyard. Mary lived at No 13 – unlucky for some, so they say. Her death certificate records it as No.1. (whitechapeljack. Accessed 23.01.23.)

EXPENDITURE

An interesting and informative blog was that of Dr Bruce Rosen, whose writings I sadly found some 7 years after he had died. They are worth viewing. [72] He wrote and quoted the financial advice that Charles Dickens has Mr Micawber offer the eponymous hero of his novel, David Copperfield.

> "Annual income twenty pounds, annual expenditure nineteen pounds nineteen (shillings) and six (pence), result ……happiness. Annual income twenty pounds, annual expenditure twenty pounds aught and six, result…. misery."

---

72 I have tried to contact the address given to seek permission to quote and to reference Dr Rosen's work, but have been unable to make contact.

One can only assume that Dickens did not just pluck the figure out of the air in 1849, and that £20 represented the sum a man might be able to live on. Unfortunately, as I recall, Micawber is unable to follow his own advice (who does) and, while invariably spending more money than he has, Micawber, the eternal optimist, is infamously remembered for living in the expectation that "something will turn up."

I wonder how many optimists there were in the East End in the latter half of the nineteenth century: how many harboured hope that something would, in reality, "turn up." I wouldn't like to guess, but it is obvious that they nevertheless just got on with life: accepted their lot, their role and their destitution without causing too much apparent noise or anything which would disrupt the natural order.

But whilst the poverty in the East End was undoubted, it was undoubtedly also present throughout the metropolis and other cities. My area of concentration focuses on London because no matter where my ancestors were from they all seemed to find their way to London in and throughout the 19th century. Few apparently owned land or property. They had no possessions it would seem that might have survive or befit themselves to be called antiques.

(I do have a shoemaker's last, which I have to say Sotheby's and Christy's are not pestering me about. Nonetheless, and although it might not prop up a bank balance, it will surely and reliably still keep the door ajar.)

Purchasing power

Dr Rosen ruminated on the salient question as to the actual value of twenty pounds at the time of Dickens' publication, and how can we determine its value: what it bought in relative terms while offering other important caveats. (All too often I have seen false comparisons made – for political reasons – even within current times in different socio-political worlds.) It is important to remember to ask ourselves: can we directly compare a former age with the present day?

Of course, wages are only relevant in terms of what they enable you to buy. However, even if we could put a figure on the income of our 19th century stonemason (at any given point in time) it is far from easy to calculate its relative value or purchasing power. A common mistake is to equate the relationship between income and expenditure with present-day figures. To do so, particularly in the area of expenditure, fails to recognize changes in the inherent value of goods. For example, as Dr Rosen asserted, if a product is new on the market, the cost will probably be higher than the price of the same product several years later, when competition may have increased and production methods improved. There are also other difficulties.

Even a staple, such as a loaf of bread, is subject to the vagaries of competition, location, quality and technology: should we attempt to compare the purchase of a local baker's loaf in 1851 with that of the modern loaf? And what, or which, modern loaf should we use for comparison? Should it be the mass produced pre-sliced industrial bread made using the 20th century Chorleywood Bread Process (CBP)? Consider also that its price may also be subject to the whims of supermarket policies and initiatives (buy-one-get-one-free/ or some other lost-leader strategies); or should we compare the Victorian loaf with some modern artisan loaf? It is further complicated because the price of both is also impacted by geographical location. In this way a modern day CBP loaf could be purchased for 65 pence in Kennington while an artisan loaf might be £6.50 in Kensington just some 4 miles away. Purchasing power is always the most relevant feature of this train of thought; nevertheless this is a subject I will leave for you and others more qualified to consider.

I wondered whether Francis Baxter, thanks to the Truck Acts, and pretty much like all his contemporaries, was paid his wages in coins rather than in notes. For a start I thought, that although a stonemason may have been prized, lauded even for his skills and talents, surely I mused he would still have been unlikely to have earned enough to warrant weekly payment which involved a banknote. In 1880, for example, the rent for one room for one night was 4d; therefore, £1 would have paid for two months' rent! [73] Naturally the stonemason was a family man and may have required more than one room, although whether he could afford it is another matter, and there are many instances of families occupying just one room.

In fact, though, Francis Baxter would *never* have seen a banknote. £1 banknotes, for those in that wealth bracket, were replaced by gold sovereigns in 1821, which was before the stonemason was even born; (and they were not reintroduced until after his death and after WW1.)

EVERYBODY COUNTS: TIMES-TABLES

'Everybody Counts: A Report to the Nation on the Future of Mathematics Education' was the title of a National Research Council report in 1989 about children's mathematical education.

---

73 I also wonder, dear reader, would a percentage of YOUR weekly wage cover the cost of your accommodation for two months?

Incidentally, poverty in London did not end with the Victorians. I had a friend who shared one room with his two sisters and their mum in 1967, where curtains provided a modicum of privacy. I believe they had shared access to a kitchen area.

Of course, arithmetic is what it is, but as times have changed so too fashions in perceived educational needs have also changed. What was required by one generation alters to the next.

Children in schools currently learn (if they do) times-tables up to 10 times 10. From that, providing you know what you are doing, it is possible to work out most calculations that you would not resort to using a calculator for. As you go back in time, though, to the post-Great War period it was thought necessary to learn up to 18 times 18; and if you step back to the fin de siècle I have seen times-tables books that cover 25 times 25. Someone must have thought it was a good idea.

In this age we use a base-10 system (called the denary system but frequently referred to as the decimal system). [74]

Under the metric system weights, liquid measures, lengths, volumes and areas are all measured in relation to a base-10 unit. It was not so easy for anyone within Britain until 1971, which includes those inhabitants of 19th century London.

Children and adults all had to accommodate all the different number bases which our ancient systems of weights, measures and coinage made necessary: such that 12 pence made one shilling, and 20 shillings made a pound sterling, and that 16 ounces made a pound weight and 112 pounds equalled a hundredweight, and 20 of those made one ton. And there were more. Many, many more....

---

[74] The beauty of the system is in its simplicity. It uses just ten symbols - 0, 1, 2, 3, 4, 5, 6, 7, 8 and 9, which are called digits, but it is the position or place of the symbol in any number which determines its value. The right-most place of a whole number contains units, its neighbour to the left contains tens of units, its neighbour to the left contains tens of tens called hundreds, and so on with each place to the left being ten times the value of its neighbour. Each digit represents a multiple of the notional value for the position in which it is placed.

Weights and measures

Francis the stonemason may have longed for a rustle of a banknote, but I am almost certain he would have known the feel of a *cartwheel* in his pocket – this was a penny coin minted back in the year his Dad (the cutler) was born (in 1797), but which continued to be used into the Victorian period.

A *cartwheel* gained its nicknamed because of its heft: it was made of 28.3g copper, was 36mm in diameter and 3mm thick. Of course those dimensions would have meant nothing to Francis, because they belong to the SI scale of measurement for weights and measures. Francis was an Englishman of the 19th century, and in England then (and until 1971) we used the different system of weights, measures and currency mentioned earlier.

By weight

All non-standardised goods, whether they were potatoes, salt, sugar, sand, or lumps of rock were sold on the basis of their weight, and this was measured from tons, down to ounces (and beyond...). An ounce is approximately equal to 28.349 grams. Sadly, most of those who might still say they preferred these "English" measurements would not be able to name the system whose passing they incomprehensively bemoan. However, in that ancient imperial scale which was the "avoirdupois" scale: the (*avdp)* ton was equal to 20 hundredweights (20 cwt); the hundredweight was equal to 8 stone, the stone equal to 14 pounds (lbs), and the pound equal to 16 ounces (oz), the ounce 16 drams, and the dram 27.344 grains: a total mixture of number bases!

By linear measure

The stonemason's work and his life, therefore, revolved within a world of imperial measurements: to him the one-penny cartwheel was just a lump: "one solid ounce of copper, one-and four-tenths of an inch in diameter, and an eighth of an inch thick." Certain U.S. American sources might give the dimension as "1.4 inches in diameter" but Francis is unlikely to have ever said such a thing as it is a combination of decimal and imperial terms, and is, therefore, neither fish nor fowl. Francis's measuring stick would have shown 1 and 4/10ths of an inch, and he would have written $1^{4}/_{10}$" where the dimension precedes the two raised strokes, similar to speech marks, which indicate imperial *inches.* Two strokes for inches and one stroke for feet, by the way, were familiar signs to Francis the stonemason. [75]

LSD: THE CURRENCY

The value of the coin then matched the value of its weight in copper, as did the two-penny cartwheel piece, which weighed 56.6g (2oz), had a diameter of 41mm ($1^{6}/_{10}$") and was approximately 5-6 mm or nearly $^{1}/_{4}$" of an inch thick. These George III coins were indeed chunky pieces.

The coinage was also quite diverse which of course reflected the nature of the pre-decimal currency system. Before the advent of the simple base-10 modern decimal/denary system English and British people had to deal with pounds, shillings and pence (£.s.d.). Sometimes this is shown as *Lsd*, where each letter represented a value or denomination. In this way the *L* was an

75 These mixtures of decimal and imperial tend to emanate from the U.S. or from dinosaurs of my particular age, who generally struggled to adapt to the new (patently superior) systems. Strangely, our American cousins incongruously labour under imperial measurements but have a largely decimal currency. Perhaps they don't understand that either.

abbreviation of the Latin word *Libra*, which currently means nothing much except to stargazers and horoscope buffs.

It was, though, a term which was a hangover from Roman times when a libra was a unit weight historically equal to a pound of sterling silver, i.e. an alloy made up of 92.5% silver and usually 7.5% copper, which was added to make it more robust and durable. So, in time, *L* came to represent the denomination value of pounds in monetary terms, while the coexisting pound weight abbreviated its name, libra, to perhaps a once familiar "lb."

The symbol for the monetary Pound of Great Britain became the £, and each pound (£) was equal to 20 shillings or 20*s*, where the *s* represented the denomination value of shillings. ([76]) Finally the *d* of *Lsd* was an abbreviation of the word *denarius* which had been the name of an old coin from the days of the Roman occupation of Britain. The *d* represented the value of pennies; there being 12 pennies to a shilling. King Offa in the 8th century AD had decreed a penny to be 1/240th of a pound, while Henry VII (reigned 1485-1509) further decreed a shilling to be 1/20th of a pound and therefore worth 12 pence. See Appendix King Offa's pennies.

---

[76] There seems to be some dispute as to what exactly the letter *s* was an abbreviation of, with some favouring the word shilling, others solidus, and others still the term, *sestertius*. To complicate coinage matters a little more the shorthand or notation version for shillings was the slash or stroke symbol "/" which when reading left to right – and coming immediately after a number – denoted an amount of shillings. Thus, 4/- signified 4 shillings, and the horizontal dash signified an unspoken "and no pence." (Incidentally the symbol "/" ***is*** called a solidus.) K.E.Bressett (1965) favours "solidus."

Libra is a constellation which takes the shape of ancient weighing balance/scales; the Collins Latin Dictionary and Grammar (1997, 2004) actually translates libra as "pound, balance and scales."

Of course, by the 19th century the coinage and currency system had evolved and, for better ease of use, coins were minted to represent not just unit values like one penny or one shilling, but also other multiples as well as fractions of a unit.

Throughout the lives of our Baxters (until 1920) any coin worth more than one penny was made of 92.5% silver. Pennies and anything worth less than a penny were made of copper. This continued until 1860 when the copper content began to exceed the nominal value of the coin; thenceforward each penny was made of bronze, an alloy made up of copper, tin and zinc. (Neither bronze nor copper coins could be attracted by a magnet. Later post-1962 coins were copper-plated steel, which could be so attracted.)

In addition to the one-shilling piece there were also multiples: a silver 2-shilling piece which was known as *a florin* or as two-bob, and for a time there was also a *double florin* - a 4 shilling piece. Then there was *a half-crown* which was 2½ shillings (or two shillings and six pence). Now I am not sure if it was so-called across the country, but certainly in London the half-crown was also known as half-a-dollar, and was otherwise recorded in the notational form, 2/6, which was pronounced "2 and six." There was also *a crown* – known as a dollar - being a 5-shilling piece.

If these denominations weren't tricky enough shillings were also divided not just into 12 pennies (12d) but into coins of different penny values, such that there were silver tanners (a six-pence piece = 6d) and thrupenny-bits (three-penny pieces = 3d). There were even occasionally minted 2d and groats, which were 4d pieces. Then for good measure there were the fractional coins: copper half-pennies (ha'pennies), and quarter pennies called "farthings." There were even - for a 27-year period ending in 1869 - half-farthings!

The children of our Baxters and all their contemporary youngsters had to learn all the names and relative values of all the coins that were in circulation, just in case they managed to lay their hands on any.

So in regards to handling solid cash in coins everybody had to know "how many of these were worth how many of those." Under our wonderful metric system we just (and only just still nominally) have one hundred pence or pennies (100p) to the pound, which is essentially base-10. But for the Baxter kids and their generation they had to know and be able to calculate using many number-bases: a pound was worth 240 pennies or 20 shillings, but it was also worth 4 crowns, or 8 half-crowns, or 10 florins, or 40 sixpences, or 80 thruppences. If that didn't test their mental agility a pound was also worth 480 half-pennies or 960 farthings. In addition to this a pound was also worth 1920 half-farthings! Naturally, a £1 in all its various divisions was also worth unspeakably vast combinations of those coins.

You may remember – and horse-racing people might insist – that there were also gold guineas worth 21 shillings, but these were last minted in 1813 and so were not strictly in circulation. The sovereign and half sovereign were gold pieces to the value of £1 and 10 shillings respectively, but for general purposes the highest value of a coin less than a pound was a crown. Appendix V contains details.

By the way there is a tradition called the Trial of the Pyx, which still takes place annually to test a sample of coinage for veracity and adherence to the prevailing criteria for size, weight and composition.

Given the above information, and testing your mental agility, suppose a Victorian-you bought an item for one pound, and you had pulled out a handful of change to pay for it. Counting the pile you find there are 2 crowns plus one half-crown plus 2 florins, plus two thruppences, plus one shilling, 5 pennies, two sixpences, 9 ha'pennies and three farthings. How much have you got and how much more would you need to make up that amount to a round pound?

(The answers are in the footnote two pages on)

TAKE NOTE

The bank-notes used in the 19th century – when they were used - were essentially of mainly £1 and £5 denominations, and these notes were white in colour. Until 1855 these were only partially printed and had to be signed and made out to a particular person, much like a 20th century cheque.

The 10 shilling note (=50p) was only brought into circulation in 1928 - well after the stonemason's death. The white fiver was still in circulation up until 1957; and it was only in 1963 that the image of a monarch first appeared on an English banknote.

Now, there are problems associated with bank-notes when used in circumstances where there is a large difference between the purchase price of an item and the value of the payment; for example, when £50 notes were first introduced most publicans and shopkeepers preferred not to accept them because in the case of the innkeeper a couple of pints then cost much less than £5, which would have required him to use up most of his "float" in giving back £45-plus in change. There was also the problem that it may have been an undetected counterfeit. For the same reasons, the stonemason – even if he had earned enough to warrant a wage which contained a pound in value – would not have wanted a bank-note: who would have been willing to change it for him? With a pint costing 2d or "tuppence" the Victorian landlord would have naturally baulked at accepting a pound-note because he would have to give back 238 pennies or equivalent in loose change/coinage. I doubt, therefore, the stonemason got to use many notes.

LAND

Anyone familiar with English horse-racing will know the terms miles and furlongs. They should know that a mile was 1760 yards, and that there are 8 furlongs to a mile, and 10 chains to a furlong. Other lengths included barleycorns, inches, feet, yards, links, rods/poles, chains etc. such that the distance between the stumps at cricket is one chain or 22 yards. When it came to areas we had acres, such that an acre was one chain wide by 1 furlong. Easy? And then we had different measurement scales for dry goods and for liquids....

77

Capital Punishment: the Bloody Code

During his life-time the stonemason had probably witnessed public executions, and with the invention of the New Drop gallows, such as was installed at Newgate Prison in 1783, the performance for the crowd's entertainment could involve 2 or three people being hanged simultaneously. As the drop was not definitely calculated to break the necks of the condemned the affair was often one of relatively slow strangulation and asphyxiation: a true dance macabre, with arms pinned, formerly known as "dancing the Tyburn Jig". (Arnold. 2012 Pg106) (This came to mind when I last saw Michael Flatley...) Incidentally executions had ceased to be conducted at Tyburn as a "concession to genteel sensibilities" as Arnold put it (ibid Pg 123.) The antics of an unruly drunken mob and accompanying vagabonds and pick-pockets were unwelcome in the thoroughfares of the fashionable and newly gentrified districts west of Mayfair, about Oxford Street and Hyde Park corner.

Francis Baxter would also have been acutely aware that such extreme harsh penalties existed not just for murder but for other acts that we now regard as petty theft and misdemeanours.

Apparently at its height the English criminal law, known as the "Bloody Code," included some 220 crimes which were punishable by death. Many of these offences had been

---

[77] It would amount to "19 ten and a farthing" or 19/10 ¼ (aka "19 shillings and 10 pence farthing"), which would mean finding some more coins to make the round pound. Scraping the dust and linings of your Victorian pockets you would hope to locate the necessary penny ha'penny farthing (or 3 ha'pennies and a farthing) to complete the payment.

introduced during the first half of the 18th century to protect the property of the wealthy classes. This was at the time of economic collapse when the South Sea Bubble burst and the effect trickled down negatively to the poor. Food was short but game (wild animals and fish) was still plentiful in the forests and on the lands of the rich; however, Game Laws and Forest Laws forbade people hunting or selling game. In October of 1721 it seems sixteen desperate/bold/hungry (or socially indignant) poachers decided to raid the Bishop of Winchester's lands, and in order to avoid being identified they blacked their faces. Other raids began to take place across a wide area - much to the displeasure of the landed gentry. One of these perpetrated thefts included the stealing of a shipment of the Prince of Wales' wine, an act deemed so heinous it provoked brutal reply. The reaction was the Waltham Black Act of 1723 which created 50 more capital offences: a person could now be hanged for various acts of theft and poaching (of deer, rabbits, hares, conies and fish) and for "blacking the face or using a disguise whilst committing a crime." Of course, blacking the face was regarded as proof of such intent. The Act was in force for a century, only being repealed in 1823 when the future stonemason was born. (See Hayward. Also Hampshire History Society.)

Crimes certainly eligible for the death penalty otherwise included shoplifting, theft of goods valued at twelve pence or more and stealing sheep, cattle, and horses. The death penalty for all theft was only abolished in 1832, when Francis Baxter was a lad. A tireless opponent of various barbarities including the slave trade was Sir Samuel Romilly. This early 19th-century MP worked to remove the death penalty for a host of minor felonies and misdemeanours, including for that of begging by soldiers and sailors without a permit! (Can you imagine our armed forces needing to beg?) In 1806 Romilly managed to end the use of disembowelling convicted criminals while alive. (See:

https://www.lawble.co.uk/death-penalty) His efforts were partly successful during his lifetime, but he certainly contributed to many great and humane reforms which were instituted after his death.

Romilly was also a supporter of the London Corresponding Society: other members included Thomas Hardy, a London shoemaker, John Thelwall, John Horne Tooke, and Olaudah Equiano. (See https://spartacus-educational. com /PR corresponding. htm) The LCS passed some resolutions in 1793 which included the observations: (VI: That it appears to us that the wars in which Great Britain has engaged, within the last hundred years, have cost her upwards of three hundred and seventy million (pounds!) not to mention the private misery occasioned thereby, or the lives sacrificed.) and (VII) That we are persuaded the majority, if not the whole of those wars, originated in Cabinet intrigue, rather than (by) absolute necessity.

Sometimes, it appears that nothing much changes...

The Seditious Meetings Act of 1795, which, had been aimed at preventing discussion of the injustice of any law, constitution, government and policy of the kingdoms was also wrapped up with the Treason Act. It limited meetings to 50 people in any place with the purpose of such discussion. Attendees and occupants inside any place were liable to prosecution and punishment. In a climate fearful of revolution it seems this again could attract the death penalty or 14 years transportation to Australia.

Later, William Ewart, a liberal MP, instigated bills which (in 1834) abolished hanging in chains and ended capital punishment for stealing cattle and other minor offences (in 1837). In 1861, the death penalty was abolished for all crimes except murder; high treason; piracy with violence; and arson in the royal dockyards. The ending of public execution in 1868 (by the Capital Punishment

Act) brought abolition just a step closer, though it would not be achieved easily or soon. The next positive step - which Francis Baxter would live to see - was the 1908 Children Act that banned the execution of juveniles under the age of 16.

All these draconian acts by the state were extant at some point during, if not throughout, the stonemason's lifetime.

CHANGES THAT ELUDED THE STONEMASON'S EXPERIENCE

Francis did not live to see other liberalising changes, which I hope not to live long enough to see rolled back; unfortunately given an apparent global swing towards right-wing politics this seems to become more inevitable than less so.

The Infanticide Act of 1922 made the murder of a new-born baby by its mother a separate offence from murder and one which was not a capital crime. The death sentence for pregnant women was abolished in 1931 and for under-18s in 1933. (These changes may be just about safe, but for the remainder, who knows?) The Homicide Act of 1957 restricted the death penalty's application to certain types of murder, such as in the furtherance of theft or of a police officer.

Strangely it would be the swinging 60's that ended the gruesome version of swinging from the gallows. In 1965, the Murder (Abolition of the Death Penalty) Act suspended the death penalty for an initial five-year period and was made permanent in 1969.

In 1998 Capital punishment was abolished for treason and piracy with violence, making Britain fully abolitionist, both in practice and in law. This enabled Britain to ratify the European Convention on Human Rights (which is also at threat in the 2020's). Those currently pressing to shred the Human Rights Acts might wish first to consider which of those protections they would wish denied to their children.

In 2021 Great Britain and Londoners have a "999" and a "111" telephone service for emergencies, but this was not available to the people of Francis Baxter's time. In fact, the telephone itself wasn't actually patented until the same year in which his wife Caroline Baxter – at the age of only 53 – gave up her mortal struggle. It was patented on St Valentine's Day, 1876 (by Alexander Graham Bell) - 8 months prior to her death and when Francis the stonemason was just about fifty years of age.

(Much of life, and all its happenstances of tragedies and triumphs {and most of the mundane trifles in between}, is a matter of timing, as one Elisha Gray might have testified. Gray, now almost completely lost-in-obscurity, had in fact applied for a telephone patent the very same day as Bell, but his application was rejected as it was said to have been submitted a little later than Bell's: it was, therefore, lower down the list of items to be considered and Gray lost out. [78] Another loser was Antonio Meucci who actually applied for a patent much much earlier than 1876; unfortunately for Antonio the system of patent-applications and importantly patent-renewals require frequent and continued payments in order to keep the patent alive. Antonio, poor chap, had run out of money before his idea was either considered or could be developed, and he wasn't able to afford even to renew his patent application.)

---

[78] Poor Gray. He couldn't even ring the Samaritans... This was an organisation which was later founded in 1953 by a vicar, Chad Varah, which provided the world's first crisis hotline: a service which offered help to suicidal or equally desperate people. It began operating from the crypt of St Stephen's Walbrook, next to London's Mansion House. By the way its telephone "number" was MAN 9000 – *MAN* being the Mansion House telephone exchange area.

Naturally telephones would soon become available - as all new technology is – first to the wealthy, but it took some time before the price dropped enough to have much appeal to the less well off. In the UK, the creation of a national network of public telephone boxes (PTB) did not commence until 1920, with the emergence of the prototype telephone kiosk (the K1) which was made of concrete. Telephones gradually began to appear in homes but not too many ordinary people had them: a situation, which persisted for many years. [79])

In Francis's day if someone had an accident, there wasn't much help beyond immediate neighbours. For example, there were also no ambulances services as we know them. Patients were usually carried on a stretcher by two helpful bodies walking the afflicted or injured to where they could be treated. (The word *ambulance* comes from the Latin ambulario/ambulare to walk or move around, and referred to where a patient had to be moved.) Later they were also transported on a wheeled *litter*).

It wasn't until 1883 that the first ambulance service began in Deptford and this was specifically for transporting smallpox victims to a place of quarantine. The service comprised 6 vehicles which were in different boroughs and these 6 – with 2 river ambulances - covered the whole of London.

By 1915, four years after 88-year-old Francis had died, that ambulance was allowed to carry accident victims; and it was only in 1930 that this was extended to serving people with illness/infectious disorders.

---

79 My family got one in 1960 but we didn't know many other people with a phone, and it was largely an ornament unless a client/customer of my Dad's rang. (It was also a "party-line", where we shared the number/telephone-cable-pairs with some stranger/ household living elsewhere. A nosey party could just listen in to your conversation!)

Ackroyd. Peter, (2000). *London: the biography*. London: Chatto & Windus. Pg 344. ISBN 9781856197168.

Ackroyd. Peter, (2006). *London under*. Pg 88

Ackroyd. Peter, (2012) London, A Concise Biography, Vintage. Pg 321

Arnold. Catharine, (2012) Underworld London –Crime and Punishment in the Capital City. Simon and Schuster UK Ltd.

Axe–Browne. Abigail (27.09. 2016) https://yougov.co.uk/topics /society / articles-reports/2016/09/27/quarter-british-swimmers-dont-think-they] Accessed 23.01.23.

Begg. Paul,. Jack the Ripper: The Definitive History, Published November 4, 2004 by Routledge ISBN 9781405807128 - ISBN10: 1405807121

Begg. Paul,. The Facts, 2nd edition (4 Jun. 2006) Robson Books Ltd ; ISBN-10 : 1861058705 ISBN-13 : 978-1861058706

BGS Minerals Programme for the British Geological Survey (https://www2.bgs.ac.uk/mineralsuk/download/minerals_in_britain/ mins_in_Britain_copper.pdf See Copper kingdom.

Bowley, A.L. (Arthur Lyon) The Statistics of Wages in the United Kingdom During the Last Hundred Years. (Part IV.) Agricultural Wages Journal of the Royal Statistical Society Vol. 62, No. 3 (Sep., 1899), pp. 555-570 (18 pages) Published By: Wiley (at Jstor.org/stable/2979937 24.01.23)

Bowley. Arthur Lyon. Wages in the United Kingdom in the Nineteenth Century (1900). Digitised by Robarts - University of Toronto

Blunden. Edmund, *Shelley, A Life Story*, Oxford University Press, 1965)

Braudel. Fernand, Civilisation and capitalism 15th-18th Century Vol. 2 The Wheels of Commerce. Los Angeles. University of California Press 1992 pp 272,282,294,600-1

Bressett K.E. 1965 A Guide Book of English Coins

British History Tithes https://www.british-history. ac.uk/no-series/london-tithe-assessments/1638-72/introduction -to-tithe-assessments Accessed 4.01.23.

Castelow. Ellen. Historic UK www.historic-uk.com/CultureUK/The-Town-Crier Accessed 24.01.23

Chadwick. Owen, "The Victorian Church", Vol. 1, An Ecclesiastical History of England, New York, Oxford: Oxford University Press, 1966.)

Chivers. Tom, London Clay ISBN: 9781529176711 Penguin Published: 16/06/2022

Clark, D. May 20, 2021 The number of people using food banks in the UK 2008-2021 published by statista.com

Clarke, John M. (2006). The Brookwood Necropolis Railway Locomotion Papers: 143 (4th ed.). Usk, Monmouthshire: The Oakwood Press. ISBN 978-0-85361-655-9

Coll. J R., On the Demise of Blood-letting. Physicians Edinb 2014; 44:72–7 http://dx.doi.org/10.4997/JRCPE.2014.117 © 2014 Royal College of Physicians of Edinburgh HISTORY 73 London, UK Correspondence to DP Thomas The Old Barn North Green Kirtlington Oxford (Accessed 26.01.23)

copper kingdom (https://copperkingdom. co.uk/mynydd-parys-mountain/ accessed 24.01.23),

Collier. Anne, The h=Humble Little Condom: a history P128 Prometheus Books, New York. 2007 ISBN 978-1-59102-556-6

Copper kingdom (https://copperkingdom. co.uk/mynydd-parys-mountain/ accessed 24.01.23),

Cosh. Mary A History of Islington, Historical Publications Ltd, 2005.)

Cunningham. Peter, 1849 The Handbook of London, Murray, London

Davis. Norman,. 1997 Europe: a history. Pimlico ISBN 0-7126-6633-8

Devereaux. Simon,: "The abolition of the burning of women in England Reconsidered." Laws Respecting Women, published London 1777 reprint Edn. Dobbs Ferry NY 1974 p 344

Draper. Dr Nick, (of UCL) 28 Oct 2010 UCL Lunch Hour Lecture: What does London owe to slavery? (See: Fowler. Naomi,)

Dylan. Bob., 1965. It's All right Ma (I'm only bleeding) from the album Bringing It All Back Home.

Encyclopaedia Britannica, Vol 26, p383 DATE????

Farrington, Anthony (2002). Trading Places: The East India Company and Asia 1600–1834. British Library .ISBN 978071234 7563.

Fisher. H.A.L,. 1946 A history of Europe, London, Edward Arnold, 1946, p. 777. (Medical History, Vol. 45, Supplement S21, Cambridge University Press).

Fussell E and **Constance Goodman**, 'Eighteenth century estimates of British sheep and wool production', Agric Hist, 1930, 4: 131-51, pp 160-1)

Fowler, Naomi: Britain's Slave Owner Compensation Loan, reparations and tax havenry. Tax Justice Network 9th June 2020 https://taxjustice.net/2020/06/09/slavery-compensation-uk-questions. Accessed 24.01.23

Francis-Devine. Brigid, House of Commons Library. Poverty in the UK: statistics, https://commonslibrary. https://researchbriefings.files. parliament. uk /documents/SN07096/ SN07096.pdf 29 September 2022 Accessed 24.01.23

Garnett. Elizabeth, 11.08.2020, https://www.museumoflondon.org.uk /discover/ curious-tale-martin-van-butchells-first-wife: Accessed 23.01.2023

Garside . M, 5th October, 2021 Statista. https://www. statista. com/topics/7156/ mining-industry-in-the-uk/statistics and facts). Accessed 24.01.23

Gerryco. That's how the light gets in https://gerryco23.wordpress.com/ 2012/10/25/the-mean-streets-of-somers-town/ reviewing the book Streets by Anthony Quinn

Gilmore. Oisín, The working week in manufacturing since 1820. Oisín Gilmore University of Groningen. (How Was Life, Vol.II. New Perspectives on Well-being and Global Inequality since 1820.) https://www.oecd-ilibrary.org/sites/ 11e27 aff-en/index. html?itemId =/content /component/

Green. Dr Matthew (2013, August 7) The Lost Coffee Houses of London. https://publicdomainreview.org/essay/the-lost-world-of-the-london-coffeehouse. Also https://londonist.com/2016/08/the-blow-job-cafe-and-the-story-of-london-s-strangest-coffeehouses. Accessed 30.01.2023

Gray. Annie, 2016 Death in the Loaf (https://musings on food history. Word press. com/ 2016/01/12/death-in-the-loaf/) accessed 31.01.23

Hartley. Dorothy, (1954) Food in England. Little Brown. London 978-0-3494-0177-5

Hampshire History. (2014 Sept 29th) https://www.hampshire-history.com/waltham-blacks/ accessed 31.01.23

Hatton. Prof Tim, et al. Statistics as given by: BBC News 2nd Sept 2013, Prof Tim Hatton et al published in the journal Oxford Economic Papers.

Hayes. David A., (David A. Hayes and Camden History Society, 2020) the Camden History Review

Hayward Arthur L, (2004 August 3rd) Lives of the most remarkable criminals who have been condemned and executed for murder, highway robberies, house-breaking, street robberies, coining, or other offences. The Project Gutenberg E-book also The Waltham Blacks: Lives of the Most Remarkable Criminals

Health Survey nhs live well healthsurvey bmi-.pdf See Rosenbaum

Higginbotham. Peter,. (2009) The Workhouse Cookbook ISBN 978 0 7524 4730 8.) History Press; and Workouses.org. uk/education /workouses. shtml.

Higham. Nick, (2022) The Mercenary River,Headline Publishing Group London

Historic England https://historicengland.org.uk/images-books/publications/iha-english-public-library-1850-1939/heag135-the-english-public-library-1850-1939-iha/

Historic UK historicUk.com The Great Exhibition. Ben Johnson. Accessed 31.01.23 And D. Appleton & Company. 1863. p. 412. New York:

Independent Laura Hampson (Wednesday 27 April 2022 10:01) https://www.independent.co.uk/life-style/love-sex/ minimum -marriage-age-england-wales-b2066398.html Accessed 24.01.23

Ingrams. Sarah, the Hackney Gazette August 13, 2012/ October 14, 2020 reviewing The Trebor Story by Matthew Crampton

Ives. Susannah. (SusannaIves.com/wordpress September 22, 2015). Frail: Tidbits on Mid-Victorian Era Menstrual Hygiene. Ives also further quoted from "Obstetrics: the Science and the Art" by Charles Delucena Meigs, published in 1852. Accessed 24.01.23

Investopedia: Julia Kagan Investopedia.com Economy>Economics Who Is Thomas Malthus? Updated June 23, 2021 Reviewed by Michael J Boyle Fact checked by Hans Daniel Jasperson. Accessed 24.01.23

Jonson. Ben, *On the Famous Voyage* (along the Fleet) - at https:// www. poetrynook.com/poem/famous-voyage

jstor 1851 (https://www.jstor.org /stable/pdf/2338356.pdffrom the royal statistical society https:// www. thegenealogist. co.uk/census/1851)

Journal of the Royal Statistical Society. Series a (statistics in society) Vol. 151, no. 2 (1988), pp. 276-309 (34 pages) Published by: Wiley for the Royal Statistical Society

Justice Stephen re www.cremation.org.uk/history-of-cremation-in-the- united-kingdom

Komlos, John. (2005 On English Pygmies and giants) publisher Ludwig-Maximilians-Universität München, Volkswirtschaftliche Fakultät, München). See https://www.econstor.eu/handle/10419/104177, (http://hdl. handle.net /10419/104177)

LCC 1952 Survey of London: Volume 24, the Parish of St Pancras Part 4: King's Cross Neighbourhood. Originally published by London County Council, London,1952.https://www.british-history.ac.uk/survey-london/vol24/pt4/pp 118-123

Lloyd. Amy J., (20007) Amy J Lloyd. Education, Literacy and the Reading public. University of Cambridge. Gale Primary Resources. Lloyd, Amy J.: "Education, Literacy and the Reading Public." British Library Newspapers. Detroit: Gale, 2007.

Lucas. Caroline, 13/01/2023 https://mobile.twitter.com /CarolineLucas/ status/ 1613914195761975296

Macclesfield Museum (2020) {https:// Macclesfield museums.co.uk/wp-content/uploads/2020/04/Victorians-Work sheet-Food.docx.pdf }

MacDonald, Murphy and Holt: (2011) Michael MacDonald and Terence Murphy "Sleepless souls: Suicide in early modern England." Reported by Gerry Holt, BBC News website: "When suicide was illegal" 3 August 2011

McRae. Andrew (1998)"On the Famous Voyage": Ben Jonson and Civic Space." *Early Modern Literary Studies* Special Issue 3 (September, 1998): 8.1-31 http://purl.oclc.org/emls/04-2/mcraonth.htm.

Michaels. L,. The Eighteenth-Century Origins of Angina Pectoris: Predisposing Causes, Recognition and Aftermath, pp. 44 – 60 DOI: https://doi.org/10.1017 /S0025 72 7300073737 https:/ /www. ncbi.nlm.nih.gov/pmc/articles/PMC2531046/ Articles from Medical History. Supplement are provided here courtesy of **Cambridge University Press** accessed 28.01.23

Mindat (https://www.mindat.org/loc-4245.html accessed 24.01.23)

Morton Eden. Frederick, (1797) The State of the Poor, published in 3 volumes in 1797

National Child Measurement nhs.uk/live-well/healthy-weight/childrens-weight/ national-child-measurement-programme/

O'Farrell. John, 2007 An Utterly Impartial History of Britain or 200 Years of Upper Class Idiots in Charge,. Doubleday.

Oldbaileyonline https://www.oldbaileyonline.org/static/ Population-history-of-london.jsp accessed 25.01.23)

ONS Old Bailey https://www.oldbailey online.org/static/population-history-of-london.jsp.

Patriquin. Larry, (2007) Agrarian Capitalism and Poor Relief in England 1500-1860 Rethinking the origins of the Welfare State. Palgrave MacMillan

Porter. Roy, (1998). London: A Social History. Harvard University Press. p. 126. ISBN 978-0-674-53839-9

Postal Museum (see https:// www.postalmuseum. org/blog/house-numbering/#) Accessed 3.01.23.

Radzinoiwicz . Dr I., (1945) The Waltham Black Act . The Cambridge Law Journal. Accessed 30.01.23

Richardson. John, (1995) "London and its people," published by Barrie and Jenkins

Rosen. Bruce, (2014) The Victorian History Blog (http:// vichist.blogspot.com/2014/ 05/income-vs-expenditure-in-working-class.html June 19th 2014. Accessed 24.01.23

Rosenbaum. S., (1988) 100 Years of Heights and Weights, for the Journal of the Royal Statistical Society. Series A (Statistics in Society). Vol. 151, No. 2 (1988), pp. 276-309 (34 pages). Published by: Wiley for the Royal Statistical

Society]. Jstor.org Accessed 24.01.23 Data from the Anthropometric Committee make interesting reading.

Sage Journals (2018) https://journals.sagepub.com Peter Greaves Regional differences in the mid-Victorian diet and their impact on health March 8th 2018. Accessed 24.01.23

Shepley. Emma, (28.03.2014) RCP senior curator https://history.rcplondon.ac.uk/blog/ georges-marvellous-medicine-rcp-archives-and-madness-king-george) OX5 3JZ, UK (Accessed 26.01.23)

Sugden. Philip, (2002) The Complete History of Jack the Ripper Rev Ed edition (21 Feb. 2002) Robinson Publishing; ISBN-10 : 9781841193977 ISBN-13 : 978-1841193977 see (https://whitechapeljack. com/the-whitechapel - murders /mary-jane-kelly/ accessed 23.01.23.)

Schofield, R S., (1972) 'Dimensions of illiteracy 1750-1850', Explorations in Economic History, 1972-3, 10: 437-54, pp. 440 1.)

Splashing in the Serpentine, The International Journal History of Sport Vol. 24 2007 Issue 5, Splashing in the Serpentine: A Social History of Swimming in England 1800-1918 Tandfonline Taylor & Francis accessed 24.01.23

Swinburne. Algernon Charles,(1969) A Study of Ben Jonson (1889) ed. Howard B. Norland (Lincoln: U of Nebraska P, 1969) p95:

Standing. Guy, (6th November 2017). Why you've never heard of a Charter that's as important as the Magna Carta. Open Democracy. https://www.opendemocracy.net/en/opendemocracyuk/why-youve-never-heard-of-charter-thats-as-important-as-magna-carta/ Accessed 24.01.23

Stow. John, (1956) The Survey of London. Everyman's Library 589, J M Dent & Sons Ltd, Aldine Press, London. Originally published 1598

The Agricultural Revolution Publication: (Nov 16, 2012). Medical History: Cambridge University Press. Copyright © 2001 ISSN: 0025-7273 (Print), 2048-8343 (Online) Editors: Dr Tara Alberts, University of York, UK, and Professor Akihito Suzuki University of Tokyo, Japan. Medical History, Vol. 45, Supplement S21: see Michaels. L

The Diary of Beatrice Webb, Vol. 1 1872-1892. Glitter Around the Darkness Within, edited by Norman and Jeanne MacKenzie) p155

The Gazette Official Public Record (www. thegazette.co.uk/all-notices).This month in History: The 1801 census. Re Thomas Malthus, 1798 "Essay on the Principle of Population," Accessed 28.01.23

The Hampshire History Society 2019 accessed 12.09.22

The Museum of Childhood . industrial-revolution-childhoods

The Museum of London https://www.museumof london .org.uk/discover/curious-tale-martin-van-butchells-first-wife (accessed 23.01.23)

Videcette. David, a former Scotland Yard man's website davidvidecette.com

Weston-Davies W H, writing in the Journal of the Royal Society of Medicine Vol. 82, 1989,

whitechapeljack. (https://whitechapeljack. com/the-whitechapel-murders/mary-jane-kelly/ accessed 23.01.23.)

Wood. Margaret, 2018 Marriage and Divorce 19th Century Style (The Library of Congress, February 23, 2018)

Appendices

Appendix I

The problem of categorising and measuring poverty
Measuring poverty.
Averages: especially to do with wages
Population worries. Too many children. Coram and Malthus.

Appendix II

The coins in their pockets. Take note?
King Offa's pennies and Henry's shillings
Further coinage for the Baxters to wrestle with

Appendix III

Family history information ----
Genesis of this work -----
Establishing identity flocking to the capital ----
who's who by generation
The 11 children of the stonemason and Caroline Gates

Appendix IV:

General Information re the stonemason's work.
Marble-polishing.
Materials used. Cement and the Romans.
"Timber!" The three little pigs
Bricks: another dimension. Quoins or coins. Getting laid

Appendix I General information

THE PROBLEM OF CATEGORISING AND MEASURING POVERTY. MEASURING POVERTY. AVERAGES: ESPECIALLY TO DO WITH WAGES. POPULATION WORRIES. TOO MANY CHILDREN. CORAM AND MALTHUS.

THE PROBLEM OF CATEGORISING AND MEASURING POVERTY

Of course, poverty may occur for many reasons, which researchers may judge as relative, situational or generational poverty. It may impact with greater or lesser severity on individuals than it does on families. For example, in the case of families there is some savings in terms of scale - it is slightly cheaper per capita to buy for a group rather than for one person. On the other hand a family has to feed non-earners and non-contributors to the food budget which impacts on the earnings to eater ratio. In this way incidences of poverty may be viewed as *relative poverty.* Within this group the relativity may involve income inequality which may include differentiation, either directly - through skills criteria - or on a simpler basis by differing levels of pure exploitation. There may also be *situational poverty* (as a result of earthquake, flood, drought etc.). In other circumstances there is *generational poverty* (where families are born into poor conditions live without aspiration, and/or are ill equipped to transcend poverty). Then there is both *rural* and *urban poverty*, with different attendant difficulties. The essential problem in all these situations is always to determine how it is possible to compare the different groups. Foremost, if research is to be valid, is for like to be considered with like. This is the ultimate criteria by which comparison, behaviours and status can be judged. These are the reasons for poverty: the degree of poverty is another matter.

How can we measure poverty in all its varieties? One strategy is to judge different people in terms of how they compare to a certain average. In Britain, households are currently considered to be below the UK poverty line if their income is 60% below the **median** household income after housing costs for that year. (Income can also be measured before or after housing costs (BHC or AHC) are deducted. Poverty levels are generally higher based on income measured after housing costs, because poorer households tend to spend a higher proportion of their income on housing. In Brigid Francis-Devine's report she states that in 2019/20: around one in six people in the UK were in relative low income **b**efore **h**ousing **c**osts (BHC), rising to around one in five once account is made for calculations **a**fter **h**ousing **c**osts (AHC). She records the Resolution Foundation estimated in early September 2022 that the number of people living in absolute poverty will increase by over 3 million people between 2021/21 and 2022/23 (See Francis-Devine. Brigid). Well, those are statistics and as Mark Twain said, "There are lies, damned lies, and there are Statistics..." (a phrase coveted by the odious Benjamin Disraeli). [80] Here, though, we must note the statistics refer to the *median* average: the middle number in a long list with a wild disparity of values. Such figures would I imagine have been far from the truth for our Victorian pre-Welfare-State inhabitants of London.

---

[80] There are curs, damned curs, and there was Disraeli. Even Winston Churchill, another shamelessly overt plagiarist, would mention Disraeli's reputation for brilliance "was growing faster than his capacity for inspiring trust." (p281. The Island Race. Cassell & Co. Ltd. 1964). He further said, "In all his attitudes there was a degree of cynicism; in his make-up there was not a trace of moral fervour." (p295) I have seen scant evidence of any moral behaviour or integrity on the part of Disraeli, Lord Beaconsfield. Both men were duplicitous shits of monumental proportions. Boris Johnson, unsurprisingly, seems to have been a fan of both.

AVERAGES ESPECIALLY TO DO WITH WAGES

Certainly there are many Victorian records, but these may contain averages or notional rates of pay which do not necessarily reliably inform an enquiry; for example, a mean average – favoured by those media people and outlets which deliver deliberate and controlled "news" - will tell you very little since it is likely that very few people earned or were paid that amount. It also skews the figures: for example consider all the people present within a particular restaurant where dinner-partying millionaire-industrialists were being served and cooked for by the same number of mostly minimum-waged earners. Here, we might well say the mean wages of everyone in that room was £250,000 a year; at which point we might need to revive the waiters....

We must be wary therefore, (and with pinch of salt at the ready), of mean averages. [81] It may be more informative to look at the modes of income at different times, i.e., the most common amount paid. (NOT to take small samples such as from a high-class restaurant...)

If we had that figure we would then need to factor in whether or not their wages were subject to other deductions and charges for materials, use of equipment, fines, cost of rent, food and clothing/livery. Then we would have to look at what people were required to spend.

POPULATION WORRIES. TOO MANY CHILDREN. CORAM AND MALTHUS.

There had been growing concern in the 18th century about an apparent trend - and the potential threat - of a rising population.

---

81 (A. L. Bowley, Wages in the United Kingdom in the Nineteenth Century). Also see the Frederick Eden report 1797

Some pondered the macroscopic view of unbridled population growth, while others who were not necessarily unconcerned about the long term instead were galvanised into action by what they saw.

Thomas Coram (1668-1751) had been appalled by the conditions children faced in London, especially as the city was in his view "a global powerhouse of industry and wealth." He was also aware that within London the child mortality rates were terribly high, and that each year some one thousand babies were abandoned by parents experiencing extreme poverty.

Coram was moved to act and to bring others along with him; and while it took him 17 years to receive a Royal Charter from King George II, he managed to establish the Foundling Hospital. Here they worked not merely in order to specifically care for babies who had been abandoned but also for those at risk of abandonment.

The Foundling Hospital was designed to care for and educate England's most vulnerable youngsters, and it gained support at the time from some notable celebrities with the artist William Hogarth and the composer George Frederic Handel, who both played a big part in realising Coram's vision. Its museum states that together, they transformed the Hospital into the UK's first public art gallery, and became one of London's most fashionable venues. (The institution has survived and continues today as the children's charity Coram,)

Jonas Hanway, who later joined the board of the Foundling Hospital, was a great organiser and administrator; he was also a great pragmatist. His view on charity was not particularly or especially driven by a sense of humanity or welfare, and instead he saw it more as a strategy to promote the interests and wealth of the country at large. In this regard he is said to have advocated Christian Mercantilism. He instigated Hanway's Act of 1767 under which all pauper children under the age of 6 from Metropolitan parishes were required to be sent to private branch-workhouse/baby farms that were in the country and at least 3 miles from London and Westminster.

These, though, were fairly local measures, while Thomas Malthus took a wider view. In 1798 he published his "Essay on the Principle of Population," which described the human population as increasing geometrically, while food production increases arithmetically. (See Investopedia: Julia Kagan) He argued that if population growth wasn't kept in check it would quickly lead to misery, vice and poverty.

Similar sentiment had been expressed by Socrates in 372 BCE who described a pastoral paradise where families were small "lest they fall into poverty and war." (Collier. P16). In his way Malthus recognized that war and disease would play a role in population control but that other efforts could be made to limit procreation. Contraception, though, which was extremely limited in effectiveness and in range, was viewed as sinful by the Church who had decried *Onanism* as contrary to God's design. Onanism has been taken to refer to masturbation but the term actually applied to Onan who was condemned for practicing coitus interruptus. Both ejaculations were regarded as being sinful as they did not contribute to procreation. Against such arguments another commentator styled as Married-Man-with-6-children declared, "God gave us beards, but Man invented razors." (Collier. P128.) Malthus's theory was controversial but with revolution in the air it fuelled and divided political debate at the time. Subsequently, with a population estimate of 9.2 million, it was decided a national census should be taken so that pernicious growth could be monitored.

On Monday 10th March 1801 a census was taken which contrived to ascertain the number of people in the country, their occupations and the number of families in each house. This and other measures were taken which were concerned with monitoring baptisms, marriages and burials in each parish, in order to help determine how fast the population was growing. The 1801 census showed that the total population for England and Wales was 8.87 million, which did not include just under 500,000 military personnel, seamen and convicts. This would give a total figure closer to 9.4 million.

This, the first reliable modern census, recorded **1,096,784 souls** in a greater London area, which represented about 12% of the total England & Wales population. (See Oldbaileyonline)

Population and poverty – with attendant child abandonment – continued to increase. While Hanway's Act was still in force, by 1844 Poor Law commissioners were attempting to persuade the different poor law unions to create district schools, such that those private institutions which covered the London area largely ceased to operate after 1850. Children in Islington, Finsbury and Clerkenwell nevertheless would still be sent to Merton for many decades afterwards.

The 1851 Census for England and Wales was taken on the night of 30 March 1851, recording more information than any previous census. London's population in 1851 was then found to have more than doubled from 1801, and had increased by 136% in that 50 years from 1.09 million to 2.6 million. The total population of England and Wales had also almost doubled from 9 million up to **17,922,768**, which meant that London's population had risen to be 14.5% of the total population. (See jstor 1851)

Of course, Malthus did not know the range of contraceptive devices and chemicals which would later become available and have such an impact. Marie Stopes, born in 1880, would not publish her famous book Married Love birth control until 1918, seven years after Francis Baxter was dead. Whilst opposing abortion she openly advocated contraception **and** enjoyment of sex. It was one of the first books openly to discuss these issues.

With a world population currently predicted to hit 10+ billion you might wonder where the resources are going to come from to feed, care, clothe and shelter them. Changes will need to be made, and while new technologies and new food production techniques will help, some billionaires are just going to have to stop opening charities that glorify themselves, begin paying their employees decent wages and start paying proper taxes.

APPENDIX II

GENERAL INFORMATION RE THE COINS IN THEIR POCKETS. HISTORY. KING OFFA'S PENNIES AND HENRY'S SHILLINGS

A brief further aside here, but it was the highly influential Offa, King of Mercia from 757-795 AD, who originally divided the currency pound into 240 parts.

Whilst not actually King of *all* England, Offa (and his Queen Cynethryth) were sovereign overlords of a heptarchy comprising all the territory of seven kingdoms south of a line from the Humber to Merseyside, excluding Wales and Cornwall. They were regarded as the most important rulers of the many kingdoms of Britain at that time; a view held certainly by Charlemagne – the "father of Europe," King of the Franks and emperor of the Carolingian Empire – who some record had a high regard for Offa and his Queen. Cynethryth has fallen through the cracks of England's history, but if for nothing else she is significantly notable for being a consort whose sole image actually appeared on coinage in general circulation. None other has achieved that distinction.

The Mercians were an Anglo-Saxon people of the "marches" (the borders) and Offa was keen to physically demark his land from that of the Welsh with a trench/embankment: Offa's Dyke is still visible (in parts), along the English/Welsh border.

Offa was obviously canny, and whilst he originally issued these 92.5% silver pennies with a value of $1/240^{th}$ of a pound the reverse side of these coins had an equal cross, enabling it to be divided into two halves or four quarters. Each quarter piece was known to the Anglo-Saxons as a feurthing (a fourth-ing, a quarter), which eventually became the "farthing." This coin was a common value in the Victorian age.

So Offa just had a pound and those pennies, which could be halved or quartered, and it would be six centuries later before Edward III, who was King of England for 50 years until 1377, would establish a coinage system with more denominations. Even then it was still another hundred years later that the first shillings were issued under Henry VII (reigned 1485-1509), who decreed them to be $1/20^{th}$ of a pound and therefore worth 12 pence.

FURTHER COINAGE FOR THE BAXTERS TO WRESTLE WITH

The forced conversion to decimalisation when it came in 1971 was, however, not popular with a great many people: this now seems unbelievable given how awkward the system was, and that it relied upon so many number-bases. (The systems for weights and measures were similarly tortuous.)

Name	value	diameter	weight	circulation
Farthing	= ¼ penny	20mm		
Half-penny	= ½ penny/2 farthings	28mm		
Penny	= 1d copper	34 mm	18.80g	until 1860
	Bronze	31mm	9.45g	
Thruppences	= 3d	16mm	1.41g	from1845
Groat	=4d	16mm	1.90g	1838-55, 1888
Six-pence	=6d	19mm	2.83g	
Shilling	=12d = 1s or 1/-	24mm	5.65g	
A florin,	=24d = 2s or 2/-	28mm	11.31g	in 1849
A florin,	=24d	30mm		1851/1966
Half crown	=30d =2s6d or 2/6	32mm	14.14g	1816/1966
Crown	=60d or 5s or 5/-	38mm	28 g	1816-1965

There was a double-florin (=48d or 4 shillings recorded as 4/-) which was a 36mm/ 22.6g coin minted for the years 1887 until 1890, but it was so similar in size to the crown it was often mistaken for the higher value. This led to too much change being given, and thus it apparently earned the nickname the barmaid's "ruin" or "grief".

The groat – a four-penny coin aka a Joey – was nicknamed after Joseph Hume. He had suggested the introduction of this denomination because it was the exact value of the London cab fare, 4d, but it did not gain favour with the cab drivers – since it tended to cut them out of their tips! I doubt cab drivers will ever change. Hume, incidentally, in 1816 gave his backing to the call for decimalisation of weights and measures. [82]

---

82 Hume was also a friend of Francis Place and James Mill, and was a supporter of Joseph Lancaster.

Francis Place, known as the 'radical tailor of Charing Cross', was born in London in 1771 and was associated with virtually every reform movement between 1790 and 1854. A member of the London Corresponding Society, one of the first working-class movements, he opened a tailoring shop in 1799 and provided a reading room of radical literature in the back room of the shop. He became both successful and influential. Amongst many other things, he campaigned successfully against the anti-Trade Union "Combination Acts."

Joseph Lancaster, the Poor Child's Friend, advocated education for all: All children have potential which can be released through education; children should be rewarded and motivated in school, not beaten; School should be free; children should be provided with food in school; Teachers should be properly trained, paid and respected. Many people disagreed with him and he faced much opposition, but through the force of his vision and energy, he changed the world. (See the britishschoolsmuseum.org)

Lancaster also designed a specific way of teaching large numbers of children. It was called the Monitorial System. Monitors were the brightest children from each 'year group', who would be trained by the teacher to deliver simple lessons to their peers. In this way one teacher could school hundreds of children in one room.

The earlier Victorian Penny was a copper coin. Facing left on the obverse ("heads") side the teenage Queen's image was at first the "young head" (with ribbon in the hair of the eighteen year old monarch) which was minted in 1837 and until 1860. In that year the penny in the Victorian pocket became lighter and smaller: from thence the coin was made from more durable bronze, and was - at 9.45g (1/3rdoz) - half its predecessor's weight, and 31 mm in diameter. Later it would bear the mark "one penny." In 1862 Britannia was flanked by a ship to her left (our right) and a lighthouse to her right which subsequently disappeared.

Victoria's portrait was slightly changed to reflect a gradual facial aging in 1874 (when she was 55) and again in 1881 (when she was 62). She must have been surrounded by obsequious creeps.... Finally in 1893 the image transformed and became the "old head" of the veiled widow. (She was 74 years old, and had actually been a widow for 31 years.) The legend (words) bore the inscriptions: VICTORIA DEI GRATIA (Victoria by the grace of God) and REG: FID: DEF: (Queen, Defender of the Faith). Post 1895 they included VICTORIA DEI GRA BRITT REGINA FID DEF IND IMP showing she was now Empress of India!

Various coins were minted for specialist purposes, such as for use in parts of the Colonies: e.g. there was the Ceylon quarter-farthing ($^{1}/_{16}{}^{th}$ of one penny) while in Malta they used the ⅓rd farthing ($^{1}/_{12}{}^{th}$ of a penny). The half-farthing originally minted for Ceylon became legal tender here in the UK in 1842. I seem to recollect these were known as mints . There was also a 3-half-penny piece ($^{3}/_{2}$ d = 1 ½ d) minted between 1834 and 1862. A 2-penny piece was only minted for general circulation in 1838 and 1848 although it was minted every year in Maundy sets.

Apart from colonial use at home specialist money was used for Maundy money: this was a set of coins given by the reigning monarch on the day before Good Friday, which was known as Maundy Thursday. This is a traditional task of the monarch and is a nod to the deeds of Jesus on the night of the last supper when Christ washed the feet of his disciples. Now whilst earlier monarchs emulated this action and also gave gifts to certain poor or deserving people, in time the feet-washing went out of favour. The practice of gifting sets of Maundy-money however continues, with each set containing 92.5% silver coins of value 1d, 2d, 3d and 4d. I think you could quite easily see that washing the feet of the poor might literally have got up a monarch's nose....

APPENDIX III: FAMILY HISTORY INFORMATION, GENESIS OF THIS WORK, ESTABLISHING IDENTITIES. FLOCKING TO THE CAPITAL: WHO'S WHO BY GENERATION THE BAXTER LINE. THE 11 CHILDREN OF THE STONEMASON AND CAROLINE GATES

GENESIS OF THIS WORK

In the beginning – a phrase I seem to have encountered elsewhere – I started with the notion of finding out a little more – just a few details, in fact - about my paternal grandparents who had died before I was born. A simple task, maybe, which I have to say is also a good deal simpler today than it was when I embarked upon it; this improvement of access is obviously thanks to the internet, to the digitisation of records and to the public's interest in family history, which has turned it into a lucrative business and further driven digitisation. Some ten years ago the sector was attracting record levels of internet activity which reportedly was outstripping the porn industry's subscribers. Don't get excited, but advertisements for "ancestry" sites seem to indicate the interest is far from climaxing.

My own interest began twenty-odd years ago and the situation developed from a simple *finding a few details* and became *following lines of enquiry*: the momentum steadily picking up as new bits of information threw up further questions which begged answers. Of course, the answers to these tended to bring yet more questions to the fore, and almost before I knew it the simple task had become first a hobby and then a compulsive endeavour: a mission. By now my interest had stretched far and wide from the original remit of paternal grandparents.

At this point it began to take the form of more formal research, which for organisational purposes required me to compile it in sections for the different streams, families and lines where my enquiries led.

It soon became clear that these ancestors were not high flyers, or captains of industry or people of any especial note: they were simply ordinary people who had lived the relatively mundane lives of ordinary folks. In fact, my ancestors' lives were a reflection of the lives of the majority of the population, whose history has fallen through the cracks of time. Tracing their simple rites of passage – those "born... married....died" details – etc., however, rapidly became less inspiring, and was too limited: these facts didn't really tell me much other than names and how old they were when they died. There were not enough records of them individually and I found instead that the era in which these people lived began to become of greater importance; such that only background and sometimes ancillary information could illuminate their story: the story of the majority.

This caused me to expand my enquiries, which in turn exposed both my ignorance of general history and also the narrow focus of what was generally taught about important dates and events in the past.

In my time children were encouraged to know the names of Henry VIII's six wives, and were applauded for being able to recall the dates of the battles of Hastings, Agincourt and Waterloo. We *had to know* the sort of thing which lends itself brilliantly to the trivia required in quizzes, but we were only rarely furnished with the really important background information: the "why?" these things occurred, and the "What was going on?" around them which led to the events, and "how did these affect the lives of ordinary people?" Cui bono? For an oft-cited example (by me) the Battle of the Boyne in Ireland is celebrated in the north as a magnificent victory of the Protestant King William of England (Prince of Orange) over the Catholic ex-King James II. In the most basic sense there is a modicum of truth to this, but it is grossly out of context because the victorious and so-called Protestant side was extensively funded by Pope Innocent XIII and had Catholics fighting alongside William's apparently and reputedly solidly Protestant force! Should you happen to find that a little baffling then perhaps you will be surprised to learn that the other (supposedly Catholic) side also had some Protestants fighting for James. It was, as ever, little to do really with religion, but instead as is usual it was **all** about power – and in that particular instance it was more about limiting the influence and power of the French King than about which flavour of deity a body bent the knee to. The powers-that-be, though, prefer to keep it simple.

Other than examples like the Battle of the Boyne, which has been monumentally and deliberately twisted, and has affected many for centuries, I suspected that a great deal of other "momentous" events had very little impact on the everyday lives of the majority of the population. People became the subjects of a series of rulers - with usually negligible change to the circumstances of their subjugation. Sometimes, though, ordinary people lived in times of greater social, economic, cultural and political change; sometimes their lives coincided with advancements such as the agrarian and the industrial revolutions which changed the landscape for nearly everyone.

The problem I subsequently encountered was how to present the information gathered: whilst a simple family tree would not tax the intellect, it would certainly test the patience of others; and that tree alone was insufficient for the amount of information I had unearthed. Thus a plan gradually formed in my head to bring all these together in a single book ostensibly for my children/descendants and for anyone else who might care or give a toss.

I admit I grossly underestimated the scale of the task, and the different streams being interconnected complicated matters. Searching my mind for a solution it occurred to me that years ago I had read a book by Harold Robbins called The Carpetbaggers, in which individual chapters introduced the life of one particular character and encompassed his or her interaction with others in the story. Over the course of the book the complexities behind simple black and white stories emerged into a technicolour tale. Well, I am no Harold Robbins, but I thought I would nevertheless try to emulate the process of some interweaving.

Essentially, though, family history is just a hobby, and I am more than a little aware that like most hobbies, it is of interest mainly to the person whose hobby it is. That being declared, I hope my expansion of it all hangs together well.

So, be aware that the focus of this section of my broader family history is a segment of our ancestors, who were part of the **Baxter** family. This particular unit of that name lived for a time in Somers Town, the area which straddles Euston Road around St Pancras Station. For a few decades the Baxters' lives and all that was familiar to them went on in Somers Town and the surrounding areas of North London.

Importantly they lived there at a time of great development, especially of infrastructure programmes that served and befitted the capital of an Empire. Naturally, these may not have actually served the local inhabitants - like our Baxters - quite as well.

Maps of the area, and sketches of the "Brill" and the "Polygon" are available on-line if you care to pursue them.

ESTABLISHING IDENTITY:

There are various records which relate and refer to Francis Baxter the cutler (the father of the Stonemason), and some of these appear to be conflicting. On some records, such as on the marriage certificates of his children, they described his occupation (at that point?) as a *cutler*, or a *surgical instrument maker* and even as a *truss maker*. In addition to this, on the occasions of the 10-yearly censuses, a Francis Baxter described himself being employed as one of those three. The problem is reliably determining whether the Francis Baxters that I have variously found (the cutler, or the surgical instrument maker – SIM - or the truss maker) are one and the same person or different people.

I do not trust other people simply choosing to accept such details without fairly substantial investigation, and as I have often said whilst there may arguably be some point to pursuing family history there is absolutely no point if a particular identity has failed to be adequately established.

If anyone is faced with this problem I can only advise that it should help if the various bits of information are collated, and then factors such as birthplace, age, job title and personal relationships can be used to determine that each is the same person (in this case Francis Baxter the cutler or otherwise). There are common links to the ones found in respect of age, which indicates birth in or around 1797-98.

In the first place on census returns a Francis Baxter (FB) is sometimes shown as being born in St George's-in-the-East and at other times in Ratcliff; as it happens these two locations are basically the same, which capably deals with that apparent inconsistency. Indeed the parish record of St George's-in-the-East shows that a Francis Baxter, son of Thomas Baxter (bricklayer) and by mother Elizabeth, was born in Pennington St, which is in Ratcliff or sometimes Ratcliffe.

This was on December 29th 1797, and he was baptised there on February 4th 1798. (Our FB therefore should be shown as aged something "times 10" plus 3 (i.e. 10x + 3) or thereabouts in subsequent censuses.)

In 1841 (Census HO 107 685 19 18 p 20 taken in Somers Town) our FB was described as a CUTLER, but a squiggle in the born in the county section seems to indicate the cutler was not born there in Middlesex. (This would appear to be incorrect unless St George's-in-the-East was then in Essex, which I do not think is right.... or unless the cutler was asked if he was born in Somers Town?). His answer, whatever it may have been, was nonetheless recorded as a squiggle, although how much emphasis can be placed on this remains open to question. His age was recorded as 40, which accords with the practice of this census, which was to round down ages such as 43 to 40. The 1841 census is very light on detail, and often contains errors – it was a relatively new venture, and I don't believe the researchers /enumerators received that much training.

In 1851, though, the census (HO107 1497 f399) shows Francis Baxter (born St George's in the East, aged 53), and Elizabeth aged 53, born Hounslow. They were at 13 Pancras Walk, St Pancras, Marylebone, with son William aged 10 and daughter Elizabeth, aged 7 (b Shoreditch - Oct 1843). Here he is described – or described himself – again as a CUTLER.

In the 1861 census RG9 108 68 St Pancras, Marylebone, the Baxter surname was misspelt as *Baxster*. Living at 13 Field Terrace, St Pancras, Francis Baxster aged 63 declared himself to be a TRUSS MAKER, born in Ratcliffe Middlesex. His wife was recorded as Elizabeth Baxster also aged 63 born Hounslow Middlesex. Here the forenames, ages and birthplaces accord. The discrepancies are the variant spelling of the surname and the occupation.

In the 1871 CENSUS, RG10 375 110 p 11 – we find FB in the list of residents in the enumeration book of the Holborn workhouse (St Andrews Holborn Bars) situated in little Grays Inn Lane. FB is recorded as a married pauper aged 74: a truss maker, born in St George's in the East. A further record shows he died there on April 3rd. The registration of Death is at Apr-June 1871 Holborn 1b 413. His wife, Elizabeth Baxter (nee Bradshaw) was elsewhere.

Unfortunately Francis and Baxter and Francis Baxter were not uncommon names, and it would be easy to claim the wrong one.

Occupations change, and a man needing a crust has to be flexible and may turn his hand to anything in order to sustain himself and his family. Job titles may also vary when basically describing similar areas of the same job. Perhaps the jobs of cutler, surgical instrument maker and truss maker were inter-related or associated?

W H Weston-Davies, writing in the Journal of the Royal Society of Medicine Vol. 82, 1989, reflected upon the history of military units' need for suitable tools in regards to making and maintaining armoury and other equipment. Their need for doctors to perform amputations and incisions required the provision of sharp-edged instruments, and the skills, therefore, of cutlers. He noted that by the early 18th Century the cutler had become the predominant maker of surgical instruments.

Weston-Davies also charted the evolution of the **S**urgical **I**nstrument **M**aker (the SIM) deriving from the Cutler, and proceeding to Surgical Appliance maker. Here we have apparent indicators that Francis Baxter may have transitioned from Cutler to SIM to a Truss maker, assuming the latter was a truss in the surgical appliance sense.

Of course it may be that people are also prone to inflating their job title and tend to exaggerate its importance, such that the bricklayer's labourer might say he was a bricklayer, and the bricklayer might say he was a Master bricklayer. Family members may do the same, and it may be of value to consider the instances where the "cutler's" children may have been required to state his occupation.

When an Elizabeth Baxter, of Charles Street in the parish of St Andrews Holborn, married a William Stuart, a paper marbler in 1840 (on March 22nd) she asserted she was the daughter of Francis Baxter, a Truss maker. We may not at this stage be able to categorically state this was the E Baxter who was the daughter of Elizabeth Bradshaw and FB; nor can we say it is the same FB, but a Francis Baxter appended his signature to the marriage lines, and we shall see later perhaps whether or not this helps.

Now, since there was no reliable contraception available, it was not unusual for siblings to be born almost a generation apart; and in the year that this E B above (born 1820) became Elizabeth Stuart her putative mum, also Elizabeth (nee Bradshaw), had a baby. So, whilst twenty years separated them, later that year Elizabeth Stuart's potential little brother, Henry, was baptised. The mother was shown as Elizabeth and the father was recorded as a **S**urgical **I**nstrument **m**aker – not a truss maker - living at Johns Court.

This is how he then recorded himself, but just a matter of months later in the census of 1841 the father of the household, Francis, described himself as a Cutler. He was shown living with Elizabeth i.e. Elizabeth Jane nee Bradshaw, in John's Ct, (i.e. at the same address as the S I M - Surgical Instrument maker) with family, including a baby Henry.

So we certainly have the cutler working as a SIM, but at the moment the proof that he was also at times employed as a Truss maker is perhaps a little circumstantial.

Let us now consider other children. Stonemason Francis and Thomas Baxter, recorded their father as Francis Baxter, a cutler, at the time of their respective marriages. [83]

In 1851 the census (HO107 1497 f399) shows Francis Baxter or Baxster (born St George's in the East, aged 53), and Elizabeth - nee Bradshaw – aged 53 born Hounslow. They were at 13 Pancras Walk, St Pancras, Somers Town, Marylebone with their son William, aged 10, and daughter Elizabeth aged 7 (born in Shoreditch - 3 Feb Oct 1843). Here he is described – or described himself – as a cutler.

His sons, however, seem to be consistent in recording him as a cutler: he was thus described on the 16th November 1856 at St Leonard's Shoreditch when Alfred Baxter married his sister-in-law Caroline's sister Phoebe Collier; and the trend continued on the 12th August 1860 at St Pancras Church when Richard Baxter married Elizabeth Holland. This – it should be stressed - is how *they* recorded him: a cutler.

In 1861, the census was taken at 13 Field Terrace, St Pancras, where they found a Francis *Baxster* aged 63 (born in Radcliffe) and his wife, Elizabeth *Baxster* aged 63 (born Hounslow). The Francis here described himself as a Truss maker.

In 1865, William Baxter, the stonemason's brother, then a coachsmith of Dorrington Street, married Susannah Dryer, a spinster at St Andrews Holborn. His dad's profession was given as a surgical instrument maker. So we still have three sources potentially giving different occupations for FB. Whilst I am tempted to believe that surgical instrument making - including truss making - are off-shoot or allied trades and skills to which a

---

83 *Family History Information: F B the Stonemason married Caroline Gates in 1847, while his brother Thomas Baxter confectioner married Caroline Collier on October 29th 1849 in the district Church at Whitechapel.*

Cutler would or could turn his hand, I still do not think I am happy to make the assertion that one and all are the same FB.

However, in December 1866 an Eliza Baxter also of Dorrington Street Holborn and daughter of Francis, a surgical instrument maker, married William Dalton Tuckwell, a mariner. (He was born 6th May 1842,) [84]

In 1871, census reference RG10 644, Eliza Tuckwell, a 27 year old mariner's wife, is found living in 5 Suffolk Place with her mother, Elizabeth Baxter, 72, the wife of a truss maker in Rotherhithe. So the surgical instrument maker IS also the same truss maker. The old lady records her place of birth as Heston, Hounslow, which corresponds with that of Elizabeth Jane Baxter nee Bradshaw, the wife of Francis Baxter the Cutler/Surgical Instrument maker / truss maker.

The same census contained a Francis Baxter, who was found to be in the Union Workhouse (City Rd – the St Luke's Workhouse). He was described as a 73 year old truss maker born in St George's in the East, which tends to confirm he was our FB. Shortly after the census was taken Francis died there. On his death certificate it shows Francis Baxter, as a 73 year old truss maker, and records that he died in that Union Workhouse of Bronchitis on the 2nd of April. (Ancestry.co.uk and the public records show it as the 3rd). The witness was W Francis, who was in attendance and whose residence was given as the Union Workhouse, Grays Inn Road.

Overall this confirms the link that Francis the surgical instrument maker and Francis the Truss maker was the same person. We have already found that the SIM was the cutler as well. Elizabeth Baxter, wife of the Truss maker, and mother of

---

[84] *Family History Information: the son of a carpenter, William and Emma, who lived in Greenwich.*

Eliza, is also confirmed as being born in Heston, Hounslow, which accords with the birthplace of Elizabeth Jane Bradshaw. Elizabeth Jane was the daughter of William Bradshaw and Martha Wilkinson; she was baptised and born in 1798. [85]

THE MATTER OF SIGNATURES

To dispel any lingering doubt we also are lucky enough to have other opportunities to identify Francis.

The marriage certificate of Elizabeth Jane Bradshaw and Francis Baxter (the Cutler) on January 3rd 1820 at Christchurch, Spitalfields, shows a signature for Francis Baxter. Then in 1840 (March 22) a witness at St Andrews Holborn of the marriage of William Stuart to Elizabeth Baxter, daughter of Francis Baxter, Truss maker, was also a Francis Baxter. Almost a generation later in 1866 (December 10th St Andrews Holborn) the marriage certificate for William Tuckwell and Eliza Baxter, shows her father as a surgical instrument maker, Francis Baxter. A signature of that person is on the certificate.

The three signatures are therefore spread over a period of 46 years across the three events. Comparing signatures, and I would not pretend to be a handwriting expert, but I would say these three signatures are better than just very similar.

---

[85] *Family History Information: On the night of April 3rd Sunday 1881 Wm (William) D Tuckwell was aboard the Gannett SS as an able seaman. His wife Eliza (nee Baxter) is shown at RG11 578. Her place of birth was recorded as Shoreditch where Eliza Baxter was born.*

RG12 503 in 1891 (at 40 Reculver Road, Deptford) shows 48 year old William Tuckwell, a Merchant seaman, with 44 year old Eliza Tuckwell and their daughter Eliza, 19. The Keir/Terry family tree on Ancestry.co.uk shows "Death of Wife: Eliza Tuckwell nee Baxter (1844–1891)". It shows her born in Shoreditch in 1844 and dying 10.06.1891 at Deptford, then in Kent and buried 17th June in Lewisham.

FLOCKING TO THE CAPITAL

Between 1820 and 1870 there was a great exodus from the countryside of people who left their homes and sought work away from the land and the mines. They flocked to industrial centres and to where the big infrastructure projects were being created, and London – being the capital – attracted a vast number. In this way and from those hordes – those families and individuals who came to London – some would become my ancestors.

The following are my known ancestors: all – back until 1842 – were from England. *Of the identified families 14 came from or were already in situ in London or else they were from parts of Middlesex and Surrey that are now regarded as London. Others who arrived in that 50-year period came from Buckinghamshire, Devon, Essex, Hampshire, Oxfordshire, Shropshire, Suffolk, Wales, Warwickshire and Wiltshire.*

My 4 grandparents were: (born 1892 – 1906)(All London born)
(*Italics represent the maternal line*)

Arthur E **Titley** & Maud **Smith**,
*Albert **Ewer** & Jessie **Smith***

My 8 great grandparents were: (born 1859 – 1871)(All London born)

Francis Titley & Phoebe **Baxter;**
Edward Smith & Grace **Harvey**;
*Henry Ewer & Jessie **Swan**;*
*James S Smith & Florence B**ackhouse***

My 16 great-great grandparents were: (born 1820-43)[$^{15}/_{16}$ English] ($^{7}/_{16}$ London born)

John Titley& Ann **Evans**;	Francis Baxter & Caroline **Gates**
Thomas Smith & Ann **Rogers**;	Jim Harvey & Martha **Evans**;
*Charles Ewer & Sophie **Kite**;*	*Thos Swan & H "Ellen" D **Coombe**,*
James Smith & ANN? ;	*Henry Backhouse & Amelia **Williams***

Nb Martha Evans was born in Wales 1842: my 1st non-English ancestor

Of my 32 gt.gt.gt. grandparents were: (born 1785–1812)
($^{10}/_{28}$ London born) (26/28 English, 2/28 Welsh, 4 unknown)

John Titley (Shropshire)	& Martha Garbel nee Speake (from Cardington, Salop)
Wm Evans (Shropshire)	& Sarah **Overton**, (Shropshire)
Francis Baxter (Ratcliff)	& Eliz'th **Bradshaw** (Hounslow, Mddx)
George Gates (Harrow Weald,)	& Hannah (Middlesex)
David Smith	& Charlotte **Harris** (both Warwickshire).
William Rogers (Wilts)	& Rachel **Manns,** (Hampshire)
George Harvey, (Bucks)	& Mehala **Smith** (Oxon),
John Evans (Newtown Wales)	& Elizabeth **Jenkins**, (Wales)
Geo Richardson Ewer	*& Charlotte **Garrard** (both Marylebone),*
John Kite (Oxfordshire aka Oxon)	*& Sophia **Sparkes**, (Oxon)*
James Swan	*& Caroline **Horsborough**, (both Clerkenwell)*
Charles Coombe (Devon)	*& Harriet **Gater** (Devon)*
William Backhouse (Suffolk)	*& Eliza **Daniell** (Aldwych)*
William Jas. Williams (Lambeth)	*& Martha **Spendelow** (Essex)*
unk SMITH,	*& unk wife*
unk2	*& unk2wife*

My known gt.gt.gt.gt. grandparents were:

Francis Overton	&	Ann **Francis,**
William Manns	&	Susannah **Mitchener**;
Thomas Baxter	&	Elizabeth;
William Bradshaw	&	Martha **Wilkinson**;
John Backhouse	*&*	*Ann (Balls?),*
John Daniell	*&*	*unk;*
James Williams	*&*	*Amelia **Reid**,*
William Spendelow	*&*	*Sarah **Clay**,*
Thomas Horsborough;	*&*	*Susannah **Sears***
John Gater	*&*	*Diana **Coles**;*
John Ewer	*&*	*Catherine **Shaw**;*

My known gt.gt.gt.gt.gt. grandparents were

Benjamin Clay	*& Ann **KETCHER**;*
James Mitchener	& Margaret **Holdway;**
John Shaw	*& Catherine Hillener/Killener?'*
Daniel Reid	*& Amelia Lomar*

Earlier generations comprised people with the following surnames:

BACKHOUSE BAXTER BRADSHAW *CLAY* *COLES* *COOMBE* *DANIELL,* EVANS EVANS *EWER* FRANCIS *GARRARD* *GATER* GATES HARRIS HARVEY HOLDWAY *HORSBOROUGH* JENKINS *KETCHER* *KITE* *LOMAR* MANNS *MITCHENER* OVERTON *REID* ROGERS *SEARS* *SHAW* SMITH SMITH *SMITH* *SPARKES* *SPEAKE* *SPENDELOW* *SWAN* TITLEY *WILLIAMS* WILKINSON

From London:

BAXTER	*(Stepney, Clerkenwell, St Pancras, London)*
BRADSHAW	*(Hounslow Middlesex)*
DANIELL	*(Drury Lane, London)*
EWER	*(City of London, Shoreditch)*
GARRARD	*(Marylebone London)*
GATES	*(Harrow Middlesex)*
HORSBOROUGH	*(Aldgate London)*
SEARS	*(Aldgate)*
SHAW	*(Hornsey London)*
SMITH	*(London)*
SMITH,	*(London)*
SWAN	*(City of London)*
WILLIAMS	*(Lambeth Surrey)*
WILKINSON	*(Hounslow Middlesex)*

From the counties and shires:

BACKHOUSE	*(Suffolk)*	*CLAY*	*(Essex)*
COLES	*(Devon)*	*COOMBE*	*(Devon)*
GATER	*(Devon)*	*KETCHER*	*(Essex)*
KITE	*(Oxfordshire)*	*REID*	*(Lambeth, Surrey)*
SMITH	*(Oxfordshire)*	*SPARKES*	*(Oxfordshire)*
SPENDELOW	*(Essex)*		

EVANS	*(Shropshire)*	EVANS	*(Wales)*
FRANCIS	*(Shropshire)*	HARRIS	*(Warwickshire)*
HARVEY	*(Buck'shire & Essex)*	HOLDWAY	*(Hampshire)*
JENKINS	*(Wales)*	*LOMAR*	*(Surrey)*
MANNS	*(Hampshire)*	MITCHENER	*(Hampshire)*
OVERTON	*(Shropshire)*	ROGERS	*(Wiltshire)*
SPEAKE	*(Shropshire)*	TITLEY	*(Shropshire)*

Francis Baxter the stonemason was a common great-great grandfather via his daughter Phoebe to this writer (Paul Titley), and to his brother Cliff Titley; and to our cousins Graham and Tracey Titley, Jill Titley (later Lennox) and Jean Titley (later Young, later O'Donoghue) from the Arthur Ewart Titley line; to their second cousins: Pete and Margaret Edwards, Marian Olive (later Potts) and Linda Titley (later Short), from the Francis Alfred Titley line; to Carol and Jennifer Walker (later Pridem and Smith respectively) from the Clifford Rolland Titley line; and to Christopher, Paul and Alan Titley from the Ernest Baxter Titley line. Apologies for any omissions from this list. The stonemason, by the way, is also g-g-grandfather to a great many others via Phoebe's siblings.

THE AUTHOR'S FAMILY LINE TO THE BAXTERS

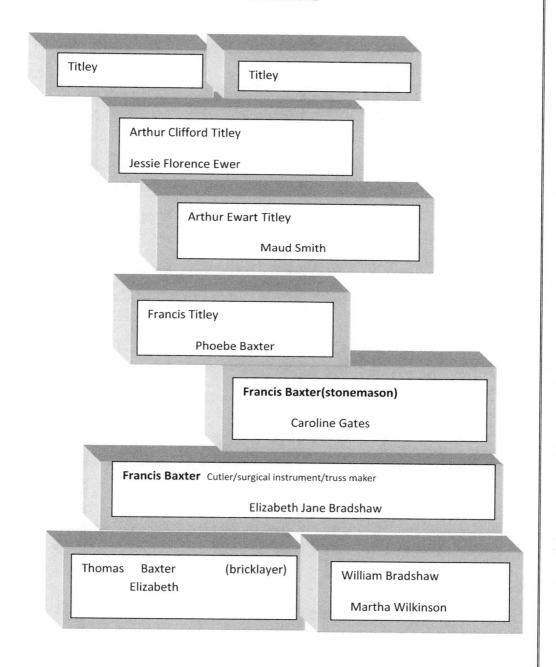

Titley

Titley

Arthur Clifford Titley

Jessie Florence Ewer

Arthur Ewart Titley

Maud Smith

Francis Titley

Phoebe Baxter

Francis Baxter(stonemason)

Caroline Gates

Francis Baxter Cutler/surgical instrument/truss maker

Elizabeth Jane Bradshaw

Thomas Baxter (bricklayer)
Elizabeth

William Bradshaw

Martha Wilkinson

Four Titley lines to Baxters

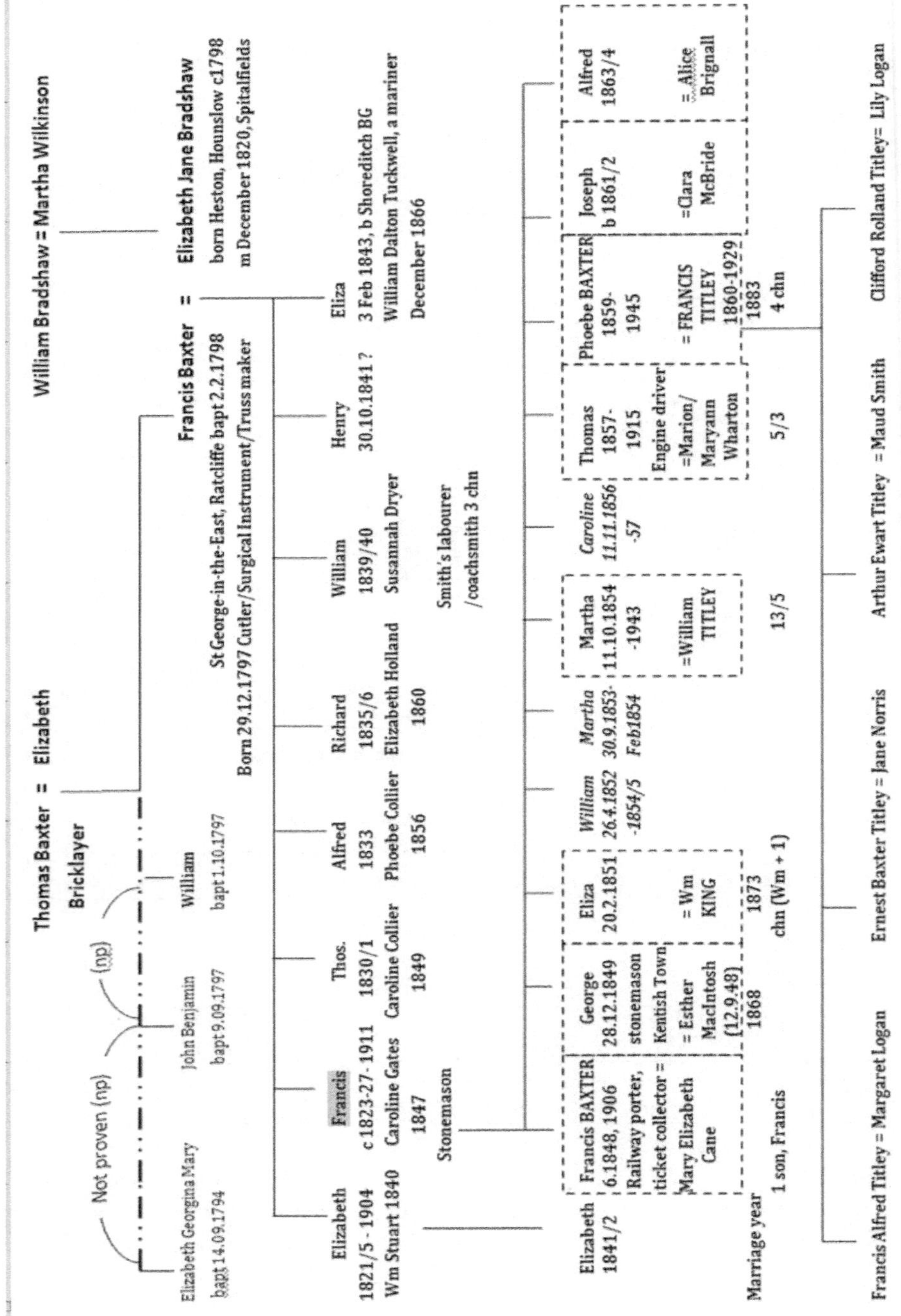

The Baxter Line

Francis Baxter Born c1823 Clerkenwell Married (1) = CG Married (2) = Elizabeth Dyde 1878 Died 10th March 1911 Union Workhouse Leytonstone Aged 88 Stonemason	**Francis Baxter** Born 29th Dec1797 Pennington St Bapt 4th Feb 1798 St Geo. In the East d 1871 aged 73 Cutler, Surgical Instrument maker, Truss maker	**Thomas Baxter** Bricklayer
		Elizabeth
	Elizabeth Jane Bradshaw Born Heston, Hounslow 1798 Married 3rd Jan 1820 Christchurch Spitalfields D 1882 aged c84	**William Bradshaw** Died St. Leonard's Heston, Hounslow Bur 30.4.1811 aged 57
		Martha Wilkinson Bur 31.07.1803
Caroline Gates Bapt 1823 Married = FB 6th Sept 1847 St Pancras Register Office Died: 22nd Oct 1876 13 Frideswide Pk Kentish Town Aged 53	**George Gates** D 26.2. 1855 Pancras Buried 4.3.1855 aged 77 Bricklayer	
	Hannah D 22.12.1844 Pancras Buried Dec 1844 aged 62	

The 11 children of the stonemason and Caroline Baxter (nee Gates).

Francis Baxter	b 10. 6. 1848, (bapt 24.1.50, St Pancras) d 1906, Railway porter, ticket collector m Mary Elizabeth Cane (March 1883) (born Sept 15th 1852). 1 son, Francis? Died 1906. No other record found.
George	b 28.12.1849 bapt 24.1.1850, St Pancras (dad Francis a polisher). George, a mason, married Esther MacIntosh (b 12.9.48) in 17th May 1868. 1c 535 at St James the Great Bethnal Green. The census of 1871 shows George as a 22 year old stonemason living with Esther in Reeds Place Kentish Town. In 1881 there is no record of George, but an Esther is shown as married (and as a nurse servant) in Antwerp House, Melrose Rd Wandsworth. She is shown as born Baker St, Paddington.(Marylebone) No other record.
Eliza	b 20. 2. 1851 married William King, 1873. She was widowed in 1887 with 2 children (Wm +). The internet states she died in Buffalo Erie, New York State 26.4.1944
William	*b 26. 4. 1852. – d 1854/5*
Martha	*b 30. 9. 1853 - February 1854*
Martha	b 11.10.1854 married William Titley, 13 born children 5 Children survived; died 1943, Yorkshire
Caroline	*b 11. 11. 1856 – died 1857*
Thomas Baxter	(1857-1915) (d1912 ? King family/tree) m Marion (Maryann) Wharton, but dead by 1915. No other record found.
Phoebe	1859-1945 m Francis Titley 1883. 4 chn: Francis Alfred, Ernest Baxter, Arthur Ewart and Clifford Rolland Titley
Joseph	b 1861/2 a general house repairer

married Clara McBride b High Barnet, lived in 85 Warley St Bethnal Green 1891; Joe a decorator in 1901. A Clara died in BG aged 47 in March 1910, buried 15 Feb Newham; Joe still in Warley St 1911. Died ? No children.

Alfred	b 1863/4 d Jan 1924? Hackney 1b 673 married Alice Brignall. No children

APPENDIX IV:

GENERAL INFORMATION RE THE STONEMASON'S WORK. MARBLE-POLISHING. MATERIALS USED. CEMENT AND THE ROMANS. "TIMBER!" THE THREE LITTLE PIGS OF 1666. BRICKS: ANOTHER DIMENSION. QUOINS. GETTING LAID.

A STONEMASON'S WORK

A stonemason's work is hard and physical; this does not suggest that Francis was a big man, but he would nevertheless probably have been fairly agile and intelligent. The work requires dexterous skills and an intimate knowledge of a range of natural materials, such as granite, slate, limestone, marble and sandstone. The types of stone Francis Baxter was likely to have encountered would I am sure have also included artificial Coade stone which had been invented/produced by Eleanor Coade. (A fine example of this is the lion on the south bank of Westminster Bridge.)

Francis would have had to know the material he was working with, particularly in regards to its application, its best uses, (for example, which could be used where, could they withstand compressive forces etc. While there have been advances in technology and tools stonemasons still have to learn to cut, carve and prepare these various types of stone in order to build or repair stone structures, buildings and monuments etc.

The job of a stonemason involved work inside or outside and he would have needed a head for heights. Many skills were required which were both physical and non-physical. You had to be no-fool to be a stonemason. Francis would need to be expert in the use of a range of hand tools, implements and diverse equipment. He would also have to know how to carry, lift, and manoeuvre heavy materials and equipment in a safe manner to get them in place and intact. He would need to know how to dress and prepare stone, making and fitting stonework (such as window, frames and archways). A stonemason would also have to be able to carve and repair headstones and statues - as well as building walls.

All this work was physically demanding, but then there was the other side to the job which would involve reading and interpreting technical drawings, thinking creatively and as we would currently term it "problem solving." All work of this type necessarily required Francis Baxter to liaise and collaborate with builders and other contractors. Then, as now, he would be required to repair old buildings and monuments and therefore Now he would need to work with conservationists and historians, but I suspect then he would have incorporated conservation into his work.

In an article for National geographic See how stonemasons keep England's oldest cathedrals standing tall published September 29, 2022, Rachael Rowe perfectly describes the importance of stonemasonry. "When the work of a stonemason goes unnoticed, it's a noteworthy accomplishment. Such is the paradoxical calling of stonemasonry, a fading craft that was not only essential in the rise of global architecture, but also one that remains crucial to the preservation of countless sacred and iconic sites."

I believe it would take 7 years for Francis to complete his apprenticeship: it currently takes at least six years to become a master mason, and the clear example of its enduring need is all too evident in the aftermath of such fires as destroyed Paris' Notre Dame in 2019. Pascal Mychalysin, master mason at Gloucester Cathedral, added that while artificial intelligence could one day replace artisans like him, he felt that would be "a loss for mankind." "It is very important to retain these traditional skills. If we disappear, it will be as bad as losing a language. That is what is at stake."

MARBLE POLISHING AND STAIN REMOVAL

Francis Baxter perhaps began – as most apprentices do – by working through different streams of the job until he gained enough proficiency to be trusted with more expensive materials. He would have to learn how to mix the various cements and mortars before even beginning to lay bricks. He would have needed to learn all about the various materials which would have included marble.

Certainly at one point Francis was a "marble polisher" which involved cleaning the stone, removing stains and slightly abrading the surface to achieve a look or to restore its original look. As marble is porous, stains settle in, such that mere polishing does not remove them. In order to reduce or remove the stain the polisher would first wash the marble with a weak or mild detergent. Francis would have learned not to use any acid-based product, so lemon and vinegars were forbidden on marble; instead alkalis had to be used in a poultice to extract the stain.

To make a poultice, Francis needed to mix just enough hydrogen peroxide into flour/baking soda to create a paste. (Of course knowing how much is just enough is part of the knowledge and skill of the craftsman.) If the mixture was too strong there was and is always a danger that it could easily bleach dark marble, so the marble worker or restorer would have to be ever ready to dilute the hydrogen peroxide paste. This recipe was, and apparently still is, good for removing organic stains. The procedure would continue with the worker smoothing the poultice onto the stain and sealing it by wrapping it. (A muslin wrap would then have been used, although in the current period I understand a plastic wrap is taped over it.) It is said to be best to leave the poultice on for at least 24 hours, although old stains often require more time. After the appropriate time the covering would be removed, and a little water would be poured over the dry poultice. Wiped with a soft cloth, the area would then be thoroughly dried, hopefully revealing a stain-free surface. I wonder how long Francis worked to perfect the knowledge and technique. I doubt he worked continuously at it, but just did it as and when required as suited the needs of his master and employer.

CEMENTS AND THE ROMANS

Francis would also have had to know the correct mixtures for the various cements, for rendering and pointing, and particularly for specialist requirements. For example, with the construction of bridges in and across stretches of water, cementing stone or bricks together might present a few problems.

Areas of water had to be shuttered and drained, but all the time the construction was at threat of water breaking through. It seems that the Romans had perfected a method with materials that even set underwater, but the knowledge had been lost. I don't know if the stonemasons of Francis's time had the required knowledge but the Romans had used "tuff", a relatively soft volcanic rock, which was common in Italy and which was ground down. A mixture of this tuff/volcanic ash, seawater and lime would set off a chemical reaction that increased cohesion with exposure to seawater, even after the concrete had technically set.

Incidentally the Rapa Nui people used tuff to make most of the moai statues on Easter Island.

"TIMBER!" THE THREE LITTLE PIGS OF 1666

Of course we all know the children's story about the three little pigs and the big bad wolf? If not, then briefly: each pig built a house to protect himself from the wolf; the first using straw, the second using sticks and the third using bricks. The wolf blows two houses down, and naturally the brick-built house proved the safer. Strangely this lesson had not been learnt or at least the message hadn't sunk in right up until the Great Fire of London in 1666 when the wooden-built structures of the City went up in smoke.

The penny dropped and prompted Parliament to decide that a more durable material might be a good idea, and thus the use of bricks to construct houses was given a boost. (In recent years, however, amnesia seems to have broken out and there has been a resurgence in "wooden" house building. Well, I'll be blowed.)

BRICKS: ANOTHER DIMENSION

All those working with bricks had to know how to make them. This included the stonemason's dad, Thomas Baxter – a bricklayer – and Francis' father-in-law, George Gates. Francis Baxter, as a stonemason, would have known how to fashion his own stones, but I suspect he would have used bricks which were pre-made and probably sourced in local brickfields. For example, a field would have its topsoil removed, and clay dug out of the ground. Then it would be mixed with chalk and possibly straw and mud. The main material from which the brick was made where Francis worked was probably London Clay. The brick-maker would compact the material to remove air, and after setting it in a mould there would be a period of natural drying before the brick was fired in a kiln. Local brick-makers used a mould of their own construction, which obviously resulted in slightly different sized bricks from one area to another and thus there was little absolute standardisation. The move towards greater uniformity came about not so much as by design as by happenstance.

In 1784 the UK government introduced a brick tax: a tax that had to be paid per brick. Now, as a device to raise more money, that left a lot to be desired because one didn't need to be an accountant to work out that if you made bigger bricks then you would pay less tax; and so inevitably the brick sizes began to grow. At one point Joseph Wilkes of Measham pushed his resistance to paying revenue a step too far by producing double-sized bricks. Well, you can only push your resistance and your luck so far, and inevitably the government set an upper limit of 150 cubic inches (10"x 5"x 3") which was still bigger than bricks had been before the imposition of the tax. This didn't quite lead to exact standardisation, but it was a step closer; nevertheless local and regional differences still made the brick height anything between 2" and 3", and lengths varied up to 13". The brick tax was abolished in 1850, although as in all economic systems, I am sure the government found a different way to extract revenue.

As brick-making became industrialised the differences generally decreased, but a standard (and metric) size would not be introduced until 1965. (Older buildings in need of renovation or repair would still require old imperial-sized bricks which has created a rather more expensive heritage-brick industry. The Victorian properties that the stonemason and his bricklaying gangs worked on were therefore built with imperial-sized bricks which, whilst they varied in size, were apparently still most commonly *9" x 4¼" x 2⅞"* or *9" x 4 ¼" x 2 ⅔"*. Note: the " indicates inches. (230 x 108 x 73mm or 228 x 108 x 68mm.)

Incidentally, Francis and Thomas Baxter would have used lime mortars, which it is accepted is a major contributory factor in the longevity of brickwork, as is testified by the continuing presence of Victorian buildings. The lime mortar allowed buildings to expand and contract with the heat or cold, and to move reasonably within windy conditions: I have also read that it has a "self-healing" property which enables any movement cracks within the mortar to repair themselves. (Possibly with the help of a pinch of salt.)

Francis would not have needed any measure to gauge how much mortar to use on each brick: experience would have seen the swipe of a trowel pick up and deposit a near exact amount to drop into the frog i.e. the indent in the top of (most) hand-made bricks which assists in the adhesion of brick to mortar to brick.

Perhaps what I find most amazing is that bricks were made by hand, with materials literally thrown together and physically squeezed by a person, and yet a great many of these still survive hundreds of years after they were laid. Of course there was a level of expertise, and while it was rudimentary technology the final product certainly did the job. Nowadays bricks are made to set specifications and must exhibit properties in regards to its soluble salt classification, its compressive strength, its water absorption, its range, tolerance and its capacity to withstand freeze/ thaw conditions. All of these are calculated and measured within set tolerances to match (perhaps) a product which the Victorian apparently just threw together.

PART OF THE SKILLS AND KNOWLEDGE FRANCIS AND THOMAS BAXTER WOULD HAVE NEEDED TO KNOW

QUOINS OR COINS

Quoins are large cuboid (oblong) blocks of masonry or brick that the stonemason would have shaped and built into the corners of a wall; and they are set so they show two rectangular faces, whereby there is a face-rectangle and an end rectangle on view at the corner. They can be used as a load-bearing feature, but they also for make for an attractive detail

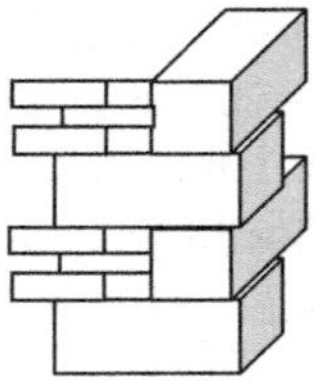

In the manner and matter of laying bricks Francis Baxter and his grandfather Thomas would have been well acquainted with the names of the brick patterns (how the bricks are arranged): these are known as the brick bonds. These have both aesthetic and practical construction-qualities and properties which must satisfy design and building specifications.

The basic terminology with regards to an actual brick concerns its rectangular faces: the longer is called the stretcher, and the smaller ends are called headers. The bricks are bound together with mortar, which is a mixture of sand, a binder such as cement or lime, and water. (The dip on top of a brick, which seats the mortar, is known as the frog.)

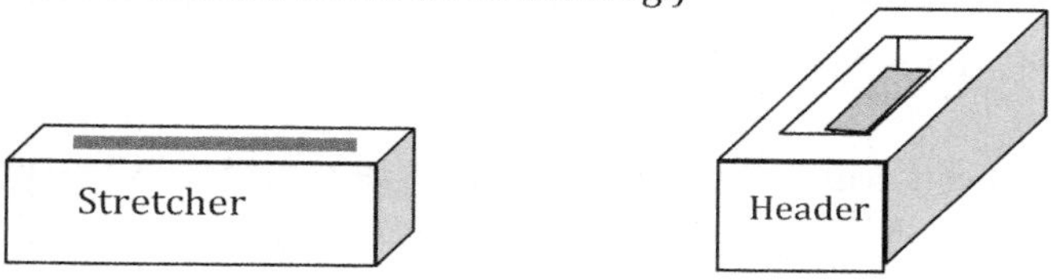

Mostly bricks are laid in horizontal rows, where each row is called a *course* of bricks. There are many types of brick bonds. (The mortar, which would be present at all the meeting faces of the brick, and usually at a thickness of 10-12 mm, is not here shown.) The following bonds are:

A *stretcher bond wall* uses less bricks, but it is not a strong bond.

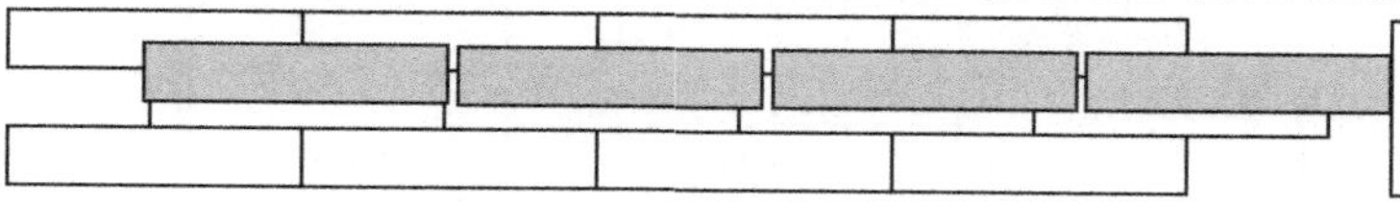

A stretcher bond wall

A *raking stretcher bond* overlaps the course below by ¼ or ⅓ of a brick

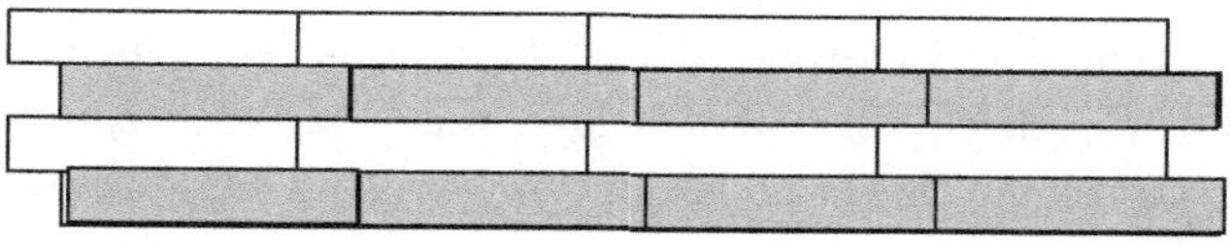

A raking stretcher bond wall

A *header bond* uses just headers in each course, off-set by half the header. This involves more materials and more labour.

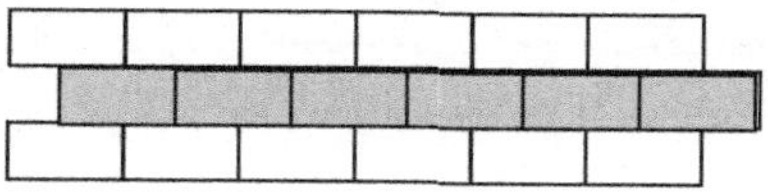

A header bond wall

An English bond alternates a course of stretchers with a course of headers: here the headers bridge the ends of two stretchers equally and from there the pattern continues

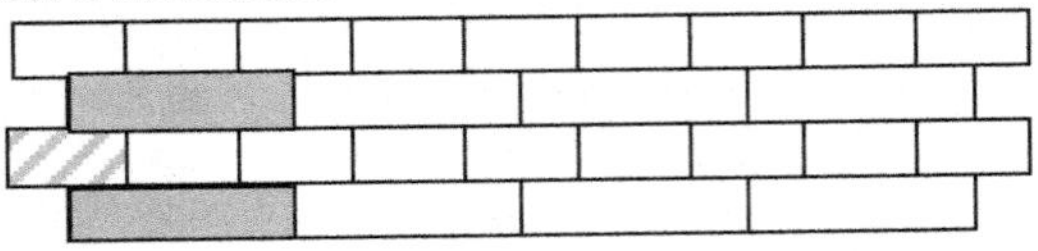

An English bond wall

The *English cross bond* shifts alternate stretcher courses by half a brick horizontally. The headers remain aligned. Staggering stretchers in this way enables patterns to be picked out in different texture or coloured bricks.

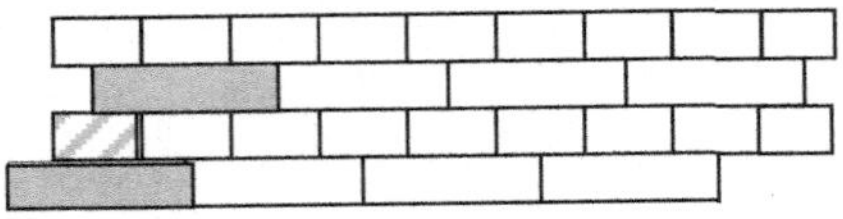

An English cross bond

The English Garden Wall bond places three courses of stretcher bonds between single rows of headers.

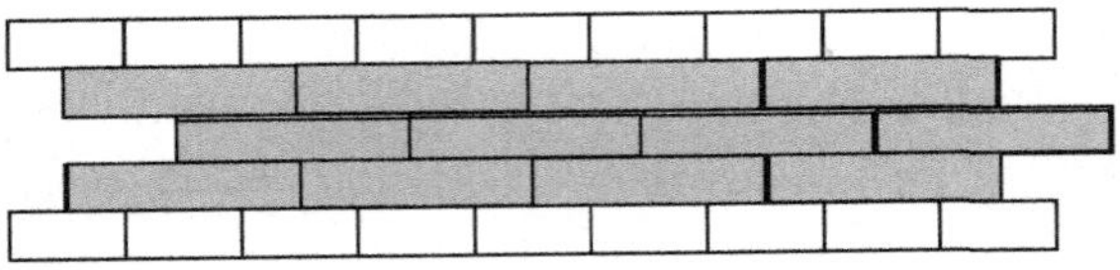

English garden wall bond

The Flemish bond is very strong and is usually used where the walls are two bricks thick

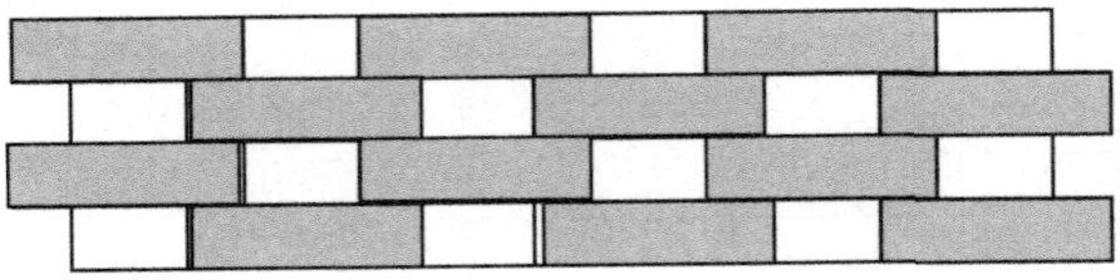

A Flemish

The Flemish garden wall bond uses one header to three stretchers along each course; the header in the upper course is then placed centrally on the middle stretcher of the three stretchers below, such that each course is offset by a quarter of a stretcher This bond is also known as the Sussex bond.

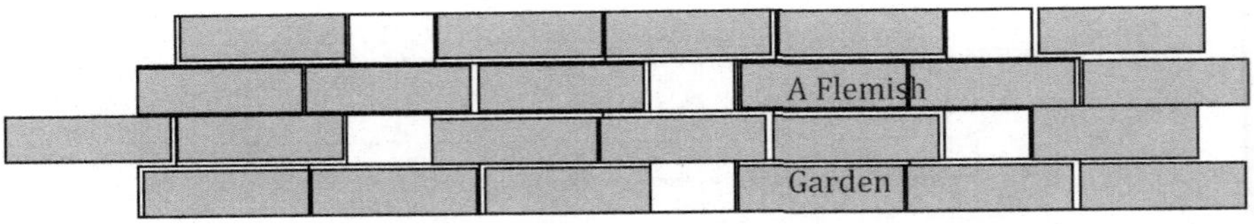

The Monk bond uses two stretchers between headers, and the header is placed across the join of the two stretchers below

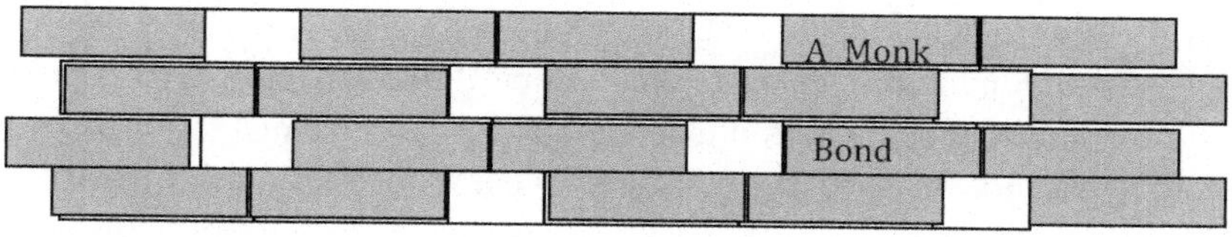

Bricklaying is not just a matter of laying one brick on top of another with a bit of random mortar in between. It is much more complex. There are five *main* types of mortar mix, assigned as M,S,N,O and K, which helpfully could be taken from the alternate letters of the words "**MaSoN** w**O**r**K**. Each mix uses a different ratio of cement, lime, and sand to produce specific performance characteristics such as flexibility, bonding properties, and compressive strength. Of course if you were building something you should check with a professional and check for recommended mixes. (The mixes listed below are for general information and are not definite formulae.)
Reference: https://www.homehow.co.uk/blog/mortar-mix-ratio

The order of the letters in Mason Work does not however signify, comply with or indicate the common usage of mortar types. The sand used for mortar mixes should be builder's sand or soft sand. Sharp sand is no good for laying bricks.

Type N is the mortar most often used by homeowners and is regarded as the best choice for general application. Whilst some slight variations of mortar types such as N-type exist, the most common mortar mix ratio for **type N** is 1 part Portland cement, 1 part lime, and 5 to 6 parts sand. This gives high compression strength of around 750 psi (typically achieved after 28-days) and allows it to be load-bearing if necessary. It is considered to be a general-purpose mix, useful for above grade, exterior, and interior load-bearing installations. It is also the preferred mortar mix for soft stone masonry.

Type O mortar mix is a high-lime mix. It is 1 part cement, 2 parts lime, and 8 to 9 parts sand which gives relatively low compressive strength (about 350 psi). Its exterior usage is limited due to its low structural capacity and it is used primarily for interior, above-grade, non-load–bearing walls. Type O mortar mix is ideal for re-pointing and similar repair work on existing structures, due to its softer consistency and ease of application. Type O mortar is softer than the older bricks, and it allows the bricks to expand or contract from temperature changes or stress.

According to "Masonry Systems," Types N and O are the most flexible and the best for bonding with older softer bricks, and is sometimes recommended for conservation work. Types M and S on the other hand are much stiffer and won't bond as well with soft brick. Either Type N or Type S mortar is recommended, though, when the brick is routinely exposed to freezing conditions.

Type S mortar is very similar to type O mortar. However, it differs in the ratio amount of cement, and is made from: 2 parts cement, 1 part lime, and 8 to 9 parts sand. It performs extremely well, withstanding soil pressure and wind and seismic loads. It has a high compressive strength of over 1,800 psi and is often mixed for strengths between 2,300 and 3,000 psi. Type S has a high-tensile bond strength, making it suitable for many projects at or below grade such as masonry foundations, manholes, retaining walls, and sewers, as well as at-grade projects like brick patios and walkways.

Type M mortar mix is the last of the four most common mortar types, and is considered the strongest on its own. Type M tends to be preferred for use with natural stone because it offers similar strength to that of stone. Made with 4 parts Portland cement, 1 part lime, and 12 to 15 parts sand it has a compressive strength of approximately 2,500 psi for most mixes. Type M mortar mix has the highest amount of Portland cement and is recommended for heavy loads and a variety of below-grade applications, including foundations, retaining walls, and driveways. While type M mortar provides at least 2,500 psi of compressive strength, it is also known for its poor adhesion and sealing properties making it unsuitable for many exposed applications.

Type K mortar can be made by combining 1 part cement, 3 parts lime, and between 10 to 12 parts sand. It is rarely used for new construction work but may be specified for restoration or for other specialty applications. It offers a very low compressive strength of only about 75 psi, and because of its softness it is primarily used for restoring the masonry on historic or ancient buildings which require a special mix that is not significantly stronger than the existing masonry.

Concrete by the way is made from sand, cement and aggregates like gravel and stone.

INDEX

Completed 01.02.2023

Printed in Great Britain
by Amazon

25874613R00245